Real Rape, Real Pain

D1714385

An (expatriate North America) Adjunct Professor in Law currently teaching full-time at the University of Canberra, who won the 2001 ACT Women's award, Dr Patricia Easteal is a nationally and internationally recognised sociolegal academic, author and activist/survivor. Through her research, public speaking and law reform submissions, Patricia has done extensive advocacy in the area of violence against women, also serving on government and community groups and acting as an expert witness. Her published work includes numerous academic articles and books.

Louise McOrmond-Plummer is an Australian feminist and survivor with 18 years' experience in activism around rape and domestic violence, and supporting survivors. Louise attained an Associate Diploma of Welfare Studies in her twenties, during which time she studied the topic of partner rape extensively, and continues in her efforts to highlight this issue through her website, Aphrodite Wounded, a support resource for girls and women raped by partners. Aphrodite Wounded is the first survivors' website to focus exclusively on partner rape, and has been applauded by trauma, domestic violence and rape organisations internationally. Louise is married with five children.

Real Rape, Real Pain

Help for women sexually assaulted by male partners

Patricia Easteal
and
Louise McOrmond-Plummer

Published by Hybrid Publishers

Melbourne Victoria Australia

First published 2006

National Library of Australia Cataloguing-in-Publication data:

Easteal, Patricia Weiser. Real rape, real pain: help for women sexually assaulted by male partners.

ISBN 1 876462 43 4.

1. Rape in marriage – Australia. 2. Abused wives – Services for – Australia. I. McOrmond-Plummer, Louise. II. Title.

362.82920994

Cover design: Ann Likhovetsky
Printed by McPherson's Printing Group

Contents

Acknowledgments

Louise's acknowledgments

My first acknowledgment must go to the brave women who lent their voices to this book and without whom it would not be what it is. My thanks to you, sisters, for having a part in ensuring that other women don't experience the same lack of understanding and loneliness that we have.

I want to thank my family too – firstly my husband Ken Plummer for his continual support throughout the long gestation of this book. As for my children: although my son doesn't really want me to spread the word, other mother-writers might be interested in knowing that teenage sons can do a better than adequate job of cleaning and childcare while you write – especially if there's a cash incentive. Thanks Nick! Thanks is due also to my girls Christina and April for preparing and cleaning up after meals as I was unable to tear myself away from winding paragraphs up. Christina, my daughter, you have been the one family member whom I felt could most deeply appreciate my passion for this book and my excitement at seeing it materialise. Thank you, darling girl. Thanks also to my babies Suzy and Finn for being the sunshine in the gloomier parts of this project and a necessary distraction.

I thank my beloved sister, Amanda McOrmond, for the continual inspiration of her courage, self-discipline and complete absence of self-pity. Mandy, if you can face what you've had to and still be so fine, there isn't a lot I can't do. And now that the writing of this book is no longer an excuse for smoking like the devil, I may actually do what you say and quit.

My two best friends, Ann Eulenstein and Helen Newman, have shown continual interest in the growth of this book as well as listening to me talk about what must have been some quite boring aspects of this process. Thank you, my friends. And thank you Helen, my teamster, for cooking me meals in the most insane periods of the last four years.

Throughout writing this book, I have had the emotional and intellectual support of the world's best people in my wonderful online survivor community, Pandora's Aquarium. I can never thank you enough, my friends, for being able to air my triggers and dilemmas at any time and for your constant wisdom, compassion and laughter. Truly, you have helped me heal and write. I wish I could name you all, and I hope this suffices in some small way.

In the time I've had my website, Aphrodite Wounded (www. aphroditewounded.org), I have had many encouraging emails from beautiful survivors of partner rape all over the world, or from the men who love them. You people have bolstered my spirit and cemented my determination. Thank you for that nourishment, friends.

Amy Drinnon, fellow traveller and writer from Tennessee, thank you for being so constantly there, loving and affirming me and allowing me to share the other parts of my life that impacted on writing.

I have had generous guidance from women who work in the areas of counselling/ domestic violence/rape. They are as follows:

Monika Ostroff LICSW (USA), respected therapist whom I am proud to call a friend, thank you for your insights as a counsellor and for your incredible generosity in purchasing and mailing American texts to me, *and* refusing any payment. You're a legend.

Sharon Peet of the Women's Information and Referral Exchange (WIRE) is due thanks for her generous help and encouragement in putting feelers out for women to share their stories with me.

Tamara Steinhubl MMFT (USA) and Jeannine Vegh, MA, MFTI (USA), thank you, women, for the insights and guidance you've given that made me reassess parts of my writing for the better, and whose articulateness just made things I was confused about 'click'.

Vicky Brown and Jill Sumner (Australia), two fine counsellors in the fields of domestic violence and rape respectively, thank you for taking the time in your incredible workloads to sit patiently with me for hours and talk to me about women and the impact of partner rape. The knowledge you shared has been tremendously beneficial.

I feel deep gratitude to the researchers/writers, rape crisis and domestic violence counsellors who have worked with partner rape in order to break the silence and effect justice. This book couldn't be what it is without the insights they have made available – and that includes my co-author,

Patricia Easteal. Thanks for *everything*, Patricia – including the many years where I knew you only by your writing and your commitment to the fight for change. How lucky I consider myself to be co-author with a scholarly and clever but very human goddess.

This book came out of my healing, and thus thanks is due to three counsellors who facilitated that: Ms Lesley Wells, who first believed me and introduced me to the possibility of social change, Ms Frances B. Sutherland, who showed me that I am bigger than my fear, and Ms Nadia Mellor, who helped me find my lost and hurt but robustly sexy Aphrodite-self and embrace her without shame.

I'd like also to say a retrospective thank you to two of my university lecturers, Robyn Mortlock and Noeline Hartwig, both terrific women at whose feet I learned much of what underpins this work. Noeline, when I wrote an essay about marital rape for your Sociology of the Family unit, you called it thoughtful and insightful, and expressed the hope that I would continue work with this issue. I have taken that comment out and read it several times throughout writing this book; it has continued to encourage me when I needed it. So thank you for a gift that has gone on giving.

And I want to thank a young Louise, who knew how to survive and who has made her presence and courage very much felt in the reopening of wounds for the purpose of this book.

Patricia's acknowledgments

Most heart-felt gratitude to the women who shared their stories with me. I know how painful it was to live through their experiences again through narrative but also appreciate the healing aspect.

Thanks to Christine Feerick and Emma Meadth for their research assistance and some funding from a collaborative research grant between the ACT Chief Minister's Department and the University of Canberra, ACT DPP, Relationships Australia (Canberra) and Canberra Rape Crisis Service for data and interviews.

Thank you, dear lovely Louise, first for agreeing to merge manuscripts, second for your brilliant insights and writing, and third for all of the validation and affirmation that you have given me over the past five years and particularly during the writing of this book. You are a true hero.

I am grateful to Simon for paying the bills while I've been living and breathing, researching and writing on partner rape. Also dear partner, our relationship has provided the sanctuary, springboard and support for my healing. Other 'Martians' who have played a variety of roles – sometimes challenging but sometimes validating – in my 'process' are my sons (in alphabetical order) Brian, David and Jesse.

So many 'Venusians' like daughter Ashley and friends Jennifer, Lynn and Meg have helped me over the years to recognise the negative self-talk, provide a positive mirror and at least some of the time a degree of self-acceptance.

Most importantly, thanks to my HP for putting me on this path.

ABOUT US: A COMMON JOURNEY

Louise's path

In late 1986, when I was twenty years old, I became free of a relationship that almost cost me my life. For two years, I had lived with a man who thought love equalled ownership, and who retaliated brutally when challenged. He had beaten me, he had threatened me with weapons and terrorised me in other ways.

Other things had happened in that relationship too. This man, who will be called 'Paul' throughout this book, forced sex on me and had done so many times, when he was angry, when he needed to assert power over me, or just because I presumed the right to say no to sex. Though it was the threats to my life that seemed most frightening at the time, I was not to realise until years later the severe and prolonged damage inflicted by the sexual abuses. I practised pretending they hadn't happened. I pretended they didn't hurt, and became so adept that I almost convinced myself that this was true. And I knew that even had I wanted to admit what happened or say that it hurt, I would get little empathy. He was my partner. Because I had willingly had sex with him, it was not wrong for him to assume he could take it by force. It couldn't have done me any real harm. It was my fault because I didn't run half naked and screaming into the streets and call the police. No, it was not real rape, I was not a real rape victim and my pain was not real pain. Just ask anybody from judges who sympathise with men who rape partners down to the next-door neighbour who believes that rape is committed by men with hairy palms and glazed expressions lurking in alleyways.

When my ex-partner was charged with murder 18 months after the end of my relationship with him, what I had tried to forget began to come back. My awareness was flooded with memories of the actions: hitting me and tearing at my clothes and each thrust like a physical taunt meant to convey my loathsomeness and powerlessness; dashing my knuckles against the walls when I tried to stop him; dirty words: slut, this is what you deserve. It daily made me sick when I began to relive these things. And still I was alone with it, my pain the legacy of choosing the wrong man. Still I believed I had no right of naming what he did to me. I tried to talk about it and found confirmation again and again that my rape was a non-event.

Even so, I developed a passion for assisting survivors of rape and when I was twenty-two, I embraced feminism and rape-activism. Even though what other women were saying about their experiences of rape mirrored my own feelings, I felt that all I could really be was a good foot-soldier for my raped sisters. I couldn't ask for support for myself because, I believed, my rape didn't matter as much as theirs.

I decided to go to university and get some professional qualifications with a view to assisting abused women. As I worked to gain an Associate Diploma in Welfare Studies, I had opportunities to study marital/partner rape and write essays about it. I was driven by a desire to end the injustice of rape, and to understand what happened to me. I remember the nights I spent shoving my textbooks and pens away from me and crying, crying as I woke up to the fact that what happened to me was *rape*. I had been *raped*. Claiming that was a hard-won victory for me, a woman whose rapist had been her partner. It hurt, sometimes very badly. But at last, I knew that there were reasons for me to feel the levels of devastation and trauma that I had. In the act of defining, naming and feeling, I began to heal.

As I healed, I developed outrage at the lack of recognition given girls and women raped by their partners. I knew that I was not the only woman who had experienced the isolation and blame. I was enraged at a society that allows some men to rape with impunity and tells the victims of those rapes that they have no right to call their violations a crime. I was blamed because I stayed with my abuser, but I saw the startling hypocrisy in the situation of other women upbraided by church, family and friends for *leaving* men who rape them. I found out that men who rape their partners are also more likely to kill them than those men who batter but don't rape. The prevalence studies I had read established partner rape as common, yet women hurt in this way were ignored.

I consider myself to be very much a 'can-do' woman – rather than just sitting and bemoaning the dearth of resources for survivors of partner rape, I asked myself what I, Louise, might do about it.

I noticed that while excellent studies had been written about marital/ partner rape, these were not always accessible to survivors. Rape recovery literature was more focused on stranger or one-off acquaintance rape and not scoped to capture the complexity of issues partner rape survivors often face. Domestic violence literature tended to view sexual assault as just another abuse and did not go into the special wounding of rape by a partner. Literature was telling us that partner rape happens, and that served an important function. But I believe that the most meaningful change comes from survivors naming, healing, and breaking the silence. We've seen how rape and child sexual abuse, once surrounded by silence and the belief that they were rare, are now much more open for discussion. We've seen survivors of rape and child sexual abuse heal and reclaim power in their lives, and we know what a difference they have made as they transform not only themselves but also the world around them.

I decided to write a book not *about* women raped by partners, but *for* them. Yet I didn't see how sharing my experiences alone could really benefit other women unless there was a range of perspectives offered. Therefore, I placed a number of requests on Domestic Violence and Sexual Assault message boards inviting women sexually assaulted by boyfriends or husbands to share their stories. Nine wonderful women, four from the US, three from the UK and two from Australia, agreed. Together with our stories, I made use of the studies, my professional knowledge, and recovery literature.

I knew the process of writing would be difficult but I didn't know *how* difficult. As I unfolded my own traumas there were certainly more demons to be faced, more fear to be conquered. However, it was also richly healing as through the other women's stories and revisiting my own story, I came to understand my experiences better. And I knew it wasn't just me who was feeling pain. I was so moved by the courage of the women who shared their stories with me, because for some of them, uncovering so much pain had come at a cost. Summer, whom you'll meet in this book, told me, 'This was not easy by any stretch of the imagination but I have to trust that it will have been worth every word written if it helps one beautiful soul in her own healing.' For this reason among others, we are indebted to the survivors in this book.

When my energy burned low, I was inspired by other survivors who had written books, faced their own ghosts, but who continued nevertheless to write. One of those authors who had gone before and whose courage continually fuelled me was my co-author, Patricia Easteal.

Joining with Patricia was a delightful development in the writing of this book. Opportunities like that just don't happen every day, and I knew that Patricia's skills, knowledge and passion about naming and ending partner rape, along with the wealth of women's voices she'd had access to, ensured that together we would create something pretty damn powerful for women seeking healing from partner rape. There's a story there too: in 1993, an Australian newspaper featured a survey asking for testimonies of rape. I responded by telling about rape by Paul. I wrote with trepidation, for I both feared and expected that it would not be seen as rape of the kind the survey requested; in other words, real rape. My fears were unfounded.

Patricia Easteal put that response into a book, *Voices of the Survivors* – along with other women who had experienced partner rape. In a very real sense, Patricia had provided me with one of my first opportunities to speak out and be validated. I had no idea then how important she would become to me twelve years later. Perhaps life has a way of arranging some things just so.

Just as other survivors of rape have stood up and said no to the silence, we survivors of partner rape can do it too. We can refuse to surrender to the myths, ignorance and shaming. We can stand on the truth of our experiences and heal from them. We have the power to be other voices in a world where women hear that their violations are not real. We will show them they are not alone.

Although my real name appears on the front of this book, in parts of the book where I share my story and healing journey, you will see me as 'Rachel'. For Patricia and me, this was a more sensible way of presenting writing specifically about me without having to deviate from the general 'authors together' voice.

Patricia's path

It was well over a decade ago that the desire to do research on sexual assault by partners began for me.

The story or its conception started in 1992 when I was sitting in a small room in the NSW Supreme Court. I was surrounded by stacks of files. Hour after hour for five days I read about the cases of homicide in which the perpetrator and the victim were in an intimate relationship. Police reports, social workers' notes, court transcripts, interviews with the defendant – sometimes tedious and sometimes horrific in the detail provided. A picture began to emerge which was further coloured in with the Victorian cases I waded through a couple of months later. In almost all of the backgrounds to these killings, with the exception of ones in which the husband and wife were elderly and ailing, there was a history of domestic violence.

I don't like to gradate violence – if you ask any survivor she'll tell you that it all hurts and that it is the emotional parts that hurt the most. However, the courts and many in the community do make gradations and perceive the physical as most serious. The more fractures and bruises, the more severe the abuse is seen. From that perspective, the prehistories in these killings would be placed at the very serious end of the continuum. And in a few of the files, mention was made of rape.

This was the first time I had read about, or even heard about, sexual assault by a partner.

In doing that research for my book *Killing the Beloved*[1] I became particularly interested in the plight of women who kill their violent partner. So I started to investigate the criminal justice response to these defendants. That's when I learned about the secrecy of rape in relationships: it was the case of an Aboriginal woman in Queensland, Robyn Kina. In 1988 she was indicted for the murder of her de facto husband, Anthony David Black. She pleaded not guilty, but didn't give any evidence or call any witnesses. After a trial that lasted less than a day, she was found guilty of murder and sentenced to life imprisonment with hard labour.

After five years in prison, a petition for pardon was presented to the Governor on behalf of Robyn. It claimed that she had not received a fair trial based on difficulties and misunderstandings in communications with her lawyers prior to the trial. The petition revealed that Robyn had experienced abuse as a child and terrible violence and trauma in her relationship with the deceased. Anthony had beaten and raped her repeatedly when she refused anal intercourse, tied her to the bed while he worked night shifts and raped her upon his return. On other occasions he had taken Robyn to the construction site where he was employed and forced her to have sex with his workmates.

She had tried to leave the relationship, but returned to their house because she had nowhere else to go.

> When I returned that time, he flogged me. I got two black eyes
> and my face was all swollen.[2]

On the morning of the stabbing, her refusal of anal sex led to violence, and Anthony threatened to anally rape Robyn's teenage niece. According to Robyn, she had picked up the knife while thinking about what he had just said.

She had not been able to disclose this to her lawyers or at the indictment or trial. She later explained that she felt scared, shy and embarrassed. Like many victims of domestic violence she believed that 'I probably deserved that', or, 'I probably caused him to do that by my behaviour'.

At her new trial this evidence was heard and she was acquitted.

My epiphany had commenced. Rape in relationships was happening in households with serious domestic violence and some of its victims couldn't talk about it.

But, there was much more to learn – both about this type of sexual assault and about myself.

In 1993, I ran a nation-wide survey (as part of the ABC *Without Consent* documentary) for survivors of rape to complete. Almost 3000 people participated. For some it was the first time that they had opened up about the experience and many took the opportunity of writing pages and pages describing the assault(s). I took this material and wrote a book derived from this material – *Voices of the Survivors*.[3]

As I sat in my office reading these letters, my skin began to crawl. I felt increasingly uncomfortable and troubled deep inside. What some were describing had happened to me in a prior relationship. I tried to talk myself out of it – who wants to see herself as a victim of partner rape? Especially when you've done research and worked in the area of domestic violence … and considered yourself enlightened, appropriately introspective and healing from other violence long identified? But denial wouldn't work for me anymore. They say that when we're ready to learn the lesson, the teacher will be there. Just as I would manage to emphasise (in my head) the differences between the woman's story and my own, I'd read another letter that used different words but described the same feelings that I had felt years before. 'Yes, but … in my case, there was no physical force …' Then another letter with the same feeling of not having consented and violation, and this time, the same type of coercion. Gradually, day after day, my denial began to crumble. Denial is such a powerful and insidious force that at least for me it required a veritable onslaught of identification to be eroded.

I suppose that it was some time in September 1993 when I was going through the first three As – awareness, acceptance and anger – that the desire to do research on sexual assault by partners was born. I had the need to do the fourth A – *action*. I have had the opportunity to do research and write a number of books after *Voices of the Survivors* and from 2002-04 collected women's stories and studied many court files. This material had been melded into a whole with Louise's research.

Coming out as a survivor

In *Voices of the Survivors* and subsequent media, I 'came out' as a survivor.

It isn't an easy process. It's like walking around naked when everyone else is dressed. You don't know who knows. You don't know what they think about it. You feel vulnerable without the usual defences. But not to do so would have been impossible, as I wrote:

> It would not have been possible to have done this work and kept one's own secrets. The pain of such hypocrisy would have far exceeded the pain of reading the letters and comments, editing them, writing bits and pieces, and coming out publicly as a survivor.

Each survivor who takes the risk and reveals that part of them to others is making a statement that we are not ashamed and that we won't keep the secret any longer.

The paths converge

Out of similar histories, determination and motivation to have the truth about partner rape told, we came together. We've done this because we don't want other women to experience the same isolation and silence that we, as survivors of partner rape have. We hope that this book demonstrates how a painful and frightening history can be made to work for positive change. Just as your authors joined on our common path towards change, we invite our sisters touched by partner rape to join us on the path towards *truth* – not that which is enforced by society or our abusers – but that which we know by our experiences and feelings. Walk with us towards the right to call our violations by their rightful names, to have compassion for ourselves as survivors of sexual violence and to heal.

DEDICATION

We dedicate this book to Helen, Susi, Stephanie, Gina, Tasha and to the loving memory of "Kate"

CHAPTER 1

Our Primary Aim: Healing

Using this book

Since not all survivors of partner rape are affected in the same ways, different recovery strategies will work for different women. We've fused literature about recovery from rape, domestic violence and trauma with experiences the women in this book have had with things that help or hinder, so it's likely that most people will find *some* things helpful. You have the right of deciding whether and when you're ready to address your issues. You will know whether you need to challenge yourself to move further. Sometimes, just developing the ability to be gentle and take pressure off ourselves is an important move forward. Remember that there's no right or wrong way to embrace healing. We each have our own unique journey.

Ideally, survivors can dip into this book, take what feels right for them and leave the rest – perhaps other parts of it will be more helpful later.

We've both found value in writing about our experiences. So we suggest that you might use a journal to write down what feelings, thoughts or memories arise as you read, perhaps with a view to sharing them with a counsellor or a good friend, or as a release just for you if you prefer.

Important: Although there are a number of chapters that examine specific aspects of trauma and healing, this book shouldn't be a substitute for professional help, but an adjunct to it. If at any stage you feel overwhelmed by panic, pain or rage, it will be a good idea to stop reading for now and seek some support.

Where and how do I begin healing?

Have you ever decided to clean out a closet that has been jammed with all kinds of stuff for years, and found that when you opened the door, you hadn't a clue where to begin? At this stage, you may not be aware of all the issues that need to be resolved. As you heal, you'll probably notice that space is cleared for you to recognise other, more hidden effects. Jodie gives an example:

> I know it was all wrong what happened, but somehow things get so ingrained in you. You don't even realise why you're feeling or acting or letting people treat you the way they are until you just stand back for a bit.

Since partner rape often goes hand in hand with other abuse, there may be other issues to heal, such as the terror left over from threats to your life or the way constant verbal putdowns eroded your spirit.

Sometimes there will be a blend of issues; for example, memories of rape may carry not only shame or betrayal, but also the fear of being physically hurt, or his murderous threats.

Here are a few actions you can take that may help kick-start and assist you in healing.

Defining and naming the rape can be a catalyst for healing (see chapters 2 and 15). Most of the women, including both of us, had trouble defining what had happened to us while we were in the relationship as sexual assault. Because we subscribed to myths about partner rape, we couldn't see the sexual acts done under coercion as assault. Rachel had to identify an act that took place after separation as rape. Dealing with that rape opened the way to recognising and healing from the other experiences. Perhaps you can choose an experience to begin with – it may be the first time or the worst time.

You could ask yourself what is niggling away at you most at the moment – is it poor self-esteem? Fear? Something that happened in the course of a rape? You may want to lay out your thoughts and feelings in a journal as a way of clearing some of the confusion and giving you some direction.

Because women raped by partners so often feel confused about whether what happened to them was really rape, they may belittle themselves for feeling pain or wanting to heal. If you feel like this, please know that the only permission that you need to heal is your own. Don't be put off by such statements as 'Why are you making such a big deal of it now?' or 'That wasn't real rape'. You owe no justification to anybody for healing. Partner rape hurts. There is nothing odd about your pain. You are strong and courageous for tackling the issues you face.

Give yourself permission to heal.

Remember too that most of us have this wonderful (survival) tendency to minimise what happened. 'Compared to so and so, it was nothing ... after all he didn't hit me ...' Violence is violence and no matter what forms were inflicted on you, there are wounds that need healing. If you think you 'should' be stronger that you feel, or if the rape was several years ago and you believe you should be 'over it' by now, you're assuming an unfair burden; so too if other people see you as strong and you believe you'll be letting them down by being vulnerable. The only way 'over it' is by healing. Challenge any pressure you feel to be 'strong', and know that facing what happened to you is in fact showing great strength.

Memories and feelings

As you heal, you may find that things you'd forgotten start surfacing. Many of us, like Kate, used repression during and after the assaults.

> I've done such a good job of blocking it all out. I can't remember very much. I hated all of it. I hated him just touching my skin, so you know, whether it was doing doggy position or whatever, that was probably oh well I hate this anyway, I hate this even more, I hate the whole thing. I think there were probably certain positions and that sort of thing that I didn't like but I think it's all a bit of blur because I just hated the whole thing, and I wasn't really present. I just literally prayed. I was in my head praying the whole time, and I don't remember a lot of what happened. I remember him talking about wanting to do different stuff and me going ugh.

Memories might entail actual experiences, or remembering how you felt when you were raped. This can be very distressing, but is normal. You may know what the signs of remembering are – for example, you feel a sense of something 'pushing through', accompanied by fear or tears. You will know whether you feel ready to explore it. Try to see the memory as something that is happening not to hurt you; rather, it's asking to be healed. In later stages of healing, any emerging memories will feel easier to take, because you'll most likely have developed skills for dealing with them.

It's a very good idea if you have support as memories emerge, because you may feel very raw, as if the abuse you remember has just occurred.

Either accompanying the memories or on their own, you may experience a number of emotions during healing. These include grief, fear, anger, shame and self-doubt. In chapter 16 we discuss what to expect and provide you with ideas on how to deal with these feelings.

Finding support: speak out

As you heal, it will be very helpful if you have a support network. This might comprise counselling, actively healing survivors or caring non-survivors who are prepared to understand the issues behind partner rape. Think of people you trust who can offer you a shoulder in hard times. If there's nobody you can think of, you may want to consider how you could go about forging supportive contacts. Call a women's organisation and see if they have support groups. Summer suggests below that an online message board has been useful to her healing.

We strongly recommend that you choose at least one person to tell about your experience/s of partner rape. Through disclosure a healing process can begin. For it is true that once you have named it, you begin to have some power. And with that power, you can begin to help others too. Shefali wanted women to know how important it is to open up:

> I'd say to other women if they feel that they can't get out of it, at least talk about it. Don't live with it without saying anything because it gets worse.

Somebody who affirms that it was wrong for you to be sexually assaulted may give a supportive push to feelings you've been holding in. It may increase your sense of a right to heal.

Talking is the beginning of *trusting* and *feeling* what needs to be felt. Sharing is the way of working through the feelings of responsibility, blame and shame. Recovery involves a lot of time and a lot of energy. Kate explains how talking about it has made the experiences real:

> I have been silent long enough and I want to tell my story and I don't care. It's time now. I've done a lot of reading on rape in the last three months and I think it's just sort of been at my consciousness a lot more. So I guess this has probably been a really big thing in just being able to say it. It's probably the first time I've actually believed it. All I know is I've always felt the feelings, like when I've heard sexual assault victims talk, I identify with every word they say, and it has always frightened me.

Jennifer wrote a poem as a tribute to the women who have supported her:

The Women of Wanjiri

My Tribute

I, a stranger
A woman crushed and alone
You opened your hearts and gave to
me
Of your time, your courage, your
wisdom
Though my need was great, you
faltered not
No criticism, no censure, no reproach
You shared of your own deepest
anguish and pain
Your loyalty and strength given
unselfishly
Your friendship never waning
Supporting me when I needed you
most
You reached out to help me
survive
Loyal, strong and brave
You remain in my thoughts
Wherever I may be
Forever part of me
We are Sisters, bonded together,
Links in a chain
The women of Wanjira

Summer shares the benefits of support through her healing:

> I have access to many positive people in my life and for that I am
> eternally grateful. I have friends who gently encourage me in my
> healing. I was always hesitant about going into a group therapy
> or support setting, but have found that through a message board
> that being around others who have experienced trauma as well
> has been life-altering for me in such empowering and positive
> ways. I learn something new about myself and my healing every
> day.

Natalie has chosen weekly psychotherapy 15 years after the one-off rape
by her then boyfriend:

I have never attempted suicide, and pride myself in attending weekly psychotherapy to assist me with my recovery. I am beginning to rediscover myself, to dig out the fun person who used to be so full of life when she was first going out with Sean: the person who stood up for herself, who was charming and confident, and had a terrific sense of humour; the sexy person who enjoyed her body. One of the most valuable things I have discovered from all of this is a trust in my instincts now, a knowledge that if someone seems threatening to me for any reason, that I need to pay attention to that. I still have a lot of work to do, but I can see the future ahead of me, and it looks bright and promising. I know I can make it on my own. I know now that no one has the right to abuse me. I have learned a tremendous amount about my inner strength, my ability to cope with adversity and succeed in spite of it. And no one will ever take that away from me again.

When you feel low, it can be hard to ask for support because it's often at these times that we feel we don't deserve any support. It will be necessary to overcome these shaming messages, and one way to do that is by attempting to reach beyond them. When you do this, they lose some of their power. In thinking about telling, affirm yourself with these statements:

I am only a victim as long as I keep the secret of what happened to me.

I am only a victim as long as I continue to blame myself for what happened.

I am only a victim as long as I remain deeply ashamed.

How can counselling help?

Counsellors often have skills that can help you overturn some of the pain and fear surrounding your abuse. When we get bogged down in terms of viewing our situation one way only, counsellors can 'reframe' or present a range of other ways of making sense of what happened in ways that no longer damage us. Counselling can help you with the management of trauma symptoms. Talking to a counsellor can be the beginning of breaking the silence and defeating old shaming messages.

Melina's counsellor gave her the validation that is so important to survivors of partner rape:

I'd started to feel proud at having survived that man and lived, but the way 'sex' had happened with him was haunting me. After years of recovering, I now knew that that 'sex' was not normal. I knew something wrong had happened. I was losing sleep with the nightmares. I needed confirmation that what I was feeling was based in reality. Finally I called the local Sexual Assault Service and spoke to a counsellor over the phone. I was much, much too ashamed to come in person, and I was too ashamed to give my real name. The depth of my shame stunned me. I could hardly get the words out. My voice cracked and faded into whispers by turns. I said that I just wanted to tell someone the story of what had happened, how it had happened. So I did. And then I said, 'This ... this isn't normal, is it?' I couldn't believe the relief of hearing that no, it wasn't normal; yes, it was rape.

I am so glad I've been able to identify the source of the flashbacks. Having someone confirm my feelings made a huge difference, I don't think I've had one nightmare since admitting what had happened to that counsellor. I've started to feel proud of being strong enough to have survived it. I'm reading empowering material. I may even get up the courage to go to a support group meeting ... maybe.

Ideally, a counsellor will understand the issues that underlie partner abuse. They should have training in grief, trauma and abuse issues. Ask a potential counsellor what their views on domestic violence/rape are, and whether they have relevant qualifications for dealing with trauma. The counsellor will know that domestic and sexual violence are about taking choice and control away from victims, and they'll be concerned with assisting you in regaining power over your life. They won't push solutions but will help you find out what works best for you.

Don't accept blame. In her early twenties, Rachel saw a psychiatrist and attempted to tell him about her relationship with Paul. The psychiatrist said, 'So, you're a masochist?' She never went back. This sort of blaming response is definitely not what you should be hearing. If you blame yourself, it could be easy to accept such statements, particularly from someone with letters after his or her name. But this is secondary wounding; you go to a counsellor to be helped, not hurt more.

Watch out also for counsellors who justify your experiences of sexual abuse as a 'family violence problem', or who spend time telling you how insecure or upset the perpetrator must have been. Counselling is for *you* to explore your issues. It doesn't matter if you're still in the relationship or not; you shouldn't be judged.

Also, not all counsellors are prepared to give you the time that you need to 'work through' some of the issues. Take what happened to Sarah as an example:

> I'd gone to see a counsellor about six months after the divorce just in case I'd missed anything and didn't want something coming back to haunt me. That's when I'd been able to acknowledge the rape. I only saw her two or three times and then it was kind of, 'Well, run along and make the most of your life.'
>
> I probably would have liked to have had more assistance at that point but it was not forthcoming. I'd said I found Stephen pretty repressive and stifling and she had asked me whether he did certain things. I wondered if she knew him but she said that it's a personality type. She said, 'This personality type is always attracted to your personality type.' I couldn't believe it. It was just so amazing. She also said that they tend to remarry very quickly and they tend to go for people who have been highly dependent on them, like women with small children.

There are many fine counsellors out there. Call domestic violence/rape hotlines to find out whether free counselling is available or, if you have the means, you can seek private counselling – perhaps the hotlines can suggest counsellors with good reputations in working with abused women.

Here are words of encouragement from Adair:

> Counselling with the right person can work miracles. I have found a fabulous counsellor, who has been very helpful in my healing. I have made a few very close friendships through two rape recovery sites online. People who know where I am coming from, understand my journey. Help from someone is essential to healing. A counsellor, a crisis centre, a trusted friend. You shouldn't keep this a secret … there are people who can help you.
>
> Caring people are out there!

Afraid to ask for help?

If your car broke down, you would want it to be checked out by somebody with knowledge about these matters. *You* are more important than your car – why shouldn't you also seek help for yourself? Many survivors struggle with asking for help. Sometimes they are afraid to be seen as 'weak' or 'whining'. They feel as if they don't have a right to ask for support. Or they feel that there's no one to ask.

Who do you tell? You certainly don't tell your parents. You can't tell your innocent and straight co-workers. I didn't have any friends I trusted. I didn't have any, and I think that was the biggest thing was that I thought well, you don't go into a strait-laced white collar group of people who you know damn well, are probably worse abused than you. Because everybody was like it just isn't happening. So I think that's why I'm here, like you know, this doesn't happen to white educated women from good families who have a good job, and that's bullshit. (Tiffany)

Yet, if you have been traumatised, needing help is normal. Trauma expert Aphrodite Matsakis has some helpful words:

If you felt powerful and dynamic just after having had it demonstrated that there are forces capable of destroying you, most knowledgeable mental health professionals would consider you delusional, mentally troubled or at least in a state of massive denial. Consequently, helplessness, neediness, and all the other feelings described above are appropriate feelings following traumatization.[1]

Linda Ledray, author of *Recovering from Rape* writes:

To other people, asking for help is a sign of intelligence and resourcefulness. To them, asking for help is a sign of wanting to do things better than they could by themselves. These people don't feel they need to be expert at everything, and they understand that they don't need to be able to handle everything on their own. They feel good about being able to find and use available resources.[2]

If you don't like to be 'needy', why not use the words 'in need' instead? This removes the negative connotations of 'neediness' and turns it into something *human*.

If you've been sitting for months with the idea of calling a hotline or you've cried alone but wished you could tell somebody how badly you're hurting, we recommend that you climb over any inner recriminations, and make a move soon. Sometimes, just knowing that you've made a time to speak with somebody can help you feel stronger. Not reaching out keeps you in isolation. You deserve support. You had to go through the sexual assault(s) alone; don't be alone anymore.

Remember: Healing is not straightforward

You may find that you thought a certain issue was dealt with, only to find that it comes around at another time for further work. Because healing often means facing traumatic experiences and feelings, you may feel worse before you feel better – but you *will* feel better. Summer provides a view of the ups and downs that healing can entail:

> The most difficult aspect of my healing is the inconsistency of it. I never know where I will be from day to day. There are days that guilt, shame, etc. overwhelm me and there are other days that I feel like I could kick the world's ass. The extremes are still hard to deal with for me. I tell myself that I am exactly where I need to be in my healing – that I am perfectly fine where I am and that sometimes I need to take a few steps back in order to pick up momentum to move forward with greater intensity.

If 'downs' alternate with 'ups', this doesn't mean you've failed in any way; it just means that you may have something more to resolve or that deeper levels of pain are presenting themselves for healing. The ups will provide you with knowledge of your own strengths. Feeling bad doesn't mean those strengths are gone.

Although healing is always beneficial, you may encounter times when you are in such deep and seemingly endless pain that you wonder whether it was worth opening and exploring your experiences of partner rape. Liz says, 'It's been very hard and painful and I sometimes wonder if it's ever going to stop.' Some therapists call this the 'emergency stage'.[3] Hang in there, taking one day at a time (or an hour at a time) and engaging as much support as you can. The pain will eventually be resolved.

However, if you're feeling depressed (see chapter 10 for the symptoms), don't neglect to get help from a counsellor or a doctor. You may find a course of medication combined with talk-therapy helpful.

Make a list of things you can do when you feel distress. If you have a counsellor who allows calls outside of therapy, use that resource. If you don't have a regular counsellor, calling a rape crisis line could be helpful – it doesn't matter if the assaults were a considerable time ago – rape counsellors understand that the wounds caused by sexual violence can feel extremely raw even decades after occurrence. List friends who are empathic listeners. If you know actively healing survivors who can offer inspiration to continue, list them too. Ask yourself what would help you feel a little better or at least hold you through the pain.

Also, sometimes, your healing may appear to stall. There may be a sense that you cannot move any further right now, or that you just can't find the answer you're looking for. When Rachel disclosed just such feelings to her counsellor, she advised, 'It's important to ask yourself whether you've done all you can with a certain issue for now.' Don't push yourself to answer everything at once.

Don't give up! If you put the hard yards in, you will heal. Be patient with yourself.

Cautionary notes: safety and coping

A necessity for healing is safety: It's hard to focus energy on healing if you are still under threat because progress can't be made if you're continually being traumatised. If you are still being raped or otherwise abused, your safety will need to be a priority. You deserve safety, and we hope that you will find it.

> No one can break your spirit. They can hurt you; they can hit you and humiliate you. But some things a man can never take away, and even if you doubt who you are anymore, know that you still exist. It's so important not to fall into a trap where you think you deserve it, or it becomes life. He has the problem; his acts of violence are his signs of weakness, not your sign of weakness. You have a voice. Use it. Seek help; even if it's a confidential telephone number, there are people there who are able to help. It's very hard to break the cycle. But women break the cycle every day, and it's possible to have a life after sexual violence. (Charlotte)

We suggest that you engage help from a counsellor who won't tell you that you have to leave or judge you, but who can help you decide what you *may* do to secure safety.

Safety is also internal. Exploring and dealing with the different dimensions of hurt that partner rape causes is rewarding, but it can be hard to initially appreciate that. Because so many of us cut our feelings off at the time of our abuses, and because society hasn't really permitted women raped by partners much space to speak and to heal, it's easy to assume that the feelings are gone. It's common for healing women to be shocked at the strength of painful feelings and memories they thought they'd forgotten. If you're aware of your pain, you may have spent enormous energy trying to fend it off. Counselling can be a safe space for you to probe frightening or intense feelings. Please, make sure your feelings, thoughts and memories are being discharged in some safe and trusting environment. Do at least one caring thing for yourself a day, and give yourself regular treats.

Although we believe that most people can benefit from having support in healing at least for parts of the process, there are women for whom this may be particularly necessary. If you experience hallucinations, severe and prolonged flashbacks, you're suicidal or actively harming yourself, it is best if you proceed in trauma work only with the guidance of a therapist. Exploring deeply traumatic experiences and feelings without assistance right now could do you more harm than good. This doesn't mean that you can never heal; it just means that you have special issues, and that you'll benefit much more from healing when your ability to cope has been maximised.[4]

If you're a woman who has used drugs or alcohol to escape the pain and fear inside you, it won't necessarily help to delve into your trauma until you have addressed substance abuse issues, and looked at other strategies for coping. Some addiction issues may require detoxification in a clinical setting. Please, speak to a counsellor about this.

Healing and ongoing contact with the perpetrator

It's often the case that because of children, women must have at least some ongoing contact with the partners who raped them. If you're such a woman, seeing him may be difficult at certain stages of healing. If you cannot avoid seeing him altogether, you may be able to limit contact with him. Perhaps you can ask a friend to do the dropping off and picking up of children for you for a while. If not, it might help you to drop the children at his home so that you have more control over how long you're in his company.

If you're a teenage girl who still sees the perpetrator at school, this is most probably very uncomfortable for you. You don't deserve to have to face that every day – it's not fair to you. Try to reach out to somebody you trust about options such as changing schools or getting restraining orders if needed. A rape counsellor may act as an advocate for you.

If he is still attempting to control or manipulate you, perhaps through children, you can talk to a domestic violence advocate about legal or other ways of dealing with it. Certainly if you're still being threatened or harmed, he is acting outside the law and this will need to be addressed.

Do speak to a counsellor about how you can minimise the impact of seeing him.

Staying and healing

If you're no longer being raped, abused or threatened, and you believe that your partner has taken responsibility for the sexual violence, you may have elected to stay, as some women do. If you're staying and seeking healing, you'll probably have special issues such as fearing that it will happen again, or sometimes being triggered by your partner's presence.

It's best if your partner knows of your need to heal – and if he's taken true responsibility for hurting you, he'll accept this. Whether you speak to him or not, do seek assistance and support for yourself.

Finding common ground with other survivors of marital or partner rape might be especially helpful. Seek out people who will listen respectfully to your perspective, and will appreciate that you have stayed for good reasons. Most importantly, they shouldn't view your rape as any less than it is – for example, they won't assume that because you've remained, the rape did not really harm you.

Some women who remain with men who raped them feel as if they are betraying their partners by sharing about the rapes with others. If he has largely been a good partner, there may be a sense of unfairly criticising him. You will need to overcome this unnecessary guilt – you're seeking to heal not to hurt your partner, because the rape hurt *you*. The positive aspects of your partner or the relationship don't deny you the right to heal.

Perhaps you are afraid that addressing the rape will mean that you have to leave, but remember that you only have to do what is right for you. Throughout the course of healing, you may feel intense hurt and anger. At times, you may wonder if you really want to remain in the relationship. Sometimes, healing does cause upheavals in a woman's relationship (whether her partner is the perpetrator or not), because as she heals, she grows in different directions to her partner. The guidance of a good counsellor will help you express your pain and clarify what you really want.

Is healing ever complete?

We believe that the recovery from sexual assault and its accompanying living issues is lifelong. In some ways it's like an onion with layer upon layer of denial and secrecy, for within, at the centre, perhaps there are many tears that need to fall. Judith Herman writes about the nature of healing:

> Though resolution is never complete, it is often sufficient for the survivor to turn her attention from the task of recovery to the tasks of ordinary life. The best indices of resolution are the survivor's restored capacity to take pleasure in her life and to engage fully in relationships with others. She has become more interested in the present and the future than in the past, more apt to approach the world with praise and awe than with fear.[5]

So while healing is never complete in the sense that if you take certain prescribed steps, you'll *never* have to deal with rape or abuse issues again, there does come a time when you're no longer dominated by the problems they have left you with.

What happened isn't so painful or frightening any more.

You'll discover a rich sense of perspective that doesn't cause you to question your worth so much. You've made sense of it in ways that no longer damage you, and you know that you're a whole person despite being raped. You will know that you are not dirty, not to blame, and you will know these things at more than just intellectual levels. You'll understand them with your spirit.

> You will feel more able to take on things that fear, depression or low self-esteem might once have led you to believe you couldn't do. Adair shares the benefits of healing in her life: 'Since counselling, I have been feeling more happy, less angry and anxious. I have started writing my poetry again, which I gave up for a long time, and I am planning on going back to school this year.'

If difficulties do crop up, they might still feel pretty awful. You may decide that you could benefit from a few more counselling sessions. This won't mean you've failed. The healing you've already done will serve you at these times.

To get back to the messy closet analogy, perhaps you have also had the experience of cleaning the closet, and after much hard work you've found treasures that you didn't know you had anymore, or thought you'd lost a long time ago. Healing is like this. We believe that you as you heal you'll discover quite wonderful qualities in yourself that you didn't know you had. You'll begin to feel proud of your victories and advancements, the great and the small. Summer shares with us moments of contentment with where she is, knowing that even though there are yet miles to go, what she has today is pretty good:

The new 'Summer' – a woman who is now, four years later, beginning to feel some degree of safety in what can be an excruciatingly painful world. When I refer to safety it is not only in the physical sense but my emotional world as well. I don't quite know about her yet but I do have expectations for her. I expect her to honor herself and her life everyday. I expect her to be gentle with herself in the face of adversity. I expect her to give to the world a little more than she takes. I expect her to be honest with those she loves, despite the fear that that may invoke. I expect her to embrace where she is in her continued healing. I suspect that I already have begun to like her and I am optimistic that I will again, one day, love her. That, as of today, will be enough for me. [Tears fall profusely.]

When you heal, 'Compassion and respect for the traumatised, victim self join with a celebration of the survivor self.' If you cannot yet celebrate your survival, one day you will. Meanwhile, we celebrate that *you* survived. We celebrate that Kuriah survived:

I am strong, no matter what others may think. I am scared, and I am not scared to admit that. I have courage, even if I don't think so all the time. I have feelings, even though many days I can't feel. I get angry. I get upset. I have cried too many sleepless nights. I have taken too many beatings. I have been treated with too much disrespect and degradation. I have needs. I have dreams. I have hopes. I am a survivor. I will survive this day and the next day … one step at a time.

As you read this book, and as you deal with your pain, take with you the promise of Adair:

Somewhere down the road of life, on your very long and tiring journey, there is happiness. For those reading this who are going through it, there is hope, there are people who care, and you are not alone.

CHAPTER 2

Another Aim: Identifying Sexual Assaults

For many reasons, not least of which is the confusion caused by social messages about what is considered 'real' rape, women sexually assaulted by partners often have difficulty defining their experiences. If you're a woman confused about sexual abuse happening in your relationship, or you wonder whether what is happening to you can really be called rape, the following chapter may offer you some clarity. If you're still being harmed, it might evoke some painful questions about your relationship and your future. Sometimes, identification doesn't happen until the survivor is out of the relationship and no longer needs to survive by burying the knowledge of what happened. If you're a survivor who is out of the relationship, you might find information that helps you make better sense of what you experienced, and aids you in your healing. Identification is a powerful healing tool.

Some women will experience deep pain as they recognise themselves in the following chapter(s). However, sometimes there are benefits in knowing that other people have experienced similar things to you, because, like many women sexually abused by their partners, you may have felt very alone, or like there's something wrong with your perceptions of what happened. As you find commonality with other women, you will know you are not alone.

> That's the reason work like this book is so important. Sometimes to hear someone else's experiences is just what a woman needs to identify her situation and feel less alone. (Charlotte)

If you experience pain, or you are still in danger, seek the support of a domestic violence or rape crisis service (see your local telephone book for numbers).

Sexual violence behaviours

We define sexual violence through the experiences of its survivors. Accordingly, we use the terms sexual violence, sexual assault, sexual abuse and rape interchangeably.

Whether accompanied by other violence or not, sexual assault and abuses by a partner are, as we will see through the voices of the women in this book, about a man's desire to disempower and dominate his partner.

We don't limit our definition of sexual violence by partners to that defined in legal statutes. The laws are both too diverse (across jurisdictions) and too narrow. As Melanie Heenan writes:[1]

> The difficulty for women lies in trying to reconcile their experiences with a cultural consensus that understands rape as sex that occurs unambiguously without their consent. According to Mahoney and Williams (1998), women know that their rapes have occurred when they have lain silent, where they have 'given in', where they have just 'gotten it over and done with', when violence was no longer necessary. They blame themselves for it. They take responsibility for it. They feel complicit in it.

We define sexual violence as the perpetration of any sexual action without consent. Our definition of consent is 'free agreement'. Free agreement means you have consented to sexual activity without the involvement of any force or coercion. It means that you must also be free to refuse or withdraw consent to sex without unpleasant or violent consequences. We will look at the variety of ways that free agreement can be made null and void shortly.

Let's first examine the range of behaviours that constitute sexual violence.

It includes forced penetration of any orifice, forced cunnilingus or fellatio and other forced touching. It is the threat to you of these actions.

> At one stage he said he was going to ejaculate on my chest and I told him to go ahead because I thought I don't care, as long as you don't touch me. Then he said if I performed oral sex on him that he'd stop, but he came up and put his legs either side and put his penis in my mouth and I was choking and I was trying to put my head to one side and I was crying and I think I just said I was choking or something. Then he tried a bit harder and he was holding me down the whole time. I just kept on trying to buck him off and it felt like it was going on for ages. All of a

sudden, I just felt totally exhausted and I couldn't stop crying. I was shaking and I couldn't believe that nobody had heard me. He'd gone down on me and there was slobber all over me and he'd made me very wet down there and was saying things like, 'Oh you taste nice' and it was just horrible. (Lisa)

Anal rape

Marital rape researchers have commented on the frequent use of anal rape by partners, saying, 'In many ways, anal rape appears to be the quintessential way for a man to humiliate his wife.'[2]

> Buggery isn't simply a lack of emotional intimacy. It reduces you to a sexual object, something (not someone) which is used for carnal pleasure with no concern for your needs or any pain or discomfort it may be causing. (Linda)

For other perpetrators, anal rape may be another way of making sure they possess all of the woman, or for the thrill of 'breaking in' a different kind of virginity.[3] Perhaps this was what Adair's boyfriend had in mind when he told her he would 'Fuck (her) little, prissy virgin ass.'

Emma informed her partner that anal sex caused her bleeding and pain; nevertheless, she says, 'That didn't stop him doing it again though – always "by accident", never asking permission.'

It is known that some survivors of anal rape feel longer lasting shame than survivors of other types of rape.

Oral rape

Women raped by husbands experience more oral rape than women raped by acquaintances.[4] Oral rape is perceived by perpetrators as a way of humiliating or punishing their partners – as with anal sex, it might be something the woman just doesn't like, or naturally doesn't like to be forced into. Nichole says, 'I was forced to give oral sex as he held my head down. This happened many times.'

Rachel, whose partner orally raped her twice explains, 'The act of having to kneel in front of somebody while they stand over you is, in my experience, a supremely submissive posture, and was intended by my abuser to humiliate me and make me feel powerless.'

The other side of oral rape is forced cunnilingus (going down on you). Because many women perceive this as such an intimate act, it can feel very violating.

Vaginal rape

Women experience dreadful attacks on their vaginas from partners who wish to degrade or hurt them. They are penetrated not only with penises, but also with fingers, fists or objects. For some women, the attacks are so vicious that they suffer tearing and laceration:

> By far, I mostly experienced attacks on the specifically female parts of my body; breasts and vagina. He punched, kicked and of course raped my vagina. It always had the feel of Paul wanting to denigrate what was woman about me. For me, feminist thought about rape as a gender-based crime makes sense when considering my experiences, because I understand that it was for him a supreme act of misogyny, or hatred for my femaleness. (Rachel)

Sexually abusive touching

This involves touching that is different than playful, affectionate lover's touching, and may be done to hurt and degrade. Forced kissing your mouth, sucking your breasts or causing you to touch him are types of sexual assault. The assault of Jodie in which her partner lay on top of her, touching her and 'pretending' he was raping her is an example.

Sexually abusive touching may be a strategy to remind a partner who owns her. Justine was sexually assaulted as punishment because somebody else, one of her partner's friends had taken it upon himself to touch her in a sexual way:

> One of his friends had walked past me and grabbed me between the legs, completely took me by surprise. I pretended nothing had happened so my partner wouldn't cause trouble. He had seen it and told his friend not to do it again … my partner kept grabbing me between the legs and dragging me around by my vagina (all this happened in the pub), telling me I had been asking for it and that I wanted his friend to do that before he got me up against the wall, strangling me.

Gang rape

Some men set their partners up to be raped by their friends and themselves. A man forcing his partner to have sex with other men than himself may be attempting to break her psychologically as she comes to feel more and more degraded.[5] Maree shares the following experience of a near-gang-rape:

And then, another episode he turned around and brought his mates home – there was four of them. As soon as I heard his car, I started cringing. And I turned around and they come in and he said, 'Maree go and get the boys a drink. They don't want coffee.'

As I'm putting the drinks and that on the tray, this guy comes out into the kitchen. I couldn't actually see but I could hear someone was walking in. I just presumed it was Alex. And this arm went around my waist, and then I looked, cause I thought, that's not Alex, cause Alex doesn't do that, if anything I'll get a slap in the back of the head or a punch in the head. And when I looked it was this bloke.

I said, 'Excuse me, what do you think you're doing?'

He said, 'Come on, you like it like this don't you?'

He was grabbing me by the arse and squeezing it.

I said, 'Do you mind? Alex, can you come here please?'

Alex come out and he said, 'What, what's going on? You are not going to turn around and keep this man happy?'

He just went whack, a backhand and I went flying against the sink. I was like oh my God, oh my God, this is going to be like those boys when I was 12 – I'm thinking this is a gang bang. But this is worse because this is my fucking husband, the man who is meant to be loving me, protecting me, caring for me, respecting me.

And the bloke turned around and pulled back and said, 'What are you doing Alex?'

He had made them believe that him and me are into swapping partners. That's what he made them believe. He said she wants it. Look that's how we are. That's the game we play. And I'm thinking, 'You sick prick.'

Luckily, one of them said, 'What are you fucking doing? That's your missus mate. She's not like that. Maree's not like that.'

Other sexually violent acts

Women are coerced to do other sexual acts. Liz, for example, had to watch her partner masturbate:

He also used to masturbate every morning and every night and it used to drive me crazy. He said to me, which I wish I'd never agreed to, he said, 'Is it alright if I do it while you lie there?'

I said, 'That's fine.'

But I didn't realise how much it would be. He got so desperate sometimes when I said I didn't feel like sex and he'd say, 'I've got to masturbate.'

I said, 'That's fine. Look can you just do it over there?'

He'd come back and beg me to hold his hand or something like that, and I'd feel guilty that I didn't want to hold his hand. I felt repulsed by it and sick of it and as if I had no space. But he would go on and on and that was part of the control and manipulation.

Shefali's husband made demands on her to masturbate in front of him and to watch him:

He started saying, 'You know I like visual stimulation.'

I said, 'Oh yeah, what's that?'

'I want you to put something there.'

I was appalled.

'You've never asked me to do that before … Okay, what do you want me to do with it?'

He goes, 'I want you to put it there and I want to watch you until I get excited.'

I didn't want to do it.

Kate was forced to participate in fantasies:

As far as sex, well, there always had to be a fantasy with it. We couldn't just have sex. It would always have to be me dressing up, or he wanted me to do a strip tease for him. Basically he wanted me to pretend to be a prostitute. I remember one of the women in the church saying if you want to keep your man faithful, and if it's prostitutes he's attracted to, then it's a prostitute you need to be. I just remember being dumbfounded.

I used to tell people, I used to say I felt like a prostitute. However the church was saying it was ridiculous to feel like a prostitute. Of course you are not a prostitute. You're a slut. It was just like being in my family.

'Sadistic' or 'obsessive' rape may involve 'perverse' acts and pornography.[6] Tiffany's husband forced her to watch such films and use sexual paraphernalia:

I didn't have control of our sex life. I would say the sexual abuse started as Peter got older. I had a lot of pain from endometriosis, and now the sex was becoming rougher. The further along our relationship was going, the less he could get sexually stimulated unless he got violent or had these pornos and I have to watch them with him, and he's stimulating himself, and then he starts to get all these gadgets and toys, and I'm asleep one night, and he had purchased this huge dildo, and he shoved it into me, and I screamed in pain, and then that made him sexually aroused, and that's how it started to go.

I told him he was hurting me, and I told him I didn't appreciate it. I wanted regular sex. I wanted regular love. Then I said to him just don't touch me anymore, and then of course all night he'd jump on top of me and just go at it, if he could. But usually he had to hold my hand up, or hold my hands behind my head.

Sexual violence also includes having sexual intercourse with you while you are sleeping or unconscious as experienced by Sarah and Jennifer:

It's at about that point that there were instances where I would wake up to find myself pinned under him. We had a waterbed – an ideal place to trap someone. It was waveless, but waterbeds, regardless of whether they have waves or not, if all the weight's in one point, that point goes to the bottom. So I would wake up and I would be pinned, because I would kind of like be sunk into the waterbed mattress, as well as the fact that he was on top of me and collecting his entitlements. I would say no but there was no choice and in the end I would just stop saying no because it made no difference.

I was very unhappy with what had happened and would be sitting in the bottom of the shower scrubbing myself and crying, and he'd go, 'What's wrong?'

I just said, 'I don't know. Just leave me alone.'

I just didn't understand what had happened. I've got two very vivid memories but I can't rule out that it didn't happen more than twice but I know very clearly that it happened on at least two occasions but it feels as though it was more than that.

I just couldn't understand why I was curled up in the bottom of the shower in really really hot water and scrubbing. It made no sense, no sense at all. (Sarah)

As far as the sexual assaults – he always insisted that I 'perform.' I was constantly pressured and made to comply with his sexual demands even when extremely ill. The most unforgivable act of this kind that he perpetrated on me was whilst I was under sedation after discharge from the hospital where I had been treated for the attempted suicide. I had taken both valium and sleeping pills this night and as I weighed only 43kg at the time I was quickly under their influence. I was unconscious in minutes. I was dimly aware of being moved but unable to comprehend totally what had taken place until the next morning when I found that Maggot had used me like a broken doll.

I was just a waste disposal for his testosterone build-up. I struggled out of bed and showered under the hottest water I could. I felt like a used dishrag. No thought for my condition or feelings. Nothing. Words can never describe how I felt. I just cried and cried. Just another item to add to the long list of atrocities I will never forgive him for. (Jennifer)

Intercourse with you while you are incapacitated by drugs/alcohol to the extent that you cannot give or withdraw consent is sexual violence too. Siobhan tells us how this can happen:

Whilst we were in the lounge room Arthur had removed my bottom clothing. He was brutal in the way he took my clothes off, tugging at them. He was rough. He then pushed me down onto the couch or the floor and had sex with me. I remember feeling so degraded and angry with him. I was telling him to stop it. I remember I was crying. I was drunk and so didn't feel so in control of my body as I would normally. After he did what he wanted to do it was over. I felt horrible after this.

I did not consent to him doing this to me. I was crying and felt so degraded by his actions.

It is sexual violence if your partner continues sexual activity after you have indicated you wish to stop. It doesn't matter if you initially consented; people change their minds for a number of reasons all the time. Your wishes must be respected. As Charlotte shares:

His sexual appetite grew tremendously and I was having a hard time keeping up – he wanted it all the time. He wasn't loving at all, he just expected it. One night, he told me to open my legs. I told him I was tired, but he demanded me to, and he told me he wasn't going to hurt me. I said I didn't want to again because I was tired. He accused me of not trusting him and got angry. Scared of his anger, I obliged and he took what he wanted.

I was starting to have trouble. Sex was painful; I was rarely aroused so that added to the pain. It hurt when I went to the loo and I suspected cystitis. Ted wouldn't let me go to the doctor's; he said it would pass in time. It got to the point where it was excruciating. I was doubled over in pain one night, when Ted came home. He wanted sex, and I told him I couldn't; that it hurt too much. He was furious at me for denying him. He threw me on the bed and tried to penetrate me. I was in so much pain that my muscles wouldn't relax, so it wasn't working. He flipped me over and penetrated me anally, despite me begging him not to. I was in more agony and devastated.

When he finished, he said he didn't understand what all the fuss was about, his ex used to love it, next time we would use baby oil, and he went to sleep.

I lay awake all night crying. I didn't know what to do. I loved him, but he was hurting me. Next morning, as usual, he had no memory. But something had changed. He was more aggressive with me, even without a drink. Sex had become him pinning me down, then finishing and not talking with me. I actually got used to it being that way.

And, if your partner goes ahead and performs a sex act that you have repeatedly stated you don't like or don't wish to participate in, this is sexual violence. Eva Jane felt betrayed after forced anal intercourse:

Yuck and I wished he wouldn't do it and why did he keep wanting to do something that would upset me if he really loved me? ... I had said no several times and begged for it not to happen, but it had and there was penetration and he would say that he was gentle. But I was still being violated in part of my body that I didn't want to be penetrated.

Other demeaning and controlling forms of sexual abuse may include:

- Denying reproductive choice to a partner. This includes denying access to contraceptive measures, or 'trickery'; putting a hole in the end of a condom before use. Forcing abortion or denying access to it.

- Leaving pornography where you are likely to come across it when he knows that you find such material repellent: pushing you to watch pornography as 'inspiration' for sex acts.

- Filming, photographing or recording you without your consent while you are naked or having sex

- Sexually degrading names, e.g. 'Slut', 'Whore'.

- Saying objectifying or degrading things about your body or sexual performance, e.g. 'you're a lousy lay', 'tits too small'.

- Commenting in a degrading or embarrassing way about you in the presence of others, e.g. 'you should see what she let me do last night', 'suck my dick, bitch'.

- Implying there's something wrong with you for choosing not to participate in certain acts; labels like 'frigid'. As Jill says:

  > He used to always ridicule me sexually. I was told how I ought to like oral sex; that something was seriously wrong with me because there were things I couldn't/wouldn't do.

- Saying that he doesn't want sex with you because you're 'too ugly' or 'until you lose weight' etc.

- Treating you in a loving way only when he wants sex.

- Boasting of affairs; comparing your physical appearance/sexual performance unfavourably to other women.

- Repeatedly (and unfoundedly) accusing you of affairs.

- Denying you the right to have friends of the opposite sex.

- Sexual innuendos about your friendships that are outside of joking.

- Open leering at other people and expressing the wish to sleep with them, or flirting in a way that suggests sexual availability in your presence.

- Controlling your clothing, e.g. 'you are not going out in that; you can only wear sexy clothes for me', buying revealing lingerie and pressuring you to wear it.

- Repeated hints or pressure to engage in sexual activities that you don't wish to, e.g. 'partner-swapping'.

- Kissing or fondling you continuously in company. This may be a sign of affection, but insecure and possessive partners may do it as a sign of ownership or as a form of control. Under these circumstances, it has an obsessive or controlling feel and can be distressing and embarrassing to you.

- Turning on you for sexual things you've done with him, e.g. 'Only a slut would do what you let me do.'

- Judging you for having sexual desires; saying or implying that there's something dirty or immoral about you for liking sex.

- Insistence on knowing about all your past sexual partners, demanding that you describe sexual encounters and 'rate' them in terms of his performance.

- Judging you for your sexual history, e.g. treating you as if you are less deserving of respect because you were not a virgin when he met you.

- Commenting cruelly about a past rape you experienced, e.g. implying you liked or asked for it; invasive questions about the rape that suggest an element of 'getting off' on it, e.g. 'How big was he?' 'Did you come?' For instance Jill describes how her husband/perpetrator regarded her assaults by a friend prior to their relationship:

> It wasn't until after we had been married about a year that he began to refer to the rapes as an affair. In times of arguments, he would bring it up. Or he would raise it in a casual conversation to prove a point. For a long time, I asked him to stop calling it an affair. Then I told him to think what he would, but that if it had been an affair, he needed to work on forgiveness and quit bringing it up. He never saw the problem in it, but finally three years ago, he quit calling it that. Yet, he still makes comments from time to time that make me believe that he still considers it to be an affair on a core level.

One-off sexual assault

Your partner or ex-partner may have sexually assaulted you many times or it may have happened once. Several of the women who share their stories with us in this book each experienced a singular sexual assault by their partner:

> One night, he came off the road and decided he was going to fulfil a fantasy of his own and 'fuck' his wife when he got home. He woke me up. I said no but he didn't care. He was nearly three times my size so when it became clear he was going to do what he was going to do, I quit fighting and probably dissociated through the rest of it. (Jill)

For Tracey, Helena and Natalie, the single rapes involved physical force. Of the five, Helena's story included several episodes of physical violence. Tracey was physically assaulted by her partner later on the same day as the rape. Neither Jill, Adair nor Natalie had experienced physical violence. What each had in common was that the rape took place almost out of left-field without any history of sexual deviancy. Natalie's boyfriend attacked her at the end of an evening out.

> When we got to his house, I wanted to just let him out and drive home, but I desperately had to go to the bathroom, so I went inside. He lived in a garage that had been converted to an apartment, and it was very small. He had a sofa bed that when it opened, blocked the entire room, so that you had to crawl across it to get out the door. When I emerged from the bathroom, he had the bed pulled open and was undressed already. He ordered me to take off my clothes and get into bed.
>
> I had stupidly left my purse across the room in his kitchen, and my car keys were in it, so my chances of getting my purse and getting across the bed to the door without him catching me were next to none. I am a very petite woman, and he was rather large and well-built, very strong, and I knew I couldn't fight him. I was scared, and decided at that point that it was safer to give him what he wanted so I could get out of there. I figured it would be quick, since he was so drunk and I knew how to satisfy him. I assumed he would either pass out after, or be so tired that I could get out before he tried to stop me. I was wrong, so wrong …
>
> I was crying, shaking, pulling back as hard as I could, begging him to stop, and suddenly he let go of me, shook his head, looked at me for the first time in hours, and asked me what was wrong; why was I crying. It was like he snapped out of a daze and was a totally different person. I sank down on the bed, sobbing, not trusting that it was over, trying to figure out how to get out of there.

If you experienced a one-off sexual assault and you find yourself thinking, 'it was only once and isn't as bad as repeated rape', please know that once is once too many. One-off sexual assault by a partner can be a terrible shock, and, as you perhaps already know, devastating in its impact.

What is *not* consent: use of physical force

Often, a sexually violent partner who is determined to accomplish a rape or other act of sexual assault does so with no intention of seeking consent – it's not an issue because he wants to commit *rape*. Or sometimes a man believes that he's entitled to sex whenever he feels the urge, and shows little or no regard for whether you want to have it or not – if you do say no, he takes no notice. Here, the lack of consent is obvious. So too when physical force is used.

He may hit, choke or use physical strength to overpower you or hold you down. Accordingly, US research has found that marital rape is most likely to occur in relationships characterised by other forms of violence. [7] Some women are beaten during the sexual violence or it may follow a physically violent episode where the husband wants to 'make up' and coerces his wife to have sex against her will.

> Eventually he couldn't have sex with me unless he hurt me first. He would explode, scream and yell and break things, batter my heart and my body and then want to make love to make it all better. Sex itself was not violent just all that led up to it. (Kuriah)

> And after the physical pain, always came the demands for intimacy. I hated it. I hated it all. (Jennifer)

These physical acts can be extreme as illustrated in the last sexual assault perpetrated by Kuriah's ex-husband:

> Just over two years ago, one terrible day he waited outside my house at two in the morning for me to come home. As I walked from my carport to my back door he was there. I reached the sanctuary of my door only to have him tackle me as I walked up the steps. As we fell, my head hit my china hutch fracturing my skull. I scrambled to get away from him and he chased after me. He caught me in the doorway of our son's bedroom and he pressed his gun against my cheek to tell me who was in control. He used his fists to beat me in to silence. He used the threat of the gun to keep me from screaming out loud. He tore my nylons off of me, loosened his pants and raped me: no preamble, no angry words; just a matter of fact action.

> When he was finished, he grabbed me by my hair and pulled me to my knees. He grabbed my face and demanded that I take his penis into my mouth. I turned my head away and he used his gun to turn it back. I took him in my mouth and within seconds he was erect again. He smiled in delight at what he had done and threw me back on the floor again. He turned me onto my stomach and sodomised me. He used his gun to penetrate me vaginally and he did it again and again.

> Over a four-hour period he performed 22 chargeable sexual assaults. He hit me, kicked me, bit me, strangled me, threatened me with his gun, and said horrible vile things about me. I was his cunt … the best fuck he had ever had … the whore he longed for

… the slut he always knew I could be … and he repeatedly told me that he had every right to be there, doing these things to me.

This time I did not buy the lie. He left my house around 6 a.m. and as soon as I locked the door, I called my advocate from Rape Crisis. She stayed on the phone with me while calling the police on her cell phone; she then switched to her cell and talked to me until she got to my house. The chief of police was on a ride along and he was at my house as well. I was covered with bruises from my collarbone to my knees and I was bleeding from my nose, my mouth, and other orifices. I had a blazing headache and it hurt to be … I walked away from the hospital the next day with a fractured skull, a stress fracture in my pelvis, a vaginal tear that required 16 stitches, three bruised and cracked ribs, a bruised kidney and a lifetime memory in the form of a sexually transmitted disease. I will live with the embarrassment and shame for the rest of my life. Forever I will have to tell my lovers about this night or at least about the aftermath. It's been 25 months and 2 days and I still have blazing headaches every morning. I still walk with a limp and I still take medication daily for a disease that will never go away.

If there's been physical abuse as there was in Helena's case, then all it takes is a certain look or the raising of a hand and the woman's shut down mechanism is triggered. Thus the actual rape may not involve additional physical force.

He may threaten to kill or otherwise harm you if you don't give in. Jennifer shares:

The difference between his sexual terrorism and the consensual intimate relationship we had was just that. When I felt I was being cared for, appreciated and loved, I welcomed intimacy with open arms. It was wonderful. However, when intimacy was being forced upon me through fear of reprisal, I hated him with all my being. But I never refused him no matter what, as the consequences were inevitably catastrophic for me.

I knew from the very beginning that Maggot's acts were sexual assault but also knew it would be next to impossible to prove that this was taking place as I was in a husband/wife relationship with him. The fact was that I was unconscious during the act and he refused the next morning to discuss it when I asked him what had happened to me. He told me, 'You don't need to know. I'll tell you what you need to know and you don't need to know.'

When I became visibly upset and tearful he became threatening and I immediately ceased my pursuit of his version of the truth.

I feared refusing his demands for intimacy. I performed so that I wouldn't be punished. He was seldom aware of my true feelings. I became an adept 'actress'. You do, if you want to survive. It all made me feel devalued, dirty and disloyal to myself as well as to him. It turned our relationship into a farce. Again he failed to see that his behaviour was killing our relationship but the truth is that he didn't care. He didn't have a problem, I did. It was always my problem.

Alternatively, he may threaten to harm another person. As Melina shares:

The sex started out as consensual. Like everything else, that changed too. Eventually it was something he demanded; something he would force me to do. What I felt was of no consequence. It always followed the same pattern. He would wait until I was sitting down or working on the floor, and he'd just come up to me and pull his pants down, standing over me in such a way that his crotch was right in my face and I was not able to stand up or move out of the way. He'd stand over me like that and just demand whatever he wanted. 'I want sex.'

And if I said no, if I didn't do whatever he wanted, he would stay standing over me and start screaming and making death threats and that he was 'going to shoot all you people' and 'blow up the town' and 'kill all you bastards!' He would keep going and going until I got frightened and just did whatever he wanted or if I still said no I would be subjected to days of threats and shouting. Sometimes he would shove me around and go and do what he wanted anyway, and I'd be too frightened by his threats to stop him. And when I did do what he wanted, I would feel overwhelmingly used and humiliated and worthless and dirty and ashamed. I was damned if I did, and damned if I didn't. This is how my daughter was conceived. And it continued until after my daughter was born and I moved out.

You may capitulate out of fear since he starts breaking furniture or other material objects:

I can remember a couple of times when I refused to have sex and he used to start smashing things and throwing things around. And he used to hit me into the wall. If I upset him, he'd be above me and I'd be in bed and he'd put his fist down on the bed as

> hard as he could and I just had to go, ' Well if I'm going to get
> hurt I'm going to get hurt now.'(Liz)

And, he might deprive you of sleep or not allow you to leave a room until you submit to a sexual demand. (Note: Sleep deprivation is a recognised form of torture).

What is *not* consent: use of other types of coercion

These are non-physically violent but emotionally distressing tactics of coercion that some men use to get their partners to have sex with them. Some authors have separated out the consequences as a distinct type of sexual assault different from rape and label it as 'sexual coercion'.[8]

Because there is a strong stereotype of 'real' rape as involving physical threats and violence, some people object to calling these types of coercion *rape*. They argue that women have a responsibility to say no even if they are scared they will be treated coldly by their partners, or that such women have a choice which is not granted to rape victims who have been physically threatened or forced. Particularly in engaging with the criminal justice system, defining this type of assault rape can be problematic. The dilemma is articulated by the US Battered Women's Justice Project:[9]

> There is no question that social and interpersonal forms of
> coercion can be oppressive and harmful. These types of coercion
> can be labeled rape for the political purpose of drawing attention
> to the violation inherent within them. Nevertheless, for the
> purpose of intervening on behalf of marital rape victims in a
> wide range of institutional settings, it is most useful to limit the
> definition of marital rape to the use or threatened use of physical
> force without the consent of the woman.

We don't believe that there is a difference for the survivor. Non-consent is non-consent, whether it is a result of physical brutality or emotional duress.

Interpersonal coercion

You may be subjected to continuous pressure from your partner; perhaps you give in to 'keep the peace', lying there passively while he takes what he wants:

> I remember having to give in to him sexually because he'd just
> be on my back every night about it. And it was just bum in the air
> and my head banging against the head board and no feeling and
> I'd feel like I'm just going to fly into the wall because he's such

> a big man. It would hurt me so much and I would disassociate. I
> wasn't there in the moment. (Liz)

Interpersonal intimidation also includes threats by partners that aren't
of a physical nature; for example, he might say he's going to leave the
relationship or stop supporting you and your children unless you comply
with his sexual demands.[10] This can be a powerful source of coercion for
those of us who are economically dependent. The words also represent a
very real threat if we have low self-esteem and feel pretty worthless. In fact,
Diana Russell found that while 70 per cent of the women she interviewed
said they were 'extremely upset' by threats of a physical nature, a larger
proportion of the women (83 per cent) were 'extremely upset' by threats
to leave or 'not love her'. [11]

Liz felt coerced: 'It was an expectation. Even if I didn't feel like it, it was
his right.'

You might feel that you have to engage in one form of sexual activity
to prevent something worse from happening; you submit to vaginal
intercourse to prevent anal rape, as Jackie did:

> He said, 'I am going to fuck you up the ass. Yeah ... fuck you
> right up the ass. You're going to like it, bitch.' I needed to control
> the situation, and I could only do it by using my head and words.
> I said, 'No, I'm about to come, keep on fucking me. Fuck me
> harder. Harder ...' until he finally came.'

Your partner might withdraw affection if you don't submit, or threaten to
sleep with somebody else:

> At that stage he was sexually very active and he had to have it
> five, six, seven times a night always. And if he didn't get it, well
> he'd go elsewhere. So for me at that stage, sex was not so much
> a loving thing, but more about having to stop this man from
> going elsewhere to get it. And also to keep him happy, because
> sometimes the aggression dropped. (Kelly)

Kate was trying to keep her husband from going to prostitutes, engaging
in peeping tom acts or cross-dressing:

> It often was painful, and I sometimes used to wonder what God
> was thinking when I was praying. Because I would often pray
> that God would help me to get aroused so it wouldn't hurt so
> much. I didn't want to be aroused to enjoy it. I wanted to be
> aroused so it wouldn't hurt. That was kind of the crux of it really,
> and praying that he'd hurry up and come. I think he was shocked

when I said I prayed through it because I usually gave a good show that I enjoyed it. I had to keep the whole pretence going that it was just great and I love it and boy what a great lover you are so that it would buy me some time so that he would not go and act out ...

I think his real skill was in emotionally manipulating me to do things. I felt very guilty and ashamed, and I always felt like I was the problem. I would often do things because I didn't know that I could say no. So he didn't actually hold a gun to my head to do a lot of things but I think I spent a lot of time doing stuff because I was afraid. I lived the whole time afraid that if I upset him or if we had a fight, he'd go and act up sexually. I lived trying to stop him, and it was thought by the church that my role was trying to stop him acting up. I was held responsible for his actions by the church and by him as well. I think he felt that too.

You may be under repeated coercive pressure to have sex before you are ready or to participate in a sex act that you have stated you don't like or would rather not be party to. To leave Africa, Helena needed her husband to sign documents allowing the children to go with her. This gave him tremendous power:

So he got angry after that and I said, 'I'm just going to bed.'

And then he raped me. He had sex with me and I was crying during it. I didn't say no. I didn't say yes. I didn't say anything except cry because I knew that that was the position I was in, and he knew that, and he didn't care.

I actually can't remember a great deal except that one conversation, and then the rape afterwards – that is kind of vague in my mind. I can't even remember how long it lasted for. I remember feeling totally devastated. Not devastated exactly; I felt powerless. I just felt like a cliché. I felt that no one was going to be able to get me out of this except me and my lies. The sex was a lie; being there was a lie; it was all a lie just to save myself and my kids and get us out of this situation. Because certainly no one was going to be able to do anything. Everyone just said, 'Too hard basket.'

Then after that he signed the papers and let me go. Not right after, but it was a couple of days I think, or three days, and he signed, but on the condition that no one witness his signature.

Social coercion

The term social coercion has been coined to encompass the pressures that society puts on us as women in intimate relationships to acquiesce to our male partner's sexual demands.[12] American research has shown that many women believe that it's their duty to comply. As one woman shares:

> When I married my husband my mother told me, 'It may seem a bed of roses but you have to lie on it no matter how many thorns'.[13]

Eva Jane understood that …

> I was very much there to satisfy him but because of the way I had been brought up and the way marriages tended to be at that time, you didn't say anything about it because you were the wife and you had to satisfy.

These cultural pressures may be even stronger for some migrants.[14]

In addition, religious beliefs can also play a major role in dictating such compliance and subordination. For instance, Kate's church dictated that a good wife was submissive and acquiesced to whatever her husband wanted sexually unless it was against the bible. Not only did the church condone his assaults but it held her responsible for his sexual deviancy:

> The church had definitely taught that you don't say no. That was part of the marriage counselling – that your bodies belong to each other and if the other person wants to do it, you don't say no. A good wife is submissive was rammed down your throat. You submit and you trust God that it will work out and God will bless you no matter how horrible it is and God will look after you and won't let anything terrible happen. You'll be pleasing God even if it's something terrible. So basically, unless it's against the law you don't say much, unless it's against the Bible or against the law like bestiality, or homosexuality, or having a third person involved …

Sarah was brought up in a religious family:

> The worse things got in the relationship as far as us being able to relate and communicate with each other, the less I was interested in physical intimacy. He would come into the bathroom and just open the shower screen door and stand there and stare at me while I was showering and I would say, 'Do you mind, I'm having a shower?'

He'd say, 'Your body's my body and I want to look at my body so I'm quite entitled.'

I'd try to shut the door and he wouldn't leave. I found that very invasive ...

So, there are all sorts of 'force' besides the physical. We strongly believe that it is important for you to know that you don't have to have physically fought or even said 'no' for an act to be regarded as sexual violence. Tears or other expressions of discomfort are more than reasonable indicators that you don't want the sexual activity. In fact, if you are a survivor of childhood assault or the victim of other violence in your life, fear may cause a 'freezing' response or 'numbing' as Tracey describes:

We got back to the apartment and he started to be interested in me for the first time in God knows how many weeks. I was saying, 'No. We're not dating anymore. No, no touching. No I don't want to do anything. No I don't want to do this,' but it just didn't make any difference. He lifted me up and put me on the kitchen bench and I said, 'No. Get your hands off me. I don't want to do this anymore. We're not dating anymore. Don't do this.'

He then picked me up, carried me into the lounge room, put me down on the sofa bed, which, of course, was laid out for a bed because I'd been sleeping on there, proceeded to lift my dress up over my head and off he went.

It was very difficult to explain to people why I didn't fight back. First of all, I was kind of in shock: 'Why are you interested in me now all of a sudden when you haven't been interested in me in over a month now?'

We hadn't had any physical activity in over a month. Why now?

I still had a gummy ankle. Then when he picked me up I was also worried about struggling in case I landed on my bad ankle. I kept on saying no, and I think I was just in shock. I was saying no and he wasn't listening to this.

It wasn't really until a few weeks later that I could see it was rape. While it happened I was just feeling so numb.

Remember that submission is not the same as consent.

CHAPTER 3

Another Aim: Confronting Society's Denial

In this chapter, we'll explore the social and historical backdrop of partner rape. Understanding that what happened to us has a context outside of ourselves is beneficial because it's another step in making sense both of our experiences of partner rape, and the responses to it that we may have seen or heard. If you are a hurting survivor of partner rape who has ever thought you are making something out of nothing, you'll find that it is actually the other way around; there are forces outside of you, which make *nothing out of something*. And they are wrong. They have asked that you accept the unacceptable. You may see that even while social attitudes towards partner rape deny it, you can find your voice and stand upon the truth of your experiences.

Rape in relationships happens fairly commonly and it damages its victims. Men who rape their partners are statistically more likely to murder them too.[1] Yet, as we'll see in the following chapter, these crimes, their danger and the psychological devastation they wreak are largely minimised or ignored by the community.

It might be tempting to believe that the social discounting of partner rape is a case of individuals who simply don't care about domestic or sexual violence, or who are just ignorant about it. But what individuals believe is often shaped by popular attitudes at large in society. There are certainly strong social beliefs about what is 'real rape', i.e. the stranger in the alleyway. Together with these beliefs, other powerful social and historical forces have worked to keep partner rape from being named and addressed, and to keep women from seeking redress and healing. It is these forces that this chapter will explore.

We have had much reliable research from three countries over the past 30 years that has verified the truth (and high incidence) of partner rape:

- In 1975, the results of an American study on many rape situations were published. Diana Russell was so appalled by her findings on rape in marriage that she decided to conduct a research project on this area alone. From the 930 interviews conducted with women from a cross-section of race and class, Russell concluded that rape in marriage was the most common yet most neglected area of sexual violence. [2]

- In 1994, an Australia-wide survivor survey found that 10.4 per cent of respondents had been raped by husbands or de factos, with a further 2.3 per cent raped by estranged partners; 5.5 per cent were raped by non-cohabiting boyfriends.[3]

- In 1996, The Australian Bureau of Statistics (ABS) conducted a random sample household Women's Safety Survey and found that 1 per cent of those currently in a relationship admitted to sexual assault by a current partner while 10.2 per cent said it had taken place in a previous relationship.[4]

- Figures on teenage girls in danger from boyfriends caused shock in research communities in the 1980s. Teen dating violence, which often involves rape and sexual assault, continues to be on the rise. Approximately one in ten high school students experiences dating violence – that figure is 22 per cent in college students.[5]

- David Finkelhor and Kersti Yllo's famous 1985 study estimated that 10 to 14 per cent of married women have been or will be raped by their spouses.[6]

- In the UK, one in seven married women reported they had been forced to have sex compared to one in three divorced or separated women.[7]

These figures are no doubt conservatively low. Those from high risk groups may not be included in the survey, and women who have been assaulted may either refuse to participate in the study, or fail to disclose for a number of reasons such as their fear, shame or denial. For instance, Canberra Rape Crisis analysed some of its statistics[8] for this project: of those who come to their service, 14 per cent present for this type of assault. Significantly, Rape Crisis counsellors report that between another fifth to a third of their other clients ultimately disclose about sexual assault by a partner during counselling.

At this stage, you know you are far from alone – you've experienced a kind of rape that is documented as sadly common. So, what are the elements that hide this common kind of rape? How do they help partner rape continue? We'll take a look in the following pages.

The male dominated rape culture

There are deeply entrenched beliefs that devalue women and, directly or indirectly, condone violence towards them. A society based on such beliefs is a rape culture. The US, UK, Canada, Australia and other western industrial countries continue to be male dominated. Each has a division of labour that relegates the majority of household chores and childcare to women. So women are more likely to have interrupted (and lower) income-earning histories. And, although more women are working outside of the home (along with taking care of hearth and home), the top brass of most occupations continue to be male. The huge array of anti-discrimination laws is unable to effectively challenge the masculine cultures of many workplaces. The institutions of society and its language and standards of 'normal' behaviour have so long excluded women and given men the power continue to do so for the most part.[9]

Rape is an inevitable part of inequality and cultures that devalue women.

Masculinity and rape

In a rape culture, male power is prized and encouraged. Sexual aggression and possession of women are the hallmarks of normal masculine behaviour.

Ideals of real manhood are endlessly churned out through popular culture and sport. Most readers will be aware that common cultural ideas about what constitutes a 'real man' lie in physical strength, aggressive competition and conquest. Boys don't cry; they are likely to be labelled 'girls' if they do. Real men fight – we've all seen the war movies that feature drill-sergeants screaming, 'Okay, you *ladies*' at platoons who aren't showing sufficient enthusiasm for war. To be branded 'ladies' is a painful insult because it implies weakness and inferiority. On the other hand, a woman who fights, takes on a traditionally masculine job or shows competitive power is said to have 'balls'. She might also be called a 'ball-breaker', which openly reveals the sense of threat that such a woman instils in some men.

Many men believe that proof of their masculinity lies in their ability to 'score' sexually with as many women as possible. They believe that a real man doesn't take no for an answer; there is a sense of entitlement to sex by any means necessary. If they don't use physical strength and aggression to force sexual activity on somebody, such men use verbal coercion or 'talking her into it'. They call this 'seduction'. It's not required that the sexual desire be mutual, just that the man gets what he wants. Such behaviour is often justified by the myth that a woman who says 'no' doesn't really mean it, or that she actually wants to be pressured a little. Men who don't hear a woman's 'no' are not confronted as rapists but are slapped on the back and praised by their friends as 'studs'.[10]

> The erect penis and the act of intercourse are generally depicted as a proud moment for the man affirming his right to call himself a man. He is 'the conqueror', the leader, the expert, the teacher, the pleasure giver. He has total power over the woman, and in this act he is at one with the idealised 'real man'.[11]

Woman as sexual property

Partners who rape often carry many of these attitudes into the relationships with the women they hurt and the relationship is seen to 'justify his aggressive behaviour or even to establish that he had a right to behave that way'.[12] Accordingly, marriage historically meant that a woman lost rights to any choice, including over her own body. A rape upon a married woman was an offence against her husband's property, but a rape by the same husband against her was no offence at all. As a US politician said to a group of women lobbying for change in rape laws in the late 1970s, 'But if you can't rape your wife, who can you rape?' [13]

Despite the existence of laws in most Western countries that now make rape of a wife a crime (see chapter 14) the idea of women as sexual property still has strong backing. Finkelhor and Yllo's landmark study found that it is still assumed by husbands and by general public opinion, that a woman trades sexual choice for a wedding ring.[14] In fact, a ring isn't obligatory; the same sense of sexual ownership can exist in less formalised relationships.

> Once a woman has voluntarily consented to intercourse, many men believe she has given up her right to refuse them on future occasions. Once again, the woman is seen to have become the man's property by virtue of having been penetrated by his penis. Like a wife, she has lost the right to say no.[15]

It isn't even necessary for sex to have occurred for lovers to think they have automatic sexual rights; Jodie and Nichole hadn't yet had sex with the boyfriends who raped them.

Rape myths

Rape myths are a fundamental part of the way rape and its victims are viewed in society. All readers will be familiar with myths about rape – those common and extremely pervasive beliefs which promote the idea that women 'ask' to be raped because of what they wear, or that women commonly lie about rape. Myths are a way to blame rape victims, and take the responsibility off their rapists. Rape myths are often based in ideas about the following:

- Female sexuality: As discussed above, women enjoy being 'coerced' or persuaded to engage in sexual intercourse. Therefore, the art of 'seduction' allows for any reservations on the part of the woman to be rightfully overcome by the persistence of the man. The media fosters this false image as we write about further below. If it's 'real' rape, she will probably have additional injuries too since in the rape culture, many see women as agreeing to sexual intercourse *unless* they resist throughout.

- Male sexuality: Rape is an effect or consequence of a libido that is uncontrollable if aroused. The man is driven by his desperate need to orgasm once his penis has been aroused by the woman's attire, manner, placement at a certain time; messages – often unknown to her – that her dress and behaviour supposedly send and of course by other intimate behaviours which she has permitted.[16]

- Harm: If a woman has had sex with the man before, then the rape couldn't be as traumatic for her.

Within the context of these and other false beliefs (e.g. if you are sexually assaulted, you will immediately contact the police) an extremely powerful continuum of what is perceived as authentic rape at one end and not quite legitimate assault at the other end forms. *If* the rapist was a stranger, *if* the assault took place in her home which he had broken into and *if* she was beaten seriously enough to get injuries, then maybe she will be seen as not having precipitated it and the reaction will be supportive. Sexual assault by an (ex) partner is not usually seen at that end of the continuum.

Social acceptance of rape myths means that society aligns itself with the viewpoint of the rapist, rather than the victim. As a result of this, the survivor of partner-rape finds that the statement her partner made in raping her, 'You are my property and it is my right to do what I will with you', is endorsed by her church, the law, and perhaps her friends, who tell her in numerous ways that she was having sex with him anyway and so what happened couldn't have been harmful.

The political scene

At a time when politicians are making the issue of terrorism a priority, terrorism against women in the home and/or by rape has been sliding off political agendas everywhere. For example, there have been funding cuts in recent years:

- In 2003, the Liberal government in Australia decided that every single household in Australia should have an information 'pack' to increase anti-terrorism awareness. This exercise cost $10.1 million, siphoned from funds allotted for a domestic violence program; $2.6 million of that came from funds to combat sexual assault.[17]

- In the UK, funding for rape crisis centres is worse than inadequate – it's nonexistent: Women Against Rape, instrumental in making rape in marriage a crime in the UK, had its core funding cut by 100 per cent in 2003; the following year, the Rape Crisis Federation was forced to close.

- Funding to the Violence Against Women Program in the US was slashed $12.5 million in the 2004 budget, reducing money for emergency shelters, crisis hotlines and other desperately needed services to protect women from violence. Three million dollars was cut in the 2005 budget for state grants that go towards improving stalking databases, encouraging arrests, reducing violent crimes against women on campus, and enhancing protection for older and disabled women.

The criminal justice system

Even if sexual assault is perpetrated by a non-family member, the criminal justice system's response is notoriously hard on the victim. We couldn't put it any better than Rae Kaspiew did in 1995:

> … Women are the outsiders because rape law has for centuries reflected the patriarchal view of human relationships and sexuality which defines woman as 'other', and that which is possessed. Rape law reflects a construction of sexuality which discounts women's subjectivity and privileges the male perspective.[18]

Now sexual violence by a partner has the added element of taking place in the home and is therefore by definition *domestic* violence. As a community and criminal justice system, we tend to use a masculine model of violence. Consequently when we think about domestic violence, a single physical assault, without much if any contextual background, may be the image conjured up.

However, domestic violence is not about a single strike. Frequently the 'incident' that results in intervention by the criminal justice system is in actuality just a small part of a complex pattern of control and *can't* be adequately understood nor its gravity measured in isolation from that background. As we'll see in chapter 14, the criminal justice system frequently fails to understand that.

As a consequence, most of the women in this book who reported the rape(s) experienced frustration and insensitivity in their contact with the police, prosecutors and the courts. This lack of 'justice' is not at all surprising; judges, police and jurors are drawn from a society that continues to adhere to the myths above.

Church

Major religions automatically relegate women to secondary status 'under man'. Central to this ideology is the belief that women must submit to men in all things – indeed, wives were at one time obliged to report refusals of sex to their husbands in confession.[19]

Sexual violence is often minimised by religious leaders who commonly see it as a problem between the couple, rather than holding the man responsible for his actions. Married women being abused have commonly been advised by clerical leaders to remain with their violators; behave better, submit more, pray harder. This has ensured the ongoing disempowerment and abuse of women.[20]

> I remember a couple of times saying to one of the (Church) women that I didn't want to be married any more and two of them got together and just blasted me for about an hour and a half about how selfish I was. How dare I even think that and what did I think thick and thin means? This is thin and you stick by him. (Kate)

Another woman, a practising Christian at the time, disclosed the rape to a church elder, who told her that the rape of a wife was perfectly acceptable behaviour.

The unmarried victim of rape by a partner may also find her violation approved by the church, but for different reasons. At the time of Rachel's abusive relationship, she was a church member. Several weeks after she left her partner, he raped her. When she attempted to tell her pastor of the rape, she was offered the conclusion that if she 'had been living right before God' (i.e. not living as a fornicator) it would not have occurred. He advised that her sinful disobedience to God meant she must accept the responsibility for her ex-partner's action.

Media

The media is an extremely powerful shaper of social attitudes. It is a primary socialiser of our children. It does have the potential to do much good. Unfortunately, it has instead commonly perpetuated inaccurate and unjust myths about sexual violence and its victims.

> The pervasiveness of rape myths and the habits of the newsroom have led the press to consistently cover these crimes with bias and, sometimes, even cruelty.[21]

News, both print and televised, has a tendency to broadcast rape cases in a selective way. For example, only the details, which cast suspicion on the victim's credibility, are presented, while facts that give support to her claims are commonly omitted. It is called 'slant', but bias is a more honest description. For instance, in one US high profile case, the victim, Greta Rideout, who had brought charges against her husband, was for the most part reported in such a way as to suggest that she was a liar crying rape for revenge, that she was after money, that she was a pawn of man-hating rape activists, that she actually liked being raped, or that even if it did happen, it couldn't have been very traumatic because she was married to her rapist.[22]

Although 'Don't believe everything you read' is a statement many people recognise as good commonsense, it is unfortunate that when it comes to the topic of sexual violence, the cliché becomes, 'Do believe everything you read' (especially when what you read brands the rape complainant a liar or a slut). It also indicates how powerful the media is.

It is rare to see sympathetic or accurate dramatic portrayals of what intimate partner rape is or how damaging it can be. Rape of partners as an acceptable activity is portrayed in movie scenes and soap operas from a protesting Scarlett being swept off to the bedroom by Rhett in *Gone With the Wind* to modern soap operas. In one 2002 episode of the soap, *The Young and The Restless*, a woman was raped by her ex-partner. The producers denied that the scene could be called rape even though there was clear force and the victim clearly said she didn't want to take part in sex with her ex-partner. Thus, we see perpetuation of the myth that rape under some circumstances is not rape.

Though talk shows such as *Oprah* have featured proactive material on domestic and sexual violence, others have not. On one *Maury Povitch* program, a couple was featured who had separated because of the husband's domineering nature. Footage was shown of this huge man thundering, 'She does what I tell her, dresses how I tell her, and has sex when I tell her.' The end of the show showed the couple reconciling, with the man saying, 'I got to look after her to keep her.' Not only did this suggest that his sense of owning his wife wasn't changed, but at no time was his admission of sexual coercion challenged or named as rape.

With the media churning out the notions that it does, it's little wonder that so many people think rape of partners is okay.

Social perceptions are hazardous to women

We grow up exposed to all of these myths. It can make it hard to define what's being done to you as rape:

> I guess it took me quite a long time to be able to use the word rape in that situation, because to me, rape was something that happened to girls who walked across dark parks in the middle of the night. I couldn't match that with what was supposed to happen in a happy and loving marriage, and particularly so early on. (Sarah)

> I did not tell anyone – I didn't know it was rape, just like I didn't know what I was going through was domestic violence. I knew it was unpleasant, I knew I was miserable, but I thought it was my lot in life and I was scared to say anything for fear of the repercussions. (Melina)

Further, as we'll see in later chapters, even if you are aware at some level that what your partner did to you is called rape; you may feel weighted down by the knowledge that sexual abuse by somebody with whom you've had a relationship is not seen as 'real' rape. Summer speaks of 'the shame of feeling half-raped'. This is an excellent portrayal of the emotional limbo many survivors of partner-rape occupy:

> How much time would have been taken off my pain sentence and those of other women if we'd been able to know sooner that our violations were not only real, but also as serious as any other? That our feelings were completely valid? It is probably fair to say that getting recognition for our experiences and accessing help and healing would have been much easier without the expectation that doing so would lead to more hurt. (Rachel)

The myths and social denial are harmful to women in other ways. Just a few examples:

- Women may be re-assaulted as illustrated in Robyn Warshaw's book, *I Never Called It Rape*. Women who clearly identified the sexual assaults as rape did not have sex with their attackers again, while those who didn't have that awareness, did so and were often raped again.[23]

- If women are getting advice from people who subscribe to the myth that what is happening is not real rape, this can have frightening implications for their future.

- Even when survivors have felt able to ask for 'professional' help, the scarcity in resources of compassion and understanding has been problematic. Until recently, many agencies fostered the view that it was either a rape issue or a domestic violence issue but couldn't be both; none of the women's services took ownership. The result was women being shunted around by services but receiving little real assistance.[24]

When we think of a war zone, we may see a picture of greyness and silence with people bustling around the bodies that lie uncovered and alone on the ground. So too the victims of sexual assault by a partner who are too often isolated and ignored.

Also, in the war zone it's hard to tell the good guys from the bad guys. In the turmoil and agony of bombings, mines and automatic weaponry, there's a blurriness in the picture and without some sound over, it's unclear who's doing what to whom or why. So too the sexual assault victim whose family disbelieves her story and attacks her for creating trouble. So too the sexual assault victim who too often finds her truth, her voice, her life, herself the object of examination and attack.

It is well past time to bring partner rape out of the closet and recolour the war zone into a society with warmer shades of support and validation.

CHAPTER 4

Stereotypes of Women Raped by their Partners

The questions asked about the victims

What type of woman becomes involved with a partner-rapist? Is there in fact a 'type'?

This question has no definite answer because *any* woman can be sexually assaulted by her husband or boyfriend. If you saw the film *What's Love Got To Do With It*, you will know that talented and intelligent women like Tina Turner experience severe and prolonged domestic violence, including rape. The women you meet in this book, including its authors, illustrate that domestic and sexual violence span all classes, races, economic and educational levels, and have little to do with the personal characteristics of the women who experience them.

A strong negative stigma surrounds women who have been abused in relationships; the stigma that accompanies rape often means that survivors of partner-rape face a sort of double whammy. Saying you were abused by a partner evokes ignorant inferences about your character, but rape, because of its sexual nature, draws additional ones that assume at worst that you must have liked being sexually abused. Negative stereotypes of abused women often contribute to the feelings of shame and inferiority that the perpetrator has also triggered and fostered:

> Maybe it's my fault I let him get away with it for too long. (Siobhan)

> I had lived for years as a non-person. I had no emotions that were not dictated by him. I had learned to bury my feelings so deeply that I couldn't recognise them. I had turned them off and couldn't find the on switch. Mentally and intellectually, I was deficient. I couldn't form a complete sentence without weighing every word. I couldn't organise my thoughts; I couldn't hold a conversation with anyone. I felt stupid and began thinking that all those things he had said about me were in fact true. (Kuriah)

Let's do a little exploring and exploding of some myths about women abused in relationships. Perhaps you've been hurt by some of them, and may even believe them to a degree. We hope you'll be less inclined to be hard on yourself after reading the following.

Are women who are raped by partners stupid and crazy?

As survivors and as people who work in the areas of rape and domestic violence, we are frequently asked, 'Why don't these women just leave?'

This question is often asked from genuine concern or honest curiosity. But at other times it is asked in a derisive way: the enquirer might just as well come out and say, 'She must have been stupid or at least a little crazy.' Rather than seeing an abused woman as somebody who was betrayed perhaps repeatedly, people resort to questioning her intelligence:

> Although the abuser betrayed you by being abusive rather than loving, you may also feel as if you betrayed yourself – your dignity, your self-esteem, your worth as a person – by staying in a situation in which you were being harmed. 'Am I a masochist?' you may wonder. You may especially ask this question if you have been exposed to psychological theories that contend that you're only victimised if you allow yourself to be. Such theories are unrealistic and inaccurate. They fail to take into account the multitude of ways in which even a bright, financially independent and psychologically well-balanced individual can become entrapped in violence.[1]

Focusing on a survivor's personal characteristics absolves perpetrators of the responsibility for the abuse they commit. Unfortunately, there's a tendency for people to side with perpetrators of violence regardless of what they have done. People seem to find it too hard to accept that sometimes other people are shockingly cruel, and in searching for reasons, they need to imagine that victims must somehow be responsible for their fate. Thus, women who have been raped or battered suffer incredible levels of insult and blame from family and friends or wider society, including the criminal justice system – we look further at this in chapters 13 and 14.

In fact, you were not stupid or crazy for staying. You may remain for many reasons; usually in part because of the dynamics of violence in relationships (see chapter 7) and the effects that has had upon you:

> But I just thought the next day ... I have to be a better woman. Why can't I get this right? So anyway, the relationship continued. (Kelly)

Violence in relationships is indeed centred on control. It is slow and insidious:

> Those things all happened slowly and subtly, so I ended up very much under the thumb and just couldn't recognise that I was under the thumb. (Sarah)

> Then you think about that. I thought it was just selfishness. I didn't think it was also control and abuse and that you're the second class citizen in the family. It didn't click. Because it was slow. (Tiffany)

It's also about humiliation and degradation:

> I've been stabbed. I've been held in a bath with an electric blow heater over me for 10 hours. I've had the handbrake pulled on in the car while I've been driving. I've been punched numerous times. He used to get me into a position in the corner of the wall in the room we lived in and he would just keep hitting me, or pulling my ears and my nose. And, he dragged me around the house by my ear. I'd rather be punched in the face. That's just humiliating; that's how you treat a dog.

> But the whole time I just wanted for him to love me more, and for him to not want to do that to me anymore. (Kelly)

Your sense of self erodes:

> So you stop fighting it, because you just can't keep up with it. But the controlling continues without a break. You adapt to it. Eventually, what was once strange becomes normal. You eventually stop thinking of yourself as a person. Your feelings are of no consequence. (Melina)

You may become increasingly isolated through secrecy and shame. Your perpetrator tells you that it is your fault he has to beat you. There's no-one to contradict him. As one woman says:

> I suppose it was partly because there was no one to validate my reality since I couldn't tell any of my friends what was going on in our house. Consequently, there's always this self-doubt; that maybe it really isn't as bad as it seems. And, there were the periods when he was charming and loving, which contributed to that type of denial.

> There was another reason that's hard to explain but it has to do with needing to stay so that he will ultimately realise that I'm OK and a good person. For years he'd been justifying his

drinking, adultery and abuse with a view of me as a nagging bitch. It became incredibly important for me to show him that his reality was not right.

On the outside I looked like I had it all together. I never stopped functioning so you see no one knew. No one had a clue. But, on the inside, each time that I failed to follow up on a threat to leave him, the self-hatred grew. It expanded within like a malignancy until I totally lost a sense of myself.

And, leaving doesn't necessarily terminate the violence. We only have to look at breaches of domestic violence orders, reports of rape and the fact that almost one half of the homicides perpetrated by husbands take place after the woman leaves the violent relationship.

Given the effects and dynamics of violence in the home and lack of informal and formal support, getting out of the relationship can be extraordinarily difficult for any of us:

It was pretty hard when I did leave him. I found it really difficult to do and society particularly unsupportive. It was so hard being on my own, it was so hard putting up with the stigmatism of being a single parent and all the crap that goes with that, the insecurity, the financial strain, his constant stuff with the kids and all the pressures with the children, and I think I couldn't have done that until I got a certain inner strength and a deep, deep, deep, watertight conviction that I couldn't go back. So I think I had to have had a gutful to leave, because it was really hard, particularly with kids. (Kate)

Are women raped by partners masochistic?

The idea that women want to be raped is a very old one. Such false myths have given rise to flippant 'jokes' such as the one that features a woman walking into a police station and saying, 'I'd like to report a rape! I'd like to, but nobody will give me a reason to!' This is another way to blame rape victims, and excuse perpetrators.

Some women may fantasise about rape. This is due in part to living in a culture where rape has been eroticised and even made sexy. Women take on the myriad of messages society gives us about female sexuality being dirty and wrong. Consequently, rape fantasies are often a way for a woman to achieve some sexual release without feeling bad about it.

In the vast majority of cases, the cause of a woman's rape fantasies doesn't lie in her desire to be harmed or victimised, nor in her supposed masochism. Rather the cause lies in the sexist notion that having sexual desires is bad or degrading to women.[2]

Rape fantasy can be triggered when a woman who has pushed down memories of prior sexual assault is having sex:

> He would laugh at my lack of rhythm and the like. I got through the first years of the marriage with rape fantasies and dissociation, but never told him what I was doing. He knew about the childhood abuse and that didn't seem to matter. He was the healthy one in the relationship. It all centred on what he wanted me to do to him, but there was never the ability to slow down enough to learn how to do it together. It would often trigger things from the past and the only way through it was by dissociation or fantasising about rape. (Jill)

If you have ever fantasised about rape you may feel guilty and ashamed and think that this somehow has played a role in you being sexually assaulted. These words from Diana Russell might be helpful to you:

> Having voluntary fantasies of being raped, and wanting to be raped in actuality are two entirely different things. First, people are in complete control of their fantasies, even if the fantasy involves a situation in which they are out of control. A woman is hardly in control when she is raped. If she were in control, the situation would not be imposed and would not be rape. Second, a person is rarely likely to feel fear in a fantasy which she has constructed. But in a real rape or attempted rape situation, unlike the fantasy version, women are usually afraid and often terrified.[3]

You may feel especially guilty if you enacted mock-rape, bondage and discipline or sadomasochistic fantasies with your partner. Perhaps you believe that such games gave him the message that actually raping you was okay. First, be assured that many couples play such games, and that it doesn't culminate in the subsequent rape of the female partner.

Let's have a look at some more fundamental differences between sex-games and rape.

Games are consensual; rape isn't. Women who are practitioners of BDSM enjoy the same right not to be raped as anybody else. If their partners have raped them, they have been betrayed. The idea that a history of sex games cancels a right to withdraw consent is wrong. Would acting out spanking fantasies give somebody the right to subsequently beat you up?

Games are about sexual fulfilment; rape isn't. It is about punishment, lack of respect and control.

Are women raped by partners weak?

Some are quick to label the battered woman as weak, passive and dependent, especially if they remained for a time in the relationship. People who take this position often proclaim in loud tones of superiority that *they* would never put up with it.

Survivors say things like, 'If I hadn't been such a coward I'd have left sooner.' Self-berating can happen for years after women end abusive relationships, often in the face of great danger. People who brand survivors of partner violence as weak may not appreciate that a woman 'putting up with it' is not weak but may be trying to survive conditions that threaten her very life, as Jennifer did:

> I told him that I was calling the police and that he would have to leave. He became very angry again but I remained calm and insisted. He picked up the computer and said he was taking it with him. I told him that he should go but leave behind anything of value as he owed me a large amount of money and when he had repaid that he could have it. We struggled and I managed to take the computer and hide it. During the struggle, my hand was cut quite badly. Eventually he grabbed me by the shoulders, looked in my eyes, punched me in the stomach twice, causing me to double over. He then brought his knee crashing into my chest twice saying, 'Maybe that will stop you.'

> By this time I had lost a child, suffered sprains, bruises, contusions, bites etc., ad nauseam. I learned never to raise my voice, cry, indicate to him that I felt pain or discomfort, regardless of what was happening to me and never to fight back. He viewed everything as a competition and if I had fought back he would have continued assaulting me until I stopped defending myself. One of us would have died; probably me.

> I know that if he had not been sent away I would either still be with him or have suffered some terrible 'accidental' death. He is a truly evil person.

Sometimes, a man may rape his partner because he feels threatened or undermined by a show of strength on her part; the rape is his attempt to take away her strength, to 'weaken' her so he can feel more in control. Accordingly, women are often raped after they have initiated a separation or indicated that they are going to leave:[4]

> When I said that I would need to speak to my lawyer, he then sexually assaulted me.

> This time he used a weapon – a pair of scissors.

> I recognised that what was happening was rape when he threatened me with the scissors, whilst trying to remove my clothing. I suppose it was the weapon that made it obvious. I fought to get away. However he is a lot stronger than me plus I have rheumatoid arthritis that affects my strength. I finally succumbed and waited until he finished. The whole process took a great deal of time. (Samantha)

It is the perpetrator who displays weakness by not choosing other alternatives to violence.

If you re-evaluate some of what you see as weakness, you might begin to see that it was actually strengths that enabled your survival.

Are women raped by partners frigid?

If you saw the film *La Bamba*, you might remember the scene in which Joey, the brother of Ritchie Valens, laments to Ritchie that he has to 'practically rape' his wife Rosie in order to get sex from her. 'Frigid' wives or women who withhold sex from their partners are often blamed for rapes perpetrated against them.[5]

Here, the perpetrator becomes the victim – a poor, frustrated man who actually has no choice but to take by force what he can't otherwise get. Remember that he has that insatiable libido too! The blame for the victim is justified by the belief that men can't be expected to do without sex, and that it is women's duty to fulfil those needs.

However, none of the 30 women in this book withheld sex from their partners.

> Carl had sex with me without my consent a lot of the time. Sometimes I felt like I had to, because I'd said no for too long. I thought if I said no he'd hit me or force me. (Liz)

The frigidity myth is confusing rape with sex. Yet, research reminds us that rape is not usually committed to have sex, but to humiliate and punish.[6]

Dispelling the myths

As we've seen, myths seem determined to blame women one way or another for rape. On the one hand, it is inferred that rape victims are 'sluts' who are raped for being too sexual:

> Unfortunately, I created a false correlation between my sexuality and Paul's sexual violence. I imagined that the rapes had occurred because I had been sexual with him in the first place. He often used to say he was doing it to teach me not to be a slut. Shit! In hindsight, how twisted is it to use rape as a form of moral instruction? (Rachel)

On the other hand, we hear that women are raped for not being sexual enough! Yet sexual boundaries are your right to set. Having boundaries is not a crime, but rape is. You can counter the blaming myths and help set those boundaries with affirmations like:

- I have a right to not enjoy sex.
- I have a right to be asexual.
- I have a right to not always be interested in sex.[7]

These myths are false and derived from parts of rape culture, including a lack of understanding of male and female sexualities, the effects of sexual assault, the dynamics and consequences of violence in relationships. Knowledge is power. We hope that you are able to use the information in these last pages to mute the voices that want to blame you for your victimisation.

CHAPTER 5

Women at Risk

While we've attempted to dispel some myths about there being certain types of women who are sexually abused in a relationship, there are indicators that some women may be more at risk. However, speaking of risk factors is in no way intended to imply that the violence is the survivor's fault – and it bears repeating that any woman can be raped by her partner.

> The phenomenon of repeated victimization, indisputably real, calls for great care in interpretation. For too long, psychiatric opinion has simply reflected the crude social judgment that survivors ask for abuse. The earlier concepts of masochism and the more recent formulations of addiction to trauma imply that victims seek and derive gratification from repeated abuse. This is rarely true.[1]

We do believe that it is vitally important for any of you who can identify with experiences and emotions shared in this chapter to be aware that you might be particularly vulnerable to violence from a partner. We are not saying or implying that abused women 'go looking' for abusers, rather, abusers may seek out vulnerability and exploit it. Looking at how earlier abuse helps shape our responses to later abuse should be an exercise in making sense of our experiences and healing, not more self-blame.

Feelings of 'not being good enough' or 'different'

All of the women who shared their growing up experiences with us disclosed that they emerged from childhood and adolescence with an impaired sense of self-esteem:

> I emerged from childhood not liking myself. I had no confidence or self-esteem. I felt like I was a failure. Even though I became a model and was quite successful, my inferiority complex remained, but I learned to hide it. (Samantha)

> Very early on I developed a real sense of the outside and was
> also very intimidated by other people, and I felt very overweight
> early on in life. And I feel very ugly, and gross, and whatever.
> You know, I did feel special early on in life, and like ... I never
> felt like I was born with no talent or nothing, or anything like
> that. But I did always feel terribly misunderstood. (Kelly)

We may wonder where such feelings of being fundamentally flawed come
from.

Some of the women like Sarah don't recall any physical or sexual violence
but believe that her family of origin was fairly normal. However, like Kelly
and Samantha, she just didn't feel 'good enough':

> I've always had a childhood memory of not being good enough.
> I don't know that it's necessarily something my parents said, or
> that it's something I assumed. My sister has a dose of it too but
> not as strongly as I do. So it could well be something we picked
> up. Whether or not my parents actually ever said that, we've
> always thought that we could be so much more ... I guess I had
> major episodes of depression in high school. When I was 16, I
> tried to commit suicide. I used to have these tablets for allergy
> reactions, because I'm allergic to grass and dust and stuff like
> that and had a lot of problems with my nose. I could only take
> half of one otherwise I would be literally falling asleep at school
> the next day. I just did my best to knock off a whole box of
> them.

> I felt I would never be accepted and loved; particularly when
> everybody else could get boyfriends and was popular with the
> boys, and I would hang out with the guys and was very accepted
> as one of the guys, but not as a romantic interest for the guys
> unless they were desperate. So here was me thinking I would
> never find anyone who would love me, never be accepted, and
> just decided it wasn't worth the pain of living, that the pain of
> dying, particularly if I didn't have to hurt myself, would be
> much easier.

Natalie explains that although there was no physical abuse in her childhood,
her self-confidence was eroded perhaps in part by having a delinquent
older sister and being cast in the role of 'good child':

> My mother chose my clothes for me, and the rest of the family
> generally took a protective stance with me, making my decisions
> and treating me as ineffective. While I enjoyed the comfort, I
> also lost esteem and confidence this way.

Mom was at home most of my younger years, but I also recall being scared of her, although I am not sure why. I recall taking over 15 minutes one time to work up the courage to ask for some ginger ale when I was sick, afraid that I would get in trouble for not being in bed. There was no physical abuse, but on looking back, my mother was very controlling (and still is), and had high expectations that I felt I could never meet ... Growing up in the early years, I remember being very anxious and fearful. I frequently cried myself to sleep, and woke up at night with anxiety attacks. I tried my best to be perfect, to make up for all of the bad things that my sister did, and so became the 'good child'. I was always on guard, waiting for the next bad thing to happen.

Kate similarly remarks on the effects of a very controlling mother on all areas of her life, particularly on her eating:

She was very controlling and had come from a very sexually, emotionally abusive family herself. She was damaged. The whole family were very damaged, all her siblings. She was mildly controlling with my brothers but absolutely obsessively controlling with me, and it was funny, because I knew from a really early age that the purpose of my life was to try and make up for Mum's crappy life. I was really young when I knew that. I was quite young when I could articulate that.

I just was so angry at her and felt so suffocated by her. She would screen all my calls and she would break up my relationships with boyfriends without informing me. She would decide she didn't like a guy and that would be the end. She would tell him he wasn't to come over anymore.

I felt very manipulated by her. I did end up doing what she wanted me to do – even in Year 12 she wouldn't let me come out of my room until dinnertime at 7 o'clock. I had to stay in my room and do my homework. I had almost no choice of subjects or any of that sort of stuff. It was what I should be doing, what was right and expected of me. I knew I didn't like it and I knew other kids' parents wouldn't do that, but I couldn't tell her. The impression that I had is that Mum would just fall apart if I told her what I really thought.

She was obsessed with the fact that I was going to get fat. So despite whether I was hungry or not, there was a certain amount I was allowed to have and that was it, and I was actually physically active and quite a bit taller than her, but she used to monitor everything in the house. She knew the bread, and if I wanted more, I was just going to get fat so I wasn't allowed to overeat. I would come home and be starving hungry after school and I was allowed two pieces of toast, and that was grudging, and that was it. It just didn't matter how hungry I was. I had to wait until 7. There were no snacks, no fruit, that was it; only a very strict certain amount of food, and all of that kind of stuff. She was very controlling about food. So, I just remember being hungry a lot, and not being able to eat enough.

Tiffany feels that she had a 'very normal childhood' and that her parents were always there and loving. However, she had dyslexia and wasn't able to perform as well as she wanted to at school. She always felt inadequate and different. The latter feeling was shared by others like Lisa:

> I went to a lot of schools but didn't have very good experiences. I felt very self-conscious and very ugly. I remember saying to my Mum once when I was a teenager, 'Do you think I'm pretty?' She said, 'Well, when you smile.'

> I think that she was trying to make me smile more, or I don't know what it is, but I just remember feeling very unattractive and very frumpy. My parents weren't the kind of parents to give a lot of compliments really at all.

> I remember being very shy of boys. I just seemed to make a few close friends and I'm not the kind of person that's very popular and has a whole bevy of friends. But I very much rely on my few friends and I'm very close to them and would do anything for them sort of thing.

> I remember feeling a bit unusual because I felt as if I had a lot of sexual energy at a young age and I didn't know what to do with it, and that made me feel a bit unsettled; made me feel I was a bit different.

For Charlotte, moving to a new place in her early teens, she experienced social ostracism and other bullying from her peers contributing to 'poor self-image':

> I believed that I was ugly, so I didn't eat very much, and I didn't notice boys as they joined in with the teasing at school. My own friends were too embarrassed to be seen with me, and I spent my days alone in the toilets, praying the day would hurry up and end and I spent my nights crying and hoping that I might sleep

and not wake up … socially I was a wreck. I was full of hate and self-loathing. I had very little faith in myself, my parents and anyone else.

Growing up with physical or sexual violence

For some the low self-worth was likely a consequence of experiencing childhood violence, either as the direct target or as a witness. As Judith Herman states, 'The risk of rape, sexual harassment or battering, though high for all women is approximately doubled for survivors of childhood sexual abuse.'[2]

Kuriah was impregnated by her biological father:

> There is nothing more shameful than this part of my life. Here is my ugly secret that I rarely disclose to anyone.

> When I was almost 14, I gave birth to a son. We share a father. My father began molesting me at the age of five and it went on until I left our house at 18. I never spoke to him or saw him again with the exception of my college graduation and my wedding day. He died a few years ago and at that time, I had not spoken to him in over a decade.

Children who are abused by people they are close to learn to equate love with violence and sexual exploitation. Rachel explains:

> Unfortunately my adult experiences of rape and battering were not new to me. Battered by both my parents since infancy and sexually abused for a long time by non-related perpetrators, I did not see being hurt as separate from being loved. My childhood sexual abuse taught me that I was dirty, that no escape was possible, and that I deserved it. These were the responses I brought to Paul. I know now that the abuse was not about me deserving no better – he abused me – he was a perpetrator. Nevertheless, I understand the ways in which my earlier history promoted acceptance and accommodation of his violence.

They have not learned to create safe and appropriate boundaries with people, and they grow up unable to see themselves as having any right to choice. Their self-image is so damaged that they may see nothing wrong with even extremely abusive treatment of them by others. It is seen as unavoidable and the ultimate cost of love:[3]

> He'd been putting negative thoughts in my life and he put me down. He sexually molested me. He touched my breasts or he

was always talking sexually to me but I guess I didn't really know these things and what he did. I'm just starting to understand that now. I can remember when I was a little girl he used to get off by coming all over my stomach and I think that he penetrated me with his penis but I'm still not sure although I have a lot of memories and nightmares. My uncle had molested me on a number of occasions when I was quite young putting his hands down my pants – that sort of stuff. So I thought ok – what Travis is going to do to me is the same as what Uncle John's done so you have to start surviving ... I feel now that all my panic attacks and my nightmares have been because of him. It's all coming back in quite severe flashes and it really does explain why I have suffered extreme dieting and fear. My childhood was filled with a lot of terror. I don't remember a lot of it still ... I remember once I was drinking at the bubbler and this bully bashed my head against the wall. I thought it was just happening again – the torture that Travis inflicted – so I just accepted it and I remember me holding my wrist out, not fighting, letting it happen.

I felt at 15 that I was sick and tired of my head ringing from my mother's blows. You know you've got to sort of steady yourself, go sit down somewhere, but the head ringing was really horrendous and you know the welts that would come up sometimes particularly from the strap, but mainly they would be where you would cover with clothes anyway; of course around the head your hair covers it. (Eva Jane)

Nichole, who had experienced a rape at age 15 before she met the partner who raped her, believes her earlier rape experience impacted on her response to her boyfriend's sexual violence:

This absolutely affected what happened, and was the impetus for the first act of sexual violence by the ex-partner. My self-esteem was terribly battered by the first assault, and having (the partner) tell me it was my fault and that I deserved it pulled me even lower.

Witnessing violence

Tracey would see her step-sister beaten:

I did get on very well with my (step) Dad. He was fun. He has a very good sense of humour; he's a very social person. But he has a lot of anger. He wouldn't necessarily yell; he wouldn't be loud. In fact, I can't remember a time when he actually would shout but he had this kind of voice that sort of built up; bottled back rage. I remember that I could feel how angry he was sometimes. I'd sort of have this anxiety about his anger and fear that he would lash out. I'd already been through that when it got to a point where he did beat me around the head.

I had really woeful self-esteem.

Siobhan witnessed her mother beaten and experienced verbal abuse from her Dad:

Mum was a shy, timid, very kind person while Dad was verbally violent. He had an alcohol problem and he was the kindest man when he wasn't drinking but when he was drinking he was a monster and very verbally abusive and controlling as well but nothing like the sort of stuff I went through in my marriage.

Sometimes on the odd occasion he'd hit Mum. I do recall that but mostly it was verbal. I don't think he was ever sexually violent towards my mother, not that I know of. I've spoken to her about it and she said no he wasn't.

So too Maree:

We were poor. I loved my parents. My father was an alcoholic, a very bad one at that. Never hit us or abused us sexually or nothing, but he did my Mum. He used to belt her. He was a good provider, I'll give him that much, but other than that as far as my Mum goes, he treated her like a pig. You would treat a pig with more respect than what he did my mother, only when he was drunk. When he was straight, he was fine.

He broke her ribs one time, another time, her jaw. I'd seen a lot of blood, but my brothers used to turn around and they'd push him or grab him saying, 'Stop it Dad. Stop it.'

And he'd just turn around and go even wilder.

'Don't interfere, your mother's done wrong, and she's not looking after you kids properly.'

She was though – she was a very good mother actually. But when he was pissed he thought she was no good; she was just rubbish. In my head I used to turn around and think, and my sisters used to say the same thing, and feel the same like me – there's no way I'll ever get married. A lot of times I didn't want to get married. If this is marriage, God they can have it. There's no way in the world I want to get married.

Melina was present when her mother tried to commit suicide:

> My mother was what is known in AA as a 'bender drinker'. Months, years could go by without a drink and then suddenly and spectacularly all hell would break loose.
>
> When I was around the age of five, my mother had a bout of drinking and slashed her wrists. She ran through the house, wild-eyed, tear-streaked and hair flying, shrieking like a banshee (an unearthly sound of animal panic and desperation that made your hair stand on end).
>
> 'I'm not your mother! I want to be left alone to die!'
>
> Over and over. As she ran, she flicked her hands so that the blood sprayed along the walls. I followed her down the hallway, and noticed blood on my nightdress, wondering for a moment amidst all this if it would come out in the wash. Then she got into the bath, and I remember seeing her lolling in what appeared to be a bath full of blood, shrieking when I looked in the door.
>
> After returning home from the hospital, I went around the house cleaning the blood from the walls (the areas I could reach, at any rate) whilst carrying on a dialogue in my head, trying to be matter-of-fact and normalise the situation, and asking Dad, 'Why does blood go dark brown when it's dry?' when I really didn't care to know the answer. I just wanted to sound cheery and make it better. I was trying to signal by my tone of voice and attitude that everything really was *all right*. Even at that age, I knew I couldn't just be a little girl and cry.
>
> The day was never spoken of again, by anyone. Years later, I tried to raise it once with my mother, but wasn't allowed to talk, for she told me I was trying to hurt her by doing so ... I emerged from childhood with a wobbly at best sense of self-esteem but no history of addiction, eating disorders or mental illness.

Keeping the secret: the three rules

The children who grow up as the recipients or witnesses of sexual or physical abuse learn the three rules of violence well; each contributes to a flawed sense of self.

'Don't talk'. The survivor is taught not to mention to anyone outside of the family what was done to her or what she saw or heard. And the family doesn't sit around the dinner table discussing the violence either.

She doesn't disclose to anyone and she takes on the responsibility for the violence. Natalie was molested by her grandfather but has never disclosed it and doesn't recall all of the details yet.

Or perhaps she does disclose but the family doesn't discuss it; the parents may believe that it is better that way. That she'll forget. She doesn't forget though and in the absence of discussion and validation, it may become even uglier.

Thus, that kernel of shame grows bigger, fed by silence and non-support:

> I never said nothing to nobody – no girlfriends, nobody at all. I kept it inside for years and years and years.

> I felt dirty, and filthy, and I kept blaming myself. I kept thinking that it was me. After so many years, I'm thinking, 'Why am I blaming myself? I didn't do anything. (Maree, attempted rape at age 12 by two older boys)

'Don't trust'. How can a child learn to trust when she has been violated with violence? How do you trust your siblings if there's only limited love and approval available which you are competing for? How do you learn to trust yourself when your perceptions of reality are invalidated?

An impaired ability to judge who can be trusted or not can also play a part in the revictimisation of a child-abuse survivor.[4] Kate experienced ongoing sexual abuse, first by her brothers and then as an adolescent and young adult leading up to the violent relationship:

> I was only in about Year 9, and I was at a party with a friend and this guy who was a couple of years older than me was at the party. He had a motorbike and was very cool. Anyway, he and I started kissing; once again, lots of alcohol at the party. He said to come outside and we went outside and he suddenly whipped out his penis and said, 'Give me oral sex.'

> I'd never even heard of this concept. And he was aggressive and intense about it and I started to get really freaked out and I said, 'No, no, I don't want to do this.'

> I don't remember how it finished. I don't know whether I tried it and just went, 'No this is terrible.'

> I can't remember the details, only being horrified by the whole concept and him sort of grabbing me and my getting away in the end.

> And I never told anyone. I don't think I've ever told anyone actually. I felt somehow that I had encouraged his behaviour. I

think I just kept all this stuff inside. The mantra in our family was: you don't talk about your feelings, ever. Sometimes if you did, you might actually stir up some of Mum's feelings and if you did that, heaven help you. She would become upset and she wouldn't speak for a day. No one would know what had happened except they all knew who did it.

The other thing that happened to me when I was a kid was that I had all these peeping toms and flashers. It was like I was some kind of magnet for these guys. Out of three hundred kids at school, I was the one that the guy flashed to at the fence in primary school, and several times there were peeping toms at our house and I'd be on the toilet or getting undressed and they'd be peeping in through the window, and some huge chase ensued. I can't tell you how many times I got flashed at as an adolescent by total strangers in the park. I've probably been flashed at fifteen times.

I did start to feel like I was some kind of magnet.

It was also a time of a lot of pain in my life. From the time that I was about six until I was about eight, I was molested by a teenage boy from the neighbourhood in a wooded area where the kids in our neighbourhood played. I remember thinking, when he no longer seemed to be around, that it didn't have to hurt if I didn't think about it and so I didn't until 11 years later.

But as I look back, I see that the impact of that experience followed me without the memory being in my conscious mind. I went from being a pretty laid-back kid to one that had to be in control of everything – not in an aggressive domineering way, but in a way that said certain things had to be on my terms. I began taking scalding hot showers and baths and in my teenage years stayed consistently underweight. Although I didn't diet or over-exercise, I was probably a good 10-15 pounds lighter than my doctor liked.

I never told anyone about what happened.

'Don't Feel.' If she lets herself feel the pain or the anger, she'll cop it worse. So she learns to keep it inside.

Young women who have been sexually abused or raped sometimes become self-destructive, and may abuse drugs and alcohol as a way of coping. For instance, Marg was molested by her uncle when she was a child and turned to cannabis and alcohol by the age of 13. She, like many of us, then engaged in risk-taking behaviours in the belief that we, and our bodies, are not worth protecting (see chapter 9). These activities can increase the risk of repeated sexual assault by perpetrators who take advantage of our pain.

Breaking the silence

We hope that reading this chapter has assisted you in understanding that some childhood experiences can contribute to a damaged sense of who we are in the world. This in turn can make us more vulnerable to predators. We hope that if you haven't experienced violence in an adult relationship but you do identify with the feelings of low self-esteem, you'll recognise this vulnerability.

There are actions that you can take. Your shame is nurtured by the three rules. We wish you the courage to break those rules. You can start by naming your childhood experiences and sharing them with someone else. We've found that counselling and self-help support groups are both of great potential value in addressing that shame core and turning the messages of self-hatred into ones of self-love.

Self-care is another important step in helping our hurting inner child to heal. (Note: The later chapters on healing from our partner violence can be used for healing from childhood traumas too.)

And, if you are a survivor of partner rape, perhaps you can now begin to refuse to wear any more self-blame or belief that sexual violence makes negative statements about who you are; it doesn't.

> Girls sexually abused in childhood and raped in their teens need to be hearing much earlier that they are not to blame, and that they deserve better. If you were sexually assaulted as a child, or before you met your partner, you may have come to believe that sexual violence must be tolerated, is your fault or is a normal part of a love relationship. None of these things is true. You deserve to be truly loved and live in safety. You'll find this out if you work through old but powerful scars you may have carried through from earlier times. (Rachel)

CHAPTER 6

Men Who Rape their Partners

Why a chapter on the perpetrators?

Carol Adams writes, 'Our language has a tendency to mask violence. It may highlight someone's victimization while simultaneously cloaking the agency and actions of the perpetrator.'[1] When we use terms like 'battered woman' or 'rape victim', there's a danger that we make battery and rape into something that is a woman's problem, which then generates theories that blame her, while the perpetrator and his actions are forgotten. This chapter is intended to be a reversal of that process. Since the sexual assaults on the women in this book are something that men did to us, we explore here some of the factors behind the actions of men who rape.

We believe that exploring rape and perpetrators can enable survivors to make better sense of their experiences, and help in giving back responsibility for the sexual assaults. If you are a woman who has blamed herself, you might find that exploring the psychological and social factors that contribute to the mindset of men who rape enables you to see that what was done to you wasn't caused by you; rather your partner operated from a set of beliefs, ideas or motivations that are common in perpetrators of rape, and were likely in existence long before he met you.

Some women may find validation in the ability to define the partners who raped them as rapists. Yet this can be understandably distressing to others who wish to continue the relationship with the perpetrator. If you do begin to feel upset, it might be a good idea to take a break from reading and engage some support. Hopefully, you will also find that the understanding you gain can help you heal. Our aim is also to challenge myths about who are 'real' rapists. Perhaps you've struggled with the fact that the public image of your partner is a favourable one, fearing that nobody would believe you if you tried to tell somebody what he has done to you. Or, because of popular notions of what a rapist is, you may even have begun to doubt your own reality.

However if you look at the table below, you will see that the reasons men give for rape are remarkably similar whether their victim is a stranger or a partner:

Reasons Given For Rape	The Partners[2]	The Strangers[3]
Power	'It gave me a certain feeling of power over her because I knew she found it unpleasurable. It was one of the only times I could best her'	'… At that time, it gave me a sense of power. A sense of accomplishing something that I felt I didn't have the ability to get.'
Anger/retaliation	'I guess I was angry at her. It was a way of getting even,'	'I met a girl at a party; she irritated me … I took her home to her apartment and I raped her.'
Insecurity/sense of inadequacy	'… She was a stronger person than I was in many ways, and I had an inferiority complex about it. '	I raped about four chicks … they all had a certain self-assurance … it used to be threatening to me.
Sexually aroused by causing pain/fear	'I had the best erection I'd had in years. It was very stimulating. I walked around with a smile on my face for three days. You could say, I suppose, that I raped her.'	Interviewer: Did her fear turn you on? Rapist: Yes Interviewer: How did you feel about her being hurt? Rapist: That was exciting.'
Preference for coercive sex over consensual sex	'I get this satisfaction from a feeling of some dominance – a man over woman thing.'	'Making a girl wouldn't do it … It was the unattainable I wanted.'
Sense of entitlement	'I have a right to this.'	'You want this, and you don't see why you can't have it so you take it

This chapter will provide many other examples of the similarities between the stranger rapist and the partner rapist. We hope that this reality will be an important step in grounding your experiences as real.

However, exploring the mindset of men who rape shouldn't be seen to offer excuses or justification for rape – there are none.

Types of partner rapists

The power rapist[4]

Many men understand that invading a woman's body against her will affords them a sort of ultimate power over her. The ability to subjugate a woman with his penis gives the rapist a sense of mastery over feelings of inadequacy and weakness; it reaffirms his masculinity.[5] If your partner was motivated by a need for power when he raped you, you may have noticed the use of interpersonal and/or physical coercion. Emma gives an example of the former:

> The best way I can describe it is that there was an unspoken threat that if I didn't have sex with him he would emotionally abuse me. He would throw a tantrum if I said no, guilt trip me. Ignore me, reject me, and because he had convinced me that I was in love with him and couldn't live without him these things hurt me a lot so in a way, I submitted to sex because it was the only way to avoid emotional/mental pain.

The power rapist intends to have his way anyhow: his position is 'give me sex or I'll take it'. Perhaps your partner attempted to verbally badger or bully you into sex but when that was unsuccessful, resorted to physical force:[6]

> I told him no, that I didn't want to do it – he kept going, when I kept saying no he stopped briefly, he started abusing me (verbally) telling me that it was all my fault and that I kept leading him on. Then shortly after he continued – I continued to tell him to stop and that he was hurting me but he did not. (Jodie)

The power rapist uses whatever force necessary to achieve sexual intercourse. He may sometimes use slapping or weapons to show his victim he means 'business', yet sexual possession of the woman to satisfy his need for power is his main aim, rather than hurting her physically.[7]

Even though the rape hurts you, your partner may not see any harm in it, or he simply doesn't care what you feel.

> During the worst incident I did cry and he was aware of this, despite the fact that I was doing my best to conceal my tears. He did not stop. (Emma)

Indeed, far from seeing his behaviour from your point of view, the power rapist often needs to believe you enjoyed his attentions.

As a means of taking control of you and the situation, he may force sex on you to gloss over an argument, or to force you not to be upset. Jennifer, who was frequently raped after being beaten, expresses it best:

> In my experience it is used to reaffirm their 'love' of the victim and that 'now everything is back to normal'. As if nothing has happened. As if the sexual act itself wipes out all unpleasantness.

When a man feels that his ownership of his partner is challenged, power rape might be an act of 'repossession'.[8] And so as we've seen elsewhere, it's not unusual for the assaults to take place or even to begin following separation:

> Sexual assault is still continuing. He is always kissing me. Feeling my breasts, in between my legs – 'just as friends'. He has had sex with me twice in 4 weeks, even though I have told him I don't want to. He has stayed at my house the past 3 nights and although I have managed to stop him having sex, he always tries. Again, according to him, this is just being good friends. I have told him that I feel as though he is still trying to control me. (Justine, after separation)

Because power rape may lack the physical violence of more stereotypical 'violent' rape, victims are often confused and angry with themselves, believing that they could have done more to stop it. The perpetrator may say things like, 'You could have stopped me', or 'You wanted it', which adds to confusion and shame. If you have felt this way, you might benefit from knowing that making the victim feel complicit is a common tactic of men who rape for power.

The anger rapist

All rape contains elements of anger, and in anger rape, there are power and control issues. But anger is the primary motivator.

> But I felt so dirty all the time. I spent hours in the shower, even when the water was running freezing, even when there was no more soap, I used cleaning products. My time in the shower angered him. Sometimes he was so angry that he had sex with

me when I got out. He demanded I leave the bathroom door unlocked, as he felt he should be able to look at me any time he wanted. (Charlotte)

Typical of anger rape, your partner may use rape to punish and humiliate you. It may have featured ejaculating on your face or in your hair to cause greater humiliation to you.[9] Anger rape commonly features forced oral and anal sex because the perpetrator perceives that you will find them painful and degrading.

He is likely to use violence to achieve sexual intercourse, which is itself typically violent with slapping or biting involved:[10]

He was sometimes very violent during sex. He would hit, pinch, or beat me during or prior to intercourse, or for refusing to submit. (Nichole)

Unlike the power rapist who forces sex on his partner after beating her in order to manipulate her feelings, for Nichole's partner beating her was part of the rape: 'He often wanted sex after beating me. The battering seemed part punishment and part foreplay.' So, too, Kuriah:

He appeared not to notice my bruises or the pain that showed with my every movement. He'd want to make love to the body he was beating only hours earlier.

'I don't want to get mad ... I am sorry you made me correct you ... again ... I love you.'

And Jennifer:

I was woken late at night or early hours of the morning and slapped across the face whilst I was in a half-dazed state because I refused his demands and asked not to be woken.

One time he positioned himself behind me and held my chin, head and shoulders. He proceeded to pull my head to the side as if to break my neck. He then pushed me to the ground and straddled me, he placed his knees on my arms pinning them to the floor, and with one hand he held his hand over my nose and mouth to stop me screaming in pain and horror. He had his other hand around my throat, strangling me, whilst he told me that he wished I were dead. He then lectured me on my behaviour and what he expected from me. He would only let me go if I indicated that I would comply.

I had to see a chiropractor because of the pain in my neck and have ongoing health problems and pain from this injury.

> Another time, he became extremely angry and grabbed me by the arms, digging his fingers into my biceps. He pushed me into the lounge room and bent my hands towards the inside of my forearms. I screamed in pain. Eventually he released my hands and punched me in the stomach several times. I fell to the floor. He then dragged me into the bedroom by the hair, throwing me bodily onto the bed. He straddled me, restrained me so I couldn't move and started to lecture me. He held my face in his hand and applied continual pressure to my face. I started to scream in fear and pain. He repositioned his hand over my face, covering my mouth and nose so I couldn't breathe. I continued to scream through his hand. He refused to remove his hand until I stopped screaming. Eventually, he removed his hand.

Like many anger rapists, maybe he forced you to take part in your own degradation:[11]

> I was forced to take my clothes off while he sat in a chair in front of me with a knife in his hand. He wanted me to take my clothes off slowly and when he felt that it wasn't slow enough he would get up and hit me again and tell me that I better 'start fucking listening'. I was also told to 'play with myself' in front of him, which I did. I was told if I didn't give him the blowjob the way he wanted it that he would have my daughter do it for him once I left … Even when I cried and begged him not to hurt me, he would become more violent in whatever he was doing to me at that given time. I thought I could make it stop but I was only making it worse. (Summer)

Your partner may show a tendency to 'snap' suddenly, changing from relatively pleasant to angry and violent:[12]

> Just when I thought I could predict him, he would react to something in a way completely apart from what I expected. We were at a house where some of his friends lived watching a movie. He had been wonderful that night – sweet and charming and why I started dating him in the first place. Then, halfway into the movie, he became moody and said it was time to go. He was angry at me and hit me and raped me that night. I later found out that it was because he thought I was flirting with one of his friends. (Nichole)

Anger rapists tend to espouse strong stereotypes of masculinity. They may act tough and be outwardly very 'macho'. But within the core of themselves this image is quite fragile. Thus, sometimes Kelly's ex-de facto partner Jack, when very drunk, would cling to her and cry for hours, saying, 'I'm nothing. I'm nothing.' She also sensed when he was violent towards her that, 'It was like Jack was angry at me.'

> I remember once on the kitchen floor being forced to masturbate in front of him, and when I refused to do it, he started tearing my jewelry off. And then he started shoving things up me, and I would beg him not to, and sex really became extraordinarily aggressive there for a while.

Perhaps due to an inner sense of fragility, the anger rapist releases rage onto women he sees as having belittled or bested him in some way. Sex is his weapon of contempt. So, even though your partner says he loves you, when he rapes you it has a feel of him 'making hate' to you.[13]

> Looking back, I can see that when he felt inferior or upset was when he tended to be more abusive towards me (like when he would fail an exam or get a speeding ticket). (Nichole)

If he is jealous or his sense of sexual ownership is otherwise threatened, it leads to an anger rape:

> The thing I will never forget is when we went to watch Robbie Williams in concert. It was his first concert and he didn't know what to expect. We were both singing and dancing around with the rest of the audience. Admittedly I was more enthusiastic than he was, although he did seem to be enjoying himself. We went for a couple of drinks afterwards, had a laugh and then went home. When we got home, he flew into one of his rages, screaming that I fancied Robbie more than him (!), accusing me of wanting to do this, that and the other with him and the usual tirade of ridiculous accusations. He then ripped my top off, pulling, nipping and twisting my breasts. My pants and knickers then came off and he went down on me, biting my vagina with such force that he lifted my bottom half off the bed with his teeth. I can remember thinking that I couldn't believe he was doing this on our daughter's bed (she was staying at relatives). Afterwards, when he had calmed down and apologised, we made love (had sex) even though I told him I didn't want to as I was so sore down below. He did it anyway. (Justine)

And, if he feels rejected, rape may be an expression of revenge.[14] In the weeks after Summer ended her relationship, her ex-partner warned her that she would be sorry if she did not return to him. Ultimately he surprised her alone at her place of work:

> I was raped vaginally, anally and was also forced to perform oral sex. He was armed with a knife that was held against me at various times throughout the rape. I was beaten very badly with a closed fist as well as an open hand. I was also held tightly around my throat, which was restricting my ability to breathe. I was also knocked into a filing cabinet which caused bleeding. He was also banging my head against the filing cabinet and the floor. I bled quite a bit from being raped anally. I was left quite bruised and bloody from the rape and the beating.

If you experienced anger rape and you blame yourself for 'making' your partner angry enough to do this to you, you are not alone. However, please know that there's absolutely no justification whatsoever for using rape as a punishment – never. Other men address anger without feeling that they have the right to commit a violent crime, especially against somebody they love.

The sadistic rapist

Though many anger rapes do contain sadistic acts, the difference between anger rape and sadistic rape is that where the anger rapist hurts his victim to punish her, the sadistic rapist causes her pain and terror in order to arouse himself.[15] If your partner was motivated by sadism, pain inflicted on you was not incidental to the rape, but deliberately inflicted. In the course of rape, you may have suffered being bitten, burned, cut or otherwise tortured, with your partner deriving pleasure from your fear and pain and his ability to intentionally hurt you. Maybe you noticed a bizarre, ritualistic quality about the sexual assault/s, or there was bondage and the insertion of objects into your body:[16]

> So he would do that. He was big on choking. Big on grabbing me around the throat. Even before we'd have sex. He was about six foot three, a very big guy, very tall, and he didn't look heavy but he was very solid, and we used to call him tree-trunk legs.
>
> I think the worst thing now that I go back to it is that not just being woken up in the middle of the night, like me being asleep and he puts his penis in and I'd find that there's some kind of large object stuck in my vagina, but also holding me down. I mean, I finally realised that that really was the part that upset me because he would hold me down in certain ways. Not quite bondage rape but there were times that he'd choke me but that was usually when he was angry, but holding my arms down, the way he'd hold my chest down, the way he'd pin my legs down,

and now, I think the thing that really upset me the most is that one, I didn't want to have sex that way. (Tiffany)

The brutal rape of (then) 16-year-old Adair by her boyfriend was an attack which happened out of the blue when Adair ran away from home with him. It contains many features of sadistic rape:

> I was awakened by banging on the door to the bedroom we were staying in. I had locked it. Only because of all the strange people coming and going, I didn't want some weirdo coming in at their leisure.
>
> When I asked who it was, he said, 'Frank. Let me in.' So, I unlocked the door and I started to walk back to the bed. He said, 'Take your clothes off, I'm gonna fuck you good.' I just chuckled and kept going towards the bed. He grabbed me and said, 'I'm gonna fuck you like the little whore you are.' I tried to push him away, but he grabbed my hair and flung me onto the bed. When I went to get up, he pulled a switchblade out and told me to 'just take it easy', that there was no reason to be scared, he wasn't going to hurt me, just 'fuck my little prissy virgin ass'. He pushed me down onto the bed and cut my panties off at the sides and then put the handle of the switchblade inside me. Not forcefully, but taunting me with it.
>
> He bit and pinched my breasts and told me to roll over. When I resisted he acted as though he was going to put the blade into me and so I rolled onto my stomach. He then proceeded to penetrate me anally, punching me in the back, calling me a whore and a little cry-baby. I tried to get up, but he would punch me right in the center of my back, it was taking my breath away. He then rolled me over and went down on me, biting the inside of my thighs and squeezing my breasts so hard, he left bruises. He kept asking me 'if it was good' and 'why are you crying' and calling me a 'fucking baby'.
>
> He then crawled on top of me and put my arms above my head, and kneeled up on my shoulders and told me to 'suck his cock'. I held my breath and he started thrusting his penis into my face, hard, and I blacked out.
>
> When I came to, he was inside me, saying, 'I thought maybe I was fucking a dead chick.' He had the switchblade at my breasts and kept asking if he could 'slice one for a souvenir'.
>
> I remember the tears rolling down the side of my face and the complete 'numbness' I felt. There wasn't any pain then. I

'removed' myself mentally from that bed, from that monster ... I wanted to die. I kept holding my breath, hoping I would just stop breathing, but I kept waking up.

He stood up over me and asked why I was shaking? If I was cold? He stood straddling me and urinated up and down my body, to 'warm me up'. I threw up and he turned my face over into it and penetrated me anally again, pressing my face into the vomit. I didn't have to hold my breath that time. I just passed out from sheer terror.

What I remember next is his fingers inside me. All his fingers, like he had his whole hand in there. I told him to please stop, that I had to pee. And that he was hurting me, that it was burning. He said, 'So piss then'. I tried to get up and he said, 'No, piss right here.' Well, his hand was still up inside me and I said. 'I can't. He said, 'Piss right here, or I'll slice you.' And he kept chanting, 'Slice and dice, slice and dice ...' over and over again. I told him to please take his hand out and I would. He did and I did. And he laughed and said, 'Look at the wittle baby pissing in the bed'. He just kept laughing and laughing. And I cried until I had no tears left.

He fell asleep at one point and I thought about getting up and trying to get away; that was when I realised I couldn't move. I was in so much pain and my head was pounding so hard I thought for sure it would explode. I lay there shaking uncontrollably. I don't know if I was cold or in shock. Probably a little of both.

I looked to the window and could see it was just starting to get light out. Morning had come after all, taking the darkness away. The sun was coming up. I couldn't believe after the night of horror I had been through that the sun had the audacity to shine. I looked to where he lay and he started to stir and wake up. He looked at me and smiled and said something like, 'Good morning beautiful', and started laughing. He got dressed and told me to get washed up and dressed and that he would be back later, so we could leave for Arizona.

The rapist didn't come back, and a broken Adair made her way home.

Police have noted that sadistic rape is the rarest and most deadly kind, but it is clear that it does happen at the hands of partners.[17] An added trauma for you may be that you wondered if you would be killed – and perhaps your partner, like Adair's, gained extra pleasure from your terror.

The obsessive rapist

The obsessive rapist shares similar aspects with the sadist, but his arousal is fuelled less by causing suffering and torment, and more by specific perverse acts he forces his partner to engage in. Perhaps your partner is preoccupied with certain types of sex acts that may be bizarre or unusual. He may read pornography, write or talk a lot about his preference.[18] Maree's description of rape by her ex-husband evokes the profile of the obsessive rapist:

> Rapes happened a few times, but this one particular time, he had this pinup on the wall above our bed, and he turned around and ripped my clothes off and all the rest of it, and raped me. And as he is fucking me, he turns around and is spitting at me and saying, 'Why can't you look like the sheila on the pinup?'

> And so for example her name is Debbie, he would be saying, 'Oh God Debbie, oh Debbie', and he is ramming it, ramming it, ramming it in me. And when he came, he did it all over my face, thinking he was blowing over her face or her tits or something.

> There were heaps of pinups but this one particular one he looked at and he would turn around and get the biggest carrots that he could get, like at the supermarket or cucumbers or the salamis and he would be ramming them up me, and I'd just be laying there, like sick. I'd feel that sick. I'd be like, 'Oh my God, when is he going to stop? Who can come and save me?'

It doesn't matter to the obsessive rapist that his partner doesn't share his tastes; he is prepared to force them on her.

> I felt abused because he wanted to play around with my private parts and put his fingers or his hand in and just do things and I'm saying, 'Don't touch me.'

> I felt worse later. Maybe before it, if he had asked, I'd be saying I don't really like that. Like to me it doesn't feel like anything exciting. I feel yucky actually, and he goes, 'Oh but I like it. I felt I had to. (Shefali)

Kate, Tiffany and Siobhan each had partners who insisted that their wife watch pornography and act out fantasies. As Siobhan shares:

> We had just woken up and were having normal sex when he rolled over onto his stomach. He wanted me to insert something up his anus. He said words to the effect of, 'Can you put a vibrator into my ass. I want you to pretend you're a boy.' ... Another fantasy

of his was for him to imagine young boys raping me. He told me that he would fantasise this while he was having sex with me. Another ongoing fantasy of Arthur's was he would ask me to take two or three sleeping pills at once to dope myself up and then he would have sex with me.

Linda, whose husband anally raped her so frequently that she developed health problems, offers an example of a partner obsessed with what he inflicted on her:

> He looked forward to it. Drove round in his (profession) van and looked forward to it, even after it was definitely without consent, when it was rape. So I felt guilty about not being good enough, of being unhappy about something he obviously enjoyed. And confused. I told him, told him time and time again, please not so often, please not tonight, please do it normally. I explained that it was not comfortable, that it hurt ... I told him this, asked him just not to do it so often. I can't remember it making any difference. It would go on, often two, three, four times a week. I remember asking him to do it less, that it was happening more than normal intercourse.

He was completely unperturbed by the pain his actions caused her:

> I had explained to him that the act itself did nothing for me sexually, nor emotionally, and that physically it had awful side-effects. And it never changed his actions towards me. His preference and pleasure came before concern for me.

Myths that perpetrators may act out

As we pointed out in chapter 3, western societies generate and perpetuate the rape of women in a number of ways, including the many beliefs and myths about masculinity, male sexuality, rape and some specifically about partner rape. Your partner may be acting out these false beliefs and/or using them to justify his violence.

Myth: men who rape their partner are out of control

Carol Adams writes, 'Men who abuse and rape their partners are men who seek to control others. In being abusive they are not out of control; rather, they establish control.'[19] Yet, there persists the common belief that rape is the act of a man out of control of his emotions or sexual urges. Understanding that perpetrators do choose to rape, and that they have control over their deeds contradicts that myth.

> My awareness of his intent to use rape in a deliberate way
> became clearer as I allowed myself to reflect on how he spoke
> to me in the course of sexual violence: 'I am going to hurt you',
> 'There's only one way to teach you not to be a whore', 'Just try
> and stop me, you bitch.' I could see that sexual violence was
> strategic; it was deliberately placed with a specific outcome in
> mind by somebody who knew he was using sex in a controlling
> and controlled way. It was an extremely painful part of my
> healing to recognise that this person did deliberately hurt me.
> But it was ultimately strengthening, and it made it easier to give
> the responsibility back to him. (Rachel)

Linda also came to understand this when her partner told her prior to a rape that he had been looking forward to it all day. She says, 'I knew then, he could control it; he chose not to. He chose to rape me. It just took a while to sink in.'

The partner who uses verbal coercion to manoeuvre his partner into unwanted sex is also behaving with awareness. Perhaps when you say no or give some other signal of unwillingness, he proceeds to manipulate your emotions until he gets what he wants. He knows that you have fears or other vulnerabilities that are fair game, and he capitalises on those. Consider the words of this man, who admits to the emotional coercion of his wife: 'I would act like I was mad at her and she would give in. It works every time.'[20] This is not the behaviour of a man out of control; it is how a man takes control.

> He would tell me that he was trained to hurt me so that I would
> have no marks to show but suffer extreme pain and no one would
> believe me because there was no physical evidence to support
> my claims. This was no idle claim and he proved it to me on
> many occasions. (Jennifer)

To make the choice to rape may involve premeditation of a few seconds, minutes, hours or weeks. It could be a question of a partner thinking, 'To hell with this "no" business. I'm going to do it anyway', or putting considerable energy into thinking about how they can get access to an ex-partner for the purpose of rape, like Summer's ex-partner who came armed with a knife to her workplace after hours knowing that there would be nobody around to assist her.

Myth: rape is part of' manhood'

From wars where the prize of the victorious is the right to rape the women on the conquered side up to present-day videogames that award points to players who capture and rape an electronic 'victim', we see that rape is depicted as the act of conquerors and heroes.

Some men think rape equates with virility and power:

> I have had fantasies of doing it, as a form of proving to the woman that I really am all man, able to get and keep a hard-on and use it to force myself on her, whether she wants me or not.[21]

Perhaps your partner used rape as a means of putting you 'in your place', that is, beneath men. Rachel describes her subjugation:

> I once went away with Paul to meet some friends of his. It is probably fair to say that the ideal of 'real' manhood was fairly extreme in this group.
>
> At this stage I was still determined to stand up for myself sometimes, and Paul's friends ribbed about his inability to keep 'his woman' under control. It embarrassed him no end. He beat me twice on this visit and refused to give me my train-ticket home. But the final punishment for being a little too big for my boots came when he arrived home one night with a friend.
>
> I pretended to be asleep as he and the friend talked for a while. Afterwards, the friend lay down on a couch in the room, and Paul got into bed with me. He immediately rolled me onto my back and attempted to mount me. I was incredibly embarrassed at having another person in the room, and I struggled with him – but briefly – I lost and was raped.
>
> I knew his friend was awake and aware of what was happening, and I cried with shame.
>
> I will never forget Paul's friend's knowing, sly looks for the duration of our visit, or how I dropped my eyes, vanquished and ashamed. It felt as if he was saying 'Ha ha, you think you're so smart, but I've seen you vulnerable. You weren't so smart then.' It did not occur to me to wonder why he had, in his silence, championed my violation, for I already understood why: Paul had needed to prove himself as a real man, one worthy of membership in his friend's group. My violation was his proof of who wore the trousers. I don't think I will ever forgive the culture of masculinity for working against me and other women in the terrible way it has.

Myth: rape is the entitlement of normal men

Did you find that after sexual assault by your partner, he behaved quite normally, as if he had done nothing wrong, in fact suggesting that it was you who had a problem because you didn't like forced or coerced sexual encounters? It's quite possible that he believed it was his right to take what he wanted from you, as many perpetrators do. Liz's husband enforced that expectation:

> An example of that was when I had my caesarean. He waited three weeks and then said, 'It's been three weeks and you have to have sex with me.' I had to hold my wound. It was very painful to have sex and yet I had to go through with it and I never felt that was right. He didn't even have enough respect for me to believe that my body was hurting. I wasn't ready so that was really sad and painful.

Kate's husband also was entirely insensitive to her recent child birth:

> Then we had our first child and I tore very badly right into my rectum and it didn't heal for six months. Every time I went to the toilet it was bleeding and I was just in so much pain. Of course the doctor had said after six weeks you can have sex and I can just remember dreading the six weeks coming around. It was awful. It was just so painful. I couldn't walk for the first two weeks after the birth. I literally couldn't walk. I couldn't sit. I was in agony.
>
> I remember dreading it. By this time I had completely lost any interest in sex and I used to pray all the way through it that God would help me to pretend that I was enjoying it and that I could just get through it, every time. Then I remember just being relieved thinking I had about 48 hours before I had to do this again.

Unfortunately, social values support such beliefs. A psychiatrist offers the following view about rape:

> It's perfectly normal for armies to rape whole populations of women. It's perfectly normal for men coming off a ship to get a bit tight, go around looking for girls and, if the girls get a bit stroppy and don't come up with the goodies, it's normal for the men to take it.[22]

Here, rape is upheld as natural behaviour, indeed, the entitlement of men. Women who don't 'come up with the goodies' should interpret their violations as a natural outcome of non-consent.

> Paul always said I was the abnormal one; prissy, prudish and uptight because he had to take what I didn't consent to by force. When he cheated on me, he mocked me, saying that at least the other woman gave him what he wanted without any of my 'bullshit'. It took thirteen years for me to understand that what he had done was not normal and that there was nothing wrong with me for having sexual boundaries. (Rachel)

Nichole says of her partner's rapes of her, 'I think he saw it as a part of our relationship that was normal. Being entitled to sex with me as his girlfriend played a role definitely.' Justine says her partner held a similar view of his sexual violence: 'I think he thought it was his right as a normal man.'

Rape is a type of making love

Did you find that at times when you were raped, your partner seemed to treat it like a legitimate sexual encounter? Justine's partner berated her for not enjoying being raped:

> Many a time, after one of his rages when he had beaten me or emotionally abused me for several weeks, he would want to make love. I would tell him that I didn't really want to (I was too tired, had a headache, too upset – if I was feeling brave enough) but he never seemed to care about my wishes. He would go ahead (usually without any foreplay) and I would just lie there, not moving or changing my breathing. Sometimes, afterwards, I would then get into trouble for not enjoying it and being a frigid/boring cow.

Did your partner want to kiss and cuddle you afterwards, or plan your next date? Diana Russell writes, 'Some rapists think they're lovers.' These men are likely to subscribe to myths that women want a forceful lover, or that they like to be raped.[23]

'No' isn't heard as withdrawing consent, but is seen as part of a game the perpetrator has every intention of winning – in fact the word 'no' may translate as, ' No, I want you to force me.' There might be initial attempts at verbally persuading a woman into sex, but their intention is to do it anyway. To these men, consent is nice but not a necessity.

Sometimes, women are confused by a rape that is presented by the perpetrator as 'making love', or after which the perpetrator was 'nice' to them:

> He stripped me naked in the lounge and raped me, having picked me up, by my breasts from behind and dragged/carried me to the settee. Afterward, while I was getting dressed, and trying to light a cigarette with shaking hands, he made me a cup of coffee, then sat down next to me to drink his, as though we had just made love. (Linda)

Also, because this kind of rape is not usually physically violent, you might berate yourself for not resisting strenuously enough. However, if you didn't give free consent, it was rape. It might be helpful to think of what happened as a product of the perpetrator's wrong thinking, and also tricks he used to get you to accept his behaviour.

If your partner held the view that forcing sex on you was trivial, this may not match what you feel about it. You can trust your feelings, and remember that minimisation of any rape is wrong.

Sexual violence targeted at children

The perpetrator's power/control issues tragically don't always stop at their partners but transfer to their children. They may inflict sexual violence.

> I found out for sure about my daughters after he'd left. I just asked the younger one.
>
> 'Oh yes', she said. 'And I tried so many times to tell you.'
>
> Then she did and we got home and checked with the older one and of course it wasn't just them; it was their friends. They started to go on about it and I just wasn't coping. I said, 'You really don't have to talk about it.'
>
> I'm not sure perhaps that actual penetration happened because the elder one asked a question that made me think that perhaps actual penetration hadn't happened. (Eva Jane)

Or the abuse may be emotional and physical:

> What Peter did tell me was that his father would ask him questions so after a couple of hours after he'd been asleep he'd wake him up. He told me he was afraid to go to sleep, because when he went to sleep Robert would wake him up and ask him questions, and that's where I got the feeling like sexual abuse and things like that. He woke up one time with a pair of pliers to his nose asking him to answer questions, who was I dating, who was I going out with, where was I going to be on the weekend?

His father was telling him that I was a whore, I was trash, that I was sleeping with men. He'd explain it to him in graphic details. The other things he did to him was he used to go by and he used to smack him on the back of the head, like with his fingers. 'You're an idiot. You're stupid. Listen to me I'm talking to you.'

Then he would say here I bought you these gifts but you can't have them until you answer my questions. So those were the mental games. He gave him a birthday present, a Playstation or something, and then he took it away from him. Then he would also grab him. He's big on twisting arms, twisting them behind your neck, grabbing you by the throat. Nothing that Peter could prove, pushing him out of the way, locking him in the apartment so he couldn't leave the apartment. He wouldn't allow him to call me. He was not allowed to use the phone to call me. (Tiffany)

Some of the women like Kate and Siobhan worry about their children's wellbeing when their ex-partner has access. Their partners were obsessed with pornography and sexual fantasy. If you have similar concerns, listening to the steps that Kate has taken might be helpful:

As far as my children and concern that Edward will harm them: I do the educational stuff about boundaries and saying no and what's appropriate for where you touch your body and who can touch your body and when. The other thing I've done, the thing I guess I've worked the most on, is having a close relationship. And that's what all the professionals I've seen have said: having the kind of relationship where you'd notice if something was really wrong, and they would feel that they could talk to you. I think I've done that, plus I've said to them that there may be times when they feel like they can't talk to anyone but that they always can. I've got them to write lists of people that they would feel safe to talk to who wouldn't be involved like Kids' Line or a couple of special people from the church who are now out of the church who I trust. And I pray a lot. I've asked enough people and all of them have said in your situation that's all you can do, and I've always prayed that if something's happening, for God to make it really clear, give me insight; that I'm not going to be one of those mothers who turns a blind eye to something.

Can a partner who rapes change?

There are patterns of sexually violent behaviour such as sadism that appear resistant to change. Treatment, if successful at all, may take many years. Some men will never be safe for women. Some abusive partners may profess change as a way of persuading women to remain in or return to the relationships only to abuse and rape them again.

However, when a man takes responsibility for what he's done, recognises women as his peers with absolute rights to their bodies, and gives up assumptions that he can control his partner or must have sex when he feels like it, change can happen. By way of example, Jackie has permitted us to share a postscript to her story: Some time after ending the relationship with the partner who sexually assaulted her, Jackie was raped by a near-stranger. Her ex-partner heard of her rape through a mutual friend of theirs. Later, Jackie saw him at a party and after expressing regret for her rape, he made a full and frank admission that his sexual assault of her had been wrong. He apologised in such a way that Jackie was in no doubt of his sincerity. This man is engaged to a good friend of hers, and Jackie relates that assumption of a right to control women is no longer part of the way he conducts his life and relationships.

Jackie's ex-partner may have had the courage to challenge the attitudes within himself that led to his assault upon her.

If you are still in a relationship with the perpetrator of your rape, and you believe he has changed, you know best. We speak of change not because we think women should remain in dangerous situations, but because it's remiss to not take into account the complexity of relationships and the love and hope that may exist. However, any responsibility for change is up to your partner; you are not required to have to be the 'helper'. Decisions about your future are also your right to make. Remember that your safety comes first. You deserve to be loved safely.

CHAPTER 7

Relationships in which Sexual Assault Happens

Getting involved

'How did someone like you get involved with someone like him?'

Most of us have been asked this. While it might be nice to think that this is some form of homage, what often underlies this question is the inaccurate assumption that only stupid or morally inferior women get involved with violent men. Also, there's a common myth that women are somehow at fault because they 'attract' men who will hurt them.

The reality is that rape happens in relationships where there are no other signs of abuse. Women form relationships with men who may genuinely love them and who are not habitually violent. The assault takes place out of left field. Maree's partner didn't commence violence until their wedding night:

> When we were first seeing each other he was beautiful; butter wouldn't melt in his mouth. Once we got married that was it; that's when it all started. I was a virgin to him. I'd never let no man kiss me, no males had ever kissed me, only my uncles or my father, or my brothers, and the kiss wasn't on the lips, it was on the cheek, or up on the forehead. And because of that, on our wedding night, Alex turned around and punched me in the mouth. 'You don't even know how to fucking kiss.'

Indeed, some women aren't raped by their partners until after they leave the relationships. Sometimes, the relationship was not violent.

And, of course, the men who rape their partners don't have 'I will eventually rape you' tattooed on their foreheads. In fact, there's little that is exceptional about the beginnings of any of the relationships described in this book. Let's have a look at some of them:

I was only 16 and working at the same restaurant that he did. I was a trouble maker and he the rebel I was looking for. (Adair)

He was the one who was originally interested in me, and I was flattered, so agreed to date him. We found out how much we liked each other, and how much fun we had together, and we became a couple. We adored each other, and were very compatible in a lot of ways. We both liked the same activities, and laughed a lot. Much of our time was spent going to movies, dancing, visiting friends, going to Halloween parties and dressing in weird costumes, going through the water parks or on the roller coasters in the pouring rain, going to the zoo and making faces at the animals, or just hanging out. (Natalie)

I met Ted when I was 18. He was incredibly good-looking, resembling Jon Bon Jovi. He stood at the bar, dressed in old jeans, a shirt with a couple of buttons open revealing a leather necklace and charm. He wore a black leather jacket, and the sexiest smile I had ever seen. There was no doubting the immense presence he had, and that women couldn't take their eyes off him. My mates encouraged me to talk to him, but I felt he was way out of my league. After a few beers, he seemed to be more in reach, so I got to talking with him. We exchanged numbers and then he left. I was so excited, nervous and expected never to hear from him again. I did ring him and leave a message and to my amazement, he called me back. He asked me out for dinner, said he would pick me up. I was able to be somewhat 'sensible' as I arranged to meet him. I said I didn't want him to pick me up because I didn't know him. He was very nice about it and said he understood. We went out and he was extremely charming. (Charlotte)

When I met my husband, Carl, he was being put down by his friends and he reminded me of me. He was 28. I knew I had something wrong with me and deep down I thought, 'I can hide here for awhile. He's not going to notice all my insecurities and I can have time to have these thoughts.' He would listen to me and he was there for me because I was very unhappy. He needed a flatmate and I was unhappy and he said that we got on well. I moved in after four months of knowing each other and I ended up being with him for ten years. (Liz)

New Years Eve 2000, the big one. I was living in an affluent [town] and I was invited to a party … by a friend of mine. We struck up a conversation. He clearly was highly intelligent, but not in a verbal way. Since I am such a verbal person, I am not normally attracted to people who don't use words precisely. Still, he was a nice guy, and had an awkward charm. (Jackie)

When I met my first husband Edward I was 20. We were at a pub keg party and got blind drunk. We slept together straight away and we just started going out. We were both doing science at uni. He was, of course, completely weird and eccentric and I thought that was fantastic. He had an odd way of looking at the world and an odd way of relating to people. I used to call him my angry young man because he was so angry at the world. (Kate)

I met him at a friend's party. He was very charming and quite a bit older than myself. I was young and naive. He was the stud of the (small) town, every woman swooned over him and thought he was so sweet. (Jodie)

Ahmad was very charming and very different. I was attracted by a whole host of qualities (the charming ones were just tricks with smoke and mirrors – tricking people and making you think what he wants you to is his art). He seemed very educated (a nice change), and had been places and seen things (jails, uprisings, wars) that I knew nothing about … His upbringing and adventurous life before coming to Australia, to my naïve mind, made him a fascinating, enigmatic personality – and wasn't it a miracle that he was such a sweet person in spite of having suffered so dreadfully! The way his mind worked was a wonder to me (in the early days). He was very clever, and a skilled and devious con-man (something I didn't appreciate until years later). (Melina)

I met him at work. He was married at the time, although living at his dad's. I was suffering from depression after a breakdown following the death of my mum. He seemed to be able to make me feel better (in the beginning) and helped get me off anti-depressants which I had been on for 3 years previously. He said he fell in love with me because I would have a laugh and was 'one of the lads'. (Justine)

Abused women often speak of their partners as having 'Jekyll and Hyde' personalities.[1] In the early stages of courtship, your abuser may have been incredibly charming, only to exhibit a controlling side later. While there are certain characteristics that may suggest abusive tendencies, such as extreme jealousy or a devaluing attitude towards women, these are often not the things most apparent at the beginning of a relationship. Those that are apparent, such as possessiveness, may be mistaken for love, particularly to women who have grown up with low self-esteem (see chapter 5). Perhaps for you, like the women in this chapter, the slide into sexual or other violence was gradual, insidious and far more than sexual or physical.

If you have branded yourself harshly for being unable to second-guess the future, please know that you are not to blame for falling in love or wanting to be with somebody who presented as a lovely person. Your attraction to him says nothing negative about you.

The good times ...

> I was never bored with him. He was attractive and smart. At first, I was very attracted to the way he seemed to take care of me. When he wasn't abusive, we had a good time together. He was talented and could be very sweet and funny. (Nichole)

> Basically he treated me like a princess. (Emma)

No relationship is 100 per cent good and no relationship is 100 per cent bad. Most men who abuse don't do it all the time. For you, the sexual abuse may constitute just a small part of the relationship, and seems outweighed by the positive times. Perhaps he's a wonderful father, or is generous and easy to talk to. Although rape or other violence is not an expression of love, there can be little doubt that some men who have raped their partners do love them, or are able to show love at other times:

> Honestly, I have to look back and say that, yes, there was love, at least on my part. I also believe, and I don't know how, that in some strange way he also loved me. (Summer)

Did you find that your partner alternated between extremes in his treatment of you, putting you on a pedestal sometimes, but devaluing you at other times? People who espouse madonna/whore beliefs see women as either 'good women' or 'bad women', and they believe that 'bad women' deserve rape. This belief system is supported by many perpetrators of sexual and domestic violence, but rather than seeing different women as either madonna or whore, they see both in the same woman. While an abuser views his partner as a 'madonna', she is treated relatively well until she falls from this unrealistic pedestal and becomes the 'whore':

> The extremes were so intense that I look back and wonder how I never lost my mind, that I never completely lost my mind. He would make love to me so tenderly. Cradle me in his arms and

sing to me, send me flowers, bring home a small gift, profess his undying love and then in an hour's time he would be belittling me. Pulling me down with his verbal abuse and sometimes, hitting me. There was one specific time when we were lying in bed. Basking in our 'glorious' love, cuddling and I triggered him by mentioning that one of his friends had stopped by to see him and the next thing I knew the mattress was flipped completely off the bed and I was lying on the hardwood floor, covered in wine among the pieces of the shattered wine glass. He put a hole through the wall and continued to rage on and on but nothing he said made any sense to me. I literally couldn't make out his words. His friend came over later to help him patch up the wall; I was asked to remain out of his sight. (Summer)

Your partner may have punctuated sexual assaults with names like 'slut' or 'whore' as Siobhan's partner did:

He never treated me as an equal. He'd come home from work and say, 'Oh hello beautiful', and then in the bedroom I was all the 'sluts' and 'whores' and 'bitches'. This was going on over the years but it was becoming more and more violent.

These names serve the purpose of reducing a woman to a 'thing', a dirty thing who deserves to be hurt. Thus, the perpetrator doesn't have to feel guilty about hurting her.

While there may have been positive moments in your relationship, they may have been mixed with abuse to the extent that you didn't know what to expect, and so you survived by anticipating the good and the normal times.

Living with domestic violence is like playing with a loaded gun. You never know when it is going to go off. You find yourself walking on eggshells, not wanting to trigger his anger; never knowing if today is the day you go too far. If today is the day he wanted scrambled eggs rather than the over easy he's eaten for the past three years. If today is the day he decides you should get a job or quit the one he's allowed you to have. With no notice, you're expected to just know when the wind changes. You have a choice – you can get hit now for telling the truth or get hit later when he finds out that you lied. Only he knows when the gun is going to go off.

Life with Ed was a roller coaster. The majority of the time it was a normal existence. We spent time with his friends, took our son to the park, went on vacation, bought things for the house, made slow sensual love. But over time things changed more and more. The outbursts went from once every few months to once every few days and then daily. He would walk through the door looking for a reason to come after me. (Kuriah)

Other abuses by partners who rape[2]

For many women, there is a range of control/abuse behaviours that set the stage for sexual assault by their partners. Types of abuse other than rape may include any or all of the following.

Control began to manifest in Tiffany's marriage with possessiveness and scrutiny of her activities. From there came the verbal put-downs and then a subtle sort of physical abuse (pushing, slamming doors on her):

> The relationship started out okay and then he started to control. 'Where am I going?' 'Who am I seeing?' 'What time am I going home?' 'What am I wearing?'

There were similar signs of control in Sarah's relationship:

> I wasn't allowed to go the dentist. That had started then, and comments like, 'You can only spend your money once', had started then. But there was nothing of any great concern. He was pro women working and he thought it was great that women could have careers. He was supportive, and we could talk about anything and I could express my opinion about anything. It was just after we got married that that all completely stopped … There was also increased scrutiny of going out. Where are you going and who are you going to be spending your time with and why? We're married. We should do everything together. We shouldn't have time to ourselves with other people. At the point where we separated and even after, he would go through the bank accounts and say, 'What's this amount for and what's that amount for?'

> I distinctly remember him saying, 'There's $20 out of the Rediteller on this date. What was it for?'

> And I was just going, 'It's $20!'

> But it was critically important to him.

It happens slowly and as the 'rot sets in', the bizarre becoming normalised. Therefore you might not even recognise how controlling your partner was until you are out of the relationship:

He's a control freak. Take my education and career as examples. A few years into our relationship, my husband decided I needed to go to Uni. He then said I couldn't go the night before I was to start. Seven years after that my husband told me I had to go to Uni. This time I did and even though I felt he kept trying to make me fail, I completed a Bachelor of Commerce with a triple major. However, I never had a career as such despite a strong work ethic. As soon as I started to do well, my husband changed his mind about his path and I was made to stop and follow along.

There was lots of violence in our relationship that I recognise as violence now. Although there had always been physical abuse, I now recognise the extent of other types that was inflicted on me constantly throughout the marriage.

For instance, I was never allowed a credit card or bank account. I wasn't allowed friends or phone calls.

I wasn't allowed to go out.

I was put down constantly.

I was made to stand on a tile for often over an hour and explain why something was not to his liking.

My problem was that I didn't see it for what it was. And I was in an extremely violent situation before I realised it. (Samantha)

It's after he left that I'd think my God, when was the last time that I listened to my own music? I never did. I was too busy doing everything that he wanted to do. Through the counselling by the Domestic Violence Crisis Centre when he pulled out the phone, I didn't realise how bad I felt. I just felt so frightened. I mean, he wouldn't leave. He was outside and he was threatening to come back in and what do I do now? It wasn't until after I kept thinking and talking about it to all the counsellors that I realised, my God, he's been telling me I'm the bossy one; that I'm the one who's controlling him, but it wasn't. It was him controlling me the whole time. I never saw it. (Shefali)

In some cases, this behaviour is an intrinsic part of a mindset of male entitlement. A man who uses male privilege believes that women must be kept in 'their place', and presumes a right to rule while he does as he pleases. Some ways in which male privilege emerges are:

- Refusing you any help in caring for the children because he believes it is 'women's work'.

- Claiming the right to go out anytime he likes while you are expected to do nothing but stay home and clean and cook for him.

- Stopping you from going out to work because he needs to be seen to be 'taking care of you'.

- Claiming the right to 'discipline' you with violence or other punitive measures.

- Claiming a right 'as a man' to expect his every sexual need to be fulfilled.

Emotional abuse

Wilson defines emotional violence as 'repeated hurtful exchanges with a disregard for the partner's feelings'.[3]

> He would often know what hurt me and say or do exactly that to upset me. (Jodie)

Emotional abuse is put-downs like 'stupid' or 'ugly', 'jokes' at your expense, or your partner withdrawing affection if his needs are not met:

> He started to say things like:
>
> 'I don't like that on you.'
>
> 'You're fat, and you're putting weight on', which I wasn't.
>
> 'What did you do to your hair?'
>
> 'You can't spell. You're stupid.' (Tiffany)

> I was told I was paranoid and stupid and had 'no idea' and that he would tell me only what I needed to know. I was always belittled in front of guests and friends to the point where they felt they had to make a comment. (Jennifer)

> And he'd make me feel stupid. Like every time we argued he'd say, 'Oh fix it yourself. You're a cow.'

> He was verbally abusive. He used to put me down too, like I wasn't worth anything as a person. I had to say I am not. If I ever did anything good at all he would say you're egotistical. He would say there goes that ego again. (Shefali)

Jodie's partner belittled her and disguised it as 'joking':

> He continued to treat other women nice but would be horrible to me in front of my friends and his – in that sly way though – where it could sort of be taken as joking.

If this happens, you may be ridiculed for being upset, or told, 'You can't take a joke'. But there is nothing wrong with you; mean or derogatory put-downs don't have to be laughed off.

Emotional abuse is blaming you for all the problems in the relationship:

> He would lecture me on the standard of behaviour that he expected from me. These lectures would continue for hours at a time and if I tried to defend or reason with him he 'beat' me down with words. He lectured me in public in the park about my behaviour and it wasn't until I admitted that I was at fault that we were able to continue our holiday. (Jennifer)

> Nobody knew about it. Nobody could know about it, because it was only my perceived problem. It wasn't a real problem, it was only me thinking there was a problem. This is what I was hearing all the time. There wasn't actually a problem, it was just that I thought there was a problem. So it was my perception that was a little bit screwy. Certainly not only did I then have this: 'If it's a problem then it's a perceived problem and it's your perceived problem and nobody else's', but then: 'If there is a problem, then you need to work harder at it, and you need to work at making it be resolved rather than just expect it to immediately happen, because you can't be putting enough effort in, you can't be working hard enough at the relationship.'

> This just reinforced quite nicely to give me a sense of I'm failing, and if somebody is happy to run with that line and give you that line on a regular basis – that you're the one with the problem and you get that message all the time, then you believe it. That sort of thing becomes so ingrained that it probably will continue to take an incredibly long time to get away from, because once you're indoctrinated as I see it, it's just so hard to reverse that stuff. (Sarah)

Emotional abuse is happening when your partner demands to know all your deepest secrets and fears, and then turns them against you. Kate had disclosed to her second husband all about her perpetrator's sexual deviancy only to later discover that he too had visited prostitutes:

> It was a big betrayal because I thought, 'Oh you bastard, you knew.' More than anyone else on this planet, he knew what I'd been through, and he condemned it. He was so angry at Edward, he wanted to kill him. He would say, 'I don't understand how men can do that! I would never do that to you.'

Then he lied about it.

Other women disclosed about past rapes, which were turned against them in some way:

> He had been pressuring me to have sex, but I was uncomfortable with it. I decided to tell him about a sexual assault that had taken place a year before. I expected that he would be understanding. Instead, he turned on me. He yelled vicious things at me and told me the assault was my fault, that I was a tease and that I deserved it. He told me that I was lucky to have him because most men hate girls like me. I wanted to jump out the car door, but I was too scared. (Nichole)

> My new partner who I told was supportive at the time to a certain extent – but I always felt as though he didn't fully believe me though he wouldn't say it. He then went on to use it against me – when he wanted to hurt me he would sometimes say stuff like he would rape someone. He knew that would hurt me more than anything. I was devastated when he pretended to rape me and would say that he would rape a girl. (Jodie)

> I have been raped previously, of which he was aware. One night, he would assault me and the next night, if I was having bad dreams, he would hold me, telling me that everything was alright and he hoped that he would meet the bastard who did this to me one day. It was always on the tip of my tongue to ask him if he knew what he was doing to me. (Justine)

Emotional abuse may involve threats to commit suicide, or to kill you if you leave.

> He threatened to burn the house down with me in it after he threw all of the couch cushions on the floor and covered them with lighter fluid. (Summer)

All of these behaviours erode the very spirit of a woman. It is degrading to be treated as if your feelings have no validity. You may find yourself apologising for everything, including things that couldn't possibly be your fault.

It may be helpful to remember that he uses emotional abuse to keep you in a place he has designated for you so that he can have control over you. He may know that while you don't know your true worth, you are less likely to challenge what's happening to you.

When you feel as if everything is your fault, or as if you are stupid or not worth any better treatment, please tell yourself that these are not statements of fact. They are symptoms of emotional abuse. The abuse is wrong, not you.

Mental abuse

Mental abuse is similar to emotional abuse, but plays with your mind as well as your emotions. In healthy relationships, differences of opinion are allowed and respected. With mental abuse, there are two ways to think: the abuser's way or the wrong way. He sneers contemptuously at all your opinions perhaps saying, 'You don't know what you're talking about', or giving you a withering 'D'uh' sort of look. What *you* know has no value.

Mental abusers lie to distort or manipulate your perceptions. If he tells you that you are crazy or stupid, you may come to believe it:

> One of the worst things was being called a 'crazy bitch' constantly. I began to believe that all my judgments, thoughts and opinions were defective. (Rachel)

He may try to drive you crazy with 'mind games'; for example, denying that something happened even when you know it did, and then calling you crazy for continuing to uphold what you know to be true.

Jennifer's partner played with her mind in a variety of ways:

> There was other psychological abuse. If he asked me, 'Would you like a cup of tea?' I would reply, 'That would be nice' and he would become angry. I would become confused and unsure of what I had actually done to annoy him. He would repeat his question and I would make the same reply and he would berate me for making the same reply instead of the required one. He would 'reason' that if he didn't understand my first answer then I should answer in a way that he would understand. I would try a number of responses, becoming more and more confused and upset until eventually he would reply, 'That is not what I asked you. I asked you a yes or no question.' He would not stop until I answered 'yes' or 'no.'

> He would put my cat in his car and drive off. When he returned he told me he threw her out along the road. I have never been sure if he actually did this or not but he always brought her back.

The perpetrator may obsessively control your thoughts, or insist on knowing what you are thinking at all times. He 'mind-reads' as an excuse for violence, and there is no right answer you can give:

> I remember sitting in our local pub and glancing up to look at the TV. He asked me who I was looking for (in that voice) and I told him I was just watching TV. He had been picking arguments all day so I thought that if I look at the floor, I wouldn't get into trouble. He then asked me, 'Who the fuck are you thinking about now?' and punched my head up to look at him. (Justine)

Like other types of violence, it often continues after separation:

> And he played little games ... mental games. Up until three years ago, he still had control over me and that was four years after the relationship had ended. I knew that if I left him, he wouldn't leave me. He would follow me to the ends of the earth, just to harass me. When he was in the remand centre I was getting phone calls like, 'Keep looking over your shoulder for the rest of your life because I know where you're going.' And he knew exactly where I was going. So I was terrified of leaving him since he'd tried to kill me twice. (Marg)

> Mark, in the month between splitting up with him and when I got the domestic violence order, was quite happy to wave at me from across the room and to play these little mind games and just to taunt me, because of whatever power it gave him.

> Although he's prohibited from talking to me, and contacting me and coming to my home or work, I could be talking to a friend and he could walk up, stand in front of me and start talking over the top of me to that friend, and that wouldn't be a breach of the order because he's contacting that person, not me. Some people would see that as very black and white; he's not contacting me, therefore there's no breach. Others would see it as being obvious provocation, which is a form of social and mental abuse, which is a breach of the order because it says that he shouldn't commit violence, abuse or harass me. (Tracey)

Mental abuse can severely erode your self-confidence. For example, you may now believe that you have nothing worthwhile to contribute to any exchange of opinions, or that if you do contribute, people will know how 'stupid' you are.

Ask yourself this: When you talk to friends who respect you, do you find you feel more confident and that your ideas sound perfectly sane, yet when you express those same ideas to your partner, you falter apologetically just knowing that he'll rubbish you?

If the answer is yes, you might benefit from knowing that since nobody but your partner belittles your thoughts, it's not *you* that is wrong. You've been mentally abused – and *that* is wrong.

Social abuse: possessiveness and isolation

In describing the earlier parts of her relationship, Jennifer says:

> He telephoned me constantly, continually wrote me poetry. Left notes on my desk, visited me frequently during working hours and extended invitations to lunch and dinner. The intensity of his attentions was overwhelming and more and more I began to believe in the things the abuser was saying and writing to me. I had never been pursued so thoroughly and obsessively and was finally convinced by the abuser that we were meant to be together.

The 'overwhelming' and 'obsessive' courtship Jennifer describes is an indicator of a possessive personality. Yet, as indicated earlier, many of us initially see possessive behaviour as romantic or loving. Your partner may use phrases like 'You're all mine' or 'I will never let you go'. Such phrases are used ad nauseam in romantic songs, but are potentially dangerous in partners. It is only later that you become aware that, far from being loving, possessiveness is actually a form of control derived from a sense that the abuser 'owns' you to the exclusion of any other people who mean something to you. He insists on being number one at all times and exhibits jealousy of everybody else you care about, including your children or even your cat. Your partner may have insisted on accompanying you on all social outings. He wants to control who you speak to and socialise with:

> He tells you your friends don't really care about you, they're just using you: Tell that male friend that if he kisses you again, I'll kill him. Don't talk to your mother again. You are not to go to work any more. What are you doing talking to those bastards, that bitch? You believe in God? That's bullshit. You have to be back in 20 minutes – hurry up. What did you say to her? What did you say that for? Are you fucked in the head? What the fuck do you think you're doing? Take all the money out of your bank account and give it to me – if you want money you ask me for it.

> Who's that bitch? What are you doing with these stupid people? You're late – you are not to go out any more unless you come with me. If they ask you anything about that, you say you don't know.

I was instructed in great detail how to act before any given social situation – whom I could and couldn't talk to, what to say and what not to say, and how to look and dress. I would be interrogated afterwards for details on everything that was said to me and what I said and did in return, and be critiqued severely. (Melina)

As time passed, he started to get really possessive and didn't trust me to leave the house. He didn't like what I wore and when he got drunk, he accused me of sleeping around. This wasn't true. He seemed to get drunk and really hate me. I loved him and doted on him and wanted him to be happy with me. I changed what I wore, and I made sure I was at the house when he came home.

One weekend, he seemed to wake up in a real foul mood, and told me I had to stay in the bedroom all weekend. He took my clothes, and was so threatening I agreed. I knew he was having problems and thought if I obeyed him, I could reassure him of my love and so I could gain his trust and could help him. (Charlotte)

Possessiveness was probably one of those things that stripped me of much of my dignity – I literally was not allowed to look at another male. He would invite his friends over and then would rip me up for looking at them in the course of an ordinary conversation. (Summer)

In order to keep you from continuing friendships or making new ones, an abuser takes the car-keys to work (even though he catches public transport). He denigrates your friends and demands that you choose between them and him. You may have become frightened of telling him about a planned social outing that doesn't include him. You may think up excuses for refusing invitations because the way he responds makes going not worthwhile:

He didn't like me to spend too much time with my friends. He absolutely hated my habit of being five minutes late for everything. However, I didn't find this overly unusual; he was the jealous type and this was apparent. (Nichole)

I used to have a lot of friends and go out regularly with them. I think I can count on both hands the amount of times I have been out without him over the last 10 years. (Justine)

He checks the telephone bill or your emails to see if you have communicated with other men. You are expected to account for any time he couldn't reach you on the phone; he interprets this as evidence that you are having an affair. He isolates you in order to increase your dependence on him:

> He kept me very isolated. The property was in the middle of nowhere. I had neighbours off in the distance and everyone was not urban, it just wasn't an urban environment, so no-one had any contact with English-speaking people, and most people there hadn't been educated and they didn't get English at school. So there was no one who spoke English in my direct vicinity, and he stopped me from going to see the family. He didn't want to go and see them himself. He said I don't care whether you go, but I really had no means of getting there. (Helena)

You may have heard statements from your partner like, 'I am the only person you can depend on.' As your other contacts fall away, he might say things like, 'You see? Your friends have stopped calling because they don't care about you the way I do.' Often women in this position don't realise that the truth is much more likely to be that the possessive abuser is far more dependent than the other way around. If this were not so, he wouldn't insist that you must love only him, nor want to close off all your possible avenues of support.

If you have lost friends or family because of your relationship, it is not too late to reach out to somebody for help and support. You may have scaled down social contacts because you are ashamed and frightened of anybody knowing you are being hurt. Although it may be difficult for you to believe right now, you have nothing to be ashamed of. There are people out there who understand what you've experienced, and will listen to you without judging. (Contact one of the Women's Services in your community.) You are not a man's property and you deserve support.

Financial abuse

Many abusive men seem to firmly adopt the creed that 'Money is Power'. They often hold 'traditional' ideas about the male partner being entitled to control finances. Your partner may withhold money from you, particularly if he sees it as a possible resource of escape:

> All money was meted out by him. Any money that came into my account had to be handed to him – even after we separated, he was demanding I give him my money, and I dutifully would. Never mind I had a child to care for. He played games all the

time, testing me. He would spend money on himself and then give me a small amount and say with great ceremony that this money was for me, to spend on whatever I wanted. Then, days later, even weeks later, he would say, 'Where is that money I gave to you? Give it to me – I need it!' And I would dutifully produce it, having been too scared to spend it as instructed and thus fail the test, and suffer the consequences. (Melina)

Perhaps you have been expected to help out in the family business for neither wages nor recognition as an equal. Or, you are prevented from seeking gainful employment elsewhere because this represents an independence that threatens his control over you. If you are a mother who works at home caring for the children, your partner might say that what you do isn't real work and doesn't entitle you to any money.

Financial abuse also involves taking any money or accessing resources that you brought into the relationship:

He constantly came up with schemes so he could get rich quick where I was required to provide the money but not receive any recompense from him. It was a constant 'dance' for me to hide my financial details and money so that he couldn't gain access to them. (Jennifer)

And, he started to say things like whatever was mine was his as of the date of marriage. He'd decided that he wouldn't financially contribute or take part in the purchase or construction of the house. But once we were married it was all, 'Well we're married now, so it's not yours, it's ours.'

Things ceased to be mine. They became 'ours' and increasingly 'his'. (Sarah)

Making you account for every cent, giving you an allowance or saying that you cannot afford to go out for drinks with your friends when he does what he likes with money, is humiliating and reduces you to the status of a child. But you are not a child, and what is happening to you is abuse.

Spiritual abuse

If your partner enforces the notion that it is divinely ordained that he as the male partner, can rule over you, tells you that that it is the will of God for you to submit to sexual or other demands, or threatens you with reminders of Hell if you object, you have been spiritually abused:

His ability to tell me what he thought or felt stopped. A sense of him having stronger and stronger views as to what I should be doing or what I should be thinking increased, although I didn't necessarily understand it. Certainly a sense of, 'Well if you think something's wrong, then you're the one with the problem', became quite obvious, and certainly I took that on. He began to use bible verses to prove his point or to remind me of where I might be erring. (Sarah)

Kate's church colluded in her partner's violence:

So it was all up to me to keep him faithful and keep him away from all this stuff and basically the message was that if he behaves this way, it's because you've blown it. You haven't met his needs. A man won't go to a prostitute if his needs are being met at home, you know ... If the male decides to stop doing his part, then you still have to do your part; you still have to submit. So women with non-Christian husbands just go through hell, because they are expected to do anything he says, put up with any amount of abuse basically, always with the blackmail of you're trying to win this guy's soul over. That was the verse they put for that, winning him over without words ... the church had convinced me that my husband was my saviour and I couldn't live without him. If it wasn't for me; he was so good to me; he put up with so much, because I was sick so much.

If there's nobody in your community of faith you feel you could confide in, please call a domestic violence service and ask if they know of any clergy that you can speak to. Scripture doesn't support abuse and control of women; rather, some clergy, and certainly some abusers twist biblical passages to justify male power or abusive behaviour.

'Spiritual abuse' also refers to the emotional and mental violence that erodes the very soul or essence of a woman.

Physical violence

Physical violence is almost always preceded by some of the controlling behaviours outlined above. You may already be beaten down internally, in your sense of self and he may promise that it will never happen again:

For the year before our marriage and the first two years we were together, it was heaven. He treated me like porcelain and I was as happy as I could possibly be. Then just six weeks after our child was born, the bomb dropped. What started as a routine conversation evolved into our first argument. All goes into slow motion as I watch what is about to happen. I remember seeing his arm pulled back, its slow approach, the smack of fist against bone, and then I feel the hard white pain of that fist, his right hand, the hand that has held mine, that has made love to me, that has reached for me, all knotted up now with rage behind it, and he hits me high on the face, on my cheekbone, just beneath my eye.

It has taken ten seconds to turn my world upside down.

My thoughts are scrambled, my hand held numbly to my face; I don't feel anything yet. I didn't see stars but I couldn't think clearly. The fact that this man who I lived and breathed for had hit me just did not compute – how did this fit into my world?

I can't remember all the details, but once it happened, he apologised, and told me he would never do it again. He followed me down the hall and told me I should leave him and go back to my family.

If I knew that would only be the beginning of years of punches, kicks, hair-pulling, guns being pointed at me, rapes, degradation and humiliation, I would have left. What stopped me then was what stopped me for the next three years ... he wouldn't let me take our child.

What I did not recognise until only recently was that long before the physical violence began, the isolation and psychological battering had been in place for quite some time. I had stopped going to school after the birth of my son and was a stay-at-home Mom. Throughout my pregnancy he had kept me isolated in a tiny town north of where I live now. It was and is a truly beautiful place. We lived above the beach, amidst the redwoods, and it was quiet and peaceful but I was home 10 to 12 hours a day, alone with no car or phone. I lived a little over a mile from the town itself so I was truly alone. I saw no one without him being there and I never went out in public without his approval and usually his presence. He stopped attending church and I was only allowed to go sporadically. Having been raised in church, this was a huge issue for me and he knew it was a means of hurting me. (Kuriah)

The onset can be subtle:

Then after that he started slamming the car door on my hand, and saying oh sorry, pushing me away from the sink, stepping on my toes – you're in my way. It just started, that kind of pushing and abusive things. You're brushing your teeth at the sink and he pushes you out of the way … I'd walk through the doorway and he'd slam the door. What were you doing in the doorway? I'd say, why did you do that? Not even I'm sorry. It was always my fault. Everything became my fault. He got in a car accident one day. I was in the car. It was my fault. So that's how it started to go. (Tiffany)

If a man is prepared to be violent outside the bedroom, it often follows that he'll be prepared to be violent in it. As we have seen elsewhere, a common feature of physical violence is that the perpetrator frequently wants sex after beating his partner:

The other abuses got worse. One time, he came into the shower and he lost it. I must have done a dissociation job since I don't know what happened but when I looked down on my arm I had a bruise this long across my arm. The only way I think that happened is … well I saw him coming towards me. I don't know what happened.

There were other times. He had me in the kitchen once and he cornered me and he's six foot three and a 120 kilos. He's a big guy and he was screaming at me. He had me cornered over something. One other time when I was denying him sex, there was this cot down at the coast and he pushed me up against that and twisted my arm and shook me and did that sort of stuff. (Liz)

Further, you may have experienced violence as not only a way of discharging aggression but also a means by which you are terrorised to the point where you believe you'll be seriously hurt or even killed if you stand up for yourself or leave the relationship:

When someone holds you by the throat until you're unconscious you know you're seriously at risk of death. He would hold me down, with one hand holding me and one around my neck, squeezing and tell me he that he hated me and wished I was dead. When you're held from behind by the chin and your neck is wrenched to the side and he whispers in your ear that he is professionally trained and could end your life with a snap of his hand/wrist you know you could die at any moment. (Jennifer)

While the husband who repeatedly raped her did not beat Linda, he nevertheless took out his rage on objects:

He used to regularly hit things when I confronted him about his behaviour: the settee, chair, walls, table etc. I especially remember the dishwasher, because I was sitting in the corner on the dresser with my feet on the dishwasher at the time ... Again, I had dared to disagree with him on something. He brought both fists down on the dishwasher within inches of my foot so hard it seemed to bounce and rattle. I was scared. It made me jump.

Linda correctly identifies the purpose of her partner's behaviour:

The message was clear enough – that could be you. It was not only a display of anger, it was intimidation.

Many of us who have been confronted by a raging man smashing, hurling or hitting things, know the terror implicit in those actions. The implied threat is the assault.

Keep in mind that assault in the home is as much a criminal act as it would be if a stranger threatened and beat somebody on the street. If you are being beaten, your life could be in danger. You may be frightened about what might happen if you try to leave. We urge you to seek help as soon as possible. Contact your local domestic violence service. They can offer you sanctuary.

CHAPTER 8

Not Dealing with the Sexual Violence

How men who rape their partners avoid responsibility

In writing about the lack of naming and acknowledging of marital rape, Carol Adams says, 'Perpetrators don't want their acts to be acknowledged through naming.'[1]

What does calling perpetrators on their sexual violence ask of them?

Abusive partners are seldom willing to take responsibility for their abuse. Confronting the behaviour asks them to do this. Responsibility is frightening because it suggests change, and some perpetrators simply don't want to stop having power over their partners. For a perpetrator of partner rape, naming may call up parts of himself he doesn't want to see or get honest about. He finds a woman's act of naming and challenging rape threatening because he understands that this is a woman rebelling.

Responding with rage at the naming of rape is a way that a perpetrator can silence his victim once again and reinforce that challenging him is futile and dangerous:

> I mentioned it once. It was during an argument, and he told me to go to the bedroom. I asked, 'So you can rape me?' I never did that again because the assault was very horrible that night and I was scared it would happen again. (Nichole)

> I once told him that I was having some trouble dealing with him having raped me. Perhaps naively, I had hoped I could make him understand how I felt about it. He repeatedly punched me about my head and said, 'If you ever mention that again I will kill you.' (Rachel)

> I remember when he smashed the chair in the kitchen. It was a Sunday afternoon and I was making the dinner. It must have been very late spring or early summer as it was quite warm

> outside and the children wanted to play with the paddling pool. He had said it wasn't really rape: 'Rape is when you're grabbed by a stranger in a dark alley and raped.'
>
> I said, "Rape by your husband is worse, because it is in your own home and by a person you love and trust."
>
> He didn't like that. He was half-way through a very loud, angry retort when Mandy walked into the kitchen: she couldn't find the plug for the paddling pool. He picked up a wooden chair and brought it down on the floor so hard it crumbled under his hands. I ushered Mandy out, reassured her and made sure all the kids were out of earshot then went back into the kitchen. He was tearing the rest of the chair apart with his bare hands. I told him how despicable his outbreak of anger was in front of any child especially Mandy, and carried on with the dinner. I didn't let on that I was quaking inside. (Linda)

Because he can't name the act as rape, you may have noticed that there are certain ways that he behaves afterwards. You may have felt very confused by the picture he presents of what happened. Let's look at some mechanisms perpetrators may use to avoid responsibility or explain away the sexual violence.[2]

Denial

> I did speak to Mark a couple of weeks after the assault. His view was that he didn't rape me. I said, 'I kept saying no, and you kept going. What does that tell you?' (Tracey)

Your partner may deny that he ever raped you. He may call you crazy, malicious, or a liar. If he appears not to remember, or tells you he has no idea what you are talking about, he's likely to be using denial.

> I just didn't know what. In the end I confronted him quite a few times and said, 'Look I'll forgive you and it's alright, but just tell me.'
>
> And he'd say, 'No, no, no, it's nothing.' (Kate)

Linda's husband used a common rape-myth to deny the nature of his assaults: He had said it wasn't really rape; 'Rape is when you're grabbed by a stranger in a dark alley and raped.' Marg's partner also denied that the act could be rape since they were married:

> But to this day he still says that it was his duty as a husband; it was my wifely duty. We'd been through marriage counselling

since he'd admitted to the affairs before. I told him it would take me a long time to trust him ever again, with the rape and that. He was like, 'I didn't rape you. I didn't rape you.'

'Tom', I said. 'No, you don't make me have sex with you.'

He said, 'You weren't struggling that hard.'

I said, 'Struggling? When you've got my hands pinned over my bloody head. We were on a waterbed and I've got a bad back.'

If he doesn't verbally deny raping you, perhaps he denies it in other ways. He may act as if nothing out of the ordinary has happened.

I was numb. I told him again what had happened, saying he had attacked me ... It wasn't until that night that he and I could talk about it, and then he had me repeat it over and over, not believing that it had happened as he did not remember anything ... He got angry with me for not trusting him, for being afraid to be alone with him, for wanting reassurance that he would not attack me again. He started talking to his family and friends about the incident, and told me that they did not believe that it had happened as I said, that I was 'overly sensitive'. So, he started to believe that I was exaggerating, too, and his concern and attempts to ease my fears dwindled. (Natalie)

Rationalisation

When an abuser attempts to justify sexually abusive behaviour, making statements like, 'I just wanted to make love to you', he is rationalising. So too when he says that it is what you want:

He would say that I wanted it; he would say that I wouldn't be here if I didn't want it. (Jodie)

On one occasion he told me that I must have wanted it or else I'd have tried harder to stop him. Rationalisation is a form of denial, because if the abuser succeeds in convincing himself that his self-serving justifications are correct, then what he has done couldn't be rape. (Rachel)

Siobhan's partner justified forced anal penetration:

Oh well, you know, we did it your way so now we have to do it in this position or that position.

So really it was always about control I guess. But in any case I went along with it to prevent further abuse.

Minimising

Minimising is a strategy that reduces the rape to something less harmful. For instance, the abuser might say something like, 'At least I didn't beat you up.' Nichole's partner minimised his sexual abuse by telling her he was doing her a favour: 'He implied that I was lucky to be dating and having sex with him.'

Minimisation also involves belittling your feelings, as Jennifer's partner did when he displayed anger that she wouldn't just 'get over' his sexually abusive behaviour.

Jodie's partner minimised his rape of her in a fairly extreme way:

> I was still a virgin at the time, although he did not believe me
> – until he realised afterwards. He tried to tell me that it wasn't
> 'real' sex and that I was still a virgin.

Here, we see that Jodie's partner first *rationalises* raping her on the grounds that he didn't believe she was a virgin, and when he found that this was incorrect, he switches to *minimising* the event.

Perpetrators often minimise because they don't want to face the consequences for what they've done. They are trying to convince themselves that what they did is really nothing. They may also subscribe to the common belief that rape of a partner is no big deal:

> He later admitted it was wrong, but has never been able to accept
> responsibility as to why it was so damaging to the relationship.
> (Jill)

Claiming loss of control

Here, the perpetrator offers excuses for the sexual abuse. He might say he just couldn't help himself because he was too 'horny':

> I remember him telling me that he went to bed determined not
> to rape me, but that when I came to bed he just couldn't stop it.
> He seemed genuinely upset about this. I completely bought in to
> that fallacy and felt sorry for him, poor chap, who desperately
> didn't want to hurt me but couldn't stop himself. (Linda)

Rachel's rapist used this type of excuse at the time of separation.

> When he raped me for ending our relationship, he said afterwards
> that he was sorry, but the thought of living without me drove him
> crazy. 'Sorry' loses all meaning when it is accompanied by the
> self-excusing 'but'.

As we saw in chapter 3, much rape mythology rests on the premise that men can't be expected to control themselves sexually. But there is no point at which a man loses control of himself. Respect for a partner's right to withdraw consent enables control.[3] There are no excuses for sexual assault, ever.

Blaming

Most of the women who share their stories in these pages were routinely blamed for the sexual violence, with the abuser claiming provocation or that his needs had been denied for too long. Thus, Jodie's partner blamed her for the rape by implying that she had led him on: 'You just can't do that to a guy and then just say no.' Linda's husband blamed his anal rapes of her on the condition of her vagina:

> After four kids I was loose, or so he said. Doing things normally wasn't exciting any more, this was new, interesting, exciting.

A blame-strategy that some abusers employ is telling a partner an act of rape is for her own good. Justine's partner called her frigid and said, "You needed it fucked out of you."

If your partner has blamed you for causing the sexual assault(s) in some way, be aware that he is trying to avoid responsibility. You are not to blame. Other men cope with frustration or other relationship problems without raping their partners. Remember that his actions are about *him* and not you.

What women do with partner rape

Women who feel unable to leave the relationship may use similar strategies to their partners to deny or justify the sexual violence, often in order to survive it emotionally:

> I simply ran damage control on all the violence. I hid my terrible home life and conditions from my work colleagues and tried in vain to hide it from my friends. I survived second by second, minute by minute. Sometimes I even got to survive day by day. I kept a low profile. I made minimal noise around the house and tried my best never to aggravate him. (Jennifer)

Those of us sexually and/or physically abused as children may have learned to survive by pretending unpleasant or frightening things had not happened. It is only natural to bring those same skills to adult abusive situations.

Denial/repression

Women's denial has been mentioned in previous chapters. Given that so much of society doesn't define forced sex by a partner as rape, why should this not also be true of its victims? You may feel you have no right to call what has happened to you rape:

> It was very frustrating later to look back on it and see the powerlessness of the whole situation in that I did not know how to respond to it. It's kind of strange in that for all that I'd been taught in school to stand up for yourself and that 'no means no' and 'what part of no don't you understand', and all those kind of images were brought up about it. You're also taught that rape doesn't have to be in a dark alley; it can be uncles or brothers or fathers but it's never really presented that it might be someone you're in a relationship with. (Tracey)

> If he came home drunk, he would take it, and this is where I see it as not being raped, because after a while you learn the process and you want the process because you know as soon as you do it, it's over. And each time I fuck him I'm getting better because he's coming faster and faster and faster, and I get it done quicker and quicker and quicker. And then if I become more sexually powerful and aggressive than he is, well then that shocks the whole system, and he doesn't know what's going on. (Kelly)

It may have become a 'normal' part of the relationship:

> I had never spoken to anyone about the abuse within the relationship. I guess a part of me had come to accept it as normal. (Charlotte)

After the first assault, some women protect themselves from the fear that they will be raped again by telling themselves it was a one-off aberration and is unlikely to reoccur. Not to deny the assault means you must face the thought of it happening again.[4]

Thus, when your partner sexually assaulted you, perhaps it evoked such painful implications for you and your future that you found it better to pretend it hadn't happened:

> I somehow just convinced myself that it hadn't happened, to the point that I made myself believe that I was still a virgin – that's what he wanted and I couldn't cope with the idea of losing my virginity that way and have anything further to do with the person that took it. (Jodie)

> Following an assault, I pretended nothing happened. I would usually shower or sleep. He would do the same, and was sometimes actually nice following an assault – he would hold me and stroke my hair. (Nichole)

Denial that what happened was rape makes continuing the relationship possible, because calling it rape dictates actions, such as leaving, that may not feel feasible. Love for your partner, or life-demands like school, jobs, or kids, may have meant that you needed to find ways to separate yourself from the pain, or just 'keep it together' somehow:

> Years ago when going through the domestic violence proceedings, I was asked if I'd been raped by my husband. I immediately said no, and at the time there's no way I would have recognised it as rape because I was in denial and would have been much too ashamed and afraid of the consequences with my ex-husband. He would have gone totally nuts, I'm sure. I don't want to even guess what that would mean.
>
> But stronger than all those feelings is the desire to protect my daughter, for if I was raped by my husband, what does that make my daughter? I did not tell anyone – I didn't know it was rape, just like I didn't know what I was going through was domestic violence. I knew it was unpleasant, I knew I was miserable, but I thought it was my lot in life and I was scared to say anything for fear of the repercussions … No, you suffer it in silence. Never would you let anyone think life was less than perfectly loving. Because your number one aim, your way of surviving at all in fact, is to pretend it's all okay. Cover it up, cover it up. (Melina)

Thus some women are unable to identify what happened as rape until after they are separated:

> I didn't know how serious it was until he left. While he was living with me, I just tried to forget it. That's why, especially when he left, I said, I don't want him to come back. I felt free. I didn't have to do it again. So that's when I felt really relieved, that I wouldn't have to do that again. (Shefali)

Rape is traumatic and may be too unbearable to deal with psychologically:

> I knew he had just raped me, stripped me forcefully and held me down. It was too awful to accept. And here he was, acting as though nothing abnormal had happened. I couldn't look at him.

I sipped my coffee, lit another cigarette and said, 'That did not happen. That never happened.' (Linda)

I just didn't understand what had happened ... It's not nice to think that it happened to you and it's not nice to believe that it did happen. (Sarah)

I guess a part of me had come to accept it as normal. It never occurred to me to seek outside help. I guess you have an image of a 'battered woman', and I didn't see myself as that image. I felt that, as long as I stood by Ted, I could help him. (Charlotte)

Denial might entail thoughts like, 'But I love this person, so how could he have hurt me this way?'

It did not occur to me until just one year ago, about 14 years after the rape, that it had been rape. I always said he had attacked me, but found it very difficult to see him as a rapist. There was absolutely no indication in the seven years of our relationship that he could be violent, and I know he adored me. I simply couldn't reconcile the Sean who attacked me with the Sean that I had known all those years. I convinced myself that he really did not remember, that he had blacked-out, possibly from the few beers he had had, although I know logically that this is very unlikely. (Natalie)

Minimisation

Because society teaches us that 'real rape' is supposed to entail violence, when we are coerced through non-physical means, we may minimise what took place. And, some of us minimise the rape not because of the level of violence, but because the rapist was our partner. Because partner rape is socially minimised, we may make it somehow less than it was. Often, we minimise not only the event, but also what we feel. For example, you may have told yourself you are overreacting by being upset about it.

Or, perhaps you minimised what your partner did to you by maximising his favourable qualities. Initial feelings of anger, betrayal and pain were followed by thoughts like, 'What am I complaining about? He's a wonderful father.'

Minimising rape by reinterpreting it in such a way so that you see it as a misunderstanding is a common reaction of women raped by men they are dating:[5]

I put it out of my mind, convinced myself it wasn't really rape, that I had misunderstood or misinterpreted the events. (Emma)

Rationalisation

After your partner sexually assaulted you, you may have tried to explain it away with such thoughts as, 'He was drunk when it happened' or 'He's highly sexed and can't help himself.' In the quest for answers to 'Why?' you might rationalise his behaviour by excusing him and/or blaming yourself:

> A couple of times I did provoke him. We were having an argument and he wouldn't listen, and I shouldn't have done it and I whacked him on his head and of course he went psycho and I suppose you couldn't blame him. I shouldn't have done it ... Maybe it's my fault I let him get away with the sexual assaults for too long ... (Siobhan)

Perhaps you thought, 'Everybody knows that real rape is what strangers do, not partners, so therefore what happened to me isn't rape.'

Rationalisation may have offered some of us a feeling of future safety because we tell ourselves that if we stop doing whatever it is we 'did' to cause the rape, it won't happen again:

> I felt that he was good for me and that if I could be a better girlfriend it wouldn't happen anymore. I always felt it would get better when I changed. Also he was the type of person everyone loves and I felt that I must love him too. (Nichole)

Like Nichole, our rationalising might be supported by other people's view of our partner: everybody else thinks he's a wonderful guy, so it must be us. Sometimes it's less painful for a woman raped by her partner to make herself the bad one and not him:[6]

> I believed with most of my heart that it was my duty to tolerate (the sexual violence), because, after all, I was the faulty one, wasn't I? (Linda)

Giving up self-blame or ceasing to excuse the perpetrator may be intensely painful because the other side of rationalisation is admitting it wasn't your fault and there are no excuses for his behaviour.

Dissociation

Dissociation is something many people who have been traumatised by sexual assault experience. We've heard many of the women talk about 'numbing' out:

> I would just feel numb. I can't explain it, and I know I was there and present mentally during the assault, but I didn't feel anything really – no pain, no pleasure, no anger. (Nichole)

> I would just cut off till he had finished. It was like I wasn't there. (Justine)

Many of us learned to do this when we were children and sexually abused.

If you dissociated when your partner raped you, you may have felt as if you were witnessing the assaults from a distance, had a sense of leaving your body, or felt detached, like the assault was happening to somebody else. Perhaps you felt a sense of time distortion where an assault that in reality lasted perhaps a few minutes seemed to go on forever. Some women focus upon a certain point in the room or upon totally irrelevant matters.[7] These are forms of 'escape' from the traumatic scene that enable us to defend against emotional or even physical pain.

Another form of dissociation is forgetting. You may have only partial recall of the assaults; for example, you can remember what happened, but not what you felt – or the other way around – you remember your fear and pain, but not what experience they go with:

> For some of my assaults, I can remember what happened before and after. Between that, I know that a rape occurred, but I know it only as an intellectual fact; I have no memory of when he entered me, what it felt like as he raped me or when he ejaculated and got off me. I can't remember what he said to me, and have no idea how long it took. Or, at other times, I remember part but not all of the assault; the beginning but not the end. (Rachel)

Forgetting can also be total – a respondent in *Voices of the Survivors* completely forgot a rape by her husband until some years later.[8] Sarah isn't sure that she remembers everything:

> I just didn't understand what had happened. I've got two very vivid memories but I can't rule out that it didn't happen more than twice but I know very clearly that it happened on at least two occasions but it feels as though it was more than that.

Blocking off memories may enable emotional survival. Later, as we heal, or something triggers a reminder of the assault, the memories may come back.

'Managing' the sexual assaults [9]

Some women employ strategies to avoid being raped again. Where we cannot avoid it, we try to limit the extent of the violence. For instance, Tiffany moved into a separate room:

> Near the end of the marriage, for the last two years, I slept in the spare room and I slept literally, and I'll never forget this, my hand was getting so cramped, I used to sleep with the phone in my hand. I bought a mobile phone and I slept with it every night in my hand with my finger on the speed dial …

> So I was just scared, and all I was doing was waiting for him to hurt me bad enough that I could get a domestic violence thing, stay in the house, protect my son, keep my job, get the money that I needed.

> Nobody said, 'Is this painful?' or nobody asked me, 'Is he sexually abusive?' I'd already said that I was unhappy and nobody was listening.

Marg slept with her child:

> I wouldn't let him near me for ages after that. I'd go to sleep on the lounge and put Tara next to me, so he couldn't touch me.

You might attempt to minimise the extent of the violence once sexual assault has commenced by manipulating the circumstances in order to maintain some control. Jackie gives an example:

> He said, 'I am going to come on your face. I can't wait to come on your face.' I was silent for a bit, and he repeated himself … 'I can't wait to come all over your fucking face.' I didn't know what to do. All I knew was that he was out of control and I needed to gain some sort of control over this situation. I said, 'Fuck me from behind.' It was the only thing I could think of, to make him not come on my face without my permission; which he would have.

Some of us pretend to exhibit a sexual response to avoid further violence:

> Sometimes I would act as if I was taking part so as not to get in more trouble. (Justine)

> I would make the right noises so that it would be over sooner and so he would not make it hurt more, or beat a response out of me. Also, acquiescing to rape fairly early meant that I stood a better chance of not being beaten as well as raped. (Rachel)

We may become fearful and placating, submitting to certain acts in order to avoid further degradation or injury:

> But I never questioned him because I was too embarrassed. I mean, it's just stupid isn't it? We're married for 16 years and I'm too scared to say, 'What are you doing?'

> But I couldn't. I just thought, 'What is he doing? Why is he doing that? He's never done that before.' (Shefali)

Survival vs. ending the violence

We've just explored the ways in which women survive or manage sexual violence by partners. While these strategies cover the pain and fear of admitting something so horrible as rape by a partner, they often serve to keep us in unsafe situations. Some women though do ultimately respond to partner rape in ways that bring about an end to it. So, what is the key to action? We think awareness. There is a link between finding the ability to define the sexual violence, and ending it.[10] Thus, in later chapters we'll look at some women who named it, perhaps fought it and in a few cases contacted the police. This suggests that when women are able to give sexual assaults by partners the name it deserves, it's possible to move out of denial and towards thinking about the safety they deserve.

Our recognition that some women do leave or end the relationship is in no way an indictment of women who don't fight or don't leave. Many of us, including one of the authors, didn't do the leaving; we were left and that's how the violence ended.

CHAPTER 9

The Wounds

Recognising the effects of partner rape

We've seen that there is a widespread notion that rape by a partner doesn't have serious impact on a woman. The truth, however, is that partner rape often carries many short- and long-term emotional and physical effects. (Flashbacks and other traumatic responses will be discussed more fully in the next chapter.) In fact, researchers have noted that women raped by partners remain traumatised for longer than women raped by strangers, with a parallel drawn between the emotional aftermath for hostages and for marital rape victims:[1]

> And they say marital rape is not as bad as stranger rape. I don't know. I have never been raped by a stranger. But I think being raped by your husband in your own home must be worse in some ways. At least if you're attacked by a perfect stranger it is not so personal. Your husband is the person whom you should be able to turn to for comfort, who should protect you. When it is the person you have entrusted your life to who abuses you, it isn't just physical or sexual assault, it is a betrayal of the very core of your marriage or your person, your trust. If you are not safe in your own home, next to your husband, where are you safe? (Linda)

We hope that by reading about the effects you may experience one or more of the following:

Comfort through commonality: Because survivors of partner rape often feel isolated, you may have felt that nobody could understand your experiences or feelings. Sometimes identifying with the feelings of another can help those who feel alone in their pain. It may also normalise your feelings, making them less scary.

Validation for your pain: If you are hurting, but have bought into myths about partner rape, you might believe that there is something strange about the level of pain you feel. Sometimes understanding that there are real reasons why you feel a certain way can bring about a sense of relief.

Identifying where it hurts: Just having words to put to an unnamed or unnameable pain can be helpful because it resolves confusion. When you are able to identify the damage, it is possible to consider where you need to heal.

Greater appreciation of your survival: Acknowledging the ways in which partner rape has hurt you may give you a sense of renewed compassion and respect for yourself as a survivor.

If you are new to considering the effects of partner rape on your life, please go gently with yourself as you read this chapter. The words of other women may remind you of pain that you might not have even been aware of or that you've tried to bury in order to survive emotionally. If you begin to feel overwhelmed, please get support if you need it. Remember: you deserve it.

All women are not affected in the same ways. Factors that may exacerbate the trauma of partner rape are the severity of the violence, as well as the duration and frequency of the sexual assaults.[2] You might find that what affects you strongly are images of the rape or there may be emotional issues surrounding it that seem to evoke the strongest effect:

> Looking back it isn't the worst rape scenes I visualise or remember most clearly. They are there, but don't necessarily force themselves into my consciousness. It is other things I remember most, snapshots of moments, thoughts or feelings. My mind numbing and the cogs slowing down from endless pointless discussions, trying to make sense of and understand what was happening. (Linda)

As you read, remember that there is no right or wrong way to feel.

Emotional effects

Partner rape can feel deeply personal. The partner's assaults are aimed at parts of us that he knows intimately. He wants to hurt *us*. In a variety of ways he is telling us the violence is our fault; this reverberates deeply into our sense of self. The sense of powerlessness and entrapment that partner rape – especially repeated rape – can cause is truly horrifying, especially for a woman who has no external resources that she can call upon to assist her to safety:

When I was living with domestic violence 24 hours a day, I did not know who I was. I did not have time to know. I was always worrying about my abuser. Plagued about his next episode, his next adventure. I did not know what I liked or disliked during my abusive years. I knew what he liked and what would upset him. His likes and dislikes became mine. Over time, I gave my life to him, not realising it. Not realising that he controlled my every move. (Kuriah)

The workers made me realise that domestic violence was just not getting bashed. It can be emotional, physical, financial – anything that stuffs your self-esteem up. I haven't drawn for years. I used to draw, I used to write stories all the time, I used to go out for walks, and I'd stopped all that, due to my marriage. I'm not stupid enough to get married again, I think. (Marg)

Not only do the rapes induce a sense of helplessness, but shame and other issues such as loyalty and self-blame serve to deepen our sense of entrapment and erosion of self. As a rape crisis counsellor observed:

Women take the blame for the relationship not working and feeling sorry for the perpetrator. They feel that they have colluded with the perpetrator and that they are responsible for the rape.

You may have found that you cannot differentiate between the badness of the rape, and yourself. Instead of seeing what happened as bad, you may believe that *you* are bad:

I feel negatively about myself and my body at times, and sex makes me feel dirty altogether. I have regained some of the self-esteem, but I have work to do still. (Nichole)

My self-esteem plummeted to the point where I became convinced that I truly was not worth loving treatment by a man – after all, I reasoned, if I had been he would not have done what he did to me. I came to believe that if people truly knew me, they would hate me as much as I hated myself. (Rachel)

I walk around with this ingrained belief that there is something wrong with me, that no one could possibly like me, that I am boring and not worth being around. At times this lifts, but not often. (Natalie)

Justine says her experiences of partner rape caused her to feel, 'Very dirty, unwanted, useless, unworthy, ugly.' So too Rachel:

My partner seemed to revel in the fact that his actions caused me to feel dirty. I can recall him raping me and saying, 'How good do you think you are now, you bitch?' Had it been more than a rhetorical and taunting question, I might have answered that I didn't think I was good at all, that I felt so dirty that I would have liked a deep disinfectant bath.

I remember quipping that if somebody who was supposed to love me could treat me in the manner that he did, I'd have hated to see what somebody who hated my guts could do. The fact that somebody who supposedly loved me could rape me definitely added to the shame. I felt that my body and my womanhood were inherently dirty, and like many survivors of rape, I found that the sense of being dirty lingered for years and took a lot of work to overthrow.

Linda captures the feeling of powerlessness some women raped by partners feel:

He was in control. He was the person who decided what happened. I had no voice. That is one of the things emotional and more especially sexual abuse does to you. It robs you of power over your own body, it teaches you that no matter what you say or do, he will do exactly as he pleases anyway ...

The knowledge that there was nothing she could do to stop the assaults brought Linda deep sadness and despair:

I remember after taking the children to school and playgroup, kneeling on the kitchen floor, sobbing and sobbing and sobbing. Total despair. There seemed no way to end it, no way of escape, no getting through to him. No hope.

Haunted women: ongoing fears of men, rape and the perpetrator

I'm frightened of men now, I have a man for massage but he's very nice but sometimes I'm a bit thingy about him touching me but I can take a friend with me if I want to, and I'm sure he's not going to jeopardise his profession. (Siobhan)

Are you afraid of your partner, or of being sexually assaulted again? This is a common fear for survivors of partner rape, for if you can be raped by somebody who says he loves you, where can you expect to be safe?

Nights when he didn't assault me were worse. Lying there, tense, waiting for him to start. I can remember wishing he would just get on with it, get it over and done with so I could go to sleep. (Linda)

Sometimes, the fear is a general anxiety and terror that seems to pervade many aspects of a survivor's life. Although Linda's marriage is over, she shares the ongoing fear the rapes have left her with:

> Tonight I will try to visit the bathroom and not flee back up the stairs from the dark. Tonight I will try to get into bed without hands gripping my feet as I climb in. Tonight I will try not to panic if my boyfriend moves in his sleep. Tonight I will try to block out the sounds of some evil thing moving downstairs. Tonight I will try to just go to sleep without curling up into a ball. Tonight I will try not to sink straight back into the country I have seen so often before. Tonight I will try not to be scared.

Women who have escaped abusive relationships may feel, for a long time after as if the perpetrator is still present and still controlling them.[3] Thus, you may carry fear or guilt for defying a violent ex-partner even if he is no longer in your life.

> For a while, I felt guilty every time I did something that was against his rules or wishes, after I broke up with him. His abuse was almost retribution for me. It made up for what I did wrong, and without the abuse it all sort of built up. (Nichole)

Apprehension may continue even when it is not realistically based. But for Summer, who is being stalked four years after the rape and Kuriah who was horrifically attacked years after estrangement, such fears are grounded in reality.

Physical effects

If you've had physical symptoms such as nausea, vomiting, soreness, muscle tension, headaches, and fatigue,[4] they may be stress-related as the presence of your partner reminds you of the rapes you've endured, or the possibility of more to come.

> I suffered through many physical symptoms following the assault – pain, vomiting, complete loss of appetite because I would trigger when I swallowed anything (including liquid for a few days), headache (probably from the trauma to the head or stress induced), chills and shaking uncontrollably, the inability to feel comfortable with clothes on or clothes off which just was making me completely break down emotionally. (Summer)

> I was unable to retain food to the point where my weight dropped to 43 kg. I was very sick for a long time. This was due to the

domestic violence situation I was in of which a part was the sexual assaults. (Jennifer)

Injuries can include rectal and/or vaginal tearing:

> I got terrible tummy cramps the following day, and diarrhoea, and piles. I remember how much it hurt to go to the loo afterwards. I was bleeding and so so sore. I had bad piles and the cream stung terribly, probably because it was an open wound. Even sitting down would be rather uncomfortable. (Linda)

> I experienced some tearing that was not repaired and can cause me significant pain. (Summer)

Cystitis, which produces a burning sensation when passing urine may be a result of bruising to the urethra caused by rough intercourse.

> I often found as well that my vulva was inflamed, with an itching and burning. Eerily, the itching and burning sometimes repeated itself years later while I was working through the rapes at particularly deep levels. (Rachel)

Rachel also experienced dyspareunia, painful sexual intercourse that can result from sexual trauma.

You may have experienced other physical effects of rape by partners including:

- Pregnancy, either incidental to the rape, or deliberately forced on you to bind you further to the abuser. Marg shares: 'He was trying to get me pregnant. He said, "I want another kid – maybe that will shut you fucking up."'

- Miscarriage if you were pregnant and battered as well as raped. Pregnancy has been shown to increase rape and other violence to a woman[5] as her partner works out his insecurities about 'sharing' her.

- Sexually transmitted diseases. Some men rape their partners to deliberately infect them with STDs so as to prevent them sleeping with other men. Battery has also been positively identified with the spread of HIV/AIDS.[6]

- Vaginismus – Like dyspareunia, this is often related to trauma and is a condition in which the vaginal muscles contract, either not allowing any penetration by a penis, or making penetration extremely painful.

Fear, shame or loyalty to the perpetrator can stop partner rape victims who need medical attention from getting it. Abusive partners may also actively prevent their partners from seeking medical assistance.

Impact on future relationships

When you enter a relationship, you have a right to believe that you won't be harmed by your partner. If you have felt a degree of safety and trust in your relationship, rape by your partner can be absolutely devastating, turning the world as you knew it upside down.

> And I say to you in my mind. Thanks. This is what you have done to me. You have destroyed my world. The world which was safe, which I knew, you took away. Time and time again you told me I was safe, that you loved me, that you would not hurt me. And time and time again you betrayed that trust, you hurt me, you who had assured me security. You took away my belief in a friendly, safe world and replaced it with fear. The most intimate, normal and known things died and were changed into evil, dangerous, threatening objects. I can't be sure that anything is as it appears to be. And you did that to me. (Linda)

Because rape by a partner involves violation of trust, you may avoid getting close to somebody again because you believe that you cannot trust yourself or your perceptions – after all, you trusted before and were hurt. As Siobhan says, 'How do I know this won't happen again?'

> I think the only thing that worries me is that because I've come out of an abusive relationship, I'm always doubting my next one. I get really worried because in counselling they say when you're in an abusive relationship the patterns continue into another one. Sometimes I do fall back and that's when my insecurity plays up, and that's when I know I'm doing it to my new husband. I say things to him like, 'Oh, you sound like this', and he's saying, 'Where's it all coming from?'
>
> So I get worried. Am I overprotective, or am I just being careful, or am I going to ruin my next relationship because of the last one? It's constant, even now. Because I'm an independent person, if my new husband now tells me, 'Don't do this' or that I can't do this, I think, 'He's telling me what to do. Somebody's telling me what to do again', and I get all panicky.
>
> I told him when I met him. I said, 'Look, I am coming out of an abusive relationship. I want a real partner. I don't want someone

to control me, tell me how to walk, how to talk, how to do this, how to do that. Just be my partner. Be with me, beside me, not on top of me. (Shefali)

In the long-term, the scars are there. It took me well over a year before I could even date anyone ... The reality of it is, I got myself caught up in a relationship that is emotionally abusive. Harry is a controlling man, one who is very dependent on me, and has managed to control me for over 11 years. I sacrificed my needs and wants to hold onto someone who was wrong for me because I felt I couldn't get anyone else. And because I was so scared of getting involved with someone who would attack me as Sean had done, I did not trust my own instincts anymore. (Natalie)

A domestic violence counsellor relates that, in her experience, the worst impact of rape by partners is that when survivors enter new relationships, 'they just can't go into intimacy':

I find myself constantly questioning my ability to select and interact with partners and potential partners. (Nichole)

The worst effect has probably been my inability to be 'me' around others. I frequently feel like I am always on alert with people, even those I trust, waiting for them to harm me in some emotional way and sometimes physically. This hurts so much because I want so badly to give these people I love the benefit of the doubt but I am always waiting for the other shoe to drop, so to speak. My inability to trust those I love breaks my heart. That my life has taken some of the turns that it has is also very disenchanting because I do believe that I would have made better, more informed choices had it not been for my rape. This truly does just feel like it has broken my spirit. (Summer)

I always tried not to like (new partners) too much because I didn't want to get hurt again. I guess if I didn't care, they could do whatever they wanted to me and I wouldn't get hurt again. I guess I thought it was a state of mind and that you let yourself get hurt by opening yourself up to them – I can see now that, that is the way that I thought because that is all I had ever experienced. (Jodie)

If you have a tendency to get angry with yourself for lack of trust, remember that healing can take time and patience, as well as proven safe behaviour from others. When intimacy exists in a relationship, it means that you are permitted to say no, and have your boundaries respected.

Because sex in a relationship is about so much more than what we do with our genitals, rape by a partner can strike deeply at many levels of ourselves, including our sexuality:

> My body will never be wholly mine again. I feel that he took from me that which was so precious. I never really had a wonderful body, but it was mine, it was what I was blessed with and he stripped away what self-love I had for myself. It wasn't much, but it was mine. My beliefs now about myself and/or my body are such that I am very self-conscious about every little part of me – physically, emotionally, spiritually. He told me that he would break me – and although I so dislike believing this, he has. Not completely, but enough so that I will never be the woman I could have become had it not been for what he has done to me and what I have subsequently allowed him to take from me spiritually and emotionally. Intimate moments are difficult in that I always feel like less of a woman, no matter how my partner may make me feel. I feel that my partner will never know the me that I was before. I'm so much more inhibited now – broken, pieces of me all over and my sexuality fragmented into slivers of the me I once was or was destined to become. I feel like my mate is cheated by what I lost. (Summer)

Some survivors, as Summer expresses in the last sentence, who find themselves unable to be sexual or give closeness to new partners, blame themselves, seeing their sexual problems as a personal inadequacy. If you recognise yourself here, you need to understand that your problems with sexuality and intimacy aren't due to a deficiency on your part. They are an effect of what happened to you.

Some survivors of partner rape feel so dirty and despoiled that sex with men who don't care about them becomes a way of punishing themselves:

> Sex became a punishment. I began to like sex with men with whom I had no real relationship. Sex with someone who cared about me was terrifying and made me feel guilty and ashamed or completely numb. I don't really trust myself with sex. I can't think of sex with someone I care about without feeling sick. (Nichole)

> I believed that it (sex) was the only reason that men wanted me. I never let myself enjoy it, though. I put myself there purely to please the men. I still don't understand why I did that. It's something I have thought about a lot. I guess back then I hated myself more than the men. (Jodie)

Perhaps you have developed aversions to different sexual acts or types of touch. Nichole, repeatedly orally raped, says, 'a blow job is completely out of the question and makes me throw up'.

You may experience sexual difficulties because, in later attempts at sex, you have 'flashbacks' to the rape/s, with accompanying terror and feelings of shame. Because sex can cause them to relive the feelings they had when they were raped, survivors develop trauma-based coping mechanisms:

> Certainly, physical intimacy with males is a problem for me. I've had a couple of short relationships. In both situations when that physical aspect of the relationship developed it was riddled with walls and panic attacks and flashbacks. Enough for me to know that if there is someone I am seriously interested in, they are going to have to be a tough nut in order to survive me and my walls and my anxieties and panics that will happen when I get close to someone. That person will have to be prepared to ride that wave, and if they're not prepared, then I will lose. So there is a high risk of me ending up in a situation where I can't win because the scars from the past are likely to ruin potential or future relationships ... Everybody has baggage, but people don't like to acknowledge that they have baggage, and I have extreme baggage, and they're sexual and physical ones. Are they going to rip me off? Are they going to be cruel to me? Are they going to hurt me? I go through a whole panic thing, and if we get past that, then the next round of panic sets in. So it has had a huge effect on me physically, emotionally and behaviourally, because I end up being this kind of split personality person. (Sarah)

Not surprisingly, if you are still in the relationship with the partner who raped you, you may experience strong and painful reactions when having sex with him:

> When we would sometimes have sex (after he had said about raping others and pretending to rape me) I would just freeze, get sick at the thought that I was having sex with someone who could do this. Sometimes when I thought about it I would just go into shut down, just rock back and forth in a daze, like a baby. (Jodie)

If your sexuality and ability for intimacy has been damaged by partner rape, you may feel that you are not missing out on anything by not having sex and closeness. The rape and sexual abuse you experienced may have come to mark all sex for you. But you can heal, and when you are ready or you feel sufficiently safe, you will be able to do so; we explore sexual healing in chapter 19.

Alcohol and other drugs: trying to numb the pain

Many survivors hurt and are full of rage. But they can't feel the pain and anger. Often, they've learned to live by the 'Don't feel' rule of violence in the family. They may use drinks and drugs to stop the pain, to medicate. Maree explains her descent into heroin addiction:

> That's how I ended up on heroin. I ended up on coke. I ended up on pills. Like people say you can't blame anyone but yourself, but listen here – when you turn around and you're driven – got fucked with for so long, for so many years, even after when we split up, he was raping me. I said, 'Can I get some heroin?'
>
> They said, 'You want to try some?'
>
> I said, 'I got money.'
>
> They said, 'No if you want to try it, you can have it for free.'
>
> See they already had it in their head, 'Oh yeah we'll get her hooked. We won't take her money now. We'll get her hooked then.'
>
> So I ended up being hooked, for seven years. Then I gave it up.

Alternatively, survivors drink and drug to let the rage come out. Emma speaks of only being able to be open about her rape if sufficiently distanced from her feelings by alcohol:

> I can type the 'r word' but have great trouble actually saying it (except when drunk – a few weeks ago I had a bit to drink and was shouting to anyone who'd listen, '(perpetrator) raped me, he RAPED me.'

But the survivor ends up feeling worse as her addiction causes more loss of self with the loss of dignity and self-respect:

> I go through periods where I do abuse alcohol in an effort to suppress my feelings and my fear. I'm only recently acknowledging this as a problem in my life. For the moment, the alcohol does tend to feel as though it can numb me from experiencing the pain and sadness that my rape has caused. I would say that I binge drink more than anything and it usually revolves around my emotional state at the time. I can and do drink socially, but notice that the deeper I find myself in my

painful emotions the more I tend to knowingly overdo it. It is becoming more and more of a problem in my recent past and I am working my way through it in therapy. I have yet to get a handle or control on the drinking. (Summer)

While I was with him I used to drink alcohol and smoke marijuana a bit. I still have a bad habit of turning to drugs when things get bad – usually it is now ecstasy – but I try to control it. (Jodie)

Immediately following the rape, I partied all the time. I would water down the bottles on my parents' bar. I dropped acid quite a lot; it usually made me pass out, which then I thought was wonderful. I wanted to party so much that I dropped out of school three months before graduation to be with the drugs and the drinking. (Adair)

Some survivors may begin a course of medication, which initially seems to help them quell anxiety or insomnia, only to find that they develop a dependency.

If you have struggled with addiction, you've possibly found that the alcohol or pills that were once a comfort now create more problems than they solve. These may be internal – facing in the morning what you did the night before or not being able to remember what you did. Or chemical abuse may cause other problems like drink-driving charges, use of illicit drugs, getting sacked, or even losing custody of children. Tragically, substance abuse also has the potential to become fatal.

Like many battered women who want to seek help for addiction, you may have been prevented from doing so by your abuser or he may have sabotaged your recovery if you were having treatment, increasing the violence until you discontinued treatment.[7] But you have a right to get help so that you can regain control of your life. Please see information about overcoming addictions in chapter 17.

Teenage rape survivors

Teen rape survivors may experience some of the above effects such as self-blame and low self-esteem and drinking and drugging. Additionally, there may be different issues for them. If you are a teenage survivor of partner rape, you may have experienced any of the following effects:[8]

A sense of loss of personal integrity: Teenage girls are busy trying to find out who they are. Rape can shatter an already fragile self-image.

A sense of loss of control: Teenage girls need to believe they can control their world. Rape can be terrifying for them as it takes away that sense of control.

Damage to emerging sexual identity: Teenage girls may start out with a healthy curiosity about sex. If somebody you loved, or liked enough to date, has forced sex on you, it might now seem ugly and frightening:

> With my next boyfriend, I often had periods of feeling dirty, not good enough, like I was damaged goods. He was a virgin, and I felt like a slut compared to him. (Emma)

Personality changes: If you were a previously outgoing girl, you might have become suddenly fearful and withdrawn or sullen and angry.

Lowered school performance: The trauma of rape may make concentration difficult, or you've become depressed and feel that trying is pointless.

Withdrawal from school or social activities: You might find that you just don't feel like going out, or you've stopped seeing friends who are part of the same circle as the perpetrator. If you are still in the relationship, the perpetrator may have deliberately isolated you from friends or other meaningful attachments.

Flagrant promiscuous behaviour: 'Sleeping around' after rape may be a sign of a sense that sex is all you are good for.

> I became very promiscuous following rape. Like I was worthless and it didn't matter who had a turn with me. I became very trampy and seductive. (Adair)

Eating disorders: Anorexia and bulimia commonly start in the teen years and may be an outgrowth of rape as you attempt to have control over your body in a way that you weren't permitted to when you were raped. Forcing vomit is also a releasing of anger:

> I ate very little and was a practicing bulimic during the relationship. (Nichole)

> My anorexia has worsened considerably since I started talking about the rape. (Emma).

> I'd battled with anorexia as a result of the bullying in my school days, so it was always there. But after Ted, and during that next relationship, with memories popping out all over the place, I struggled with bulimia. And even now, despite being so much stronger, if I start to get very stressed out, I have a tendency to binge. (Charlotte)

Self-destructive behaviours. Because you may believe that being raped again is all you deserve, you may visit dangerous places alone or walk alone at night. You may not care what happens to you or your body:

> I have very little fear of rape. I have often walked home alone from clubs at 2 a.m. without a second thought – my attitude is 'oh, here we go again'. Another one to add to the collection. I'm sure this isn't a good attitude to take, but I honestly believe that if some guy is busy raping me, at least he's not raping some innocent girl who isn't used to being treated like that. (Emma)

Other behaviour may include involvement with another violent man or self-injury in the form of cutting or burning. Self- injury is often a way for young women to affirm the sense of badness that the rape has left them with.

Alienation: Maybe you feel an inability to relate to family and friends. A morbid sense of utter loneliness sets in as you believe that nobody will understand about the rape, and that it is a malevolent secret you must do your best to hide.

If you are a teenage girl, be assured of these things:

1. You are not alone.

2. There is help available for you. Please call a crisis or domestic violence line.

3. The pain you are experiencing won't last forever.

4. You are not bad or flawed; bad things have happened to you.

If you have been raped, don't wait to get checked for STDs and pregnancy. A rape counsellor can advise you on how best to go about this. Talk to at least one trusted adult about the rape.

Isolation: increasing the effects of partner rape

A domestic violence worker reports that she has heard many disclosures of partner rape from abused woman clients, but that this is almost always the last type of violence to be disclosed. 'Where battering is thought of as something private and shameful, what happens in the bedroom is even more so.'

> If an assault had been particularly humiliating, I found it hard to be among people. It was very hard to serve coffee for somebody from the local church, while I tried to shut off images of the night before; difficult to focus on conversation with remembered

hisses of 'slut' in my ears. The shame was horrible, and I used to imagine that people present could see how disgusting I was. At its worst, I actually felt afraid to meet people's eyes. The shame silenced me, because I knew that if I told of the assaults, my dirtiness would be confirmed. (Rachel)

The isolation that survivors of partner rape feel is a factor that makes it more traumatising than stranger rape or battery for some women. Because of social perceptions that regard partner rape as less serious, or in fact not rape at all, we will see in chapter 13 that some women attempting to disclose their experiences have had their pain discounted, increasing their sense of shame and isolation.

As we heal, we learn to take back control over our lives. We can step outside our silence and isolation; we can acknowledge our pain and claim the right to heal. If you've read through this chapter and recognised yourself in any part of it, you might feel a little daunted. Please know that you *will* be able to heal. For the moment, you have hopefully come a little closer to knowing that there is nothing odd about the feelings and issues that rape by your partner may have left you with.

CHAPTER 10

PARTNER RAPE AND TRAUMA

Survivors may experience a range of symptoms often found in survivors of other trauma situations such as war, terrorism, rape and domestic violence.

Many assume that when a woman leaves a violent relationship, she will be safe. Because some people downplay the seriousness of women attacked by their partners, they don't realise that a woman may experience ongoing violence and/or residual emotional difficulties for a lengthy period after leaving:[1]

> I did have a brief moment where I came out of an elevator and was walking out of the building just as he was coming in, and even though I had a friend sort of step in between us so we couldn't see each other, and we did a sort of circling a pillar as he went into the elevator and I went out the building, I was shaking and in tears just being near this person, just sort of looking up and there he was. (Tracey)

If people underestimate the seriousness of battery and death-threats by a woman's partner, they are, as we have seen, even more inclined to do so with rape by partners. All too often, survivors hear that what happened to them wasn't serious, or that they should 'get over it'. Consequently you may not understand why you still feel rotten years after a violent relationship.

In fact, many of us may experience Post Traumatic Stress Disorder, more commonly known as PTSD. We devote a chapter to describing PTSD (with specific consequences for rape survivors)[2] due to our own experiences and awareness that although having a name for something doesn't necessarily make it easier, naming it can demystify the feelings and thoughts:

> You should not judge your response as right or wrong, good or bad. Rather, it is important for you to understand why you feel as you do.[3]

The nature of trauma is that it turns a person's assumptions of a safe world and of control over their lives upside down so that they no longer feel safe anywhere:

> The normal, everyday items that hang around the house are ready to change, to turn into something terrifying, sinister. A doll, propped up against the computer table is staring at me as I walk by and as I turn my back I can see it jump down looking evil, after me. The plant on the sideboard shivers slightly in the draft near the door, and I start, expecting something or someone to jump out from behind the curtain. The slice of roast beef I pick up and eat, folded between my fingers, as I dip it in the juice on the plate will leave bright red blood. I reach into the fridge to pull out a can of Guinness. Just opening the fridge was bad enough, as though something unexpected was lurking inside. Now the can I want is at the back, I reach further in but it is stuck in the cardboard packaging. But my right hand holding the door feels exposed, I can't see the other side of the door and my fingers tingle, waiting for something to grab them. I take the can at the front and shut the fridge quickly, panicking. Turning the lights off as I progress back through the house is terrifying, as the lights go out, my back faces darkness, an unknown danger.
>
> Mirrors must be avoided, what will I see behind me when I look into them? Darkened windows are scary from the light inside. Will there be something or someone the other side or will they show something approaching me from behind. I go up the stairs, the wood creaks beneath my shoes and behind me. They don't sound like my footsteps. In the children's bedrooms I turn off the lamps and the huddled shapes under the duvets are monsters which will spring out to attack me as I walk through the door. A sleeping bag on the girls' floor is a dead body.
>
> I can't sit with my back to a door or open space. I need to see everything around me to check constantly that it has not changed. I am always ready to fight or flee. Startle at the wind pounding the window, the drip in the water tank, the cat jumping off a top, a knock on the door and the ring of the phone. I lie in bed tense, too tense to sleep, late into the night, wide awake. Then come the dreams, deformed cats appearing between stairs, an island which keeps changing, and I wake more tired than I went to bed. At work the chink of glass as I misjudge the distance between the pumps, the bar door opened by punters I saw coming, the

sudden squirt as a barrel runs out, the click of the glass-washer as the cycle ends, the sound of a crisp packet being suddenly torn, [workmate] touching my waist as he walks past. When will they stop startling me, making my heart miss a beat and my pulse race?

Nothing is safe. Everywhere danger is lurking. Everything is a threat. (Linda)

Some survivors interpret the symptoms of trauma as negative personal characteristics, but they are nothing of the sort. We hope that by the time you've finished this chapter, you will know that there is nothing wrong with you for feeling as you do. Just like the survivor of a bloody battleground, you have been wounded:

> Perhaps you have heard a doctor talk about head trauma, bone trauma, or trauma to some other part of the body … Just as the body can be traumatised, so too, can the psyche. On the psychological and mental levels, trauma refers to the wounding of your emotions, your spirit, your will to live, your beliefs about yourself and the world, your dignity and your sense of security. The assault on your psyche is so great that your normal ways of thinking and feeling and the usual ways you have handled stress in the past are now inadequate.[4]

If you are suicidal, or struggling with urges to harm yourself in some way, *please don't wait to get help*. These feelings can be a symptom of trauma survival. If you recognise yourself in the following chapter, or you suspect you may have PTSD, it's a good idea to seek help and clarification from a counsellor or physician with appropriate qualifications.

The stages leading to rape trauma

Rape Trauma Syndrome is similar to PTSD, but recognises that there may be rape-specific symptoms.

The immediate aftermath of rape (acute stage) tends to entail disruption of the victim's world. It includes such symptoms as shock, memory loss, emotional swings between grief and denial, social disruption involving distancing from friends, memory reorganisation giving you a flawed view of having more power or control than you actually had, and self-recrimination. Natalie portrays the shocked state encountered by survivors immediately following rape:

> I am a bit sketchy on the details of what happened; I have blocked out a lot of it over the years. I know that I was terrified, that he

was tossing me around on the bed like a rag doll, putting me in different positions, entering me from behind, attempting anal sex, pinning me down. I was crying, saying no, and begging him to stop, but he didn't even respond. I had an asthma attack at one point, but he just flipped me over on my back and entered me that way. It lasted over two hours. And then he dragged me out of the bed, up on my feet, and was trying to drag me towards the bathroom for some reason. I was seriously petrified at that point. I had seen straight razors in there on the sink, and I truly thought he was taking me in there to hurt or kill me … I got out of the door, with him promising to pick me up at noon the next day to take me up to school. I drove away as fast as I could without raising suspicion. I have no recollection of the drive home, or going to bed, I am sure I was in shock. I have no idea if I cried or not. I got home at 4 a.m., and was up early the next day to make preparations to leave for university.

The crying, hysterical rape victim is a popular stereotype. But, while rape trauma may manifest that way, other women may feel detached and calm:

Initially, I was upset, shocked, yet I had a sense of calm in that I felt I was in a shell deep inside but watching out through my eyes. I also had a great deal of energy. I couldn't sleep. I kept scrubbing the house and I have lost lots of weight. (Samantha)

The periods of calm may alternate with bouts of terror and uncontrollable crying.

Now I'm terrified. I want to run. No energy. I am constantly crying. My emotions are running rampant. I'm on anti-depressants although I fought them for a long time. I still have trouble sleeping. I have an inability to relax and to leave the house. I am physically drained and have a great deal of pain from my rheumatoid arthritis. I am extremely emotional. (Samantha)

Later stages include 'regaining control' with the woman outwardly coping well. You may function fine at work or in your family responsibilities. After having control taken away, you naturally want to feel more 'normal' and in control again. Sometimes, when a rape survivor appears to 'bounce back' fairly quickly after an attack, others may view her with suspicion or less empathy than she deserves:

Pretending things were okay and that my life was perfect, I kept myself busy so I wouldn't have to think about anything. (Nichole)

At this stage, some rape survivors make major changes to their lives such as moving cities or changing jobs. They may have a radical change of hairstyle. Again, this is about taking control – but you may also be seeking to escape reminders of what happened to you.

Pseudorecovery

Despite the fact that you may 'act fine', you may be experiencing an internal struggle to keep feelings that you know aren't resolved under control. You just want to 'put it behind you'. You may have gone into 'pseudorecovery' – that is, a false sense of being 'over it' *before* traumatic memories and feelings have been dealt with. Indeed, you may believe you have nothing to get over because of notions about partner rape not being real rape. If you don't identify what has happened to you as rape, you can hardly 'get over it' in a real sense. Pseudorecovery may seem the only option because of issues like love for the perpetrator, or wanting the state of your relationship to return to what it was before this terrible event was thrown into it.[5] Also, survivors who will be beaten or otherwise threatened for not 'being fine' with rape, are having pseudorecovery forced on them.

Survivors who can't successfully process their memories, or who have not had support may begin to feel helpless, anxious and depressed. Your self-confidence and your ability to judge people and situations may have faltered, and, without intervention, you may have developed long-term post-traumatic symptoms.

The symptoms of trauma

The impact of trauma can generate such powerful emotions, pictures and sensations that it often feels as if the trauma is happening all over again.[6] You may experience the reliving of your traumas in some or all of the following ways.[7]

Triggers

Triggers are reminders of your rape, which may cause the 'back then' feeling, along with panic attacks and flashbacks. Eva Jane who was anally raped repeatedly, says:

> I've had some bowel problems, which of course means anal examination is necessitated and I have been absolutely petrified. I've had to say to the doctors I don't want to know about this and I've been trying to relax while they've been looking and I've had a couple of procedures done but that's been ok since they've knocked me out. I can't tolerate it but I know they have to look.

> I just say to them I'm sorry I'm going to be this way and this is why and this gives them some insight. They've been pretty good and talked me through what's going to happen and I'm fine so that's a mega thing.

Triggers can be many things such as certain words and phrases, colours, certain sex acts, a time of year, news reportage about rape, odours or a touch:

> I feel sick when I see someone being raped on TV or videos. Or if I read something in the newspaper I just get nauseous. I go a bit crazy. (Jodie)

> Sometimes, if I smell Adidas Cologne (which he wore) I get sick to my stomach. (Adair)

> It does still haunt me. If my husband now just accidentally puts his arm a certain way it triggers me. He understands. He says what did I do, but I didn't mean to hurt you. I could be fast asleep and I wake up and he's put his leg over me and he could do it the same way 20 times and then the one time just the time of night, I don't know, I just freak out. I just say don't do that. Don't touch me like that. Move over, you're squashing me or whatever.

> Particularly if he ever comes up behind me. Every time he comes up behind me and he gives me a hug from behind, I tense up. If he's anywhere near my throat from behind, it's panic. (Tiffany)

Triggers are often confusing in that you may feel fear or other emotions associated with your rape, but have no idea what the trigger was:[8]

> My emotional symptoms are certainly more intense when I am in some way reminded of the assault, but they can also creep up on me out of nowhere, with no identifiable trigger to account for them … I re-experience the event and when I do it often seems to be accompanied by a new memory that was somehow triggered by something I am unable to identify. Often I have no idea where these come from and that is extraordinarily uncomfortable and frightening. (Summer)

Triggers can be terrifying, but it's possible as healing takes place, to identify them and become less fearful of them. Although triggers are naturally unpleasant, they are indicators of what still troubles you about your experiences, and can be guideposts to where you need to heal.

Nightmares

Nightmares about your traumas may come out of the blue, or may have been triggered by a reminder of your abuse:

> I had a dreadful dream once in which I was performing consensual oral sex on my current partner. All of a sudden, he began slapping me hard around the head and shoulders – I could feel the pain and see the white explosions in my head in exactly the same way I had when I was orally raped and beaten by my ex-partner. (Rachel)

Natalie's PTSD was triggered years after the one-off rape by her boyfriend. The trigger? Within a context of emotional abuse by her current partner, nightmares and flashbacks broke through her denial:

> So, here I am, 15 years after the assault, and only now looking at it and the impact it has had on me. Over the years I have suffered depression and anxiety. I have very low self-esteem, and I am only now beginning to trust my instincts and realise that I have needs, wants and feelings that deserve attention. I started having flashbacks and nightmares about the assault eight months ago, but they have receded now as I deal with the end of my marriage.

Such nightmares can leave you feeling not only emotionally, but also physically as if the rape just occurred:

> I still have nightmares that leave me with physical disturbances, such as soreness in my jaw. (Nichole)

You may also dream in ways that symbolise the trauma; for example, a dream of your car careering out of control reminds you of the loss of control you experienced when you were abused.

Flashbacks

A flashback is a memory that is unlike ordinary remembering. It is a memory of trauma. You feel as though you are there again. You may have vivid mental 'pictures' of the abuser's face or smell his aftershave, and/or 'hear' inside your head the things he said to you as he raped you. It may last anywhere from seconds to hours. It may be a quick sensation or you may go fully into reliving the trauma:

> I have had one 'flashback' and it was what lead me to counselling two months ago. It was so vivid and so terrifying. I started to

> hyperventilate and get dizzy, I was sick to my stomach and I
> threw up. (Adair)

Flashbacks may vary in the way they happen:

> I have a mild form of flashback. I don't think or feel that I'm
> there, but I can see myself on that night as though I was watching
> it on TV. (Emma)

Sometimes, you may experience purely emotional flashbacks – the same intense feelings that you felt at the time you were hurt. This can be triggered by a present-day situation that reminds you of the trauma in some way.

You might have intrusive thoughts about your experiences of sexual violence, finding that no matter how hard you try not to think about them, the thoughts force their way into your mind anyhow:

> During the course of day-to-day living, I have recurring
> memories of the assaults. There are some things you just can't
> run from, and one of these is your memory. (Jennifer)

With physical flashbacks, sometimes called 'body memories', you may experience the sensation of a penis inside you, or pain that corresponds with the areas of you that were abused. Some survivors who were orally assaulted feel themselves choking or suffocating. Sometimes the details of another person's story, or something else connected to your rape, may trigger these flashbacks.

If you try writing or speaking about the flashback, this may ensure it loses much of its power to hurt or frighten you. Call a trusted friend or crisis line. If you belong to an online survivor community, you can post there anytime of night and ask for support.

> I had an awful post-traumatic dream some years ago, and
> woke up extremely disoriented and frightened. I wanted to call
> somebody just so I could have some assurance of a sane world.
> I felt really embarrassed about calling Rape Crisis; I thought,
> 'How dare I tie up a counsellor's time over a stupid dream when
> there are probably women who have been raped right now trying
> to get through?' However, I made the call and the counsellor
> was terrific. Because she understood trauma and the plethora
> of feeling that nightmares can leave, she gently dismissed my
> apologies and then skilfully talked me back into the present.
> (Rachel)

If there is nobody you can go to, know the terror will pass. Do some self-care – perhaps a warm bath, sitting in the garden or listening to soothing music. Remind yourself that although it *feels* otherwise, the trauma isn't happening now. This too will pass. As you heal, these symptoms become less frequent and less frightening:

> I have learned how to manage flashbacks and they don't haunt me like they used to. When I had a long-term sexual relationship with a partner following my breakup with the abuser, I would cry during sex, and eventually I would dissociate again. I would occasionally think he was my abuser. Sometimes [my ex-partner] is on my mind a lot when I see someone who looks like him or something that reminds me of him. The thoughts are intrusive but I have better coping mechanisms through time and some therapy. (Nichole)

Numbing

Your mind may have 'anaesthetised' your emotions to protect you from the impact of the trauma. Perhaps the feelings around your partner having raped you were so sad or frightening that you couldn't afford to feel them, or expressing emotion was physically dangerous and you learned to suppress your feelings.

You may not yet have recovered the ability to feel. Some survivors believe that because they have no feelings about the assault, there are no feelings to have, only to later find that when they are engaged in healing, or they are triggered in some way, powerful emotions do surface.

As you work through your trauma, you might find that numbness alternates with raw feeling. This can be confusing, but it is possible that your psyche is defending you for the moment against any more pain:

> I spent the next several days after he left basically ignoring what had happened, and studying for my upcoming exam. But, I was hardly sleeping, and I was in tears much of the time … My emotions, of course, got overwhelming for me. There was no way I could keep up the façade, and a day or so before my exam, I 'crashed', crying constantly, very anxious, unable to sleep. I nevertheless made it to my exam, and managed to pass all but one section, achieving very good marks; but unfortunately, the section I failed was a key one, and I was not eligible for entry into medical school. I couldn't face the thought of repeating that exam, so my dreams of medical school were gone. (Natalie)

Avoidance

Do you attempt to avoid thoughts, feelings, and reminders of the sexual violence? Perhaps you find that you suppress thoughts of your rape/s with frantic work, drink, or other activities. Or maybe you physically avoid doing things. Women who have been orally raped often find trips to the dentist terrifying, or may get to the stage where putting anything in their mouths causes retching. Forgetting all or part of the trauma may be a means of avoidance too (as we saw in chapter 8).

While 'trying not to think about it' might sound self-preserving, it means that the issues left by the trauma aren't being dealt with. The old saying, 'If I ignore it, it will go away' is unlikely to be effective forever. Only you will know when you are ready to deal with feelings around your trauma, or to face down triggers. With time and support, you will gradually learn to be able to work through thoughts of the rape without needing to avoid it.

Sense of a foreshortened future

Sometimes, abuse robs you not only of your past, but seemingly also your future. If you were repeatedly sexually and/or physically assaulted, it could be that you stopped looking forward to anything because when you did, only bad things happened.

You may have a constant sense of impending doom and even avoid making plans because you fear they will never materialise. You may interpret any physical symptom as a sign of a terminal illness, or just not expect to live much longer.

If you are experiencing these fears, you may want to seek help from a counsellor, as Rachel did:

> Sense of a foreshortened future was for me the most terrifying symptom of trauma. I was obsessed with the thought that I was going to die. With my counsellor, I explored and faced the terror of times in my life I'd received the message that I couldn't expect to live long. My ex-partner had physically or verbally threatened my life many times – and even though he was gone, my psyche still behaved as if it expected a disaster to happen.

Fight or flight and freeze reactions

Perhaps, when you were assaulted, you either felt an adrenaline rush that provoked the impulse to escape, or alternatively, you may have felt hypnotised and frozen into immobility as the events unfolded. You may have experienced your traumas in a kind of 'slow motion' way. Triggers may evoke similar feelings.

Anxiety and panic attacks

Anxiety is a general feeling of dread or worry. You may find yourself worrying about your health, your loved ones, the return of your rapist, or being assaulted again. Sometimes, you may just feel an unease that you try to fight for fear it will get stronger and overpower you.

Panic attacks are feelings of sudden terror for which you may or may not recognise the trigger. It feels as if a disaster is about to occur. Your heart palpitates. You experience shortness of breath, sweating, dizziness, shakes, and perhaps nausea.

If you are experiencing anxiety and/or a panic attack, it may help to be close to somebody you trust and to remind yourself that you are experiencing a PTSD symptom. If the symptoms are severe and causing difficulty in your life, you have lots of options, including relaxation, meditation and/or a course of anti-anxiety medication.

Irritability and anger outbursts

> I have been so angry ... this raging fury!! Lashing out at everyone
> for the last 13 years ... I have really been so angry!! And so sad
> ... (Adair)

Anger at rape, or perpetrators, is justifiable. But sometimes it can overflow onto the wrong people:

> When I was recently out of the relationship with my ex, male
> anger was very triggering for me, because with him, it meant
> danger. Consequently, I became frightened whenever I perceived
> my new partner to be even slightly annoyed. From that place of
> fear, I would go into an immediate and defensive rage, screaming
> at him, 'What the hell is wrong with you? Why are you talking
> like that?' I felt as if my anger could provide me with armor. I
> needed to often apologise for misinterpreting signs of danger.
> (Rachel)

If you are a mother struggling with PTSD, perhaps you have found that there are days when you feel that one more request for a drink or to be driven somewhere will drive you to explode. This is part of parenting, but that extra angry irritation is also part of PTSD.

It may mean that you need to learn some calming techniques; releasing that anger onto those around you isn't a good thing. If you find yourself responding to current situations with far more anger than is justified, it is a good idea to speak with a counsellor.

Difficulty concentrating

You may sometimes feel muddled and daydream, repeatedly letting sink water overflow, forgetting appointments and not knowing what you did with your car keys. You cannot remember conversations you had five minutes ago, or your boss gets angry because you forgot an important job task.

If you are experiencing this response to stress, you can make notes about appointments or say to yourself, 'Watch and remember. You put your keys *here.*' You can also give yourself a break and understand that there is a reason that you are forgetful.

Hyper-vigilance

For some traumatised people, being on the lookout for danger is not always conscious, but may have become an automatic way of functioning. Some examples: a slight change in a person's manner or voice may remind you of the ways your partner's voice or manner changed when he was going to hurt you, and even though it is safe now, you feel intense fear; you check and recheck locks; if your partner woke you suddenly before or during the rape/s, you might wake at even slight noises. Sometimes, you have a sense of somebody behind you when nobody is present.

If you are feeling particularly fearful, you may see black shapes darting about out of the corner of your eyes. When you feel like this, it may help you to do a 'reality check' to convince yourself that your environment is safe. When you've done this, try to do something that you find relaxing.

Sleep disturbances

You may be afraid to sleep because of the fact that we are more vulnerable when we sleep, or because of nightmares. Perhaps you experience insomnia because of intrusive thoughts of the rape, or if you are still in the relationship, the very natural dread that it will happen again. Some survivors find themselves repeatedly waking up at the exact time they were raped.

Lack of adequate sleep can cause problems in other areas of our lives. If you are experiencing insomnia, it's a good idea to talk about it with your counsellor, doctor or naturopath, because there are strategies such as meditation, or a short course of (non-addictive) sleep medications that can help.

Besides the risk of developing a chemical dependency, drinking alcohol to help you sleep isn't a good strategy because, while it might help you relax in the short term, it actually disrupts sleep two to three hours after it has been consumed. Because alcohol dehydrates your system, you are also likely to wake with a dry mouth, powerful thirst, a full bladder and sometimes a bad headache.

(Clinical) depression

Depression may be a feature of PTSD. It may happen as part of the grief you feel at being betrayed by your partner's rape or the loss of safety it represented. However, the sadness that comes with grief tends to get better over time, while depression either worsens or shows no sign of letting up. Clinical depression is an illness. If you have it, you are not a bad person but an individual with a health problem that is treatable. It is different from sadness; instead of just feeling sad and being able to express that, you feel hopeless and helpless:

> I cried a lot, buried myself in my schoolwork, and tried my best to convince him that we needed help for this. Fortunately, I did not turn to drugs or alcohol, and the self-harm described previously did not occur during this time. I believe I was clinically depressed; a reaction to the assault. (Natalie)

You may feel tired all the time, perhaps finding that you just don't feel like getting up and facing another day. Sleep problems such as early awakenings, or difficulty falling or staying asleep also occur with depression. You have difficulty making decisions; thus, simple tasks like going to the supermarket can be a nightmare. You may feel as though you are looking at everybody, including those you love, from a distance (almost like there is a pane of glass separating you from them).

Be aware that depression may have the 'masked' presentation of anxiety. You may also develop some degree of agoraphobia and have difficulty leaving home.

Depression gives you constant messages like, 'You are stupid and worthless and that's why nobody loves you', or 'The abuse was all your fault.' Additionally, you might have suicidal thoughts like 'Everybody would be better off if I wasn't here', or 'It will never get better. I will always feel like this':

> Depression followed as did lack of any self-care or self-worth. Though I am so ashamed and afraid to admit this, yes, suicide did enter my mind on many occasions and thankfully I was blessed in my life by my daughters because they were my reason for surviving and pressing on even when I could barely stand my existence. I am still frequented by many of these emotions and

am now just beginning, through therapy and a strong support
system, to work through them. (Summer)

Remember these inner messages are the products of a feature of clinical
depression called 'cognitive distortion', which is another way of saying
that the messages that depression relays about your worth are *lies*. There
are excellent medications available, or you might prefer to try a natural
remedy. Naturopathic remedies usually need to be taken for some time
before they get into your system. Medications vary in their working time.
Bear in mind that some medications work in different ways for different
people; speak to a doctor you feel you can trust and is known to have
knowledge about domestic violence and sexual assault. If you try one anti-
depressant that doesn't work for you, don't give up. There are a broad
range of medications that work on different parts of our biochemistry.

Talk therapy with or without medication may help if you are depressed:

> I have recently gotten into counselling for my anger and severe
> bouts of depression. If I have to remember in detail my rape
> … I cry. When I hear of others, I get angry. I have in the past
> been given medication … Prozac, Zoloft, Depakote. But I am
> trying not to use any medications at this time. Only talk therapy.
> (Adair)

A good counsellor can help you uncover and resolve issues that underlie
your depression. The depression of rape survivors is often an expression
of destructive anger turned against *themselves*. In blaming themselves for
the rape, or being unable to be angry with the perpetrator, the anger turns
inwards and emerges as helplessness, hopelessness and self-loathing.
Sometimes, depression derived from anger and self-hatred leads survivors
to inflict harm on themselves. Talk therapy can often be extremely useful
for assisting a survivor in turning that anger away from herself and giving
it back to the perpetrator.

At this time, you may feel as if you cannot reach out to anybody, that
you'll be a burden or that you don't deserve help, but you do. If you are
depressed, it is most important that you seek help *now*. You have absolutely
nothing to be ashamed of. As often happens to depressed people, others
might tell you that your depression is 'self-pity' or that you should 'just
snap out of it'. Don't listen. You are not choosing to feel this way and it
doesn't make you weak.

Disconnection

> Traumatised people feel utterly alone, cast out of the human
> and divine systems of care and protection that sustain life.
> Thereafter, a sense of alienation, of disconnection pervades
> every relationship from the most intimate familial bonds to the
> most abstract affiliations of community and religion. When trust
> is lost, traumatised people feel they belong more to the dead than
> to the living.[9]

If you are a survivor of partner rape, you may understand the above
paragraph all too well. The sense of a right to be safe with your partner
underlies the experience of loving and trusting. What you thought was
true about love and safety has been shattered, perhaps leaving you with a
sense that it will never be safe to be close to a man again, or that loving
itself is dangerous. You may believe that you don't even deserve to be
loved safely.

Your trauma has disconnected you from the things you have a right to,
such as love, or respect and safety from the people you have relationships
with. This is a profoundly sad and unjust effect of trauma. In healing,
however, reconnection is possible. We shall explore this more closely in
chapter 18.

Self-destructive behaviours

The desire to self-injure is a symptom of trauma, which has made you feel
worthless and dirty. This is often a way that survivors 'punish' themselves
for 'asking' for the rape:

> He just didn't get it. He became very angry. The next morning
> I just couldn't face another day. I took first one sleeping tablet,
> then another and another. I was talking to a friend on the phone
> and the next thing I remember was being placed in an ambulance.
> I truly didn't want to die; I didn't think about what I was actually
> doing. I just wanted it all to stop and the effect from the pills was
> enabling me to become remote from it all. (Jennifer)

Survivors of multiple traumas, particularly abuse-related, are more inclined
to self-injure.[10] If you self-injure, or you want to, it's a very good idea to
get counselling and support. Rape crisis counsellors have understanding of
self-injury as a problem faced by rape survivors. Even though you might
find this hard to believe right now, *you don't deserve any more pain.* As
you heal, you'll come to understand this. If you'd like support from other
survivors who have self-injured, or successfully managed to overcome it,

you might want to join a rape survivor or self-injury support group – either offline or online. You can also make a plan for what you will do instead of cutting when those urges arise.

Drug and alcohol abuse can be ways of attempting to shut down on feelings around rape/sexual assault. This was discussed in the previous chapter.

Other addictions may include frequent gambling or spending much more than you can afford on 'shopping sprees'. These often create a 'high' or rush, but will also cause more problems for you. They can also be discussed with counsellors.

Prognosis: healing

A simple diagnosis of PTSD is often not appropriate for the survivor of multiple traumas because it doesn't account for the sometimes severe disruptions to personality that can happen in prolonged trauma or captivity.[11] If you were exposed to repeated trauma, your PTSD symptoms will naturally be more severe and the period of recovery may also be lengthened. But this is no reason to despair; you can still heal and experience joy and peace.

The earlier you seek help the better. It is known that earlier intervention can prevent long-term trauma symptoms. Even if you've had symptoms for a long time now, obtaining help can enable you to establish control over them in ways that will prevent them from continuing to rob your life:

> The PTSD is pretty much gone. I don't have the panic attacks anymore, my depression is lessened, and nightmares are far less common. (Nichole)

There are excellent books available that contain structured exercises and in-depth discussions of what can help (see Appendix 3).

Try to remember that awareness is the key to change and you have taken that step by reading this book. Please don't be hard on yourself for feeling as you do. It's not your fault you were raped, and it is not your fault that you have been traumatised. Be gentle with yourself. If you have had a rotten day coping with flashbacks, or panic, do at least one nice thing for yourself, even if it's just to relax with a cup of something, listen to some music that makes you feel good or go for some exercise.

In between managing symptoms, remember that you are a competent, beautiful and worthwhile woman.

This too shall pass.

CHAPTER 11

Staying with a Partner Who Has Raped You

There are many reasons why women may choose to remain with the man who has raped them. Some women who do so are no longer being abused. For some, it happened once and although once is once too often and devastating, it can sometimes be 'integrated in a non-destructive way'.[1] As the next section describes, for those of you living in an active domestic violence situation your ability to make choices may have become seriously compromised. We hope that information and identification may be a first step to getting back that power.

In this chapter, we briefly look at a number of the reasons why women stay. We do this for two reasons: We think it's very important for workers, friends, family members and policy makers to understand what is actually going on instead of making victim-blaming assumptions that women remain in abusive relationships because they like the violence, or are happy for it to continue.

We also believe that if you are a survivor who is co-habiting with your perpetrator, assessing your reasons for remaining will hopefully help you to think outside of any sense of entrapment these reasons present. We hope that it won't be an exercise in blaming yourself for staying for the 'wrong' reasons. Whether you choose to remain or to leave is ultimately your choice. Certainly we don't recommend remaining in an environment that is unsafe, and we will provide several safety tips.

As we saw elsewhere, some women resist thinking about the sexual violence because they believe that doing so will mean they have to leave. Again, you don't have to do what isn't right for you and your circumstances. However, if you've acknowledged the sexual assaults, it will be better for you to make an *informed* decision instead of one that relies on suppressing the truth because it's sad and frightening.

Dynamics and effects of domestic violence

It seems that the worse the violence inflicted, the harder it is for many people to comprehend a woman's apparent apathy or return to her abuser. Yet, the paradox is that the worse the violence, the greater her inability to leave. Most people could probably understand this in the context of political hostages. The more serious the psychological and physical brutality, the greater the power of the captors and the hostages' inability to free themselves from the almost magnetic control. It's widely accepted that war hostages or kidnap victims suffer personality changes in an environment of trauma that result in them expressing loyalty or even love for their captors. There is even a name for it: the Stockholm Syndrome.[2]

Yet, people fail to equate the reality of domestic violence with political terrorism or war. They don't understand that the battered woman's situation is similar, that she is a hostage in the home. They don't comprehend the numerous ways that control is exerted (as we saw in chapter 7) or the range of effects that we experience (as discussed in chapter 9 and 10). Her behaviour is therefore seen as unreasonable. Where the political hostage's actions are not seen as signifying innate weakness or dependency, battered women are labelled as weak, passive and dependent. It is said that it's because women are that way. The political hostage is not described as masochistic. Yet, haven't we each heard someone speculate that women must stay in violent relationships because they enjoy it?

As a hostage in the home, you may have developed traumatic bonding with your perpetrator.[3] This is a condition experienced by people exposed to violence or threat in many contexts. It arises out of the type of cycle that often takes place with domestic violence: periods of remorse punctuating the violence:

> Some harbor hope for better times. The cycle of tension, abuse, relief; tension, abuse, relief has periods in which optimism is rewarded. Hope for the cessation of battering is realised and the relief experienced in the periods of peace is profound. Animal experimenters and human inquisitors know there is nothing as powerful as relief from torture as a positive reward for desired behavior. For some battered women the thin thread of hope and the episodic experience of relief reinforces her decision to stay.[4]

Perhaps your partner appeals to you with statements like, 'But you know I really love you' or 'You know I'd never *really* hurt you'. These comments may have helped you cope with the violence, because they promoted a belief in an end to it. And, some perpetrators do make efforts to change their behaviour, and stop abusing. However, an abusive man often skilfully manipulates his partner by appealing to her belief in his love and her hope for change.[5] In this way, he continues to get away with repeated violations of his partner without having to demonstrate any real commitment to change:

> He used to remind me how long he spent waiting for me before we started going out, and say that I should give him at least that amount of time to try and work things out. He would often threaten suicide or self-injury if I tried to break up with him. He also cried – it is an awful thing to feel that you have made a grown man cry from fear of losing you. (Emma)

> Any time that I tried to leave the relationship he would manipulate me through false love and tears. (Summer)

Your partner may love you and be capable of goodness when he is not hurting you. Being raped, battered or otherwise abused should never be a cost of loving or being loved. Giving up beliefs that have sustained us through violence and trauma can be painful, because it means facing the fact that the abuse may not stop. The pain is worth it, though; we are better able to think about our future safety in a way that is real, rather than based on broken promises:

> If I could advise other survivors, I'd say, 'Recognise it and get out.' (Samantha)

If you feel shame, remember that traumatic bonding happens to women who are taken captive and raped by men they *don't* know. If captives who have no initial positive connection to their abusers come to express love or loyalty for them, why should you, for whom there *was* an initial positive connection, feel ashamed?

Cultural contributors

We know that for many women the sexual assaults are not a part of other domestic violence. For some, it is a one-off experience. For these women and for those who are living with the ongoing disempowerment that is part and parcel of violence in the home, there may be aspects of the culture that work against leaving. As we see next, these include both values that we have been programmed to believe and also a lack of support. Liz and Jennifer, who left violent partners, explain why they returned:

> It's like, where do you go? You think your mum's going to be supportive? She didn't want to talk about anything that was

on my mind. She just said get on with it, which she does. No support; just nagging me for things I hadn't done around the house or whatever. I thought it's probably better going back to him in some ways. So I did. (Liz)

I realise now that is the reason I took him back again. I have always hated being a burden in any way to anyone. I'm very independent. It's a dreadful thing to feel you have no one to care for you; to feel unable to tell your family. (Jennifer)

Internalised beliefs about relationships

In chapter 3 we learned about internalising myths about women and rape. There is also often much we each internalise about relationships:

I guess it's fairly easy to now say you don't have to stay in the relationship. You can get out. But I appreciate it's not easy. I didn't get out. I was left and that's how I got out of it. (Eva Jane)

It is sad but true that much of society has been less concerned about the violence we experience, and more concerned with impressing upon us that a failed relationship makes one a 'bad woman', a bad mother, somebody who can't keep a man; a failed *person*. The combination of internalised messages about sexual assault and relationship responsibility creates a potent mix of self-blame and self-negation.

Having internalised the belief that it is our duty to keep a relationship together, and that the onus for resolving the problems is on us, our self-care often becomes the lowest priority:

I stayed and kept trying and trying and trying despite the severity and constancy of the abuse. I was confused about my own position, my duty to my husband. How far does it go? The only way to tolerate (the sexual violence) is to deny your own feelings, your instincts, your right to object, your personal being. (Linda)

Some women feel guilt because they believe that leaving means breaking marriage vows, which they view as sacred. If you are such a woman, remember that you didn't vow to have crimes of violence committed against you. In fact, partners who rape are breaking a vow to honour and cherish. If you are feeling guilty and responsible for hurting your partner, remind yourself that it is important not to confuse compassion and caring with your need for safety.[6] Instead of viewing yourself as responsible and as a failure, you might begin to see that the actual failure lies in a society that expects a woman to be responsible for upholding its values at the expense of her safety.

Religious reasons

If you embrace a spiritual belief system, you may have found it a source of great comfort and sustenance throughout your abuse. Nobody should ever make light of your religious ethics and concerns. Yet, as we saw in chapters 2 and 3, there are women like Kate who are encouraged or even pressured by communities of faith to remain in abusive situations. They have been blamed for sexual violence they have been brave enough to disclose. It is these women that this section concerns.

In one study, religious leaders were asked how severe violence would have to be to justify a woman leaving; almost one-fifth believed that no amount of violence would justify it.[7] Many religious leaders preach a theology of unconditional forgiveness and mercy, which means that anything a woman's partner does to her must be forgiven at the expense of her safety, or even the risk of her life.

> (It was) My duty to stay married, to try to keep to the oath I had made before the Lord and before man. (Linda)

If religious tenets or advice have taken priority over your safety, you might find this quote from Carol Adams helpful:

> If you have been given advice to stay or submit because that is your duty, or because God ordains it, if you're told to forgive the rapist, you have talked to the wrong person. If you are given this advice, no matter who the counsellor is, no matter how inspiring or spiritually attuned he or she is, you have the wrong advisor. It is not you who are mistaken for resisting this advice; it is the counsellor who is mistaken for suggesting it. You have the right to be safe.[8]

Linda was still able to stand up for herself despite pressure from her church:

> I remember a call with (church associate). He was on about my attitude towards Roy was wrong. I told him he should go home and bugger his wife for 4 months and the see what her attitude to him was like. I think his response was that there was no need to get funny with him.

Similarly, Shefali defied the directive of her imam to appear before six other imams and justify her divorce:

> I said, 'I'm not repeating this again. I've already told you and
> I'm not going to repeat this in front of six men. I'll leave it at
> that and I'll go to Hell.'

Since her liberation from a sexually violent marriage, Linda works to help other women living under similar circumstances. Her words are important and encouraging, because they illustrate that freedom is possible without having to give up your faith:

> Funnily enough, the abuse has not dented my faith in God, just
> Man … and my experiences with the Church have made me very
> aware of how misunderstood DV and especially marital rape
> are, hence my determination to work on raising awareness. How
> many more women are stuck in abusive relationships, forgiving
> in what they believe to be a Christian manner, praying more and
> harder and waiting for a finger to come out of heaven and point
> them in the right direction, sure of eternal damnation if they
> even think of divorce?

Sex and ownership

Many people still believe that the lack of a woman's hymen somehow lessens her as a person, 'spoiling' her for a decent man. Girls are told that if they give their virginity up too easily, they forfeit the courtesy and respect that 'pure' women are entitled to. Subsequently, even if the man to whom a woman has lost her virginity has raped her, she feels compelled to remain:

> It's strange but I felt as though since he had taken (my virginity)
> from me, I had to stay with him and try and make the relationship
> last. (Jodie)

As we've seen, men who want to stake ownership over a partner often use forced sex to achieve this. There's a common notion that sex with a woman gives a man proprietary rights over her, even if that sex is rape:

> Some women have internalised men's perceptions and made
> them their own. A few even accept the notion that completed rape
> means successful conquest, and that marriage to the conqueror is
> the only way that some virtue can be restored.[9]

If a pregnancy results from the rape, a woman may see marriage to the rapist as her only choice. Family or friends may encourage that view.

There is nothing wrong with equating sex and commitment. However, commitment is not the same as ownership. Intercourse, especially forced, doesn't mean that you belong to somebody. You always have a right to leave the relationship.

Social invalidation

We'll see in later chapters that when women seek help for the issue of partner rape they often are unable to find understanding and validation. You may have had people to whom you turned for support say or imply that the sexual violence is due to a problem in the relationship, rather than something the perpetrator does to control and hurt you. Instead of hearing that rape is a criminal act and a terrible betrayal of you, it becomes watered down to something far less, and you receive 'advice' that instructs you to view it as less too, along with suggestions about how to improve yourself:

> The main responses I remember are the 'yes, but's': 'Yes, but your behaviour hasn't been perfect either.' 'Yes, but your attitude to him is wrong.' 'Yes, but you have to hand the problem to the Lord.' 'Yes, but you have put him under a lot of pressure.'
> (Linda)

You may have returned to a sexually violent man because other people's positive feelings for him caused you to doubt your own perception of the violence.[10] Perhaps friends or relations of the perpetrator have persecuted you for disclosing abusive behaviour. This can be a frightening prospect.

Abusive partners can manipulate family, friends and even counsellors so that the abuse becomes the woman's fault:

> In our community everybody saw him as a really lovely gentleman. How could he be abusive? He told people he had to go because of my aggression – the fact that I was always saying things like 'you lazy piece of shit', 'you bastard', that kind of aggression. He's been telling that to everyone in my community, in the Muslim community, and everyone looks down on me.
> (Shefali)

Invalidating advice often has a 'He raped you – so what?' feeling about it. You might have heard things from even well intentioned people, like 'So he gets a bit aggressive when he's horny? Aren't you glad he finds you so desirable?' Or it becomes a lecture that appeals to indebtedness to your partner: 'Oh come on. *Rape*? He's your children's father for heaven's sake. He loves you. He works hard to give you a good life. You should count your blessings.'

Those who give this kind of advice often place values such as keeping families together above a woman's safety. They may have extremely limited views of what rape is, or they have stronger loyalties to your partner than to you. This actually means that they are probably not best qualified to give you advice.

On the other hand, you might have had advice that goes to the other extreme: 'Rape? You have to leave him right now!' When you don't follow that order, such a person might imply that the rape couldn't have been all that serious, or may make condescending suggestions about your mental health. If you love your partner, or believe that the relationship can be salvaged, this will be hurtful and invalidating in another way. It could make you feel frightened and ashamed of speaking about the rape again. When people give such responses, they have forgotten that this is about you, not them. Your thoughts, feelings and wishes aren't being heard.

But it is you living with the reality of sexual violence. Try not to discount what you know to be true (especially about your safety and that of your children) just because other people hold a different view. Seek out people who are able to listen and help you decide for yourself what you need to do.

Nowhere to go/financial concerns

Women who are dependent on their partners for a place to live may have few options in terms of anywhere else to go, and this may be made more difficult by the presence of children. In Diana Russell's study on marital rape, all women who were the sole providers of household income left the husbands who had raped them, while 90 per cent of the women who remained were those whose husbands were the main source of income.[11]

Sometimes, we have no access to money for other accommodation, or we have no contact with family or friends who could help us. While Justine earned a wage of her own, she was penalised by being required to pay prohibitively expensive rent when she sought alternative accommodation:

> I tried to leave on several occasions but was unable to stay in a
> hostel as I was earning and would have had to pay full rent (£250
> per week).

Lack of adequate living quarters may bring with it the fear of having your children removed. Certainly if you have never worked outside the home, have dependent children, or your husband has always controlled the economic side of the union, you may not feel confident that you could manage without him.

The presence of refuges and shelters has created alternatives for women, and should be viewed as an option. If you have no other safe alternative for living, contact your nearest shelter and discuss the problem. Another alternative you might want to explore is whether your abuser can be made to leave the home.[12]

Non-mainstream cultural factors

Because of issues such as racist discrimination from service providers, immigration policies and language differences, non-Anglo women may face greater hurdles in getting out of a violent relationship.[13]

Cultural pressures to remain in the marriage are coupled with isolation and a lack of awareness about the resources available and the relevant legislation. The abusive partners of immigrant women may deny them the freedom to learn English, or may threaten to have them deported back to their country of origin if they leave. These problems may be exacerbated for brides in arranged marriages and Asian women sponsored by non-Asian men. [14] Also, women may face total rejection by the communities they have grown up within for reporting domestic violence, or for seeking to leave the situation.[15] For instance, after Shefali severed the relationship, she suffered ostracism from the local Muslim community who did not believe that her husband had been violent.

If you are a migrant woman, please know that domestic and sexual violence are illegal. If you face discrimination or other improper treatment from police or other agencies of help, you have the right to make a complaint. Consider taking a telephone counsellor into your confidence.

Fear of sexual assault outside the home

A study on rape in marriage found that women sometimes stayed with husbands who raped them because they feared sexual assault outside their homes.[16] It is common for some of us to initially view rape by a partner as less bad than rape by a stranger. Perhaps you believe that if somebody you love could rape you, you cannot expect to be safe anywhere else.

Your fear is only natural, but you deserve much more than living with the threat of rape *in your home*. We strongly urge you to discuss your fears with a counsellor or other trusted person.

Personal factors

Where the sexual violence figures in the scheme of your relationship

Perhaps addressing the sexual violence in your relationship has not been a high priority. This could be due to many factors: for example, you have only recently identified the sexual assault, you may be ashamed, or you want to preserve this relationship because you love your partner:

> Keeping the relationship intact was important to me at certain times because I thought that he was 'saving' me from much of my past – that the love he was giving was somehow compensating for all of the love I didn't receive when I was younger. (Summer)

Survival of her partner's *physical* violence was Justine's highest priority:

> You spent so much time being careful, not saying or doing the wrong thing so as not to provoke him, during the relationship, you just didn't think about things like that.

At this point, the sexual assault may feel too hard to address because you have to maintain yourself for family or other responsibilities. This is not wrong, but your safety and your healing are important priorities too.

Genuine love of your partner

As we saw in chapter 7, many men who rape their partners are also capable of exhibiting very loving behaviours outside of the sexual violence. These are the qualities that women love about them. Moreover, an act of betrayal or violence doesn't automatically switch off the love a woman feels:

> Hatred would have been easier. With hatred, I would have known what to do. Hatred is clear, metallic, one-handed, unwavering; unlike love.[17]

Though this quote comes from a story about childhood bullying, it articulates the confusion that victims of partner rape often feel about loving the person who raped them.

If you love your partner even though he has sexually assaulted or abused you, you are not wrong for doing so. Even if you love your partner, though, it is a good idea to resolve the questions that the sexual violence might present you with. They are not going to go away and will need to be addressed sooner or later.

Other barriers to leaving

Children

Some women, like Tiffany, are told by the violent partner that if they leave, they must leave the child(ren):

> The actual sexual assaults where I'd be awakened in the middle of the night lasted about a year. The thing that really irritates me and makes me angry is that I was still in that marriage because I couldn't leave my son. I actually had put my body on the line for my son. I'm so mad that that the law didn't allow me to get out to protect my son, and women reach the point where they have to go. They can't stay. But in my case I'm still at that point where I was physically putting myself to save my son. I think it's horrible that you can't take your child and prove this without having physical scars, like I could open up my chest and go, 'Look at these scars, in my heart and my head.'

Others are warned that they'll lose custody of the children if they leave:

> We got into an argument because I was unable to find a ride to work. He began beating me and telling me to leave. I packed a bag for the baby and myself and again he said, 'You can't take my child ...' so I didn't leave. (Kuriah)

If you have children, you may feel guilty that leaving will mean you are depriving them of their father. This might be all the more heart-wrenching if your partner is a good father. Jill's husband raped her once; she conceived her second child:

> I would have left him then if I had not been pregnant. I have tried to make the relationship work for years. I have gotten a great deal of help and am at a healthy place emotionally and have done a remarkable amount of healing in my own life. My husband has not participated in that process – largely due to his choice.
>
> I have recently made the decision to leave but am hoping to be able to carve out some financial security before doing so. He is afraid of me leaving, but is not able or willing to deal with the issues that have to be confronted ... If we didn't have two children together, it never would have made it this far. I am about to mandate personal therapy for my husband if he wishes to try to save the marriage.

Certainly, relationship breakdown can be hurtful to children, and any loving mother feels pain if her children are distressed. However, staying 'for the sake of the children' has been a huge burden imposed on abused women. Also, children are likely to be more negatively impacted upon by exposure to violence.[18]

Taking steps to end the violence is a responsible act. You don't have to be sacrificed to repeated rape or other abuse to uphold an ideal of selfless motherhood; *you count too*.

You may want to speak to a lawyer about pursuing financial obligations your partner has to his children. Also seek legal advice or domestic violence advocacy if your partner has blackmailed you with threatened removal of your children should you leave.

Loneliness and losses

We've seen that some abusive partners deliberately isolate women from their family and friends in order to have greater control over them. You may have lost friends who don't understand your experience and gave up on the friendship. Also, if you are ashamed of the abuse and trying to conceal it from family and friends, you may avoid them, and this sometimes leads to the erosion of relationships that might have been good resources. You may feel that your partner is all you have.

Perhaps you are worried that good relationships with friends or with your partner's family will be lost if you leave. You may also face grief over the loss of the perpetrator and all the positive things that sustained you even as you were abused.

> [I felt] Fear of being alone with the ongoing physical injuries I have. I feared losing his love, such as it was. I feared the loss of intimacy and the possibility of affection. (Jennifer)

Fears of loss and loneliness are realistic, but they will pass with time and support. If you are thinking about leaving, prepare some strategies in advance for coping with loneliness.

Blackmail

Blackmail may take the form of threatening to expose embarrassing secrets to your family, friends, or church community if you leave. Or, if your partner coerced you into criminal activity such as drug abuse or prostitution, he may threaten to turn you in and have your children taken away.[19]

Ask yourself how likely your partner is to tell the police of crimes that he himself has been involved in. Also, your safety and that of your children is the most important issue. If you are worried about criminal charges, talk to a lawyer through legal aid perhaps; try to find somebody with a background working with domestic violence or cases of duress.

Teenagers' views

Many teenage girls see jealousy and possessiveness as normal parts of a relationship, or even as romantic. The more traditional views a teenage girl holds about relationships, the more likely she is to accept sexually violent or coercive behaviour. Further, repeated experiences of sexual assault and coercion may degrade a young woman's self-esteem to the extent that she feels that she deserves what her partner does, and this may undermine her ability to escape.[20] Teenage girls have fewer social and legal resources and may not be in a position to change schools or neighbourhoods, which can increase their sense of entrapment and leave them vulnerable to the perpetrator.

If you are a teenage girl caught in an abusive relationship, know that what happens to you is not normal. You may feel very lonely and think that nobody could understand. This is a feeling that many girls and women who have been sexually assaulted by their partners share, *but that doesn't make it true*. Sexual assault is not your fault. Do consider telling somebody, even if you begin with a confidential hotline.

Making a choice: safety first

We are not responsible for the abuse that has been done to us. However, since abusive partners cannot be forced to take responsibility for the violence, it is important to consider that our own lives are ultimately all we are responsible for. Taking control over our lives often begins with choices we make.

You know what is best for you, and if or when you need to act, but you may want to consider the following advice from Lissette and Kraus's useful book, *Free Yourself from an Abusive Relationship*:

> If you are considering staying with your abuser, it is important to make sure you are realistically evaluating the level of violence and danger in your relationship without denying or minimising it.[21]

First priority should always be given to the issue of your safety. While many men plead remorse to coerce their partners into forgiveness or remaining, several possible indicators (but not guarantees) of his sincerity and your increased safety might be:

- He has taken responsibility for the sexual violence. He acknowledges that raping you was wrong and he doesn't offer excuses.

- He allows you to vent what you feel without becoming defensive – for example, he doesn't say, 'Well I said I was sorry, didn't I? Why are you still carrying on?'

- He no longer practises former patterns of controlling, possessive or sexually coercive behaviour. If he has difficulty altering these patterns, he is prepared to seek good, confrontational counselling.

- What your instincts tell you – you know best.

Counselling

You may like to talk to a counsellor or other trusted person as you work your way through confusion, and decide what you need to do. If you consider seeing a counsellor, please check what their position is on relationship rape – ideally, they shouldn't minimise your experience in any way, and will appreciate that your relationship has many dimensions.

Any counselling you undertake if you are still in the relationship, should be centred on your safety and should acknowledge that your partner is responsible for his violence. Be very wary of suggestions to get couples counselling. If your partner has not acknowledged responsibility or made a real commitment to change, couples counselling is not a safe or useful option for you:

> Marriage counselling before has been a joke because he is not
> honest and refused to go along to any sessions. (Jill)

One problem is that some couples counsellors tend to treat partner abuse as though it is a mutual problem, rather than something the abuser does to control his partner. Also your partner may control the interactions, responding with violence to you for telling about the abuse.

Remember that if you choose to remain, you are no less entitled to compassionate support than any other survivor of rape. Your decision to remain doesn't erase the need, or the right, to heal.

Safety tips for women who are staying with a violent partner

There are no guarantees that you can avoid violence if you continue to live with an abusive partner. However, here are some things that could increase safety:

- Make a list of people you can call in a crisis.
- Be prepared to call the police if the violence starts again. Work out a signal with the children or the neighbours to call the police when you need help.
- If you need to flee temporarily, where would you go? Think through several places where you can go in a crisis. Write down the addresses and phone numbers, and keep them with you.
- If you need to flee your home, know the escape routes in advance (see Appendix 4).[22]

It may be more helpful for you to discuss with a domestic violence counsellor a safety plan that has the best chance of working for *you*.

CHAPTER 12

Leaving and Safety

Many abused women make several attempts to leave, but are drawn back by promises, guilt or fear. There are also often emotional issues such as depression or loneliness that contribute to women returning to abusive relationships. Trauma, grief and the multitude of issues that impact on leaving can make it hard to think clearly. As well, it's true that leaving doesn't by itself guarantee safety, but may escalate the risk of violence. In this chapter, we'll explore strategies that *may* reduce the risks to you.

This chapter also presents common psychological snares that perpetrators use to get their partners to return, together with strategies for seeing your way through some of the pain and confusion you may experience.

We hope you will be inspired and comforted by reading about the experiences of other women who were frightened and who made it to the other side:

> Even as I knew the violence would not stop, even though I was terrified, and even as I survived from day to day, I never stopped cherishing the dream of freedom. Far from haplessly accepting the violence, thoughts of 'when I find a way, I will go', were a consistent part of my experiences and were a form of internal rebellion that sustained me. (Rachel)

> My batterer was served with restraining orders. It was one of the toughest decisions I've made in my life. The fears and confusion I was feeling made me cry. I cried when he left. I cried when he called. I cried when I held my child and told him that his daddy was not going to live with us any more. It was okay for me to cry. What wasn't okay for me to do was to take him back. I had had enough pain from this person. He had caused me plenty of suffering and sadness in my life. Enough was enough! I had finally hit my bottom.

Enough was enough, when I put my wellbeing ahead of his. Enough was enough, when I allowed reality back into my life. Enough was enough, when I told myself I could make it without him. Enough was enough, when I set boundaries for myself and did not extend them for any reason. Enough was enough, when I realised I loved myself enough to take that first step. I hadn't loved myself in so many years that it was strange at first, but then felt good. Enough was enough when I discovered I was worth more than this, that I had a right to be safe ... (Kuriah)

If you have a dream of freedom, hang onto it.

The importance of a safety plan

Do you believe that if you disengage from your abuser in the nicest way possible, taking time to explain everything reasonably and gently, you'll be safer? Have you tried to reason with him after a separation only to be harmed? There is no way to let a possessive partner down gently; in fact, as we will see, it is often safer to leave without telling him, or to announce the separation in relatively safe circumstances:

I made several attempts to leave Paul. Far from wanting to live with his violence, I alternated between wondering if it would change, and knowing this was unlikely. My attempts to leave were often subverted by guilt, or just as frequently, violence. He often told me he would kill me if I left, and I knew that he was capable of doing it.

One night, after several months of living with the violence, I told Paul I'd had enough and that I wanted him out of my life. I began to pack his things. He looked at me as if I was crazy and asked what the hell I thought I was doing. Determined, I restated that I was throwing him out, and continued to stuff items of his clothing into the bag. Paul said, 'I'm not going anywhere, bitch', knocked the bag out of my hand and slapped and punched me all the way to the bed. He raped me and when he finished, told me that this would be repeated throughout the night until he couldn't 'get it up' any more, or until I changed my mind. He told me the choice was mine.

I covered myself with a sheet and cried as he taunted me about how good it would be to repeatedly rape me. When he pulled the sheet away and told me to get ready for the next round, I gave in. He stayed. In doing what he did, he repossessed me and reasserted control.

One other time after a particularly severe beating, I opened my back door and fled. He chased me, dragged me back by my hair, and shut me in the bedroom. He smashed a mirror with his fist, picked up a shard of the glass, and held me at the point of it, running it all over my body until I promised never to pull a stunt like that again. These are just two examples of what I faced in trying to leave – there were other times that were similar. Sometimes, all he had to do was cry. (Rachel)

Rachel wanted to leave, but had thought of no plan for keeping herself safe. Announcing the desire to end the relationship without any means of protection from violent retaliations was a doomed mission.

Others, like Liz, were more secretive. She pretended that she was just taking one of her children to school and headed to a refuge:

I said to myself, 'I'm getting out of here. My time is up. I've done my time. I'm getting out.' My plan was to leave the house looking as if I was taking Mark to school and having Tommy with me pretending we're just going for a drive. I didn't take any clothes. I nearly blew it since when we were leaving, I had a bit of a panic attack and said to the boys to come and say goodbye to their father and that was a bit final. I was terrified inside. It was like I was betraying him. I just kept talking to him about things we had to do in the next few days like take the car into the shop so that he wouldn't get suss. Inside it just didn't match the outside.

Jennifer did extensive planning and shares this advice:

Plot, scheme, save, save, save. Money is the power to make choices. The right/better choices for you and yours. Don't tell him you're going. Get support but be very careful whom you trust.

What worked for her?

I knew I had to be very, very careful. I had incredible support from my employers (the same as his, though a different division) and from our friends who actually came and helped me move out and have supported me ever since. I hid money and resources from him for quite some time. He finally went away for two months. I used this time to escape to a place where he couldn't find me. I refused to take his phone calls. I called his employer and asked them to intervene. He is a military police captain and they took the circumstances very seriously. I took out a restraining order just before he came back and made sure that he couldn't ever come near me again. He kept trying to contact me. I took steps to stop this but he kept breaking the orders.

Her next step was to relocate and go into hiding, where she remains.

- Safety was her number one priority.
- Leaving was planned in advance and without announcing it to her partner.
- Jennifer made the fullest use of any resources she had, including help from employers.
- Jennifer refused to compromise her safety by giving in to the abuser's demands for contact.
- When one part of the plan didn't work, i.e. a restraining order alone was not sufficient to protect her, Jennifer relocated, revealing her whereabouts only to those whom she could trust.

For some women, going underground (hiding and/or assuming a new identity) is an option because their ex-partners are so dangerous that they are unlikely to be safe otherwise. This often means massive upheaval, but like Jennifer, they recognise it as a better option than being killed.

It's possible to respond to fear in self-protective ways; for example, instead of giving in to more demands from her abuser, Jennifer used the fear as a guide to what she needed to do to get safe. What she did is just one example of a safety plan. Different things will work for different women.

> Don't let anyone persuade you to leave until you're ready and know you're safe. If you can, take the precautions: get credit cards cancelled, find a place to go, make copies of the keys, withdraw money, etc. There are lots of places to help you through this, but you best know how to do it. (Nichole)

If you fear ongoing danger from your partner, here are some steps you can take:

- Seek advice from the police.
- See Wilson's safety plan in Appendix 4.[1] It contains information that may help you minimise the risks to your life.
- Discuss a plan with a counsellor. Since some abusers find out whom their partners have been calling via bills, you may need to call a counsellor from somebody else's phone.
- Find a survivor support group. This might be through your local women's shelter, or it might be an online community. There are

many women out there who have made it and who will be happy to share advice with you.

- Keep any letters or emails in which you or others have been threatened, as these will be useful to show to police. If other people have heard the threats directed either at you or them, ask if they will testify in court for you.

- Either apply for a restraining order yourself or ask the police to do so. (Appendix 5 discusses restraining orders.)

I went to court on Tuesday; he was served on Wednesday and the hearing was on Thursday. He never turned up, and I got my protection order, the final one, for two years. I got protection for two years, which means: don't talk to me, don't ring me, don't write to me. (Shefali)

Leaving in crisis

Some women leave immediately before or after an act of violence. It is recommended that when you know your partner is escalating towards violence, you exit as soon as you can if possible. You may be familiar with signs of impending violence; for example, there may be a change in his facial expression, breathing, or tone of voice, combined with things like pacing or name-calling.[2]

It is still possible to have a safety plan in place for such a situation. Think about what is most likely to work for you should a violent episode occur. The following tips could be helpful in constructing a crisis safety plan:[3]

- If an argument seems unavoidable, try to have it in a room from which it is easier to escape.

- Try to avoid rooms in which weapons might be available.

- Identify in advance the exits from your home that offer the easiest means of getting out.

- Ask trusted neighbours to call the police if they see or hear any signs of a disturbance coming from your home.

- Have a code-word for children, friends or family that can be used when you need them to call the police.

Exercise: assessing your strengths and vulnerabilities

To prepare for leaving an abusive relationship, make a list of things that are likely to help you and another list of things that could impede your process.

On the first list, write down personal and social resources; for example, if you have a friend whom you know will help you without judgment, list that person. Even if you don't feel very strong, there are bound to be qualities you have that can help you – for example, determination. Write down anything that can be an asset to you at this time.

Exploring your vulnerabilities can give you more power over them. When you list them, look particularly at what might draw you back into the relationship or expose you to further violence. For example, you might write something like, 'When he cries and pleads to see me, I feel bad and I want to give in.' Now, ask yourself how you would *like* to respond in future. For example, you could write, 'Next time I'll tell myself that I'm not responsible for his feelings and act on that instead. If I'm finding it hard, I'll ask for support from friends/my online community/counsellor.'

List your fears and in turn, what would help you feel safer. You might look at physical vulnerabilities. If you are afraid because your ex-partner still has a key to your home, you might consider strategies such as getting locks changed. Make a safety 'to do' list.

Do you have a friend or counsellor with whom you could do some role-play? Practising what you might say or do in possible future encounters can be extremely productive and equip you with skills for managing the fear.

The snares set by men who don't want to let go

We've seen that violent men who want their partners to stay (or return) play all sorts of mind games and make declarations of love and promises of change. Your partner may truly believe he can't live without you. Faced with your refusal to reconcile, he may move, often quite swiftly, from loving behaviour to violent or abusive behaviour:

> He bounced back and forth between sorrow and anger, crying and
> violent outbursts, 'I'm sorry' and 'You'll be sorry.' (Summer)

When an abuser doesn't get what he wants, he begins to devalue his partner. He thinks, 'She's only a bitch anyway. I'll show her she can't humiliate me.' At this time, the danger of violence increases because he blames her for his feelings, and wants to punish her. Therefore, it may be safest for you to limit communication to third parties, such as lawyers:

> The other thought that is weighing heavily on my mind right
> now is that when women are able to make that break that they
> don't turn back, that they not maintain contact. I think once I did

that I gave him the sense that he could continue to manipulate
and control me. (Summer)

If you do feel that you must give him a hearing, it might be best if you
aren't alone with him, or if communication is not face-to-face. A man
unwilling to let you go is likely to take the opportunity to manipulate or
harm you. That is what happened to Rachel:

> When my mother, with whom I lived at the time, had gone to
> work her night-shift, I heard the front door opening. It was Paul;
> he had returned with a knife and waited until my mother left. For
> the next two hours, he held the knife on me, threatening to cut
> my throat or cut off my breasts. He forced me to say I loved him;
> he liberally sexually and physically assaulted me with the hand
> that was not holding the knife. Eventually, like a fever breaking,
> he dropped the knife, burst into tears and said, "I came here
> to kill you tonight. I was going to kill you.' I consider myself
> fortunate to be recounting because, as we know, women held to
> siege by angry ex-partners are indeed sometimes killed.

You can establish a telephone plan with a friend or neighbour whom you
trust and will check on you regularly. You can develop a code like turning
on a particular light or leaving a blind or shade up – some visible or vocal
sign that lets someone know you are in danger and need immediate help.[4]

Rape/sexual assault

As we have seen, sexual assault may be a way to force a woman to change
her mind about leaving, or to trap her into going back. The perpetrator
may believe that if he can have intercourse with his ex-partner, she will
belong to him again. Women who are raped under these circumstances
may also interpret themselves as reclaimed property, and return.

We read earlier about Kuriah's horrific assault by her estranged partner,
which offers evidence that sexual assault by an ex-partner isn't a spur-of-
the moment explosion of his frustration, but may be premeditated, as also
occurred to Summer:

> During the rape he did, in fact, bring and use a knife. He never
> really carried one around with him, so my mind tells me that he
> had planned this out.

Traps that ex-partners might employ in order to commit a sexual assault
include:

- Coming to your home and pleading that he 'just wants to talk'
  about his feelings, the children etc. (It is wise to be careful of this

at any time of day, but quite often pre-rape visits happen late at night.[5])

- Coming to your home on the pretext of visiting the children.
- Surprising you in your home, or like Summer, at your place of work.
- Abduction.[6]

If you believe you are in danger, go over the safety plan in Appendix 4.

Stalking

Stalking is a serious problem. Statistics estimate that 90 per cent of women in the US murdered by violent ex-partners were stalked prior to their deaths.[7]

Stalking is a deliberate pattern of threatening or intrusive behaviour, such as:

- Following you;
- Continual phone calls that involve threats or silence and hanging up;
- Letters or emails;
- Sending 'gifts' such as flowers, or macabre items like dismembered animal parts;
- Driving by your home;
- Approaching you or your property;
- Hanging around your workplace;
- Surveillance – watching you or tapping your phone;
- Text messages to your mobile phone.

The stalker may desist periodically in order to lull his victim into thinking the stalking has stopped, only to begin again weeks or months later:[8]

> There were times when he was angry and would call me around the clock and scare the shit out of me. He would continually call me at work and harass me and would often show up, unannounced at work when I was done. My co-workers were extremely concerned for my wellbeing and would often walk me to my car and have me call them when I got home safely. Most of this occurred during the first week or two after the relationship ended. Then there seemed to be a cooling-off period where I wouldn't hear from him at all. I was beginning to feel a false sense of safety. On the few occasions that he did call during

those final two weeks he was calm, somewhat reflective about the relationship and filled with a sense of sorrow that it ended the way it did and why it did ... The stalking and harassment began full-force after the rape and continues today – albeit in cycles. (Summer)

If you are being stalked, watched, threatened or intimidated in any way, please ask the police or a domestic violence advocacy service about a restraining order. You can also lay charges, if stalking is a crime in your jurisdiction. Evidence is important, so try to always: [9]

- Record dates and times of incidents;
- Preserve emails, letters or gifts;
- Keep telephone messages;
- If possible, ask your workmates or neighbours to tell you if they see somebody fitting the stalker's description near your home, school or place of work. Ask any witnesses if they are prepared to testify.

Remember though that if you get an order, it is not a *guarantee* of safety, particularly if the police and courts are not supportive:

Unfortunately leaving him did not mean I was safe. He continued to stalk me and show up unannounced and terrorise me.

My experience with the justice system and the police has been nothing but tiring and frustrating. I deserve as much time and consideration as other victims of other crimes. I pay taxes. I am a human being who deserves to be treated with dignity and respect. They are too quick to judge abused women. Just because I know my abuser doesn't give the courts the right to make me feel like I'm the bad guy or that my justice is less deserving! Just because I was paralyzed by fear for years and was not willing to fight him in court doesn't mean that I don't have a right to justice.

I once said to an assistant prosecutor, 'Am I not the victim? The abuser gets more justice then I do!'

Her response (yes, a female prosecutor said this). 'This is a vicious cycle with these types of men. Keep changing your phone number, have your child call from a pay phone so your ex-husband can't get your number. We can't put a police officer outside your door.'

How many complaints did I file over the years? Probably too many to count. (Kuriah)

The ongoing threat implicit with stalking can make it hard to move into healing. Please get as much support as you can.

The coercion factor

The *coercion factor* is a mechanism by which an abuser continues to terrorise his ex-partner. He knows that she is still afraid of him, and he exploits this in order to go on exerting control over her, sometimes for years after the end of a relationship.

Maybe you have noticed that even when you give in to demands to see your ex-partner because you are afraid of frustrating him, he still beats or otherwise threatens you for refusing to return to him. While you may be scared and surviving by giving into his demands, as long as he has contact with you but doesn't get what he truly wants – your return – he's likely to be frustrated anyhow, and ultimately just as dangerous to you.

Taking steps to combat the coercion factor can be extremely frightening at first. You will know if and when you feel ready to do this. If you decide that you are going to refuse a dinner invitation or not return a phone call, please ensure you have the support of a good friend or family member. Make a safety plan. For example, if your ex-partner is likely to become angry because you won't do something that he wants you to, look at what steps you might take in the interest of your safety. If you are threatened, consider calling the police. Ask about a restraining order.

In identifying and challenging the coercion factor, you have taken another important step towards the freedom you deserve. Congratulate yourself.

Emotional blackmail

Has your partner fostered guilt in you for hurting him by leaving or wanting to leave? Do you feel responsible for his happiness, or cruel for leaving?

> One night, several weeks after I ended the relationship for good, Paul came around to my home early in the evening and told me that if I didn't go back to him, he would kill himself. I refused to buy into that, and he said, 'They'll find me tomorrow, and my blood will be on your hands.' He left, and I dismissed his threat as typical manipulation. (Rachel)

Your partner may be genuinely upset about the end of the relationship, but you should not allow him to make you responsible for his feelings or choices. He does have other options: he could seek counselling or somebody else to talk to.

You could be struggling with internalised learned ideas that you are supposed to be nice to somebody who is hurting. Even though it is you who have been hurt, perhaps you find that you maintain contact with your ex because you feel that you 'hurt him enough' by leaving.

If you are struggling with unwarranted guilt, remind yourself that even though it feels very strong, you don't need to feel guilt for somebody who is trying to control you. He likely knows that the softer parts of you are fair game for getting him what he wants, and he'll play them as much as he can. Because guilt-trips can delay your freedom, try to resist acting on guilt. If you need somebody to talk with about it, call a hotline, speak to a friend, or post a message to your online survivor community. Remember too, that the guilt will pass the further away you get from your abuser.

Using children

As we saw in the last chapter, it's common for abusers to get back at their ex-partners through their children.

If your ex-partner threatens suing you for custody of the children unless you return, this can be extremely frightening. If you believe this is a real possibility, talk to a lawyer. Domestic violence services may know of free legal services. Melina's ex-partner made those threats plus he threatened to kidnap their daughter.

> He assured me he would pay me a divorce settlement, yet threatened that if I went to court for the settlement the judge would award him custody rather than leave a child with her single mother. I believed him, as I believed everything he said. He strung me along for months and months, alternating promises of settlement with kidnapping and death threats and mind games. I couldn't take it anymore, and moved out myself.

Child abduction may be a very real danger at this time:

> Talk to your child regularly when he or she is visiting the other parent's home. Listen for any hints that abduction may be planned, especially talk about visiting faraway places or people. If you fear abduction, try to obtain knowledge of the whereabouts of family and friends of the other parents who live out of state or in another country.

> Some courts work with victims of violence to offer supervised visitations in these situations; they may also be willing to order that children not be taken out of the jurisdiction of the court. Some schools will only release children to people authorised by the custodial parent. Consider implementing these and other

safeguards, from simple measures such as fingerprinting your children, to obtaining injunctions for protection. Let the other parent know you will follow through with any and all legal measures necessary to prevent abduction, and give children instructions on approaching others for help if an abduction occurs.[10]

Since perpetrators of violence often don't care who their behaviour affects, your ex-partner may play the 'bad mother' card with your children by telling them the separation is entirely your fault:

> His father was telling him that I was a whore, I was trash, that I was sleeping with men. He'd explain it to him in graphic details. (Tiffany)

While it's a good idea to avoid participating in those destructive games by responding in kind, you could feel very upset and angry because this hurts your children and it is extremely unfair. Have a counsellor, good friend or survivor peer-group to express your anger to, and to discuss ways of responding that are best for the children and afford you the maximum dignity.

Because some ex-partners use child visitation as a pretext for harming or harassing the children's mother, your safety is important at this time too.[11] Even if the court has asserted that he has the right to a relationship with his children, your safety must still be a priority. Perhaps it is possible for him to see the children on neutral territory.

Sometimes, there may be grounds for him having no access to the children if he is dangerous. You will need to seek legal advice about this.

Wooing and more promises

Abusers who are faced with loss of their partners often become intensely loving. At this stage, you may have received letters or speeches telling you that you are the only person he will ever love, and that he wonders how he could ever have hurt you. He may tell you that he will do anything for just one more chance to prove he can change. You may have heard this so many times that you know it cannot be trusted. However, if you are grieving over the end of the relationship or you still have feelings for him, his words might be incredibly seductive. There's appeal in believing that somebody that you've invested emotion in really loves you, and is sorry for harming you. You may want to remind yourself that once again, he is trying to draw you back to a place where he can control you.

Be careful about acceptance of gifts at this time. Under some circumstances, people who have separated buy Christmas or Mother's Day gifts for their children to give to their ex-partners. This is acceptable and even praiseworthy if there are appropriate boundaries; that is, if the buyer of the gift has accepted the end of the relationship and such gifts are really intended to be from the children. But if there's a history of violence, possessiveness or manipulation of you, acceptance of gifts is likely to fuel his hope that you will return to him. Continued gifts, letters or phone calls may constitute stalking; check the stalking laws where you live.

Sex with your ex

Some women are lonely after the end of an abusive relationship, and when the abuser appears with declarations of love and entreaties to go back, they find it difficult to resist going to bed with him. You may feel that he basically owns you anyhow, or your self-esteem might be so eroded at this point that you feel affirmed by the fact that he still wants you in some way.

If you go to bed with your ex-partner, he is likely to see this as an indicator that you don't really want the relationship to be over. Though sleeping with him in no way whatsoever justifies future violence against you, it won't help if you are trying to break free from violence.

If you have had sex with your ex-partner you may feel obligated to go back, or you may be so ashamed that you feel as if you deserve him. But having had sex with a man doesn't make you his property, nor do you have to go back into an abusive situation. It's not too late to start setting clear boundaries. Remember that you are entitled to make choices at any stage.

On that note, *was* there choice? If you have had sex with him because of the threat of violence, it is rape.

But what if he's really sorry this time?

Some abusers do genuinely regret the abuse. If you still love your partner, you may hope that he's truly sorry, that he's really changed and that you can reconcile with him. Only you know what to do with his promises, but if they have been repeatedly broken in the past, it isn't a favourable indicator of future change.

Do you feel manipulated? Is he really hearing what you need, or do the promises have a desperate sort of, 'Yeah yeah sure, anything as long as you come back' quality? Do you think there's any real responsibility being taken for hurting you, or is he trying to justify it?

One sign of remorse and commitment to change may be that he doesn't pressure you to return and trust him immediately, but displays understanding of why you cannot do so right now. Lissette and Kraus advise too that:

> If an abuser truly means to change, he ... will demonstrate that by participating in personal, not marital counselling or batterer programs and demonstrating nonabusive behaviours.[12]

Actions speak louder than words: watch what he does, not what he says.

Coming through ...

Judith Herman describes the inner state of women who have escaped violent relationships as one of ambivalence: there is often an alternating between fearing the perpetrator of their abuse, and feeling 'empty, confused and worthless without him'.[13]

> I had left on two previous occasions and gone back. Both of those two occasions were so emotionally exhausting. I wanted out of the relationship but there was also an addictive quality to it so I went back. I wanted to feel loved, I thought I could change him, that I could make him forfeit his control. (Summer)

If you have experienced mixed feelings around your decision to end the relationship, you need to know that this is a common response to what you have been through. Sometimes, things are just not straightforward or as logical as we would like them to be, and it can take time to unravel and understand the emotional ties you may have brought away from your relationship.

> For the next few weeks, I was miserable, I cried all the time and it took everything I had not to call him back. It made me realise how dependent on him I had become. (Charlotte)

Instead of condemning yourself for how you feel, or being tempted to respond in ways that will open you to further danger, consider that your ultimate freedom will be quicker if you don't act on any urges to see him. Emotions lessen with time. Get support from people who can affirm for you that you deserve to live free from violence.

Also remember that women who *leave* abusive relationships experience more depression than women who stay.[14] When you were in the relationship, perhaps the struggle for survival was so much a part of your everyday existence that you couldn't afford to feel or address the reality of your experiences. When we are safer, these realities begin to dawn on us, and this can be an extremely painful process.

Depression may arise partly as a result of grieving for the good parts of your relationship, or that your children can no longer grow up with a father. The end of the relationship may represent the shattering of dreams or wishes that you cherished. There are often many things to mourn when emerging from a relationship, even if it was violent.

If you are feeling that you really cannot make it without your ex-partner or that you are a worthless and horrible person who probably deserved to be hurt anyway, tell yourself that even though the bad feelings you have about yourself feel true, they are actually symptoms of depression and trauma, not statements of reality. Perhaps you might read, like a mantra, the words below from women who left safely and have successfully come through the post-relationship/violence emotions and the perpetrators' snares. Their voices offer advice, empowerment and hope:

> You are just worth so much more than the hell you're living in. You are special and a human being and life has so much to offer. It must be very hard to turn and walk away … afraid, possibly alone and with no money. But there are shelters and safe havens to keep you (and children) safe. And they care! Someone outside of your nightmare cares … (Adair)

> I would definitely tell other women living like I was to do something. Go to the police before it's too late, or you'll wind up dead. (Siobhan)

> Good luck! If you can find the strength to do it, please, please get out. (Emma)

> My sisters, please don't make my mistake of thinking that another assault on your body and spirit won't matter. It does, and do you know why? Because you matter – you're far too precious to have any more pain inflicted on you. I found that out for myself, and I hope you will too. (Rachel)

Good luck!

CHAPTER 13

Secondary Wounding: Surviving and Healing from It[1]

Survivors of rape can and do benefit from having loving or caring support from others:

> After getting involved with my current partner, I was able to refer to the past relationship as the 'abusive relationship', but I never wanted to define it as that until I met a woman I was working with, and she confided in me that she was in a bad relationship and I was able to tell her that I had been too. I was able to talk about what happened with her. She was so relieved to have someone who really understood what she was feeling, and not just repeatedly telling her she should get out of it. (Charlotte)

It's also true though that other people's reactions can significantly disrupt a survivor's healing. For instance, if anybody has told you that it is your fault you were raped or that you are lying or exaggerating, perhaps this has deepened shame and isolation for you.

Such responses are called *secondary wounding*. Secondary wounding compounds the trauma you have already experienced, causing you to feel ashamed both for having been harmed, and for being affected by the harm:

> The secondary wounding that was inflicted post-trauma was almost equally as degrading as the assault itself. (Summer)

It is important to understand that these hurtful experiences are not about who *you are*; they are not about you being dirty, hopeless, stupid or any of the other things implied. They are about the other person whom you've confided in; sometimes their cruelty[2] but more commonly the consequence of the individual's parroting of the rape culture myths, which as we saw in chapter 3, are unfortunately deeply embedded in our culture.

Some people do not wish to believe that men in their peer-group, family, or church congregation would rape somebody. They may be a little naïve and find it inconceivable that a man could brutalise his partner. It is often too frightening for them to accept that people do horrible things to another with the aim of disempowerment. So they unintentionally wound you.

> She approaches life as I did, believing every Brother and Sister
> to be trying to follow the example Christ has given us. Believing
> all people are rational and would not purposely hurt or humiliate
> or manipulate. (Linda)

Others may believe that a truly morally superior or intelligent woman would not be assaulted by her partner. In order for their own worlds to be safe, they actually need to believe that people who get trouble have asked for it in some way. So they unintentionally wound you.

It is often easier for people to believe the respected male community member than his wife, who might be a traumatised, nervous mess living in a refuge. It is easier to discount the credibility of a sobbing teenage girl than her boyfriend, who might be the handsome, well-liked star of the football team, especially if she has any reputation as 'promiscuous'. So they unintentionally wound you.

This chapter will explore the nature and effects of these wounds. (The next chapter will look at secondary wounding inflicted by the criminal justice system.) A benefit of reading about the harms and their impacts is that you may come to identify and understand how certain comments or situations have hurt you. We'll look too at some strategies for overcoming the damage caused to you.

Don't be surprised if you find yourself experiencing strong waves of memory and emotion. If this happens, think of somebody you can trust to support you, or call a sexual assault helpline and talk it through.

Forms of secondary wounding

Disbelief or denial

Has anybody implied or outright stated that you are lying about your rape? They might say things like, 'He couldn't have done that to you, he's just not the type' or 'You are making it up because you are vengeful. Are you jealous of his new girlfriend?'

Linda, who left her husband to live in a refuge, was visited there by his mother and sister, where the following took place:

> I am not sure exactly what I expected from them. I thought they
> would be shocked and rather upset, maybe they would want
> confirmation from me that he really had done as (I thought) he

had told them. I was nervous and really felt sorry for (mother-in-law) especially; imagine being told your son is a rapist. Her initial question completely blew my mind: 'You need a good reason to go to a refuge, they don't just accept anyone. What lies did you tell to get in there?' Said with a fair bit of attitude too. I replied that I had told no lies. I had told them the truth. 'What is the truth?'

Tracey's friends were just as unbelieving:

I have had a pretty clear message from most people that they didn't want to get involved and one of the catchphrases has been, 'Even though Mark's the weirdest, I just can't imagine it. I've heard what's meant to have happened but I just can't imagine him doing that. Both of you are our friends and we don't want to choose sides.' I know that Mark has a very different story about what happened, and I sat there and I almost laughed at them because I felt like saying, 'Well what do you expect him to say? Do you actually expect him to say, "Yeah, I raped a girl. I raped someone who I'd dated, who I'd lived with, who I wanted to marry and have children with"?'

How do you say with pride, 'Yeah, I beat someone so that they had bruises all down their arms and legs.'

It was all very unbelievable. Some of my friends who had seen the bruises down my legs totally ignored that the bruises existed, and were happy to just do the, 'We weren't there, so we don't know what actually happened', routine despite the fact that they had seen the bruises and those sorts of things.

Discounting and minimising

If you spoke of rape by your boyfriend/husband, you might have been told something like, 'It's not as bad as if he was a stranger'. Discounting gives your pain other names such as 'self-pity'. Thus Rachel's feelings were discounted when she disclosed rape to her pastor and his wife:

I uncharacteristically broke down crying, and the minister's wife said, 'I think there's a lot of self-pity going on here. You'd better save the waterworks.' This was tremendously humiliating, to say nothing of hurtful. Believing my pain to be a manifestation of self-pity was to affect me for a long time.

If you say the sexual violence has harmed you, discounting is being told that you are overreacting to something that isn't really a big deal: 'It's not real rape so why are you making such a fuss?' Or, people overlook that you might need some TLC and expect you to carry on as normal. For example, you may have told somebody about your rape, and that person tells you that you should get over it quickly since it wasn't 'really *that* bad':

> I told a few of my friends, including my roommates (I lived with five other girls in a house), and their basic reaction was initial concern for how upset I was, but pointing out that he had not hit me, and he had never done anything like this before, so I had no right to be upset for longer than a couple of days. I stopped talking to them about it, and kept to myself ... I was left alone to deal with the aftermath, with friends who didn't want to hear about it and minimised my experience. (Natalie)

Or somebody might tell rape 'jokes' in front of you, and then say, 'Awww, come on, you can't expect everybody to walk on eggshells – get over yourself.'

Your pain is also being minimised when people say, 'Well, you returned to him, didn't you? It obviously couldn't have hurt you that badly.'

> My secondary-wounding was riddled with insinuations that it just 'couldn't have been that bad' that because I chose to stay in an unhealthy relationship, in a relationship that I had been warned repeatedly to get out of, that that somehow was me asking for 'more of the same'. I've also been told in no uncertain terms that had I decided to report, that it would not be considered rape. (Summer)

Minimising statements may also be prefaced by a *denial* of the minimisation to come: 'I don't want to minimise what happened to you *but* ...'

Blaming the victim

Sometimes people state quite openly that because you stayed in the relationship you must have wanted or allowed yourself to be raped. Other times, blame comes in the form of uselessly retrospective advice like, 'You should have left', or 'You should have called the police'.

> An example of this is where my mother recently, even though she was trying very hard to be understanding and compassionate, stated quite bluntly and I quote, 'It was your fault he hurt you because you stayed' unquote. I smiled gently and said 'No, it wasn't my fault.' (Jennifer)

If you are still in the relationship, you might be told that if you don't leave, you don't deserve any compassion.

People with traditional views of marriage, or male entitlement might ask if you were not giving your partner enough sex. Or, a woman raped by her partner might be blamed simply for her choice of a certain partner:

> I suppose there's some sense that you allowed it to happen, and certain people, like a female minister with no idea have suggested that – that I allowed myself to be in or encouraged an abusive relationship because I was obviously unstable since I had one, attempted to commit suicide when I was 16 and two, been in an abusive marriage. Therefore, there must have been something wrong with me that made all this possible. (Sarah)

Tracey's mother blamed her due to her own history of violence:

> I told my mum. Her first reaction was, 'What did you do to provoke it?' At the time that she said it, it really made me step back and go, 'Whoa. Hang on a second. Did I do something to provoke it?'

Blame creates moral equivalency between rape and something the woman has allegedly done to provoke it, or between rape and her lack of perfection as a partner.

> My mother-in-law said he was in a dreadful state, and if he had an accident or did something stupid, it would be my fault. She also told me that I had forced him into raping me by putting him under so much pressure he was guaranteed to break.
>
> I appeared to be going completely against the Lord's will. My attitude was wrong, there must be another option, a better way, I was unforgiving, I should pray better and wait for the Lord's answer. She even gave me an example of the type of prayer I ought to be praying. But how can she know? She has not been in my shoes, my home, my bed. (Linda)

There is, however, no moral equivalency between rape and something else; your own mistakes or shortcomings *never* justify the commission of a crime against you.

Stigmatisation

With this type of secondary wounding, you are given a psychological label. You might be told that you are neurotic or that you are just trying to get sympathy: 'Oh, you are just hiding behind that PTSD thing you are supposed to have.' If you have said your partner raped you, it might be implied that you are 'one of those crazy women who accuses men of rape'.

You might be ridiculed or condescended to. People may treat you like a fragile victim, or like a nutcase who no longer has a valid point of view. People often confuse trauma with mental illness:

> When I confided in my mother regarding the rapes (just a month or so ago; it's five years later or more and I've only just been able to admit it to myself), I only did so because she was insisting on my first daughter's 'right to know' of her 'father.' She actually did say she was sorry, yet then said, 'You can become too introspective, you know.' (Melina)

There's also an unfortunate tendency for some men to think that because a woman has been raped, she 'likes it rough'. This form of stigmatisation is actually dangerous.

If you've been treated this way, remember that being raped and being traumatised are *not* negative personality characteristics.

Denial of assistance

There are stories on record of women being denied help by Rape Crisis services because, 'It's a domestic violence matter' only to find that battered women's services also denied them assistance because they were 'only raped' and therefore a 'rape crisis issue'.[3] In Australia, for instance, it is only in very recent years that women's services have attempted to bridge this gap by convening conferences that umbrella both domestic violence and sexual assault agencies.[4]

Families and friends might have refused to shelter or support you, saying things like, 'You made your bed; lie in it', or 'What goes on in your bedroom is not our business'.

Women may have problems accessing help too if their perpetrator has possession of the documentation required to apply for government assistance:

> However, my phone is now cut off. My finances are depleted and I can't even get anything from Centrelink since Gary still won't provide me with any of the financial documentation required, including my group certificate. (Samantha)

Shefali tried to get help from her local religious leader to get a divorce under Islamic law:

> The imam of the mosque, he was having a good time. He said he'd never heard of it. He wanted me to come to Sydney, go to this big mosque in front of six holy men, imams, and tell them why I wanted my divorce.

Betrayal of confidence

This happens to the teenage survivor who finds out her friends are talking about her rape or scoffing at her pain behind her back. It happens when the survivor of partner rape tells her church leader what has happened, and the pastor tells the perpetrator about her disclosure. For Rachel, it was her mother who betrayed her confidence:

> Worst of all, my mother began to tell anybody who would listen about my rape – even people she barely knew. Because people often responded by saying, 'Oh, you poor dear thing, aren't you wonderful for caring so much', it gratified mother's need for pity and heroics. It had nothing to do with caring for me in actuality, because my feelings did not count. Meanwhile, I learned, once again, that my needs, my pain and my right to the dignity privacy might have offered me, were unimportant.

Because of betrayals of confidence, you may have been exposed to further danger from the perpetrator. Or you may feel as if you've lost control again, which can trigger the same sense of powerlessness you felt when you were raped.

The betrayal of confidence may also have opened you up to more secondary wounding experiences. Perhaps you feel as if you can't go out and hold your head up now that everybody knows. Unfortunately we have no control over the responses of other people. However, please try to believe that your rape is nothing to be ashamed of; rather the shame belongs to the person who couldn't be trusted to keep your confidence, and to those who would use it as the subject of gossip.

Siding with the perpetrator

This form of secondary wounding encompasses many of the above to a certain extent; aligning oneself with the perpetrator includes disbelieving the victim, blaming her and minimising her experiences of abuse:

> The most amazing thing was how the women of the church leapt to his defence. 'It's so good that he's told you.' 'It's so good he wants to get help.' 'You need to stand by your man.' 'You need to forgive him.' 'Don't you realise what the poor guy's going through?' (Kate)

Many people, from members of her church to her best friend to her own father, turned against Linda. When she disclosed the rapes to family members, her father-in-law and brother-in-law were, she says, 'too angry with me to even see my face'.

In many cases siding with the perpetrator happens because people simply dismiss the victim's disclosure of rape.

Silence

Saying nothing implies a lot. There are non-verbal ways of displaying compassion, such as a gentle press to your hand. But when a disclosure of rape meets with blank silence and nothing else, this can be just as hurtful in its own way as getting a cruel verbal response. Many of us know the pain of the blank stare and awkward silence, accompanied by the listener either changing the subject or walking away.

> My family seem to be having difficulty with the situation. They can't talk about it and are obviously uncomfortable when on the phone. (Samantha)

The feeling of being unheard can certainly be experienced as a secondary wound as well as a trigger – just as we are not being heard now, neither did our abusers listen to us.

Making it all about them

While friends or family who love and care about you might be justifiably very upset about you being raped, ideally they won't expect you to be accountable for their feelings, or to comfort them. However, there are people who will seize any opportunity to place themselves at the centre of a drama, or make themselves somehow the victim.

> When my mother found out I'd been raped, she began to mope about the house, sighing and expecting me to be apologetic for the burden placed on her by my rape. Sometimes, she burst forth screaming and yelling at me for being stupid enough to have been raped – then she'd tell me how stressful it was for her. Sad to say, I bought into the guilt she wanted me to feel. I was at her elbow with constant cups of tea as she complained about how hard it was for her. I ran her hot baths, I cooked her meals. I hope I don't come off as harsh here, because many mothers are upset by raped daughters – naturally so. My mother, however, was the same mother who called me a whore and continually accused me of liking to be raped. I knew her; I knew her motives. (Rachel)

Some people are self-centred, and engage in 'one-upmanship' like, 'Oh but wait until you hear what happened to *me*. You don't know what suffering is until you've been through what *I* have.' This both minimises you, and gratifies the other's need to make it about them.

Other examples of people 'making it about them' are storming about telling you what you 'have to' do, without asking what *you* need.

Your rape is about you. While this doesn't mean that the feelings of others merit no consideration at all, it does mean that you are not responsible for what they do with their emotions.

Intrusive questions about the rape

Unless you are making a police statement, nobody needs to know the details of your rape unless you wish to tell them. Certainly, nobody should be pushing you to tell him or her exactly what happened. Unfortunately, there are people who 'get off' on hearing about rape; their questions have a 'tell me every dirty detail' feel. Others who want to know what happened may be quizzing you in order to pass judgment on what they believe you did or did not do to stop the rape. Some people may just be after something to go away and gossip about.

Other people may have kinder if somewhat misguided intentions, believing that if you talk about it you'll feel better. However, only you know when you are ready to share details, and with whom you feel most comfortable sharing them. It is very okay to say, 'I don't want to go into it'. Feeling pressed to give details if you are uncomfortable or before you are ready could be traumatising for you; don't forget, this is about you.

Effects of secondary wounding

Immediate responses you could feel to secondary wounding are helplessness and depression, as if what the wound implies about you is true. Rage and the desire to retaliate against the person who wounded you is another common effect. Secondary wounding can compound the low self-esteem you may already have.[5] This is likely to be particularly true (and you are more susceptible to secondary wounding) if you are already convinced that the rape was your fault.

Perhaps you have started to believe that there is something wrong with you for telling of the rape; that you are as hysterical or as overreacting as other people say. You may conclude that there's nowhere to turn with your pain, and continue to suffer violence:

> I felt completely alone. A major effect for me was fear of more secondary wounding, and so I decided never to tell anybody again of what Paul had done to me. Silence seemed the only alternative. (Rachel)

Alternatively, self-destructive ways of dealing with your pain may emerge.

Linda shares how she became so used to negative responses that she no longer expected fairness or kindness:

> The positive responses are more difficult to accept. I know how to deal with accusations, antagonism, disbelief and open hostility. I don't know how to cope with concern or belief. It is scary.
>
> My solicitor believes me. And I find myself crying. I don't know how to respond emotionally with him saying 'I believe you', 'what happened was terrible' (with no but's attached). I think this is partly because I so desperately need that belief, reassurance and concern from people like my dad, and it isn't there. The only way I can cope with the pain of the betrayal is to shut myself off emotionally, build a hard wall around me to protect myself.

In a perfect world, we could adopt a 'sticks and stones' mentality towards secondary wounding and just let it roll off, recognising that it says much more about the person inflicting the wound than us. But it hurts – for very good reasons. Please remind yourself that you will worsen your pain if you try to suppress it with 'shoulds'. Once you let yourself feel the anger and the pain, their intensity may be lessened.

Secondary wounding that silences a woman will ensure that the trauma of her rape festers without any relief. You are allowed to tell the truth about your life and say that it hurt. It's essential that you do so, despite what you may have heard.

Closeness to the person who wounded you

Because the opinions of those closest to us often seem to matter a lot, secondary wounding may feel more painful if it comes from somebody you have a close relationship with.

A well-intentioned friend might say, for example, 'Now I *know* you've had an awful time, but everybody has problems, and you have to see that wallowing in your past isn't going to help you.' Since the remark is coming from somebody who cares for you and genuinely believes they are acting in your best interest, it might make you question yourself. You may feel ashamed and confused since you felt that you were making progress with your healing.

Some people don't understand that in the course of recovery, a survivor often feels worse before she feels better, and they may be genuinely alarmed when the survivor doesn't 'get better'. No matter how much somebody loves and cares for you, this won't make them immune to rape myths, nor do they become experts on the survival and healing of rape and domestic violence.

Importantly, their concern does not mean that their judgment is correct. You may want to thank them for caring, but remind them that this is your journey, and it's really important for you to find your own way through it. You can ask them to respect you for having the sense to know where you need to go with your pain.

Protecting and healing yourself from secondary wounding

It is a good idea to be selective about whom you tell about your experience/s of rape. Obviously, you wouldn't want to confide in somebody who holds erroneous beliefs around rape and domestic violence, or who is likely to hurt you. You may want to test the water: instead of making a full disclosure about yourself, mention a recent news story about rape or domestic violence, and see what reaction you get. Or without being too specific, you could say that you are a survivor of domestic violence. Ask yourself if the response is an empathic one. Does this person seem to be somebody you could trust to talk to?

If you are in regular contact with people who are hurtful, you will find it harder to heal. It may be time to think about the best way to take care of *you*. Limit or end contact with the person or persons who continue to be disrespectful to you about your rape. Your healing is worth that, and you deserve better.

Surround yourself as much as possible with supportive people. Support has proven to be vitally important for us to heal from the trauma of the sexual assaults – so too the healing from secondary wounds. *Nothing beats support and validation from others.* You could call a hotline, share with a (online) survivor support group or a good friend who will listen. If you have a loving supportive other in your life, this can help. Such people can help you reaffirm that you are a strong, intelligent, worthwhile woman, who doesn't have to take on board the ignorance or cruelty of others.

Writing⁶

Identify your secondary wounding experiences. Write down as many as you can remember, and what forms they took. For example, were you stigmatised, or disbelieved? Then think about how you felt at the time. Were you hurt and/or angry? Ashamed? Do you still feel that way now? Do you need support?

Next, look at how secondary wounding has altered your attitudes. Do you feel as if nobody can be trusted to hear what happened to you? Identify attitudes you wish to keep, and which ones are actually hampering your life. Think about ways that you might be able to find support in overcoming secondary wound scars of shame and fear.

Now, look at how your secondary wounding experiences may have caused you to avoid activities. The main point to realise is that, unlike the original secondary wounding experience, you do have a choice now. Focus on the situation you fear, and ask yourself whether you could engage support to help you tolerate this activity.

Another writing exercise you could do: draw up three columns. In the first, list your experiences of secondary wounding. In the second, list how you responded. The third will contain ideals about how you'd *like* to respond should anything in the first column happen again. Please, though, don't allow it to become an exercise in beating yourself up because you didn't respond a certain way; instead, let it be a helpful tool for dealing with any future secondary wounding.

Confronting the person who wounded you

Think of somebody who has been insensitive or judgmental. What would you like to say to them if you could? Do you think it's worth raising the issue of the secondary wound with the person who has hurt you? If there's a chance you'll get hurt again, it's better to save your time and energy for other ways of healing.

If somebody has been insensitive or ignorant, this doesn't necessarily mean they don't care, just that they lack understanding. Some people are open to new information about rape and trauma. If you can have a respectful exchange of ideas that aids their understanding, that's great. Of course not all people are open and you may get hurt again. You need to decide what is in the best interest of your emotional safety.

Consider writing a letter, and then decide whether to send it or not. Sometimes, just the process of writing it can be helpful. If you do decide to send it, write and rewrite until you are sure you have said all that you want to say.

> I have confronted secondary wounding by letter, and I can attest that it was most satisfactory. About ten years after the minister and his wife episode, I saw them in a supermarket. The wife gave me a nod of recognition. I was instantly full of rage. After

examining my anger and becoming aware that it was the product of an untreated secondary wound, I wrote a letter reminding them of our interactions a decade before. I told them it was disgraceful to treat raped female parishioners they way they had treated me. I let them know that ignoring the pain of rape survivors, and blaming them was likely to drive women away from the church. The wife got a very hot sermon on accusing me of self-pity. I informed her that the pain of raped women is real. It was very empowering, and I felt that at last, I had corrected a great wrong. I had done something to prove to myself that I was worth standing up for, and this was immensely healing. (Rachel)

If you write a letter, or otherwise confront the person who inflicted the secondary wound, it is most important that you be clear within yourself that you are doing this for *you* to address your grievance and not with expectations of their remorse. It is important to accept that you cannot make another person change; you can only choose what you do with the secondary wound.

Also, if you feel the need to retaliate in an aggressive way, it is strongly recommended that you don't act on this, but talk it over with another person. No matter how angry you feel, don't say or write anything that could be construed as threatening. Use 'I' statements, i.e. 'I felt angry/hurt/other when you said the rape was my fault'. It's better first to state the issue, and then later, relate your feelings of anger and disappointment. Perhaps you'll find it empowering if you are able to tell the person that you have triumphed over the wound; for example, 'I felt silenced by your words, but I've overcome that and I'll never be silenced again.'

If you want to confront a secondary 'wounder' by phone or face-to-face, you could try some role-play or writing to prepare you for possible responses.

Sometimes there might be official options open for you to address secondary wounding. For example, if you have a work colleague who knows of your abuse yet makes slyly barbed comments about marital rape in your presence, this constitutes harassment and you don't have to put up with it. Complaining isn't being 'precious'; you are worth acting for.

If a health or other professional has treated you inequitably, it could empower you to look at avenues of complaint. Sometimes, a rape crisis or domestic violence worker will advocate for you in such matters.

Self-talk

Another way of countering the negative messages imposed by secondary wounding is with positive self-talk messages. Here are some possible mantras:

- Not everybody thinks the same way as the person who hurt you.
- Ignorant or cruel responses say more about the person issuing them than they do about you.
- You cannot change another person. You can only change what you do.
- Nobody has the right to tell you how you should feel about your rape.
- There is no time limit on pain or anger.
- It is your journey and nobody else's.
- You were raped. Your feelings are valid, despite what somebody else might say.
- You are not weak for being traumatised.
- You are not weak for being hurt by secondary wounding.
- You are not weak for asking for help.
- Inequitable treatment by courts, police or other professionals calls for social change, not for you to feel that you deserved it.

You are strong. You are worthwhile. You will get through the pain of a secondary wound.

Humour works well too. Draw on your own wicked wit or that of your friends for something that will expose the silliness of secondary wounding comments and give you some comic relief.

What you deserve

Summer experienced some awful secondary wounding; however, she also received some lovely support:

> I think the most profoundly loving and uplifting experience I had was about three months after the rape. My fellow co-workers and I were visiting another co-worker who was living at the beach at that time. This co-worker was a male and we were extremely close. He came down to the beach early one morning while I was there, crying, feeling all of these powerful emotions and he just held me, for hours he just let me cry. The only words he spoke were that he loved me and that we would get through it. He had

very strong emotions himself about what had happened, but in that moment, he never once let his own emotions get in the way of mine.

He just was allowing me to 'be' in my feelings and not trying to have me fight them. There was so much serenity in that gesture. Although we have taken separate paths in life I will forever be grateful to him for those moments of unspoken concerns, those moments where I could just gently ease through all of my emotions without having to explain them or, more importantly, explain them away. There was a sense of peace, that sometimes there just truly don't have to be words.

Just because you may not yet have had such a supportive response doesn't mean you don't deserve it. You do. Look for people who are capable of understanding and compassion, and of honouring you in your pain.

Believe in yourself.

CHAPTER 14

To Pursue Justice?

We know that only a small proportion of victims report to the police.[1] Fear of the perpetrator is the most common explanation provided for why women choose not to. In addition, not contacting the police is contributed to by our concern that we will lack credibility, and our confusion in defining the rapes. This self-doubt can be even more powerful if physical force was not a part of the coercion. Of the 30 women whose stories make up this book, the only ones who disclosed the rape to the authorities were Jennifer, Siobhan, Kuriah, Lisa and Samantha. For each, the rape involved physical force. A number of the other women, like Tracey, Tiffany, Marg, Maree, Summer and Kelly either contacted the police or their neighbours did about domestic violence and stalking issues. None of them disclosed the sexual violence to the officers.

It is completely up to you whether to report the rape(s). You might want to speak to a rape crisis worker or a legal worker about your feelings and options. Do remember that delayed reporting can lead to the disappearance of evidence and is sometimes used against you in court in an attempt to discredit you.[2] The rape myth operating here is that the 'good' victim reports immediately.

If you do decide to take the criminal justice route, know that in many places, such as all Australian jurisdictions, the immunity of husbands from prosecution and a 'license to rape' have been abolished.[3] However, it is not illegal in all States in the US.[4] For instance, in March 2005 in Arizona, a House panel defeated a Bill that would have made spousal rape punishable by up to 10 years in prison.[5] Alarmingly, the arguments against that legislation included concern that even fewer women would report if their partner would go to prison for a decade and that men needed to be protected from false accusations.

You need to know whether rape by a partner is against the law where you live. Contact your local rape crisis service or a centre that provides legal advice for women.

Even if you find out that the rape by your partner is illegal in the jurisdiction where you live, be aware that there is often a huge gap between the black letter law of statutes (the theory) and how they are actually applied (the practice). We will look in this chapter at the very low rates of prosecution and conviction and we will see that beliefs about a partner's conjugal rights are not so easily changed.[6] We see the rape culture myths like 'once his, always his' alive and well in some courtrooms. For instance, one Australian judge presiding over a case in which a man raped his estranged wife, made the observation that 'the respondent probably hoped to repair the rupture and resume living with his wife'.[7] Here, the rape seems to be regarded as an act of loss: a sort of wooing. It also implies an entitlement based in ownership. The judge's other comments reflect more myths about male sexuality and rape.

> However, the fact was that the parties were living apart, and this cannot be explained as the case of a husband losing his self-control during the continuance of the cohabitation.

The notorious comments of another Australian judge in a 1993 South Australian trial reflected his (and undoubtedly others') opinion that some types of coercion like 'a measure of rougher than usual handling' are acceptable with marital sex since ... '(S)ometimes it is a fine line between not agreeing, then changing of the mind, and consenting.'[8] The 'rougher than usual handling' in this case involved forced anal, oral and vaginal intercourse as well forcible insertion of a bottle into the victim's vagina.[9]

We look in the following pages at the law 'in practice' largely through the experiences that the few women in this book who reported the rape had with the police, prosecutors and court. Also, one of the authors had the opportunity to read through 23 prosecutor case files.[10] For the most part, we do not find 'happy ending' stories and most involve some secondary wounding.

Hopefully if you go to court, the process and outcome will be more positive. However, we believe it is important that you have an understanding of the worst-case scenarios. Forewarned is forearmed! Perhaps you can use Jennifer's method of emotional detachment as a model for going beyond survival and achieving success with the criminal justice system:

> The hurdles I have faced have been, at times, insurmountable. However, I persisted and allowed nothing to dissuade me. I

forced myself to face each issue as a business issue, nothing to do with me personally. I disassociated my emotions from the task at hand, treated them as if they were happening to someone else and pretended I was liaising on their behalf. I believe this was the key to my success in dealing with each and every challenge.

Contact with the police

The police may treat you with a lack of sensitivity. They may minimise what happened to you in a number of ways, including their choice of words in questions they ask. For example, in an interview with one woman whose ex-boyfriend was charged with 'unlawfully confining a person', 'sexual intercourse without consent' and 'intentional threat to kill', the officer asked, 'How did he come to rape you?' After she responded that he had forced her legs open, the officer asked, 'How long did he lay on top of you in that position making love to you, fucking you, whatever words you want to use … raping you?'

Most of the women in this book who turned to the police either to report physical assault or sexual assault did not feel wholly supported. For Jennifer, it took three years for the police to actually lay the 16 charges:

> The police failed to follow up obtaining reports from counsellors, medical practitioners etc. which has delayed proceedings significantly.

She feels that if she had pursued the rape charges, she 'would have received a better service from the authorities.'

Samantha, however, has felt supported but recognises the limitations of what the police can do:

> I reported the rape to the police as soon as I felt it was safe. Unfortunately this was not until he left for work the next morning. I also contacted the Crisis line, and SARCS. I had a medical examination. Gary was arrested and charged with the rape. The police have been good. They have provided me with advice on all my options. Yet they are relatively helpless with the pressure that he is applying now.

How the police treat you can have an effect on your decision about whether to continue legal proceedings:

> The manner in which the police deal with a complainant will obviously affect the way she feels. Even if they do not tell her

to withdraw her allegation in so many words she might be left feeling that it is her only option.[11]

Lisa first had contact with the police in an informal interview at her forensic examination. She felt pressured to make a formal complaint:

> The policewoman [at the forensic exam] was there talking to me and she took a few details and it wasn't that she wasn't interested but she made it very clear to me that if I decided to give a full statement it would give them carte blanche to do what they wanted to do. At that stage I wanted to go to see somebody and I wanted to tell them that I didn't want the decision of whether we were going to prosecute or not made at that time.
>
> I wasn't in the right mental frame of mind to make that decision then. I was too shocked and everything. So she took some information off me, but it was just like a chatty conversation; it wasn't a formal statement. She said if I wanted to make a formal statement I had to get in touch with them and she gave me her number.
>
> I felt frustrated because I just wanted to get there and blurt it. I thought I was going to be able to just blurt it and then realised I couldn't without worrying about what I was saying or that it was going down in a formal statement.
>
> I think that's what's very wrong. We should be able to blurt it and then go back and do a formal statement at another time without feeling like anything we say may be taken down as evidence. Because it's such a formal process, and you're going there for forensics and they tell you they've got to match all this and they've got to do this, it's all got to be done, and they've got all these bottles and a double match and they're taking it and writing your name and they're talking to each other and it's all very formal. You don't really get a chance to just talk. You only answer questions.

Like Lisa, you may have several interviews with police officers. It may be wise in the hospital not to say anything to a police officer until you have decided to make a formal statement. Sadly the courts (and the defence lawyer deliberately) often don't recognise the impact of trauma or minimise the trauma, and search for any discrepancies in your accounts.

Remember, you have choices here. It's wise to have as much support as possible and try to always have an advocate with you when you are interacting with police officers.

On to the prosecutor

There is a high rate of discontinuances or dropping of charges in all sexual assault cases,[12] but it happens even more often in partner rape.[13] As one prosecutor admits, 'There is the issue of consent where there is a complicated history of violence and consensual sex.' Indeed, the so-called archaic view of wives as chattel or property and as granting an irrevocable (lifelong) agreement to sex[14] continues to appear in sexual assault by partners cases – not always spelled out but certainly one can read between the lines in some comments by judges:

> There are special difficulties in reaching a just verdict where the rape or attempted rape is alleged to have occurred in the matrimonial bed or the bed of parties to a continuing sexual relationship. There is the risk of motives, disclosed or undisclosed, arising out of tensions in the relationship. There is the risk of misunderstandings as to consent arising out of the habitual physical contact inherent in the relationship. The opportunities for corroboration are slight and an accused can do little to defend himself apart from denying the allegation.[15]

If there are any differences between what you said to police between different interviews and/or in your preliminary hearing testimony, the prosecutor may pre-empt the defence raising these discrepancies at trial by labelling you as 'not reliable' and discontinue or drop the case.

> Most of these types of offences are committed behind closed doors with no witnesses other than the complainant and at any hearing it is generally oath against oath.

How the victim's reliability is seen is therefore very important. As already discussed, your credibility as a witness unfortunately is equated with your consistency. Thus, Lisa was encouraged by the prosecutor to withdraw:

> I went straight in to see the police prosecutor. He sat me down and said, 'Right. I thought I'd get you up here face to face, because I wanted to tell you that I don't think we're going to win and I wanted to see if you wanted to drop it.'
>
> I was just so angry I burst into tears straight away.
>
> I said, 'Why?'
>
> He said, 'Oh, I told the DPP officer to have a word with you, because there's a chunk of your statement that doesn't match, and they're just going to completely discredit you as a witness. It

says the people that heard you shouting out, then saw you come out of the flat and have a cigarette.'

Now that is wiped from my brain. I have been known to have a cigarette when I've been very distressed. I will just cadge one-off somebody if I'm very distressed, or if I'm out socially and really merry, but I don't smoke, and I can't smoke. They said they saw me out.

'They're just going to jump on that. They're just going to discredit your testimony completely, discredit you as a witness and it's not worth going ahead.'

I told him that I still wanted to go ahead and thought that he should ask for a continuance to another date to get the witnesses all organised. You never know what goes on behind closed doors because you are not allowed into the court until you give evidence but apparently they did ask but they weren't allowed for it to be delayed so we went ahead.

In a significant proportion of cases, the victim plays an active role in requesting that charges be dropped.[16] There are a number of reasons why you may decide to withdraw your complaint or to not testify. Jennifer explains why she withdrew her complaint of rape:

I view intimacy between a woman and her partner as something that should be beautiful and totally sacred. Maggot had violated my trust in so many ways and to have this aspect of my relationship with him put on public display was something that I just could not do. The humiliation would have torn me apart, never to be repaired.

Some women may be convinced (sometimes subtly and sometimes very directly) by the police or the prosecutors that there is little hope of a guilty verdict. For others, their cross-examination at the committal hearing has been an ordeal and they simply don't have the energy to continue.[17]

If something like this happens to you, don't beat yourself up. The criminal justice process can be extremely traumatising. Only you know your inner capacity. Don't try to do it alone. Most rape crisis services offer advocacy support.

If you didn't initiate the dropping of the charges, then having the case discontinued can be very demoralising. It can contribute to inner doubts about the seriousness of what happened to you.

The charges against Siobhan's husband were dropped. She found it especially distressing because of minimal communication from the police or the prosecutors.

> I think more contact with the police would be better so that you know what's going on; whether the charge is going to be dropped. So often when you ring up you get the feeling they're not talking; they know something but they're not talking. It would be better if they could tell you that the case has been dropped than being left not knowing and feeling more victimised, I think.

Ultimately, she was advised that lack of forensic evidence was pivotal in the decision to drop the sexual assault without consent charge.

> He got away with the sexual assault – there was no forensic evidence, I think, because I was going to the toilet a lot and he never got to do the 'back door stuff' he was trying to force on me but on that night I don't know if I mentioned it, I bit him a couple of times and how else do I fight this big overweight man. He's so strong.

This illustrates how important forensic evidence is in decisions about whether to 'run' with a matter and a reminder to have an examination. If this happens to you, we hope that you don't let that minimise what you have experienced. It's not a reflection of you and your trauma but a mirror of the flaws of our criminal justice system and the difficulties in prosecuting rape cases.

Going to trial

If the case makes it through the prosecutors' filtering, be prepared for more challenges. First, there is the issue of time.

Lisa spent 18 months waiting for the trial; it was cancelled twice. Jennifer has waited more than three years just for the indictment. The wheels of 'justice' move very slowly (if at all). A lack of expectations and some of that elusive virtue, patience, will help you bide your time.

Secondly, the complainant does not have a lawyer or anyone advocating for her in the courtroom.

> I kept on trying to talk to my QC and he kept on saying, 'You are just another witness. If you tell me anything that's not in your statement I'll have to tell the other side so I don't want you to tell me anything.'
>
> After we agreed it would go ahead I said, 'I suppose you want

to go through my statement now and get a bit more background information.' He said, 'No I don't. I don't want you to talk to me.'

He was like that at court as well. He kept on saying, 'I'm not your QC. You're just another witness.' (Lisa)

It can be frustrating for you if the prosecutor does not cross-examine the defendant about matters that you have told them about:

Bill would lie on the stand, or the witnesses would say something and I would catch him in the break and I'd say this isn't right, and he'd just say, 'How many times do I have to tell you? I am not your QC.'

The background stuff that I'd been feeding the DPP officer all these months hadn't got through to the police prosecutor.

I got so angry about the whole process and about the unfairness of it all. It was bad enough sitting in court listening to Bill lie through his teeth but the prosecution missed opportunities. The prosecutor didn't even attempt to discredit Bill as a witness even though he had lots of opportunities. Bill while on the stand said things about counselling and the house and the car that were complete lies and the prosecutor could have questioned him but he didn't.

The whole process was terribly frustrating.

Similarly, the judge may not allow certain evidence like history of domestic violence and you have to sit there and quietly accept such rulings. We know from the women in this book how common it is for domestic violence to be a part of partner rape. Therefore, evidence of prior abuse can be vital. Unfortunately though, not all judges see it as relevant.[18]

Testimony or other proof of prior violence being ruled as inadmissible may play a role in acquittals. One prosecutor, who expressed the view that evidence of this type should be allowed if relevant, noted that history of prior violence was generally admitted in committal proceedings but usually objected to at trials in his experience. Indeed, it was clearly an issue in at least three of the acquittals in the ACT Australia sample:[19]

Judge: But how did the prior history operate to her consent?

DPP: As to her fear of the accused.

Judge: Well, why would that fear be any different? I mean if the Crown case is the accused grabbed her by the throat with a view to apparently forcing her to have intercourse, I would have thought previous history would be pretty – well, furthest from your mind under those circumstances.

DPP: Well it goes to the relationship that existed between the parties; and it is on that basis that it is proposed to lead the evidence, your Honour, The whole story was –

Judge: Well, what has the relationship got to do with it? If the accused had intercourse without consent, it does not matter what your previous relationship is.

...

Judge: Well no is the obvious answer. Well, why is it relevant? I am not saying it is not relevant to the relationship; but this is not the relationship that you are trying to prove, is it? You are trying to prove a particular crime.

DPP: Well, your Honour, to show the relationship between the parties – to take this instance in a vacuum – would not give a true picture of the relationship, and it is admissible in my submission, on that basis to establish the relationship between the parties leading up to this incident.

Judge: But what issue does it go to?

Secondary wounding on the stand

As is so often the case in rape trials, the complainant's word ends up being on trial.[20]

Melanie Heenan[21] puts it this way:

Securing convictions in male partner rape cases remains difficult for prosecutors. Like most rape trials, the defence is likely to devote considerable attention to attacking the victim's character and credibility. Where there has been a relationship history, the defence has a greater pool of information about the complainant to draw on in reconstructing a version of events set on undermining what she alleges happened. At best, the approach is designed to raise a reasonable doubt about her veracity in the minds of the jury. At worst, she will be exposed to a gruelling process of cross-examination that will remain transfixed on the detail of previous consensual sexual activity she once engaged in with her partner – the man she now accuses of rape.

Accordingly the partner/complainants in the Heenan study were cross-examined about previous consensual sex.[22]

The aim of defence barristers in these cases was unashamedly directed at suggesting that consensual sex was more likely to have occurred on the occasion in question, just as it had in the past. Across the five trials, women were asked how often they had sex, when they started having sex, and whether they could speak to the general health of their sexual relationships. They were challenged about their versions of the regularity of sex, their alleged refusals to engage in sex, and their claims to often appease their male partners through submitting to sex.[23]

One hung jury seemed to pivot around the credibility of the complainant or specifically her inability to remember all the particular details of the assault.[24] The defence barrister's cross-examination was exhaustive and managed to get her confused about a number of details.

> Q: And you are not sure whether the instrument came out from your vagina or your anus, are you?
>
> A: No.
>
> Q: In fact, you are not even sure if the instrument was inserted into your anus or vagina, are you?
>
> A: No
>
> Q: You disagree with me, or you agree with me?
>
> A: No, I'm not sure that there was. There was something inserted in me, but I don't know what it was.
>
> Q: And you don't know where it was inserted, I suggest, whether it was in the vagina or the anus, do you?
>
> A: No.
>
> Q: Do you agree with me, or are you agreeing with me?
>
> A: I'm agreeing. I don't know.

Lisa's experience was equally traumatic:

> I was on the stand for a day and a bit, really a day and a half. It was a terribly traumatic experience.
>
> The defence tried to trip me up on the fact that I had said things during the forensic exam that had been included in my statement later and I had to just keep on saying that I was told it wasn't a formal statement. I wasn't given the opportunity just to talk. I was asked questions and I responded to the questions I was asked, and if it was different it was because when I gave my full statement I gave a full statement of everything that had happened.

I was asked a question at the forensics, 'Did he penetrate me anywhere else', and I said no because he hadn't. I'd told them about the oral sex but I hadn't told them about that because he hadn't. They ask you a question and you say no and that's it. Bill had tried to put my legs right up over my head and tried to enter my bottom and he hadn't managed it but because I was so embarrassed about it, I didn't bring it up until the formal statement. I didn't even bring it up until the second day of giving my formal statement because I was too embarrassed the first day. They tried to bring that up in court implying that it hadn't really happened – I'd thought that it would make my case better and had brought it up later.

It's like they said to me at Forensics, 'Have you washed the clothes that you were attacked in?

I said, 'No. I left them at the place. I took off my nightdress and put on the sundress that was hanging over the seat and put my knickers on and just went.'

When it came out in court it sounded as if I had kept the nightdress but I hadn't washed it. So where was it? The officer hadn't written down that I had told her that I had left it there, that's why I hadn't washed it. So when the question was asked, 'Did you wash it?' and I said, 'No', that was what was documented. It wasn't documented that I didn't have it, so I couldn't wash it.

These are the type of questions you may be asked. The object is to confuse you and make you appear as unreliable.

You may be asked questions that you can only answer 'Yes' or 'No' to but which are impossible to answer in that way. You may be asked questions that seem to be all over the place chronologically – they are. The defence is trying to mix you up.

Be prepared.

Do plenty of role-plays with a support person and with friends. Have a plan for things you can do if you get confused in the cross-examination. For instance, you can ask the judge for time out for a glass of water. If possible make eye contact as much as possible with a support person. Get a 'reality check'. You can do that by developing some signals with the person before hand, e.g. If she touches her forehead she is saying to you, 'This lawyer is trying to play with your head'. If she clasps her hands in front of her it is a message of strength and union.

If you do get confused, don't be hard on yourself. High-priced lawyers are trained to do this. Do not count on the prosecutors for support. Again, it is really important that you have someone or several people there for you. Also find out if your jurisdiction allows you to give your testimony in another room or with a partition. You will feel more comfortable and safer if you are not in the same room as your perpetrator.

Outcome

The conviction rate in rape trials is very low. For instance the Australian Bureau of Statistics found that sexual assault and related offences have the highest acquittal rate for defendants in higher courts.[25] In partner rape, the convictions are probably even rarer.[26] As one prosecutor observes:

> I have a low expectation of conviction on partner rapes. If they're separated but seeing each other, even when they haven't had sex, he'll still claim it was a romantic consensual event.

Samantha's husband was acquitted of the sexual assault in which he threatened her with a pair of scissors:

> Well he got off. It's incredible how he managed to do that when there was so much evidence. The court case was worse than anything I could imagine. As a victim I found that the courts are set up for the defendants and it is terrible that the victim is put through trauma both inside and outside the court.

There was no conviction for Lisa's ex-partner either:

> They never explained to me how they tied together the charges. He had to be found guilty of the aggravated sexual assault in one charge, not just the sexual assault. I thought, 'Well I didn't ever agree to that, and that's not fair.'

> The jury even came back and asked if they had to do that. They were obviously having problems proving beyond reasonable doubt the aggravated part – because of the bad forensics taken by the police and the way that the woman doctor fluffed it on the stand. The other side were jumping up and down with glee when the judge instructed them that they couldn't split it and it had to be all taken as one. So that's when they came back as a hung jury. I was furious. 'What's happening? Why is it like this? Why can't we separate it?'

> It means if they don't believe you about one part of it, then they're not going to believe you about any of it. It's like, we're just going to go with this all or nothing, and that was the prosecutor's sort of cavalier attitude.

I just found the whole thing very distressing.

Although the cases that are prosecuted are the most violent, UK research shows that for the most part lower sentences are given when there is a previous sexual relationship between the offender and victim/survivor.[27] Accordingly, an appeals judge, in reducing a defendant's sentence, stated that:

> ... the fact that this was not a rape of a strange woman or a woman hardly known, but the rape of a woman with whom the appellant had lived as man and wife – initially no doubt very happily – for upwards of 10 years. This does add a different dimension to the case and puts the sentence at the lowest end of the bracket.[28]

However, sometimes justice does emerge as the victor. Remember Kuriah who was savagely attacked after years of being stalked by her ex-partner?

> How many complaints did I file over the years? Probably too many to count.

> He was arrested; his mother bailed him out. For the next months he violated the restraining order repeatedly and yet spent no time in jail. The trial was postponed time and time again. Then one night I got a phone call from the District Attorney who told me that he was going to plead to two aggravated misdemeanours and that he was going to be given formal probation. That's it???? Twenty-seven felonies, nine misdemeanours and that's it?? My life had been hell for the past months and that's all he gets?

> No. I would not accept that and did not. Some very powerful women in my life went to bat for me and called the system on its lies and the plea bargain was withdrawn. We went to trial almost a year after the original rape. He was convicted on 18 charges.

> Then he filed and won an appeal.

> So here came round two.

> Seven domestic violence charges against him, 20 sexual assault charges, two false imprisonment charges, one assault with a deadly weapon. I couldn't stop my anxiety attacks or my legs shaking, but I made it through a second trial, thanks in no small part to a wonderful group of incredibly strong women who have held my hand all along the way. He was convicted on all but three charges and given the maximum sentence. Because of the

laws in my state (he was convicted on two counts of special circumstances – lying in wait and using a gun in the commission of a felony) his sentence was mandatory life. He has to serve 51 years before parole is a possibility. He made an apology to me in open court, which I will never believe or accept.

Thus, Kuriah persisted in fighting for justice (successfully), as have Jennifer and Lisa. We don't know the final outcomes for their perpetrators yet. Each has experienced some secondary wounding but they continue to fight. Like them, you can use the knowledge of the games that are played in the criminal justice system as a suit of armour to protect you to some degree from the wounds.

CHAPTER 15

Healing: Naming the Wound

If a woman does not recognise that she has been raped, it follows that she'll have trouble naming it. However, some women who can recognise that they have been raped find that there is a difference between *knowing* it and being able to *name* it.

Survivors do often go to lengths to avoid using the word rape, instead preferring euphemisms that feel easier to say.

> I would say I was 'attacked' in the beginning, or 'what he did to me'. (Adair)

> Naming rape goes beyond simply naming an act; it often seems to make a statement about oneself. For me, this had its roots in the sexual violence itself. Saying 'I was raped' felt equal to proclaiming 'I have no dignity'. If I did not say that word, I could retain at least the pretence of dignity. (Rachel)

> When I did go to leave my husband, at the time I had a student who was working for me as a casual worker, and I knew she was doing law, and I said to her, 'Can you tell me what information there is on kinds of sexual abuse stuff?'

> She just kind of looked at me and she said, 'In marriage?'

> And I said, 'Yes.'

> 1991 was when the laws were changed, and I got married in 1991. She brought in the pieces of paper photocopied out of textbooks. She'd gone and looked it up for me, and it said that consent wasn't given if you were asleep or unconscious or a few other things and I thought, 'I think I fit into that category.'

> At that point I understood that technically that fits, but it has always been a battle to use the word. (Sarah)

Difficulty in naming what happened to you as rape is often due to numerous social and personal factors; we have looked at most of these in previous chapters:

- You may have learned that in our society rape says negative things about the victims.
- Due to the myths, you feel self-doubt or that people will see you as hysterical, or 'making too much out of nothing'
- You may feel that calling it rape will mean that you should leave the relationship.
- Your partner may have threatened harm if you tell, or you know he will retaliate violently to an act of naming.
- You may be aware that there will be little social validation for your naming.
- Not naming your rape is a way of distancing yourself from the deeply traumatic feeling it holds for you.
- You may possibly be scared or embarrassed about hearing things like, 'You didn't make a big deal of it back then. Why are you calling it rape now?'
- You may be afraid that you'll become lost in frightening or painful feelings.
- If you define your experiences as rape, you have to face your vulnerability to further rape.[1]
- You may find defining your rape difficult because the perpetrator says things like, 'You really wanted it', 'You could have stopped me', or 'But you know I love you.'[2]

These are just some of the many reasons for survivors of partner rape not knowing what to call their experiences. The following chapter may help you shift some of these fears around naming. We'll look first at some of the rewards of naming, then at the process of recognition and how to help it along.

Why name?

Carol Adams writes, 'A problem inadequately named cannot be adequately addressed.'[3] Naming can achieve the end of denial and with it the end of the violence. When we name rape instead of using language that obscures, we give responsibility back to the perpetrators.

> It has helped for me to define what happened as rape because I now accept less responsibility for what happened. I can be angry instead of depressed about it. (Nichole)

Some women find it liberating because it validates the level of pain they have felt, or eases burdens of shame and guilt.[4]

> For me, wanting to name was like taking a run-up to a hurdle, but being held back from the leap by shame and fear. However, it is my sincere belief that if I had never made that leap, I would still be hostage to fear and shame. The other side of the hurdle is a better and much more powerful place. While it is true that not naming protects us from things that we fear, not naming the rape affects and hurts us anyway. I would far rather have faced the rawness of naming than still be tormented by pain that I could not give a name to. (Rachel)

To name can be a deeply healing exercise in taking back power and control. Until you define it as rape, you may not believe that you have a wound for which you deserve empathy, support and healing.

On a broader scale, it is a powerful act of defiance against the social denial of partner rape. Naming defies fear left over from abusers; it breaks their rules.

Looking at obstacles to naming

If you are afraid to name, ask yourself why. What do you fear it will say about you, or your partner? Is it shame you are avoiding, or hurt? Are there false beliefs about rape telling you that you haven't been raped?

Consider that the only real measure of whether what happened to you was rape or not is whether it happened without your consent. If this was what happened, you *can* call it rape. Integration of truth is what happens when what we *know* catches up with what we *feel*. If you know that you were raped, but still question yourself, you may have become engaged in an exhausting cycle of belief and disbelief, knowledge and denial. Integrating the truth of what happened to you means that you know you were raped *and* understand it with your spirit, rather than a state in which you feel hurt and frightened, but your head keeps chattering rape myths – or where you know in your head it was rape, but feel ashamed of seeing it as such.

Here are a couple of 'hands-on' exercises you can do to help you confront these hurdles.

Exercise one: Write your fears down and discuss them with a trusted counsellor or friend. You could do this with a list that goes something like, 'If I name what happened to me, I'm afraid of /that [insert all of the feared situations and/or thoughts].'

You may find that there are great benefits in addressing these fears. You can begin to challenge them fear by fear. For example, if one of your fears is that naming means saying you are a bad woman, then ask yourself if that is true or does rape say more about him having issues of control and power? Does calling it rape really mean you must have been stupid or crazy for not leaving, or does it actually mean that you loved him or simply didn't recognise at the time that it was rape? Does labelling it rape mean that you are disloyal or that partners can be rapists?

Exercise two: Develop a sort of checklist of all the reasons you cannot name your rape and confront the myths that underpin each. We list ten of the most common thoughts that may be stopping you from naming your rape. Add your other doubts and go through a process of examining where those ideas are coming from; identify the myths that underpin those ideas as we have done for those below.

1. I can't call it rape because he was my partner. (See chapter 3 for a discussion of this myth.)

2. I can't call it rape because a relationship grants automatic consent. (See chapter 14 for a discussion of the law.)

3. I can't call it rape because it wasn't violent. (See chapter 2 on types of coercion.)

4. I can't call it rape because he was upset. (See chapters 6 and 8 about how perpetrators justify and chapter 13 how others may give you this message.)

5. I can't call it rape because I stayed with him or returned to him. (See chapter 7 about the relationship and remember how the cycle of violence affects the very spirit of its victims. Also chapter 11 discusses this myth.)

6. I can't call it rape because I love him. (See chapters 7, 8 and 11 – all refer to this myth.)

7. I can't call it rape because I didn't scream or do enough to stop it.

8. I can't call it rape because I didn't say no.

9. I can't call it rape because I was aroused.

10. I can't call it rape because I sometimes really enjoyed having sex with him.

We'll look next at the last four in the list since they haven't been explored in other parts of the book.

Tip: On days where you start to question your reality, you may find it helpful to reread this section and the relevant parts of the other chapters, or to talk to somebody whom you know will not put your reality down.

I didn't scream or do enough to stop it

When your partner raped you, did you freeze, go limp, or otherwise submit? You have no doubt heard that 'real' rape victims are expected to respond by fighting and screaming; anything less is seen by many as proof of consent. Because of stereotypes of how a rape victim should behave, you may feel guilty because you see yourself as having failed to do all you could to prevent the rape. Perhaps you feel that because you submitted, you have no right to even call it rape.

> One of the most terrifying aspects of rape for women who did not fight back is confronting their own passivity. Therefore, it's important to realise that if you were passive during the rape, your passivity was probably a combination of sex role conditioning and a defensive noradrenaline reaction, resulting in a freeze or numbing response.[5]

This might have caused a frustrating and distressing pendulum of self-doubt:

> At times I often feel as though I am 'blowing it up out of proportion', that it wasn't really rape, that I'm making it up, that it wouldn't have happened if I'd done 'something'. I don't know what this mysterious thing is, but if I'd done it everything would be ok, I'm sure. (Emma)

If you froze and felt shocked like an animal caught in the glare of oncoming headlights when your partner raped you, you were not 'allowing' yourself to be raped but were in fact experiencing a normal response to a traumatic situation. Perhaps you felt unable to believe it was even happening or that your partner could hurt you this way. By the time the shock allowed you to register what was happening, the rape was well under way.

A passive reaction can be caused by many other factors as we have seen in previous chapters. You may have submitted out of a misplaced sense of guilt for having led the perpetrator on. This is a guilt that perpetrators often encourage. You may believe, through your indoctrination and experiences, that forceful or coercive sex are normal parts of a relationship. And, if you are a mother, silent submission may have been the only choice for you to avoid your children being awakened by sounds of violence.

He was getting up and down drinking, and he came to bed and forced me to have sex with him. He rolled me over and he grabbed me by the wrists and because I've got small wrists he was able to just use one hand and hold me down. And I was trying not to yell because there was a baby in the house. He pinned me down, and I had bruises and everything, and in the end just succumbed. I didn't want to scream. I didn't want to struggle. But I had bruises on my wrists and bruises on my thighs, and I felt very violated. (Marg)

If you feel contempt for yourself because you think you 'chose' to be raped, how about turning it into compassion that you were in a position where the only choices were violation or something else that you feared? You can turn any self-blame into understanding that social myths and sex-role conditioning perhaps made you question whether it was even rape.

I didn't say no

If you have felt hurt and confused because your partner used coercive tactics, or just commenced intercourse without taking any care to make sure that was what you wanted too, you may be reluctant to call it rape, or you may have been told you don't have the right to do so. Some survivors struggle terribly with the gulf between what they feel, and how rape has traditionally been defined.

Putting aside notions that if somebody doesn't actively say 'no' they must be consenting, we can look at the different ways of not consenting that exist. Remember that there are other ways of saying 'no;' for example, did you cry, or go limp? Why were you afraid to utter 'no'? Did your partner actively encourage these fears? What 'punishments' did you face for not wanting sex? Remember that consent means free agreement, not a grudging yes given in anger, frustration, fear or anxiety.

I was aroused

Women may have trouble viewing their experiences as rape if they experienced sexual arousal or even orgasm during the event. This was a hurdle that Emma had to overcome to recognise and name what had happened to her as rape: 'I had an orgasm so I must have wanted it.'

Although women often feel deeply ashamed of it, sexual arousal in rape is well documented and is nothing to be ashamed of. For some women repeatedly raped by partners, arousal may be an adaptive response that makes repeated rape more survivable.[6]

> I used to say to myself, 'Dear God. Let me get wet down there or just please just let me get through this.' The pain used to be so bad sometimes because I'd be dry and he'd be going quickly and it was probably rubbing on that scar, and my body's remembering what it's like to be raped, over and over again as a child. (Liz)

If you lubricated or orgasmed in the course of forced sex, and this makes you question whether you were raped at all, perhaps you will benefit from the following:

> Before you chastise yourself for one minute longer, remember that your sexual organs do not have a brain. They cannot distinguish between a mauling rapist and the gentle touch of a lover. They simply react to stimulation the way they were designed to respond.[7]

We have seen that some men attempt to stimulate a woman in the course of a rape as proof of their sexual skills, or so they can use it as proof that she 'wanted it'. However, involuntary arousal is not the same as liking to be raped, or wanting it to happen. The issue here is consent. Regardless of what your body did, if you did not consent, you were sexually assaulted.

Sometimes I really enjoyed having sex with him

This thought is based on stereotypes of what is considered real rape, and what is deemed appropriate behaviour for a real victim. There is an assumption that a woman is either 'sick' to go willingly to bed with somebody who has raped her, or that if she does go to bed with him another time after the assault, she was not actually raped.

If you recognise yourself here, first, see that you are not just the victim of rape but also of false beliefs that are unfortunately alive and well in our community and even in our courts.

> Although the complainant suggested, during evidence in chief, that – following the events of September 1997 – she had thereafter submitted to the applicant out of fear, those claims rang somewhat hollow after her cross-examination, during the course of which she conceded that they would, on occasions post September 1997, have intercourse several times per day in the course of which she would 'fellate him' repeatedly.[8]

Previous or later consensual sex does not constitute a man's license to take sex from you. Don't be hard on yourself, and remember that a myth cannot turn a rape into something less than it was.

Helping you to recognise and name it

Aside from challenging our fears and the myths that we have internalised, there are other processes and/or experiences that can help you to identify and name partner rape.

Comparing partner rape to other rapes or sexual relations

Sometimes, looking at other experiences of rape in our lives can promote the ability to name experiences of partner rape. This was a catalyst for Nichole: 'Naming it began with naming an earlier sexual assault and dealing with it.' For Kate, it was having 'normal' sex with her second husband:

> Until I remarried and was completely in another relationship I didn't know that there was any other kind of sex. I didn't know that it was possible. I thought that the experience I had in my first marriage of hating every minute and praying every minute was normal. I didn't know that there was any other kind of sexual experience available to women so that's another reason why I never thought to bring it up or to talk to anyone about it, because I just assumed that that was the common experience. When I suddenly experienced something different in my second marriage I think it hit me how awful it had been in the first. It wasn't until I saw that contrast that I was able to see how bad it had been.

Similarly, Charlotte was able to recognise and name her rape several years afterwards when she was in a loving partnership:

> This was another thing in my life that I wanted to forget about. I made new friends and moved on, never thinking about Ted or what we had.
>
> I under-estimated the effect that the abuse had on me. I had another relationship a long time after, but there was never any trust, and we certainly lacked closeness. I almost thought that was the way relationships were meant to be.
>
> Finally, my priorities changed, I had this overwhelming desire to travel and meet people, and be alone ... actually get to know myself again ... Nick and I connected almost immediately, spiritually, emotionally and intellectually. It was through our relationship that I understood that what was before was not right. With the benefit of hindsight came the grief, and the hurt that I had stored for so long.

Identifying with others and receiving validation

Noticing the commonality between yourself and other survivors of rape can enable naming. Have you had conversations with other rape survivors or read survivor accounts and had a sense of relating to their experiences and feelings? If you have, this is not happening because you were *not* raped, but because most likely you were.

Hopefully, hearing the women in this book will provide you with a source of identification and validation. Plus, there are other survivors' accounts in other books. Or you can join or visit an online survivor message board. The last is what enabled Natalie to identify what had taken place as rape. (See Appendix 3 for a list.)

> It just suddenly hit me one day that it had in fact been rape, when I was discussing it with my therapist and used the word. It shocked me to say it, but after doing some research on the internet, mainly the website Aphrodite Wounded, I realised that I was in fact, correct in calling it rape. Since then, there has been no doubt in my mind about how to characterise what had happened.

Some women come to recognition through TV programs like *Oprah* that serve the important function of bringing the crime of rape by partners 'out of the closet'. They relay to women that what they thought was private and beyond the understanding of anybody else is in fact recognised; they are not alone.[9]

This illustrates how important external understanding and validation can be in slicing through mythology and assisting women in defining rape by partners.

> I never really considered it until it was pointed out to me that what he did was wrong. At the time, I would not have used the terms sexual assault or rape to describe anything that happened in the relationship. (Emma)

Ideally, we grow to a point where *we* know what happened and that is all that matters. But in those painful stages of confusion, hearing that 'Yes, it was rape', and 'No, you are not crazy or exaggerating', can make a huge difference.

Despite that you may have felt isolated, if you are reading this book, you know by now that there are women who have felt the same things you do. Find people who will support you in your naming. Doing it alone is not impossible, but it is harder.

Becoming aware of the dynamics of rape

Coming to understand sexual violence itself may be a key factor in being able to more fully recognise that what happened to you was indeed rape:

> I read material about rape and why it happens, and in doing so, it became clear that many of the elements of rape I was learning about applied directly to my own experiences. (Rachel)

Think about what was actually happening when you were raped. Does closer inspection reveal themes of control, retribution or determination to have what he wanted no matter what you did or did not do? What did he say? Perhaps there are indications that the rape was planned.

When you get some clarity about what rape is, particularly noting how it is different than ordinary sex, you may come to understand that you are not overreacting in seeing your experiences as rape.

Trusting yourself

When you think about the sexual violence you've experienced, do you feel torn between a sense of 'making too much of it', and the painful emotional awareness of what happened to you? Because of the social view of partner rape, you might 'feel like a liar' in calling it rape.

> I find myself feeling as though I am lying when I know I am not. Feeling guilty for telling what happened as though I was spreading malicious rumours. (Linda)

This is an additional but falsely assumed shame for the survivor of partner rape. Remind yourself that the myths that lead to you feeling like a liar are themselves lies!

Trust of the self can be particularly difficult after partner rape, because the betrayal it represents may have left you with a sense that your perceptions cannot be trusted. Also, you may have had people stating with unwarranted authority that your rape is not real. We are often taught to discount our feelings as silly or invalid, but you *do* know what happened, and that knowledge is more valid than a bunch of myths. You can trust it.

Watching the inner self-talk

See if you can catch yourself when or if you think, '… but what happened to me is not as bad … not as real … was only my partner … etc.' If you hear yourself thinking like that, you may want to substitute those old and untrue messages with new ones such as:

- I no longer discount my own pain by believing other rape survivors are worse off than me because my rapist was my partner.
- My experience is as valid as anybody else's, and putting it down does not help me.
- My invalidating self-talk is based in myths, not truth.
- My rape was real, it hurt me, and I deserve to heal.
- Violence is violence; rape is rape. There is no hierarchy of seriousness.

You can try thought-stopping. Catch the thoughts and mentally say 'No!' or 'Stop!' When thoughts such as, 'My experience wasn't real rape', intrude, you may want to visualise a big red neon sign flashing 'No' at the thought. Or, imagine banging a door shut. Give the thought a darn good telling off. You could do it playfully: 'Gotcha! Get the hell outta here!'

As you come more to believe in the validity of your experiences, you may find that thoughts that negate them intrude less often.

Recognising that it mattered

When you realise that your rape mattered, you may find you are less inclined to feel foolish about seeing it as rape:

> The impact of the moment when I realised that my rape mattered is still emotional for me. I was 24 years old. The rape support group to which I belonged offered attendance at court with women who had charged their rapists. I was very good at flanking women into court with sisterly solidarity, all the while believing that my rape did not count the way theirs did.
>
> One day, I attended a trial in which the victim had several supports. After the case was over, her supporters crowded around her in a truly loving and protective way. It was obvious that what had happened to her really mattered to them. While I kept my supportive face up, I felt the emergence of a terrible pain. I did not for one second begrudge the woman the loving support she was getting, but a deep craving opened up inside me; I wished that I had had it too; that people had thought my rape mattered the way they thought hers did.
>
> I realised at that moment that it mattered to me. I got home, tore off my court suit and ran the shower, sobbing. I had never cried like that about my rapes – indeed, I'd never felt that what happened to me was worth expressing pain for. Though it hurt, I recognised that it was healing pain. No longer smothered by

myth and shame, I could now acknowledge that I had been raped. It happened; it hurt me; and that mattered. My need for recognition had become bigger than the droning platitudes about partner rape not being real rape. Recognising that it mattered was the beginning of having compassion for myself. (Rachel)

Others may discount what happened to you but you can begin by not doing this to yourself anymore. You can come to realise that your feelings aren't overreactions – they are there because something bad did happen to you.

Recognising that you matter

Perhaps the sexual violence you experienced damaged your sense of worth to the extent you feel that you don't matter, much less anything that is done to you.

This isn't true. You matter, and what happens to you matters.

As you heal around your sense of worth, it may become easier to see your rape as a real wound for which you deserve healing. Because you may not have realised that what you experienced was rape, you may not have been able to care for yourself after it happened. You may not have felt that you deserved care. You do, and it's very important that you give yourself that now.

When women name the rape

Women may be more inclined to recognise their experiences as rape if they have ended the relationship.[10]Justine, who experienced ongoing sexual assault after ending her relationship, saw it as, 'Definitely, more of a "real assault" after I had left.'

It is also more likely to be recognised when a partner's behaviour becomes overtly deviant or violent:[11]

> I knew it was rape. He'd forced me. I'd said no and I'd said no. I didn't say no like messing around giggling, and going, 'No, no, no.'

> I said, 'No. I don't want to do this.' (Marg)

Because anal or oral sex are seen as perverse or taboo by some women, they may more readily define these acts as rape than vaginal intercourse, which is more 'normal' – though vaginal penetration with objects may also be a critical factor in defining an act as rape.[12]

The recognition that you were raped, and that it is real rape, may occur as a blinding flash of revelation. Jill, whose husband violently raped her once, says, 'I labelled it rape right away.' Or, it may be more gradual, like degrees of recognition. That was the process for Melina whose daughter was conceived in a violent rape:

> I began to feel strange if forced to refer to Ahmad as my daughter's 'father' whenever I filled in paperwork. In particular, when enrolling her in preschool, I had to fill in questions that I'd not had to look at for a long time. It felt so intrinsically wrong, even sickening. I never investigated these feelings or questioned them until recently. Since the birth of my second child, the desire to give Sonja a surname that is significant has become even more important.
>
> I think it's simply time that has brought on the realisation. And being in a healthy relationship. With the question of Sonja's surname, I suppose it brought back memories that I'd left buried. I'd become haunted with nightmares and flashbacks of life with Ahmad. I knew my feelings weren't just down to sour grapes – I have no time for that.

It could be that you will go through a cycle of accepting that what happened to you was rape and then doubting it several more times before you come to terms with the fact that it was in fact rape:

> I acknowledged it only once, four days after when I lashed out at a friend who said the wrong thing at the wrong time. I remember crying to my friend Lee. 'Why didn't he stop? He knew I was crying, why didn't he stop? Surely if your girlfriend is crying while you fuck her you know she's not enjoying it?' After that, I put it out of my mind, convinced myself it wasn't really rape, that I had misunderstood or 'misinterpreted the events. (Emma)

You may be ashamed or embarrassed about changing your mind and calling it rape, and this may be underpinned by myths you may have heard such as 'women frequently 'change their minds the morning after' and label sex as rape.' Plenty of survivors shut down on their pain and address it later when they have more resources for doing so. If you are in the cycle of acceptance and denial, you have nothing to be ashamed of. Changing our minds and giving our experiences the name of rape is an *essential* part of healing for many survivors of partner rape.

A degree of recognition

Some women know that something sexual took place that they did not give consent to, and ask themselves if it could be called rape. Personal distress or social messages about what is real rape may intervene at this point, so that what happened becomes demoted to something that was like rape but not real rape:

> I think I knew fundamentally that it was sexual assault/rape but I was of the mindset that it wasn't the same as being raped by a stranger – that I was not as bad off as women who had been raped by strangers. It was reinforced by some people I chose to share with and that packed a whole new punch. It was bad enough having that thought in my own head but having society continue to validate that misconception just made it so much worse. I still struggle with this to this day. (Summer)

Summer was beaten, tortured and raped at knifepoint – yet people minimised it because the perpetrator had been her partner.

Imagine how absurd it would be if you were thrown from a horse and broke your leg, and people said, 'Don't cry. That's not a real break; after all, you *did* choose to get onto the horse in the first place, yes?' You would hardly respond by saying 'Well, there must be something wrong with me that it does hurt. I'd better splint the leg up and try to walk as best I can.'

Think about the absurdity behind the social view of partner rape. How can one woman be 'less raped' than another, or 'only a little bit' raped? The fact is that while being raped and/or beaten once is a terrible trauma for any woman, survivors of partner rape have often experienced these things more than once. Your wounds need to be acknowledged and healed, not lessened.

Emotional readiness – naming in your own time

Women often come to a place of defining their experiences when they have built up sufficient resources and inner strength through healing:

> I never really let thoughts of the relationship enter my consciousness until I was healed enough to define what happened as rape for my own sake. I know completely that what happened was against my will and was assault. I am older, smarter, and I now have the resource to deal with what happened. (Nichole)

It's very common for women who have experienced partner rape to first disclose with words like, 'He makes me do things in bed that I don't want to.' Sometimes, saying that much can be hard enough, and your timing needs to be respected. You will know when you are ready to attempt more explicit naming.

Rape survivor Patricia Weaver Francisco, in her beautiful book *Telling*, uses the words, 'Fearlessness without recklessness'.[13] Rape survivorship is about reclaiming choice, and setting boundaries. Don't allow anybody to push you into naming, or to imply that if you don't name, it didn't happen. Just because you cannot yet speak, it doesn't mean it isn't real. It means that owning it is painful. On that note, the first few acts of naming are likely to make the rape more 'real' and, while naming is a healing step, you could feel a lot of emotion, some of which could be frightening. Please engage the support you deserve. Tell your survivor friends that you named it – they know that naming rape can be tough and they'll be proud of you.

Maybe you'll find that naming begins internally – for example, you can say silently to yourself, 'It was rape', but still not feel okay about saying it out loud. After awhile, you may move on to say it to people you especially trust. Perhaps you can write it, but not yet say it.

If you can name your experience through pain and confusion and social denial, you will know that saying, 'I was raped and the perpetrator was my partner' is much more than a string of words. It is a hard-won victory. Congratulate yourself.

CHAPTER 16

Healing: Your Feelings

Counsellor: What are you feeling?
Survivor: Fear and anxiety.
Counsellor: That's good.
Counsellor: What are you feeling?
Survivor: Grief and deep pain.
Counsellor: Good ones.
Counsellor: What are you feeling?
Survivor: Anger and rage.
Counsellor: Excellent.
Counsellor: What are you feeling?
Survivor: Self-blame, shame and self-doubt
Counsellor: All good.

Someone once said that if people were sent to prison for their feelings, there'd be no one left on the 'outside'. Feelings are not bad; although remembering and feeling can be an undeniably hard part of recovering from abuse, they will help you heal. When we bury emotions or memories, they tend to hurt us anyhow, sabotaging as they do our present life with shame and fear. In sharing the memories, you'll probably find it easier to put them behind you. Rather than losing control, you'll be able to gain more control.

In this chapter, we focus on ways of acknowledging and accepting feelings; however, remember that this is *your* healing, and nobody should push you into feeling before you are ready. That would be like ripping the top off a scab before sufficient healing has taken place underneath it. The same is true for memories. Not everything needs to be remembered in detail for you to heal. If you experienced many traumas over a number of years, you may have 'representative memories' of a certain period of time. You can still heal without revisiting every trauma.[1]

Respect your pace and your process.

Feeling fear and anxiety

When we are over-exposed to repeated threat, we may feel ongoing heightened anxiety for some time after the relationship, as if parts of us are unable to believe we are truly free. If your relationship entailed a culture of ongoing terrorism, you may find it hard to relax even years later. You may feel anxious when you are touched in a certain way as we heard from Tiffany elsewhere. Medical or dental contact that triggers memories of the rape due both to the area of examination and/or similar feelings of powerlessness over what somebody is doing to our body can cause profound anxiety. If you add PTSD symptoms such as hyper-vigilance, it isn't surprising that you feel on edge, almost as if you will be punished for letting your guard down.

You may have a fear of men:

> I still remain afraid, knowing that other people can turn on you without prior warning, but I also know that that is not a fault in me. (Natalie)

Specifically in the context of the abuser, many women find that even when they have effectively severed contact, they still fear the return of the perpetrator, sometimes for decades. This is one of the grimmest legacies of domestic abuse. As mentioned in chapter 12, some women go into hiding because it is a sad reality that they will never be safe from their ex-partners any other way. For Summer, ongoing safety concerns are a reality because she continues to be stalked by a perpetrator the police cannot locate. Jennifer also hides:

> I have had no contact with him other than in court. He cannot find me so he cannot hurt me. I live in hiding and am very careful not to be complacent about my safety. I have had several near misses with journalists taking pictures of me, which would have been displayed nationally on TV and in papers. I did not allow the journalists to take my picture or do any stories on my involvement in various community activities. I do not allow my guard to slip. Until he has gone through the court process I worry about him finding me. He is supremely arrogant and would actually think after all this time that I would welcome his attention.

Many rape survivors fear seeing the perpetrator again; for the survivor of *partner* rape, this is often a very real possibility. Such fears are *not* unreasonable as they are derived from painful and violent experiences:

That has been very difficult in that I feel this anxiety, fear: almost agoraphobia. What if he was walking through the city and he follows me around the shopping centre? Who's going to know? It means that I don't go to places that I would want to go to normally because if Mark turns up I can't guarantee that he won't be taunting me from the other side of the room. I would feel uncomfortable just having him being around me. (Tracey)

I had a support person from the women's centre in the courtroom with me. This helped immensely. When I had to speak, I couldn't get the words out. It was a tiny whisper, my throat clamped shut painfully. I just kept thinking of my daughter, and eventually managed to speak more or less audibly. It was horrifying being in the same room with him, where he could see how scared I was and get his jollies from that. Just a screen so he couldn't see me would have been wonderful. I didn't want him to see how I looked now, how I'd changed my hairstyle so I was less recognisable by him, how I'd lost weight. I felt so exposed. (Melina)

Dealing with your fears and anxiety

An important part of self-empowerment is realistically assessing your fears, and dealing with them:

For many years, I played down my fear of Paul's release from jail. I told myself it simply wasn't worth being terrified while he was out of the way. Eventually I had to face the fact that I was frightened. A year before his release, I did some very good work with my therapist. We looked at what my fears were, and what I needed to feel safer. I was trying furiously to dismiss my fears as the product of hysteria, and my therapist brought me back down with a much-needed and validating bump when she said, 'Some fear is wise fear. Just as you would fear a poisonous reptile because it is unsafe, you know very well from experience that Paul is unsafe.' I am thankful that my fears were unfounded – nevertheless, it was helpful to confront and examine them. (Rachel)

It's likely that after facing your fears, you will feel more in control and better able to relax.

Acknowledge your fear. Try not to pretend you are not scared if you are. It's not 'weak' to be frightened, particularly as you have been harmed. You'll benefit from openly admitting the fear and getting support to deal with it.

Identify the trigger. Try to identify what the trigger for the fear is. Has there been a reminder of the past? Or have you had approaches such as a phone call out of the blue or a threat? Perhaps you are distressed by news that your ex-partner is in your area. Or is your fear coming from a current experience over which you have little control?

Determine if the fears are realistic. If you are experiencing strong panic attacks or other trauma-based fear, this will cloud the issues. In that place, thoughts of the perpetrator's return are naturally terrifying. When you've moved through the bout of PTSD-related fear, you will then be in a more rational frame of mind, and can assess whether your fear is realistic or based in PTSD symptoms.

Take safety steps. If you determine that your fears are realistic, you will need to take any steps necessary to care for yourself. Talk through safety strategies with other women who have escaped violent relationships. Keep trying ideas until you develop a plan that is workable and is likely to increase your ability to protect yourself and feel safer. You may feel safer beefing up your home security and going to and from work with an escort, at least for a while. If there have been threats or other harassment, you could contact the police.

If you are feeling generalised anxiety and hypervigilance, here are a few tips:

Learn to relax. Create a relaxation space for yourself, surrounded by things that help you feel strong and safe, such as pictures of good friends. Sit or lie down in a comfortable position. Put on some music. If you begin to feel anxious, start telling yourself, 'I am here in the now. I am safe now. I can relax now. Nobody is going to hurt me now.' If you start to feel frightened or panicky, ground yourself by noticing the weight of your bottom on the chair or rug, and repeat the above words. Tenderly hold yourself, and say, 'It's okay for me to relax. There are no needs to cater to right now but my own.'

You may also want to think about relaxation and meditation classes. Yoga may be useful, focusing as it does on finding a place of inner peace.

Change your surroundings. Learning to feel safer may mean getting rid of physical reminders of the violence. For example, if you've separated from your partner and still sleep in the bed you were raped in, buy yourself a new bed. This could be a pleasant and positive venture; choose sheets and quilt covers in your favourite colours.

Have some faith. Faith is the antidote to fear. You don't have to have a religious epiphany or even a spiritual experience. You can choose to have faith in the power of other women who have gone beyond mere survival to healing.

Feeling grief and sadness

Since partner rape shatters basic assumptions we hold about love and safety, the betrayal involved can cause you to feel as if something has died. Summer grieved the losses of safety and the sense of self she had before her rape:

> I am trying to gently release the 'Summer' that I was. I loved her to some extent and I am currently mourning and grieving her loss in my life. Perhaps more than anything I am mourning the passing of her sense of safety in this crazy world. I am grieving the loss of her naiveté and the innocent woman I once was. The woman that I lost because I had love to give and love that I so desperately needed to have in my life.

Sometimes, the sadness felt in healing is not necessarily grieving a loss, but feeling deep sorrow for the conditions imposed by the relationship:

> As I developed compassion for myself, I felt terrible sadness about the abject loneliness that I had experienced while living with Paul. I had had nobody who did not condemn and shame me to go to. I was being raped and abused and covering it again and again because I was so ashamed and frightened. I cried for that young mother, who kept feeling sorry for him at her own expense; a young woman who might have died for loving the wrong man. (Rachel)

The grief may be about the loss of the relationship:

> I must confess, I still think about him often, and I am still grieving over the loss of the relationship we had before the assault. I think about what we could have had together, and I sometimes fantasise about seeing him on the street and going back to those good times. It is so difficult to reconcile who I knew him to be for seven years with that one night. Just a month ago I tried to look up his phone number, to call and just hear his voice. But, I have never ever questioned my decision to break up with him, I know it was the only thing I could have done for myself. (Natalie)

Despite the fact that your grief and sadness may be deep and perhaps frightening, it will be necessary and beneficial for you to acknowledge and express these emotions when they come. In this way, you'll move past them. Experiencing your feelings is for many people an important part of coming to terms with traumatic experience. Validating your losses by giving yourself space to grieve honours what you have lost and how you have been hurt.

Your pain likely will not emerge as one big crying session, but will linger for several months and lots of crying sessions. This may alternate with periods of numbness, which will offer temporary relief from active pain. Possibly, you will face separate pockets of sadness months or even years into your healing as other aspects of your experiences emerge, and you will cry some more.

Note that there is no statute of limitations or timetable for grieving. Years may pass and something takes place in your life that is a reminder, a trigger, and a wave of grief runs over you. Remember that this is normal; a sort of emotional recycling process.

Grief and sadness naturally do not *feel* good. At certain stages of healing, however, you may come to appreciate that your tears are 'good tears'. You will know the difference between the hopeless, uncontrollable crying of despair, and the cleansing release of healing tears. You may come to appreciate that feeling is preferable to operating in constant numbness. You'll realise that while pain doesn't kill us *not* feeling it is far more harmful.

At times it may feel endless; each time you dry your tears, you know that there's more where they came from. You may have entered the 'emergency stage' we spoke of in chapter 1.

You may even wish that you could put it away again. But it *will* get better. You will get through. When you do, you will know you don't have to run away from your feelings any more. You've faced them, and they will be less frightening.

What can help you through grief and sadness

Support. Please, try to get help from people who will not say that you are 'feeling sorry for yourself', or 'When are you going to let it go?' At times, you may just want to say to somebody, 'I was raped and it hurts very badly. I need to talk to somebody.' Who is in your life that you can do that with? There's no support better than another survivor. Telephone counsellors are often very helpful in the absence of others.

Don't negate your pain. In grieving, you will possibly need to overcome inner voices that tell you that you are on a 'pity-party' or some such untruth. You have a right to your pain. If you find yourself feeling sad about different things some years into healing, don't put yourself down as 'malingering'. Understand that with deeper levels of healing, the tears may need to fall again for a little while.

Hugs. Would you like to be held? Think of somebody you trust who will do that for you.

Holding yourself. Imagine holding and rocking the self that was raped. Put your arms around yourself, and speak loving words to her.

Allowing yourself space and time to 'go with it'. Naturally, if you are actively feeling grief, you may be scared that you will start crying at work or school. You won't always be able to leave to give into it, and may find that you feel embarrassed about being near tears around others. You are right to be cautious; not everybody understands. Make time to give your feelings space.

> Sometimes I feel myself slipping into a dark sea, where I start to doubt myself and feel ashamed. I used to write in order to gain some perspective, or go for a walk, to take my mind of things. But now, when the mood takes me, I go with it. This means, that sometimes I break down and cry, other times I shout and scream. I get myself into such a frenzy, I exhaust myself. The thing is, I am allowed to feel that way. I give that to myself. If I want to cry, I can and I will. I don't have to hide those feelings for anyone; after all, they are my feelings. (Charlotte)

Don't talk, just feel. You may be a little over-analytical and concerned with trying to 'talk' the pain away. But grief does not always need words. Sometimes, those big, gulping, wordless cries are the most cleansing.

Don't fight it. Once grief and sadness arise, they are very difficult to suppress again. If you try to push your pain back down, it only means that you are staving off the inevitable. Unless you absolutely must put it away for a while because of other responsibilities, it is much better if you get support and allow those feelings to come as they will.

Keep an eye out for depression. In grieving, you may experience some depression. This is often 'situational depression' or a normal response to your experiences. However, if you are feeling constantly hopeless and helpless, guilty, suicidal, or other debilitating impacts are impairing your ability to function, discuss this with a counsellor, and see your doctor. Also, remember that it will pass – however deep and terrible. Hang in there.

Take it one day (hour) at a time. Grief can seem like it will last forever. Instead of worrying about whether your pain will still be with you tomorrow, next week or next month, take it one day at a time. Each day, do the best you can to take care of yourself as you move through your pain – just for that day or even for an hour at a time or five minute increments! You may find that this breaks the enormous task of getting through down into a more manageable size.

Use your imagination to see the end of grief. Imagine yourself free of pain, and celebrating that fact, even if it seems distant.

Remember that this too will pass.

Feeling anger and rage

For many women, anger at their husbands and at the rapes is the most vividly recalled feeling:[2]

> He made an apology to me in open court, which I will never believe or accept … Why did the man who claimed his love for me hurt me? Power. Control. Because of his childhood problems that he carried into our marriage. Because of jealousy and lack of respect for himself and for me. It doesn't really matter. More reasons are not needed, there is no reason that would justify or explain what he did. I hate this man that I once loved. I have more anger than I can contain at times. (Kuriah)

Yet for a number of reasons such as self-blame or having learned that it isn't 'nice' for females to feel it, you may not have allowed yourself to experience that anger. It is not sinful to get angry with somebody who has hurt you; it is human and fair. Another obstacle to feeling your anger is that despite your brain knowing that the abuser cannot hurt you, perhaps you have been traumatised to the extent that anger automatically carries fear of retaliation. You may also be afraid that if you get angry you will go crazy and hurt somebody. A counsellor can help you look at and resolve fears of loss of control.

Feelings are feelings, pure and simple. In healing, expressions of anger can be extremely positive. Healthy anger honours the fact that you have been hurt or treated unjustly. It is not 'bitterness', or feeling sorry for yourself. Your anger not experienced may turn inwards and turn into depression, so feeling it is extremely therapeutic.

Perhaps you are in a situation where you don't feel heard. Or maybe someone is telling you that you are feeling or being a certain way and you know you are not. A person may be 'in your space'. If these types of situations trigger a tremendous amount of anger or rage, it is a clue that this is about more than the current situation. Anger about the rapes may be set off by people treating you with the same lack of respect that the rapist did.

You may find that you are not only angry in hindsight, but you can also recall being angry when you were sexually abused. If you touch any rage you felt when you were raped, you may experience cathartic tears. Find somebody who can hear your rage. You deserve to put that anger out where it will be understood and empathised with.

You may know that there is some anger below the surface that you just can't get at, and perhaps you feel depressed about this. It's OK. When the time is right, your anger will come.

Some strategies that may help with anger

Feeling your anger can become a courageous statement of triumph when you realise that you have a right to your feelings and that the perpetrator can never take that away from you again.

Put boundaries around your anger. If you feel that anger is on its way, take time out from your surroundings whenever possible, and remind yourself that although you have a right to be angry, releasing it onto the wrong people is unfair to them.[3] Remember that you can be responsible for choosing what to do with your anger. Even if you are enraged, it will not become something that takes over and 'makes' you act violently.

Get professional help. A counsellor will be able to help you explore safe and productive ways of validating and expressing your anger. This may be particularly important if you are experiencing fantasies of revenge that you are considering acting out.

Physical ways of discharging anger. You may find that rigorous exercise helps you discharge your rage. Try pounding a pile of pillows with a baseball bat. Or, take a length of garden hose and a telephone book and beat the daylights out of that phone book; call the perpetrator names with every hit.

Watch out for generalised anger. If you are angry with all men, this may be an important indicator that you are angry at some level about the rape. Ultimately however, it will need to be directed at the perpetrator; he is the one who inflicted this on you.

Directing anger at the perpetrator. Your anger can be expressed through writing (see chapter 17) or the spoken word: If you are still in the relationship, and have determined to the best of your knowledge that you are safe, it will be useful if your partner understands that he needs to be prepared to hear your anger, which is a response to what he did to you. Again though, stay safe.

Dance and music. Movement helps discharge anger. Do an anger dance – and imagine stomping the stuffing out of your abuser. Do you have any anger-music to yell along with? Alternatively, music can be calming – it isn't for nothing that it is said to soothe the savage beast within.

Screaming and yelling. If there is a safe place to verbally vent your anger at your abuser, go for it. You can do it at home or in the car alone, or in the company of survivors. Reclaim the Night marches can be excellent opportunities for venting loudly – there is a conscious release of righteous anger as you shout with the other women, 'However we dress, wherever we go, YES MEANS YES AND NO MEANS NO!'

One anger at a time. As you heal, different things to be angry about such as battery, emotional abuse, or the way that you invested time and love in a relationship with somebody who kept making false promises of change will probably arise. Secondary wounds that once simply hurt or shamed you will suddenly make your blood boil.

You don't have to address all your anger at once.

Humour. Laughter often helps dispel anger. Imagine yourself getting back at your abuser in a way that is powerful as well as funny. How about chasing him with a whirring chainsaw and saying 'Okay you bastard, rape *this*?' Or tattooing, 'I'm a rapist' on him and parading him down the main street?

Forgiveness. Linda Ledray writes, 'It is okay to stay angry at the rapist. You never need to forgive him, forget what happened or feel sorry for him.'[4] Some survivors, though, find forgiveness healing. Forgiveness means different things to different people. However, it does *not* mean saying that what that person did was okay, or that you have to love them.

A level of forgiveness may feel appropriate if you have chosen to remain with your partner (and the violence is not continuing).

> About Travis and after almost 20 years apart: I know the gentle person that is there and I know if something was to happen to him I'd be there like a shot, possibly more for my children's sake than anything else. I've gotten to the point where I can accept him as a person. I certainly can't accept the things that he's done. They're really out of line and all the rest of it and I really loathe and hate and detest, but as a person I can be civil to him and in

fact in some ways I do feel sorry for him but at the same time I
still blame him. (Eva Jane)

However, forgiveness must be something that you come to in your own
time, if you do. It cannot be forced by belief systems or others' ethics.

Feeling self-blame and shame

The line between blame and responsibility is blurred for many abused
women. Blaming ourselves for the abuser's violence and/or for staying in
the relationship is a thing some of us fall into often, and overcoming this
can be a long, hard struggle. Shame is related to self blame, but where
self-blame is a product of *thoughts* about why it was your fault, shame is a
feeling of intense humiliation, like a perpetual stain and sense that you've
done wrong. In place of self-worth is a core of shame, which continuously
says to you, 'You are the one responsible for this. You are flawed. You are
bad.' The source of shame is often a mix of things that the perpetrator did
or said to you, our childhoods and internalisation of social views about
rape.

There are particular areas of shame for women raped by partners; these
include shame for returning to the rapist, or for continuing to enjoy sex
with him outside of rape. However, as we've already examined in previous
chapters, this doesn't make you disgusting or weird; in actuality, you have
responded normally to an abnormal situation. Nothing you did or didn't do
makes you responsible for the sexual assaults.

Dealing with self-blame and shame

Survivors often believe that they will always feel dirty and ashamed. When
you get stuck in self-blame and shame, seek help from your counsellor
and from other healing survivors, who can encourage ways of challenging
notions that weigh on your self-esteem. You can also try asking yourself
if you would blame somebody you loved for being treated as you were
treated.

> I forgive myself and realise that it is not my fault for not seeing
> his potential for violence. (Natalie)

Accept that you were powerless. Sometimes, it's not enough to know it
wasn't your fault – this knowledge only begins to make a real difference
when you understand *why* it wasn't your fault. Summer shares the benefits
of understanding what happened to her:

> I have attained some level of healing and inner peace and I can
> settle for that 'some' right now. As far as understanding what

> happened to me – well, I got involved with someone whose own
> self-worth was so low that he had the need to bring me down
> to that same level. He needed to control me because he was not
> capable of looking at himself.

As you make sense of your experiences both emotionally and in a wider
social context, the self-blame will begin to shift. Faulty logic often lies
at the heart of self-blame. Blaming ourselves is a form of denial of how
powerless we were or how badly betrayed we were. In order to stop self-
blaming and the resulting shame, we have to give up imagining that if we
caused the abuser's behaviour, we could have stopped it.

Converting weaknesses to strengths. A truly excellent tool for overcoming
self-blame and shame is revising what you have defined as weaknesses,
and recognising that they were actually strengths. As you understand
this, you'll develop respect for yourself for knowing how to survive.
For example, if you are blaming yourself for giving in to your partner's
wishes, perhaps you can begin to see that this kept you from being further
harmed, or even killed.

Many women hate and fear whatever they believe it was that attracted an
abuser to them. Yet, Jennifer says, 'I have not really changed as I have
maintained those qualities that attracted the abuser to me.' This is a wise
and self-affirming choice. Rather than reject and blame herself, Jennifer
hangs onto the beautiful traits she had when she met her abusive partner.

Reclaim truth about yourself. Dealing with shame will mean coming to
understand that rape does not define you. Make this your mantra: *'I am not
what he did to me.'* Reclaim truth about who you are. Remind yourself that
what may have been true for the perpetrator, or what is true for society,
does not have to be true for you. Imagine yourself parcelling up the shame
and giving it back to the perpetrator. *He* raped you. The shame is his. As
you deal with issues of self-blame, and begin to rid yourself of internalised
messages of shame, it will become possible to view yourself with more
compassion. Summer shares the growth of compassion for herself:

> When I look back I see a young woman (accompanied by a little
> girl in her heart) that was seeking love and acceptance in the
> worst of places.

Challenge myths that blame and shame. Begin to challenge beliefs that
are placing the blame on you. You may need to dig out anything you've
internalised – for example, when you start to believe things like, 'He raped
me because I'm a slut', ask yourself whether that is a reflection of what he

said about you. Have social notions about rape and bad girls contributed? If you believe it happened because he was sexually unsatisfied, ask yourself just where you got the idea that a man should have sex with his partner whenever he feels like it, regardless of how she feels. Is that really fair to you?

Remind yourself that the rape was the result of forces inside him, and encouraged by forces outside him like rape culture. You did not cause them. It was not your fault:

> Leaving these words here, knowing they will be displayed before you makes me feel shameful. Yet I know it's not my shame; it belongs to him. (Kuriah)

Affirmations: Recovery is an inward battle between the voices we have learned who whisper of shame and self-hatred and another voice that talks of self-love and exoneration from blame. Use an affirmation like, 'I am a beautiful, capable and loveable woman who is not responsible for the violence.' Have a regular 'meeting place' with your affirmation, like the bathroom mirror.

Feeling self-doubt

Self-doubt is an emotion that integrates two other feelings we've already looked at: fear and shame. Rape survivors often feel as if the perpetrators are still controlling their thoughts for weeks after an attack.[5] We know that the same is also true for survivors of partner rape/domestic violence. As we saw in chapter 9, it's very common for a woman abused by her partner to feel as if he has left a part of himself behind in her, often for a long time after the relationship has ended. She automatically feels fear when making decisions the perpetrator would not have liked, and may internally 'hear' him sneering things like, 'You are stupid. You can't win.'

If you identify with this, you will know that at times when you are vulnerable, this can feel really daunting. You may even have come to automatically accept these negative messages as part of who you are. In healing, there will come a time to identify and counter those internal exchanges. That sense of still being controlled can be driven out, with your own power put in its place.

Dealing with self-doubt

Using visualisation. The next time you hear 'that' voice inside your head, telling you that you are worthless, or that you can never overcome fear, actively identify it as psychological leftovers from your abuser, and decide to fight back. You may visualise yourself having power over the perpetrator.[6] Imagine yourself rising up and him shrinking before you.

> A friend of mine once handed me an effective tool for dealing
> with negative internal voices. I was to visualise pushing Paul
> into a yellow cab, slamming the door and paying the driver a
> one-way fare. I finished the visualisation laughing instead of
> frightened. Select a destination; perhaps somewhere full of
> exotic man-eating animals. At other times it has helped me to
> visualise pointing a gun at him and saying 'Bang!' (Rachel)

Techniques such as this actively take control of fear and vicious internalised messages.

Being defiant. Taking control of your life back may mean not listening to the self-doubt and *actively defying* your partner's rules. Do what he wouldn't have liked anyway. Defiance increases your understanding that this is your life; his rules are old rules. They are not *your* rules, and he can't dictate to you any more. You can make your rebellion fun. Imagine telling him where he can get off as you defy his rules.

Defiance can also increase your self-esteem. Suppose you've had a tough few weeks dealing with self-hatred. The last thing you may feel like doing is making a gesture of care towards yourself. Try to do it anyway. If you keep refusing to obey the dictates of negative thoughts, they will begin to lose some of their power.

Wholeness and feeling

Try to trust that whatever you are feeling today is OK. Trust in the process of healing. As you allow yourself to work through all of the feelings discussed in this chapter, you may find that you feel more whole, more together than you did when you were numb, frightened of your feelings and disassociated from them.

> I now see a woman who wants to feel validated and believed
> and trusted and loved. A woman who occasionally shares space
> with more emotions in one hour than some spend in an entire
> day, week, month or year. Facing these emotions has made me
> stronger. (Summer)

After the fear and grief passes, you will likely discover that it is possible for you to feel joy that you are here, and that you survived. You will know your strengths, and be proud of them. You will notice the enjoyment of doing things that it was not possible to do when you were afraid of your partner. You may even choose to celebrate with a ritual – quietly, or noisily.

Your survival is a real reason to celebrate. If you are in a state of deep grief, you may sometimes question whether surviving was worth it. Moving through your feelings will lead you to the sure knowledge that it was.

> I remember that when he lay on top of me in the act of rape, I felt such humiliating, impotent rage that I couldn't make him stop. He gleefully mocked my pitiful struggles, and raped me with all the more relish. After the relationship, I continued to feel the emotional sense that he was still on top of me; still holding me down and degrading me and there was nothing I could do.
>
> But that was then and this is now. The freedom to remember and express my fury has given me a true sense of finally having gotten him off me.
>
> This power is ours, sisters. (Rachel)

CHAPTER 17

More Healing Steps: Making Choices

In earlier chapters, we explored essential healing themes such as perpetrator responsibility, recognising that you have a wound, feeling your feelings and, most crucial – safety. Hopefully, this has laid foundations for further healing. This chapter explores another major area or theme in healing: giving away responsibility for the things we cannot control (other people, such as the perpetrator) and taking responsibility for the things we can (you and your healing).

You were in no way responsible for the rape(s) perpetrated against you. You didn't have control over your partner's behaviour but as a consequence of the violence, you may feel as though you've lost your power as a decision-maker and believe that you are responsible for other people's wellbeing and actions. An important step in your healing journey is divesting yourself of this unfair and inappropriate responsibility, and accepting that you are responsible only for you.

After having somebody else force his will on you, it can be hard to realise that you now have control over your life. Especially at certain stages of healing, you may feel so depressed that you don't feel like lifting a finger to help yourself. Bills pile up, appointments are not kept, and surroundings are cluttered and chaotic. The longer it goes on, the worse you feel. It becomes a self-perpetuating downward spiral. But our personal histories cannot be allowed to become reasons for continuing in self-destructive and self-defeating patterns. You are the only person who can make a decision to call a counsellor, to begin tidying up the mess, or to take a brave leap into treatment for an addiction. So, admit if you feel terrible. Make the choice to go to the doctor about your depression and anxiety. Call a counsellor if you feel self-destructive.

It is healing and life-enhancing for you to recognise that you can now make choices for yourself. This is an extremely important and rewarding part of taking back control.

When I self-injured, I believed that I was doing it because I was raped and needed to punish myself for being dirty. But the day came when I realised that there was another part of the equation in this cause-effect relationship; I began to understand that I could make a choice not to cut. It was not my fault I was raped. It was not my fault I was depressed. However, while these factors could make me feel like cutting, they could not actually force me to do it. Instead, I could choose to talk to somebody about my feelings and the urges to hurt myself. These choices were very real ones. (Rachel)

As you read this chapter you will see that there are many choices that you can make that will assist you in self-care and empowerment. You can incorporate the ideas and actions that feel right for you and leave the rest behind. Your healing is personally custom-made and designed (by you)!

Making safety choices

One of the most frightening things rape survivors face is the fact that we live in a world where things happen beyond our control. In healing, we need to come to terms with the fact that there are many things we cannot control and find ways to stop this fact from limiting our lives. Essential to this is looking at what we *can* control in the interest of our safety.

Assuming that you are no longer in the worst danger – that is, still with somebody who assaults and threatens you, consider what else might help you feel safer.[1] Perhaps you may start with security measures in your home, such as an alarm system, good locks and security screens. You may feel more secure with heavy drapes or blinds closed over windows at night. If your working hours include evenings or nights, find out if there are security patrols for night workers, or well-lit and highly visible parking areas. If not, arrange to walk with someone else; there is safety in numbers. See if your neighbourhood has a crime watch program. If not, perhaps you could find out how one is established.

A course in physical safety is something else that may increase your sense of control. Does the thought of a martial art or self-defence course appeal to you? In the US, the Rape Aggression Defence (RAD) course comes highly recommended. It is run by women, which is less triggering for survivors. You may want to shop around and find something that suits you.

Women's fears, particularly of rape, are often discounted as 'hysterical' and we learn to discount our inner voice. Yet, listening to your instincts will also be an important part of taking control of your world. For example, if you sense that somebody may be following you, instead of attacking yourself as 'silly' or 'paranoid', act on your intuition and take steps to get safe. If your gut tells you that the guy who wants to walk you home from a party is a creep, you may worry that you will be seen as neurotic or an unpleasant bitch if you refuse. Getting away from somebody who is creepy is much more important than what he thinks of you. If your instincts tell you something's not right, and you are wrong, what will you have lost by listening to those feelings? You are worth any precautions you need to take to keep you safe.

Choosing to set limits with other people

After partner abuse, some women have trouble setting boundaries with other people. That can mean that we have trouble separating ourselves from another person. We feel responsible for their happiness (and everything else). Focusing on or obsessing about another person's wellbeing and tying our energies to them can be an unconscious means of avoiding our own feelings of pain.

Choosing to accept our powerlessness over other people is therefore a really important step in our own healing. Sound easy? Well, it isn't. Most of us find this a very hard habit to break; we 'let them go' and then 'take them back' regularly. It's a choice we have to make consciously each day.

A lack of healthy boundaries can also translate into people walking all over us. We may feel controlled or directed, used, ridiculed and/or belittled in some of our relationships. You may find when this happens that you feel triggered by reminders of how your abuser treated you, and you may feel powerless and fearful, as well as angry and hurt.

You can work your way towards saying 'no more'! Remember, this is *your* life. You have the same rights to consideration and respect as anybody else.

> I have distinct boundaries and never apologise for making them
> clear. (Jennifer)

Your partner trampled over your dignity and rights when he raped you; taking control of your life means weeding out others who do it you in different ways. It is healing to actively take control of situations that are eroding your self-confidence. You can say, 'No.' You can tell the other person that their advice doesn't feel OK for you. You can tell the other person how their behaviour feels for you:

- 'I feel used when you …'
- 'I feel abused when you …'
- 'I feel hurt when you …'

It is then up to them if they will change.

While you cannot change another person's behaviour, you can change how you respond to it. You can follow through by enforcing your boundaries: 'What we do needs to match what we say.'[2]

If someone continues to be hurtful, exploitative or abusive directly or indirectly by trying to control your healing and life, you can limit or end contact with them. (Of course, this strategy is more problematic with your children when particularly during adolescence, they may disregard limits and boundaries and try to dump their shame on to you.)

Here are a few more tips on boundary setting:

- Be clear and succinct.
- Tell yourself how this situation today is different from the violent one with your rapist.
- Tell yourself that asserting your wishes is not the same as being rude and selfish.
- Imagine telling the person firmly that you know what is best for you.
- Examine your fears – are you scared of anger, loss of love, or being seen as selfish?
- Consider an assertiveness-training course, or do some role-plays with a therapist.
- Do some reading on codependency. There are a slew of books out there that are devoted to boundary setting.[3]
- If there's one in your area, try a self-help support group that looks at boundary issues; for example, Alanon, CODA (Codependents Anonymous) and ACA (Adult Children of Alcoholism and Other Dysfunctional Families) are relevant 12-step programs.

If you are unable to extricate yourself from a situation or relationship or you have trouble standing up for yourself, try not to beat yourself up. Your self-esteem may have been damaged to the extent you believe that what you want doesn't matter. But your freedom will grow as you practise responding to yourself as a person whose rights and needs are as valid as anybody else's.

It's a day at a time and perhaps tomorrow or next week, you will be able to set that boundary.

Choosing to put your healing first

Another boundary or limit setting issue is that as survivors of violence, we often tend to put other people's needs ahead of our own. Possibly, your life once revolved around the abuser's needs and consequently, you always came last.

But everybody is not more important than you, and sometimes it has to be *your* turn. You may need to spend money on quality therapy. This is an investment in your future. If you live with other people, there may be times you need a little peace and quiet so you can think through some things that came up in counselling, or read and do some healing exercises. Don't be afraid to ask for this. *Insist* on it. It's really important to own some time that is yours.

If you feel guilt for being 'selfish', you may benefit from knowing that the original meaning of the word 'selfish' is 'with self'. In healing, it will be essential to be 'with self' sometimes. This is completely different from not considering anybody else at all; rather, you've discovered that your needs are at least as important as those of others, and should not be ignored. Don't worry that your children will suffer because mother needs space sometimes. Establish it as a pattern and they will get used to the idea that 'This is mother's time'. You are teaching them an important lesson for their own futures: when they need space, they will be more inclined to know that setting boundaries is okay. Also, you are replenishing your emotional reservoir so that you have something to give to those you care about.

Choosing to end isolation by reconnecting

We have seen that an effect of trauma is disconnection. You may feel unworthy of friendship, believing that if anybody truly knew you, they wouldn't like you. Perhaps you feel that you simply cannot trust anybody enough to get close to them. They may harm you or end up abandoning you. Your abuser may have sabotaged relationships, or any friends you had were mutual friends of yours and the abuser.

But if trauma is disconnection, healing involves reconnection.[4] For some of us, this means literally rejoining the human race. It means overcoming an inner sense of innate badness – shame – and developing the sense that we have a place in the world and in the scheme of humanity and fairness.

You may also be a person whom others see as strong, and because of this you are afraid that by being vulnerable or asking them for help, you will let them down. The reality often is that people who really care for you are honoured that you are able to share your pain with them. It also helps them to listen and get 'out of their own heads'.

Don't continue to deny yourself the support you deserve.

Disclosure

We are only as sick as the secrets we keep. What we keep inside continues to hurt us. You possibly feel that you could never tell anybody of the brutal or disgusting things your partner did to you. Although it is necessary to exercise choice in telling or not telling, isolation and silence will not offer any relief from shame or fear. Indeed, isolation, silence, shame and fear are the best friends of sexual violence and its wounds. Healing is better not done alone. Reminder: Be cautious about secondary wounding and test the waters first.

There are other ways of breaking the silence; for example, you could write about your experiences for a women's health newsletter. Some survivors find that breaking the silence begins with sharing with other survivors in safe and private online forums. Disclosing there may be somewhat easier since you are writing rather than face-to-face.

Let the person or people you are confiding to know what you need. For example, you can say, 'I'm wanting to get this off my chest to somebody I trust, and I'm grateful to you for listening. That's what I need.' Ask for hugs if you feel safe (if it's face to face). Tell the listener that you'd like their thoughts, or conversely, that they don't have to say anything.

Breaking the silence will give you more practice in breaking any rules around telling that the abuser may have imposed over you. In choosing to use your voice, you are once again taking back control from him.

Making friends

Making new friendships is an essential part of the healing and rebuilding process after violence.[5] You could meet new women in a support group or, like Rachel find like-minded people, when doing a course in something you have always wanted to do:

> One of my loveliest memories of reconnection is of when I trained in a group to be a court supporter of women seeking restraining orders against violent partners. Many of us were survivors and some of us had difficulty with confidence. In that intense and wonderful time, we did everything from cry on each

other's shoulders to laugh about nose-picking. The sense of bondedness was so amazing that I cried like a baby when the course was finished. I gained a glimpse of myself as others saw me – a funny, warm, trustworthy and switched-on sister who was worth having as a friend.

While it may be hard for you to believe sometimes, you are good enough for loving friendships.

Making it work for you and others

This can be an important means of reconnection. Some survivors of marital rape have said that 'making their experiences work for them' by helping others has helped them heal:[6]

> I did an internship with women survivors of domestic violence which was helpful. I have several good friends who come from similar pasts who are very helpful giving me someone to talk to. I maintain a website for sexual abuse survivors (welcometobarbados.org) where abuse issues often come up. (Nichole)

> The only good thing I've found so far is in being able to help others in the same situation by talking and listening to them. For example, recently a good friend of mine who I met over the internet through a chat room for 'survivors' wanted to kill herself – her story is similar to mine but she has only just left him – and I talked her out of it. Although I know it's a bit selfish, that has made me feel better about myself and it has also suggested to me that maybe some good can come of what my ex-partner did. (Emma)

> I guess the most positive thing has been me getting into feminist organisations. I work on the phones helping other women and I know that while I am helping others I will always be learning about myself also. (Jodie)

Think about what you would like to do. Many rape survivors build websites and share about their experiences. There are plenty of free web-hosts out there; you get to indulge in your own artistry as you build. Next time you see a judicial comment that suggests a woman raped by her partner cannot be harmed as badly as a woman raped by a stranger, you may want to write to the newspaper that reported this comment, or to the judge who actually made it. This is anger translated to action and transformed to power. You can do this with domestic violence or rape-related groups, or on your own. What you have to say and contribute is important – very much so.

Choosing a creative (and fun) healing journey

Healing does not always need to be approached as something that is heavy and dark. Parts of it can and should be *fun*. Laughter is restorative. Perhaps you have spent so much time in grief, fear and self-hatred that there has been little laughter. As you heal, you will find your sense of humour again:

> I have to kind of laugh though, because life or God or the world has taken its own revenge. She (ex-partner's current wife) told me that he has been impotent for a while. I thought, 'What revenge would I need after that?' (Sarah)

Any ridiculous trait your abuser had? Poke fun at him, and imagine him shrivelling under your withering scorn. Coin silly, ridiculing names for him.

Make up a silly song about PTSD. Make a joke about your symptoms: 'Knock knock.' 'Who's there?' 'Nobody. You just *think* there's someone there because you are hyper-vigilant.'

It is much more difficult to be scared of what we can laugh at. This does not mean laughing fear away, but it certainly can reduce its strength.

Art and writing

If you draw, paint, use sculpture, or write poetry and prose, these talents can be harnessed to help you heal.

Therapeutic writing can include keeping a journal of your daily thoughts, trials or progress in healing. You could write about a rape in as much detail as you can remember. If you write exactly what happened, including the surrounding circumstances, what he said, and how you felt, you may gain a much deeper appreciation of your actions and emotional responses. You become aware, for example, of just how threatened you felt, which can lead to less self-blame and an understanding of why certain things are triggering for you.[7]

You can also use writing to express your anger at your perpetrator. Imagine what you would like to say to him, and express it in a letter to him (not necessarily to send). It can be as cold or insulting as you like.

Adair's letter:

> All of the monsters I was afraid of as a child, I always imagined all hairy, or with sharp teeth, long, ugly nails, jumping out of my closet or hiding under my bed. I never imagined a man with beautiful black hair, and blue piercing eyes. You are a monster

of a different kind. One mommy and daddy couldn't scare away. I came to you for help and you turned on me, you RAPED ME. YOU BIT MY BREASTS. You made me SUCK your filthy cock, you PINCHED MY BREASTS. You bit my thighs. YOU RAPED ME ANALLY. YOU FUCKING PISSED ON ME!!! YOU ARE A MONSTER! A SICK BASTARD. YOU TAUGHT ME HOW TO HATE … because I HATE YOU! But I am finding my way back! I won't let you win!

NOT THIS TIME! I'M A SURVIVOR!

Summer's letter to her abuser (fragments):

… Now, I have some things I want to tell you …

You never accomplished your ultimate goal of having no other man want me. I am still beautiful, perhaps more beautiful than before. I am desirable and I am able to have wonderfully intimate moments that fulfil me and give me back some of the beauty and power of my womanhood … For each time I re-experience the pain you inflicted, I make a new memory of warmth and love. For each time I hear you I listen to something empowering, something more powerful than you. For each time that I taste you, I recall a time when oral sex was something that was shared safely and intimately in loving … I thought very early this morning that for each time your face appears in my head I am going to put you in a vehicle behind me at night, so when I look back all I can see are the lights on the car and you are invisible even if I feel like you might be there. Besides, like a friend told me yesterday, when I let the light in, my darkness fades. For each time that I touch another man your hands will burn, if nothing else in my mind. I will hold safe, warm, cuddly things in my hands and think positive thoughts. For every time I feel you touching me I will envelop myself in someone else's arms. If none are avail,able, I will be there in my mind. I let you walk and I still struggle with that – but because I did, I do not have to allow you to walk through my soul, through my mind …

Writing or pictorial art are effective ways of clearing out issues that are stuck inside you, or for expressing a particularly painful memory.

Dreamwork

In healing, you may have powerful and vivid dreams. Some of them will be frightening and traumatic, particularly with new layers of healing. However, your dreams, even the frightening ones, may carry helpful messages. Discuss your dreams with a counsellor. Record as much of them as you can remember in a dream journal. Notice common themes, people, words, songs, colours or other things that appear. It is likely that these will mean something to you.

As you move through fear, you will probably find that your dreams will depict you as having more power … and you do!

The anniversary of violence

If there was a particular date or time of year when you were raped, you may find yourself becoming anxious and distressed around then. You may also experience flashbacks or nightmares. This is called 'Anniversary Reaction' and is a common feature of PTSD.[8] Get support from a trusted friend, counsellor or your online survivor community.

Many women choose to do something good for themselves on their rape anniversaries: curl up and eat chocolate, buy that CD you've been hankering after, commune with nature. On the anniversary of her rape by a near-stranger, Jackie parachuted from a plane. Take the day back from your rapist and make it your own again.

If you don't know the anniversaries of times you were raped, it's possible that if there are days that you feel fearful or distressed for no apparent reason, an anniversary could be behind it. While you don't know the date, your psyche does. Be good to yourself. You deserve it.

Choosing self-care

Initially it may feel uncomfortable to do things to take care of you. You may need to do battle with feeling undeserving. That inner voice will get quieter as you learn to treat yourself with kindness and love.

So, when you have had a hard day dealing with your past or in living in the present, run yourself a bubble bath, sit outside and look at the garden, or talk to a friend whom you know cares about you. Don't silence or dismiss your needs any more as your partner did. When you were raped perhaps you had to 'do normal' and answer constant demands. You do not have to do so now. It's okay for you to go easy on yourself and explain to those you live with what your needs are. You don't need to be superwoman anymore. Hang up the cape!

Giving up unhealthy coping mechanisms

If you have 'coped' and 'dealt' with your feelings through abusing (or obsessing about) alcohol or other drugs, spending, eating, sex or gambling, you deserve to replace these patterns. Unhealthy coping mechanisms may be working frantically to push away the pain. Your inability to see that this is what you are doing may be contributed to by cross-addiction (switching substances or processes). Whether you are a teenager, in your 20s, 30s, 40s, 50s or older, you may for instance give up alcohol only to develop some type of eating disorder. When you lose your sense of having control over your life, controlling what goes into your body can be a coping mechanism.

Forcing yourself to vomit, spending money that you cannot afford and doing things in an altered state that you would never dream of doing if sober do not help us to build our self-esteem. In fact, they do the opposite. They feed the self-hatred that is a barrier to healing.

Accepting that you have a problem is an essential first step followed by willingness to do something about it. It's likely that you will need help beyond that decision; addiction can be 'cunning, baffling and powerful'.[9] Sometimes recovery requires detoxification and ongoing monitoring. Check your telephone book for appropriate services. You are not alone. Most communities around the world have a variety of self-help programs to help you – people who are trying a new way of living, one day at a time. If there are no groups in your area but you have an internet connection, you can participate in a cyber-self-help program.

If you are using alcohol or something else to 'medicate' feelings of pain, anger and fear, you could work on getting support to feel the feelings (see chapter 16).

Taking care of your body

Your body is a temple. Try to treat it with kindness and respect.

Sometimes, women who have been raped view their bodies as not worth demonstrating care for. We may neglect our physical or dental health, and disregard our physical needs.

Eat something good when you are hungry. Try to get adequate rest; fatigue can make it that much harder to cope with trauma. If you are cold, get warm. If you need to pee, don't wait. Cuddle up with a hot water bottle when you have menstrual cramps. If you have a broken underwire in your bra that pokes and hurts your breast, stop wearing it. Go and buy yourself a good new bra and make it a better quality one!

Pick a form of exercise you enjoy, and do it regularly. It can help you to get in touch with your body and be comfortable in it. It can serve as *your* time to be doing something for *you* plus depending on the type of exercise you choose, it can be a connector to the outside world and a way of making friends.

If your body has been misused and violated, that is all the more reason to care for it now. Listen to it and treat it with more regard than your abuser did.

Listening to music

Do you like music? Are there songs that lift you up, help you feel more powerful, or alternately comfort and calm you? Songs that make you feel good as a woman are terrific. Many survivors of rape love Tori Amos – not only because she is a marvellous, strong and sensual performer, but also because she has made a sexual assault in her history work for her and others.

If you don't already know what works for you, you may like to experiment with different types of music. Burn yourself some compilations for specific moods.

Playing

In healing, you may experience times when working through your rape and other abuse experiences seems to preoccupy you most of the time. You will benefit from balancing this with family activities, socialising, study, or just plain fun. Be sure to take time out to do things you really enjoy. Go for a walk or jog and get the double benefit of exercise and the great outdoors. Watch comedies with your kids, spouse or friends. Play.

Not actively being with your traumas at all times doesn't mean you aren't still healing; it just means that trauma work is not all-encompassing. Take those breaks. You've earned them.

Positive self-talk

Reclaiming a positive view of yourself is hard work.

> I am slowly beginning to acknowledge and embrace my good qualities – but I will say it takes incredible effort not to get stuck back in my old feelings. It is a daily challenge for me to stay focused on the positive and not revert back to the negatives. (Summer)

You may be giving your rapist and other perpetrators in your life space in your head rent-free! As a consequence, you may speak to yourself as they did – far more unkindly and harshly than you would talk to anyone else.

Here's a simple action you can take. Imagine that your brain is a car radio. When those self-deprecating and toxic voices are 'on', reach over metaphorically and change the station. Practice talking to yourself as you would to a dear friend or to your child – with love.

Also, try to become aware of 'all or nothing' thinking. 'My healing sucks!' 'I'm the worst.' 'I'll never get better.' This is a relic of living with abuse. You can change your thinking patterns. Awareness is the key.

Another positive step is to develop a list of the things that you feel good about yourself. How about strengths that you have? Do you cook well, have a good sense of humour, personality trait, or a physical feature you like about yourself? Have you achieved something terrific? On that last, you can start with your survival. As you heal, the list will grow, and in times of self-doubt, you can remind yourself of your positive attributes.

So much of healing is learning to accept ourselves, warts and all. We are neither saints nor demons, just human beings.

Other positive steps

We have read about the control that violent partners have exerted. While in the relationships, some of us were not allowed to study or fulfil occupational or other dreams. Making decisions like Eva Jane, Adair, Jodie and Linda, Helena, Rachel and Natalie to do further study can be self-actualising and help to repair the flawed sense of self:

> I guess the first really piece of life that gave me some self-esteem was passing the Uni entrance course. Then I studied Information Management as a major and I did History as a second. (Eva Jane)

You can make other life choices that are positive. Just making the decision can be empowering and therefore a plus in healing. Thus, Tiffany decided to move from the US to Australia, Charlotte to travel around the world and Kate and Natalie to get divorced from a subsequent (abusive) partner.

Choosing to respect yourself and your process

Our survival in a violent relationship often involves trying desperately to have control in a situation where tragically we have none. We walk on eggshells, tiptoeing around the abuser (unconsciously) believing that if only we can be the perfect woman, wife, mother, person, he won't be violent. When he is, we then feel responsible deep inside. And the core of shame expands.

As we take our healing journey, we may impose the same ideals of perfection on ourselves and similar tapes play in our heads. 'Now,' we say to ourselves, 'I really am making choices and so they *should* be the right ones!' For some of us, also there is urgency to healing. We want to get through the problems so that we can have a better quality of life. We become frustrated then when emotions recycle and ashamed that our healing seems to be retarded in contrast to others we know. What we thought were well-constructed boundaries one day appear either as walls or non-existent the next. The idea of taking care of ourselves is ludicrous at those times – the critic (abuser) within says we don't deserve it.

Easy does it. Be gentle with yourself. You are doing the best that you can and that's enough. Remember that when you are comparing your progress to others, you are comparing your 'insides' to their 'outsides'. Of course they look a lot better!

Healing cannot be rushed. Certainly, with practice and experience, some problems become easier to get on top of. But it does take time, particularly if you have been exposed to repeated and severe abuse. Rather than getting frustrated at what seems to be an endless process, remind yourself that healing often happens in layers.

Survivor: 'I just want to get on with my life.'

Counsellor: 'Healing *is* getting on with the rest of your life.'

CHAPTER 18

Relationships after Partner Rape

The most important part of a relationship is for you to be safe and to feel safe. This chapter provides some strategies for ensuring that safety. The material is intended both for women who are no longer with their perpetrator partner and for those who are still with the partner who raped them. It's designed to help you to determine whether you are safe or not. Security, trust and intimacy are closely related, for only when safety has been reasonably established, can the trust that fosters intimacy grow.

In addition to safety, another important component for a healthy relationship is to have a partner who is able to be there emotionally for you and capable of intimacy. We'll explore what that means so that you know what to look for, expect and deserve.

Another ingredient in the positive partnership recipe is you. In earlier chapters, we have seen that great damage is often sustained by survivors of partner rape in the areas of trust in men, love and relationships. Your healing is therefore an important part of being able to be a part of a functional relationship.

> Unfinished business, unresolved anger, blocks to our past and thus blocks to us, prevent intimacy. If we haven't tackled our historical work, if our old messages are driving us, we may be unable to attain intimacy and closeness.[1]

We will look at some of our old survival thinking and acting patterns and how you can change them and develop healthy ways of being and responding in a relationship.

There is a definite message of hope in these pages. If you live with fear and mistrust or believe that you can never have a loving relationship, we hope that you will come to believe that some resolution of these issues is possible.

Making choices

We have seen that healing is about taking back the power in our lives as decision-makers. When we were living with violence, life happened to us; we were victims. Now we have the freedom to choose what steps we are going to take; this includes in the context of relationships.

Same sex or heterosexual

One choice made by some survivors is to identify as lesbian or bisexual and find a same-sex partner. The underlying motives are probably multifaceted as Helena discusses next; perhaps having experienced rape by a male partner, the idea of intimacy with another man is abhorrent. Some women have always gravitated towards other women but were in denial.

> I've always identified as bisexual but I'd never acted in or participated in a same sex relationship before. When I moved here my main friend was a lesbian who introduced me to people. There was one particular friend of hers, Tania, and we got on really well, and she kept visiting me and supporting me, and just kind of taking me out. She'd say, 'Come on. Let's go out. You need time off.' … Then a year and a half later something just kind of happened with me. I turned to Tania and I thought, 'Who is this person. She's amazing, and I really like her.' I guess I kind of felt like I'd hurdled something and she was there. She was right in front of me the whole time, and it was the same for her. It did make me question what it is now that has made me see a woman in that way and fall in love with her. Is it because she is a mind that I've fallen in love with, or is it because she's not male? I think the answer to that question is that I've fallen in love with her mind, and the sexuality of someone doesn't matter to me, and it never has.

If you do choose to have a lesbian relationship, be aware that sexual, physical and emotional abuse can take place. Therefore, much of the material below on safety should also apply to potential lesbian partners – you can switch the 'hes' for 'shes'.

Choosing whether to have a relationship

As we saw in the last chapter, taking control of one's life is an extremely important part of recovery from rape. If you came from a violent relationship, it is possible that you experienced a world that could change suddenly and be blown apart in ways that you had no control over. It's natural that you will want to maintain control over your life now.

> I can get to a certain point and then I get panicked because what
> if I get in a relationship and they rip me off, or what if I get in a
> relationship and they reject me? It was 1991 when I got married.
> I was married for two years so that's 1993. So let's call it ten
> years plus and the baggage is still very much a barrier. (Sarah)

Because your experiences of partner rape may have left you afraid to get
to close to somebody, you will need to observe whether you push people
away when they get close. This is not choice-making.

Perhaps you are seeing somebody to whom you feel as if you would *like* to
commit, but fear of the unknown (or your instinct as discussed later below)
pulls you back from doing so. It may help you to take your dilemma to a
counsellor who has worked with abused women. He or she can help you
weigh up the pros and cons and make a choice.

You may have friends or family who believe outmoded ideas about a
woman needing a man and who tell you that 'the best way to get over one
man is in another man's arms'. They may say things that minimise the
violence like, 'Oh, come on, I know you've had an awful time but you
can't let that turn you off men forever.' Be firm with such people about
what *you* need. As a survivor of partner rape, you've been hurt badly. You
need time to achieve a degree of healing. It's your right to take the thought
of another relationship just as slowly as you need to.

On the subject of making choices, we must note that some women who
leave abusive relationships grow to love their new-found independence so
much that another relationship feels like the last thing they want or need
right now. As Tracey shows, this can be an empowering and affirming
choice – it does not need to be 'healed':

> I'm quite happy to not have a relationship for a very long time,
> thank you very much, even though I've got the emotional scars.
> I just want to get on with my life. I don't need a man to feel like
> my life is complete. I'm quite happy just to be me for a while
> and leave it at that.

Safety in future relationships

For any woman entering a new relationship, determining safety is a
practical issue. Whether you are a woman who cannot trust at all, or one
who has given trust before it was deserved, you may be confused about
what is safe or unsafe. Here are some pointers as to how safety may be
determined.

Let's look at dating first. Here are some precautions you can take until you know your date better:[2]

- Don't have a date for dinner alone at his home or yours, but in a restaurant or other public venue.

- If your date has suggested doing something that you are not comfortable with, decline by suggesting an alternative. Think ahead of time about options that feel safe to you.

- Arrange for your own transport to and from the date venue; ideally, directly from the venue and not from an out-of-the-way car park that requires him to walk you there.

- Have sufficient money to pay for transport home.

- Have a mobile (cell) phone with you.

- Drink moderately and not to the extent that your judgment may be impaired. Also, observe whether he has a tendency to drink too much.

- Keep an eye on your drink until you've finished it – this guards against the possibility of drink spiking.

- If you've met his friends, what are they like? Do they seem like 'meatheads' who regard women as conquests? Does he seem to share that view?

- Use the first few dates to make observations about him. Does he want to control everything? Is he crude or denigrating about women? Emotionally immature and clingy? Or do you believe that this is a person who respects your opinions and your boundaries?

- Trust your gut. If you feel that something isn't right, it probably isn't.

- Maintain your independence and insist on paying your way. This will knock on the head any sense he may have of being entitled to sex because he paid for the date (though even if he does pay, this doesn't mean he is entitled to sex – or that he has the right to become hostile and commit a crime against you).

- If you feel any sense of danger at any time during the date, remember that you do not have to be afraid of his response and you are not being rude if you terminate the 'date'. The importance of your safety far outweighs etiquette.

It's a question of balance. While you don't want to be nervous that every date is a potential rapist or ruin your time out with hyper-vigilance, neither should you automatically assume safety.

Testing the waters: take stock of red flags

Once you are past the first few dates, and are thinking about actually having a relationship with someone, you can be attuned to signs of abusive personality characteristics or behaviours. Please remember though that such traits aren't always apparent at the outset of a relationship. Some men are better than others at covering up abusive tendencies. Plus, partners who don't appear to be abusive in other ways can rape.

One domestic violence counsellor offers this advice to abused women entering new relationships:

> I tell them to test the waters. Does the man want to make all the decisions? Does he tell her what to wear? Is he jealous about the time she spends with friends? If so, she will need to remind herself that this is not romantic – as it can initially seem – but it suggests that he is controlling, and may become sexually coercive or physically violent.

Start looking for 'red flags' by asking yourself the following questions:[3]

- Are my values violated in this relationship?
- Am I afraid of how this person will act with my children?
- Does my helping this person hurt me?
- Do I find myself doing things I truly do not want to do?
- Am I ever in fear in this relationship?
- Does this person touch me when I do not want to be touched?
- Do I doubt my abilities when I am with this person?
- Does this person keep me from my friends and other interests?
- Do we argue and disagree too often?
- Does this person respond disrespectfully to my wishes?
- Does this person trigger old sexual assault memories?
- Does he continue to do something that I told him was a trigger?
- Has this person used my confidences about past rapes as a weapon against me and/or did he respond in a way critical of me?

If you answered yes to any of these questions, it's *possible* that your new partner is showing signs of inappropriate control and emotional abuse.

There are other danger signs. Ann Jones, who has written about domestic violence, warns women to:

> Stay away from a man who disrespects any woman, who wants or needs you intensely or exclusively, and who has a knack for

getting his own way almost all the time. Any of the above should put you on guard. And if, when you back off, he turns on the solid gold charm, keep backing.[4]

Indeed, making you the centre of his world can suggests instability and dependency – and the potential for danger if he is thwarted.

How he deals with boundaries that you set will be another possible indicator. If you make it clear to him that you want to spend your Sundays alone or with your children, yet he calls incessantly or comes over unannounced, he is not respecting your boundaries and this does not bode well.

Also, be cautious of a man who says, 'Trust me.' If he insists early in a relationship that you can, should or must trust him, and acts slighted when you don't, you may feel confused about whether he can really be trusted, and feel badly for doubting him. However, a man who truly cares for you, and who is emotionally healthy, will not try to strong-arm you into trust that you are not ready for. *Trust must be earned.* Even if the potential new partner seems very nice, there need to be other signs of safety since there are abusers who initially present as 'nice guys'.

If you have children, watch for 'red flags' in his contact with them. For instance, an abusive man may pretend that he likes your kids in order to impress you but you may have a gut feeling that says otherwise. Be alert for signs of jealousy of the time you spend with them, or accusations that you are 'spoiling them' because you disagree with his ideas of punishment.

He hasn't had a relationship with your children; like any other relationship, it will have to be built. He shouldn't try to fill a father role immediately, but should treat your children in an appropriately friendly and respectful manner. In time, he may, as with Melina's second husband, fulfil the role of Dad.

> Sonja does most certainly have a father. She adopted her step-father as her father herself when she was a baby of 20 months. And he couldn't be more devoted or loving a father either – she has good taste!

Red alert: thoughts and feelings that can compromise your safety

You may have developed certain ways of thinking and reacting that are the result of past victimisation and its relics. As you will see next, some of these thought patterns can compromise your safety. However, once again, awareness is the key. If you identify with any of them, you do have the power to change the self-talk, which will then change the thinking.

'It's relatively better.' Sometimes, a woman who has been physically and/ or sexually abused thinks that despite signs of emotional abuse, the fact that the next man doesn't hit her means he's safe: 'At least he doesn't get physical. I'm lucky this time.'

You don't deserve though to be abused in *any* way, and if you are being controlled, you may still be in danger. Don't ignore control or emotional, financial and social abuse just because they aren't followed up by hitting or don't seem as drastic as the violence you experienced in your last relationship.

The same principle applies to sexual coercion. If you were violently raped by your last partner, and a new partner uses interpersonal coercion (see chapter 2) when you don't want to be sexual, you may believe that it is not as bad as your earlier experience. Rape is rape though and as we've seen in numerous chapters, victims are affected whether there is physical force or interpersonal coercion.

'I don't deserve decent treatment from a man.' Thoughts like this are not statements of truth; they are signs that your self-esteem needs some improvement. When asked what she would say to her rapist-partner if she could, Justine's answer was, 'Fuck off – I deserve better.' She does indeed, and so do you. Give yourself time to heal, and with more self-acceptance and self-love, you'll be drawn to people who treat you with respect and dignity.

'I desperately need a man to want me.' You may feel so unlovable and empty inside because of a past partner's abuse that you almost crave a 'romance fix'. Affection or attention from a man makes you feel a little better about yourself for a while. That's OK up to a point – many of us like compliments; it's nice to have our egos stroked occasionally. Remember though that trust must be earned. If you are very lonely and feel a lack of warmth in your life, be careful about heading into the arms of another man before you've taken the time to establish that you are safe.

'If I sense it, it can't be right.' If something doesn't feel comfortable in the relationship, it would be wise for you to take a step back and re-think.

A common problem for survivors is that although we may sense something is wrong, we get into self-doubt because of our past abuse. If you have any doubts about your safety with someone, please try, like Emma, not to dismiss your concerns as paranoia:

> I had a brief romance with a lad in halls here at uni – he'd had
> a lot to drink on this particular night, and when it came down to

it he couldn't perform. He was very frustrated, naturally, but he reacted by slamming his fist down on the pillow, inches from my face. I have not returned to his bed.

Your last relationship can be your teacher. You will know control and abuse when you experience them. Don't belittle that knowledge – it has been won at great expense. Make it serve you.

Contributions to a 'healthy' relationship

After having been hurt by a partner, perhaps for a long time, or by more than one partner, you may find the land of love and respect a strange one whose language you don't understand. You are vigilant, waiting for it to be ripped away from you, almost as if you aren't allowed to relax and enjoy something wonderful. Sometimes, you may feel like you want to sabotage the relationship because you are sure it will go sour anyhow. Continue to work on your self-esteem and your ability to accept healthy love will increase. In healing, you are likely to develop a deeper sense of your positive qualities, and to know that you don't deserve ill-treatment. This will give you deeper conviction about the types of treatment that you will not be prepared to tolerate. There's a continuum of course; relationships, like everything else, are not 'all or nothing': healthy or sick. One sign, though, of health in a relationship is lack of inertia and a commitment to working on problems as they arise.

We can never truly know what will or won't happen in the future, or even if someone initially appears safe, how long he will remain that way. However, sufficient safety can take place for a survivor to open herself to trusting and loving again. It's a fact, and an encouraging one, that survivors of partner rape do go on to have caring, safe relationships with men.

Here are just some of the things you can look forward to and expect from a non-abusive partner, from yourself and in the dynamics of the relationship.

What you look for and expect from your partner[6]

He's non-threatening. He talks and acts so that you feel safe and comfortable doing and saying things.

He's respectful. He listens to you non-judgmentally and is emotionally affirming and understanding. He values your opinions and gives you space.

He's supportive of you as a person. He supports your goals in life. He also respects your right to your own feelings, friends, activities and opinions.

He's accountable for himself. He accepts responsibility for himself and will admit being wrong when it's appropriate.

He's responsible but not controlling in family decisions. He's open to discussion about the day-to-day and the major event decisions that you need to make together.

He shares in parenting. He shares parental responsibilities, acting as a positive, non-violent role model for children.

He shares the domestic workload. He agrees on a fair distribution of labour.

He's respectful sexually. He doesn't force sex or pressure on you for sex before you are ready. He understands and respects that you will not always want sex when he does and does not withdraw affection if you refuse to have sex.

If you find a partner that fulfils all of these attributes *all* of the time, you may be eligible for the *Guinness Book of World Records*. Just as we are neither saints nor perfect, so too our partners. Remember the continuum and that real life does involve ups and downs. If he has shown himself to be trustworthy and you have learned to feel safe around him, then he's doing something right!

Changing what you can – yourself

We have survived the most horrific attacks on our very core. As we know, these leave their calling card on our personalities and behaviour. Hopefully, you are somewhere on a healing journey and through that process the effects of violence on your self-esteem and actions are waning. Unfortunately though, healing is a process and we don't graduate. Many 'survival tools' of thinking and behaving in the violent relationship often recycle. It's good to recognise when the old tapes start to play and replace them with the following practices in order to be a part of a healthy partnership.

We work on detaching. In the last chapter, we acknowledged that an artefact of living in abuse is trying to maintain control (of just about everything, including partners). Some survivors go into chronic 'people pleaser' mode to avoid abuse, learning to be a mind-reader and anticipate every need and want before the partner even knows he has them!

Just like our ex-partner's control, these survival behaviours, although not violent or abusive, are not conducive to intimacy. Adair wisely and honestly acknowledges her control issues, and seeks help for them:

> I am hard to please ... my way or the highway and I am trying to ease up through counselling.

Perhaps you too may benefit from some help in relaxing control and caretaking behaviours that are harming your relationship.[6]

We learn to trust. Trust is a huge issue for those of us who were betrayed within what we undoubtedly had hoped was a secure space. Telling about your past abusive relationship will be an important part of building trust:

> I am currently in a wonderful relationship, he is very empathic and understanding of my rape. We can discuss it openly and honestly. He hurts for me. It makes him angry that he didn't know me when the rape occurred, because he says he'd have gone after the asshole. (Adair)

You may find that you 'test' your new partner to see if he will betray or hurt you too. As you trust, you are more likely to relax and stop testing him.

We deal with triggers without dumping on our partner. Some triggers are unavoidable, and suddenly you feel sick, angry or scared. It's a good idea to try and calm yourself down before you speak to your partner so that you don't end up lashing out at him. If you know what the trigger is, and that whatever he did was unintentional, explain it to him. Is the trigger something that can be avoided without too much trouble, or is it one that is better being faced and defused?

You don't want to let the triggered feelings dictate a helplessly fearful response to the present situation. Acknowledge that what has happened is triggering, get support if you need it, but then address the issue behind the trigger.

We set boundaries and expect them to be respected. After having a partner who trampled all over your boundaries or responded with violence when you tried to set them, you may be frightened of asserting clear limits with future partners. But doing so will help you heal and strengthen yourself so that there is less chance you will be walked on. Pick a boundary you'd like to set, and give yourself a loving nudge to do it. It can be anything from what type of touching you will or won't allow, to asking him to stop calling you a pet name you hate. You have the right to set these limits and to have them respected.

We maintain some independence. There is little doubt that financial and other dependence on a man increases the entrapment of women who are being abused. Keep your own money at least in the early days of the relationship, and do not give up your dwelling to live with your new partner until you feel ready, if at all. If you own your own home, and you sell up to merge with your partner, make sure there is equal decision-making capacity, and that your name is alongside his on any property purchased.

Be sure to maintain social independence. Keep seeing your own friends, maintain contact with family and continue to pursue interests that don't include him.

We see ourselves as equals. You are an adult of the same standing to any other person. Any idea you have that the man 'should' take charge, or that you should have sex when he wants it, needs to be challenged. Take stock of what myths about men and women and about control or sex that you may have internalised.

If you are lucky to have a good person in your life, remember, *he's lucky to have you too.* Value yourself as an equal, for that is what you *are*. This knowledge can take some time to integrate, but just keep practising. A sense of one's rights can be empowering.

Communicating happily ever after ... ?

You are not two halves forming a whole but two wholes forming a partnership.

In any good relationship, there will be some healthy dependency on each other. Neither person is dependent in an unhealthy way; both have their boundaries and respect each other's. Positive dependency means knowing that you can depend on the other to keep promises, listen to you, or not touch you when you don't want to be touched. With interdependency, each partner has awareness that they can depend on one another for support, care and friendship. The giving isn't one-sided. No one is expected to know intuitively what the other needs or wants but is open to listening and responding. So, honesty and communication are necessary in developing interdependency.

Mutual trust, deepening intimacy and a sense of harmony with your partner will be the fruits of good dependency, or interdependency.

No relationship is perfect, though. Healthy relationships do tend to involve conflict. Let's face it: men are from Mars and women are from Venus. An example: many men will look at a kitchen and actually see it as clean; women look at the same room and see the dirty dishes waiting to be loaded into the dishwasher, the dish drainer needing to be emptied and the loaf of bread on the counter-top. When you live with someone who actually is perceiving the world differently from you, disagreement is not just inevitable but is healthy. Living happily ever after means safety from physical, sexual and emotional violence but it doesn't mean an absence of disagreement or acrimony.

If and when you decide to enter a new relationship, we hope it will be loving and safe with none of the fear and oppression you have experienced in the past. If you take things slowly and bear in mind that trust must be earned and learned, it may be possible for you to see that being hurt in another relationship does not have to be an absolute given. This is what you deserve.

Because sexuality is both an area of damage for survivors of partner rape, and an important part of relationships, this will be addressed in the next chapter.

Sexuality after Partner Rape[1]

Rape survivors often experience problems with sexuality. Those of us sexually assaulted by a partner may face special areas of confusion and self-loathing given that the violation has come from somebody who was supposed to care for and value us.

Women who have been sexually abused often, through no fault of their own, come to view sex in a certain way: as uncontrollable, hurtful, secretive, as a commodity and having no moral boundaries.[2] These attributes are true of *rape* – but not *sex*. Some survivors have trouble differentiating between the two, though. Jodie came to see sex as something separate from caring while Nichole, as we saw in chapter 9, was terrified of sex with a *caring* partner and saw sex as a punishment.

The possible effects on you as a sexual being that are presented in this chapter may seem insurmountable but, with healing and energy, and by integrating the ideas that are provided in these pages, you can do a lot of work in overcoming them.

> I got remarried three years later to Samuel, a person in the same church. With him, there were periods of very satisfying sexual times, and I was astonished by that, because it was the first time I'd ever experienced sex as a pleasurable thing, and I couldn't get over it. (Kate)

Gentleness and patience are needed, though.

> It's taken me ages to enjoy sex, and in fact, I have had to re-educate myself on what sex actually is. And now, I am kinda enjoying it! (Charlotte)

> Even though I made great strides in healing in other areas, I still could not imagine that there would come a day when I would view sex with real desire, and myself as a sexy woman who no longer needed to feel shame and fear. But that day did come

– after commitment to hard work. I say to survivors who believe
there is no way to recover sexually, that it is possible. (Rachel)

A counsellor trained in assisting survivors through the sexual impact of
rape, will be able to help you identify triggers, deal with hurt, and reframe
yourself and your body in your own terms rather than the abuser's.
Contact your local rape crisis centre for the name of a therapist who has
done productive work with survivors. The internet may provide lists of
reputable counsellors in the field.

The effects of partner rape on you as a sexual being

You may feel upset, frightened or ashamed if you identify with the
thinking and behaviour patterns described next. Remember that these are
an outgrowth of sexual violence, and many survivors experience them.
You are neither to blame nor alone.

Automatic reactions

These are feelings, both physical and emotional, and thoughts that may
inundate us when having sex, thinking about sex, or even just when dating.
Automatic reactions may last from seconds to hours, and can trigger other
reactions. They may include:[3]

- Intrusive thoughts and flashbacks of the rape triggered by touch
  or sound.
- Flare-ups of beliefs about sex, i.e. that you'll be punished if you
  don't say yes.
- Instant fear, shame, or 'dirtiness' when touched in a certain way.
- Conversely, a numbness when confronted by sex, very little
  feeling.
- Sexual arousal that simultaneously causes fear and panic with
  shortness of breath, dizziness and shaking. You may experience
  sexual arousal when somebody reminds you of the abuser or at
  reminders of the abuse itself.
- 'Body memories', for instance, the thought or the act of oral sex
  on a man makes you gag even if it is happening gently. Or:

  > I unconsciously contract my vaginal muscles while engaged in
  > sex. I only know this through my partner though – somehow
  > it must be extremely noticeable or perhaps enjoyable on
  > his part because he has mentioned it. I think he thinks that
  > I am intentionally doing this although that isn't the case; it
  > seems to be more of an unconscious response to penetration.
  > (Summer)

Self-injury

Self-injury can be expressed through certain sexual practices. You may masturbate to abusive fantasies, ask people to hurt you in the course of sex, or have indiscriminate sex with people who don't care about you. There may be a compulsive, driven sense around these behaviours. You may find that when participating in them, you have a detached or numb sort of feeling.

As a sex worker who specialises in group sex and rape fantasy, Kelly is not only emotionally self-injuring but has also been seriously harmed physically:

> What I find is that I actually give service. I go above and beyond to satisfy the man sexually. There is no laying around; there is no sitting there and taking it. I give, and I'm hard when I need to be, and I'm soft when I need to be – certainly very perceptive, very professional. When I walk into an intro I have to be able – which is where a lot of girls go wrong – to know what that man is there for, so I can play up to it straight away; so I can convert it to a job. I have to know if he wants affection, or whether he is looking for a bit of sex or fetish or whatever.
>
> I go very well with the fetish and rape fantasies. I do group bookings of up to 20 men, where I will be fucked for an hour by 20 men. This happened a couple of weeks ago at a buck's party and they said at the Gilmore clinic it's probably worse than any rape case they've ever seen. I was split in my episiotomy. I was bleeding cervically for two weeks afterwards. I've only just stopped bleeding now. I was so swollen, they couldn't give me an internal; it took about a week for the swelling to go down. I was so ripped and torn that it was such a mess that they actually didn't know for the first week where the bleeding was coming from.
>
> But I am unable to feel pain there while the service is happening. I feel the pain but all of a sudden it is transformed to knowing if you ease off now it's going to take longer. You've got to get hard, so for me I go harder, and the more it hurts the harder I go, or the more full on, or the deeper down the throat. The only thing I cannot do is anal – and that's probably since for me, it would tip me over the edge pain-wise. I don't know, it's just something I'm really scared of.
>
> I do like the group bookings, because I have the personality that

carries them. Certainly in that sense I find they go faster, and are more interesting. I'm finding it harder and harder to pretend to be affectionate, so I'm finding it easier to go with bookings that are more about fetish and more about rape.

You may have come to believe that sexual abuse is part of being *loved*. This is understandable and a sad legacy of partner rape. But unless you take steps to change, you will continue to suffer pain. Indiscriminate and unsafe sex practices make you vulnerable to STDs, including life-threatening ones such as HIV/AIDS. You deserve much better than that.

Other behaviours that deny or harm your sexual being

Using sex as a commodity. Perhaps your abusive partner was only nice to you in the course of sex, so now, you see sex as the only way to receive affection. Or, you learned that you had to make yourself sexually available in order to avoid anger. Having sex in the hope that you will be loved may have led to feelings of exploitation and disappointment.

Avoiding sex and intimacy. You may, like some partner rape survivors, feel able to be sexual only outside intimacy because you believe that the less you care, the less likely you are to be hurt if something goes wrong.

> I suffer strong feelings of loss in my intimacy yet I am able to go through the physical motions and actually find pleasure and enjoyment in those moments. What I think I may be lacking is the emotional tie, the bond, the attachment that comes with trust. It is bothersome in that I feel like I can have the physical part without the need for the emotional involvement – that somehow it is even safer that way. (Summer)

Avoiding relationships or sex. You may resist relationships because you don't want to have to be sexual. Or, if you are in a relationship, you resist situations where sexual approaches may happen, such as staying up until your partner has gone to sleep.

Numbing out. You may have deadened your feelings in order to protect yourself during rape or other inconsiderate, abusive sexual behaviour. While this was adaptive then, it's a major barrier to establishing intimacy in a non-violent relationship.

Using sex to hurt others. Sometimes, the anger, revulsion and scarring caused by rape and betrayal can contribute to projecting them onto other people in hurtful ways. Some examples are having affairs or saying sexually denigrating or personally offensive things to your partner.[4] These behaviours may contribute to your self-hatred.

On to healing

Favourable relationship conditions

As we have said elsewhere, current sexual abuse by a partner isn't conducive to healing since you are exposed to the same environment that caused the original damage. Also, you need to feel safe since a part of sexual healing is about recovering the ability for intimacy – emotional closeness and caring that is more than connection of bodies. If you are unsafe and cannot trust your partner, you will naturally find intimacy difficult if not impossible to foster:

> I tend to hide in a shell when I feel I am threatened, emotionally or otherwise, and Harry's need for control and dominance, and his dependence on me played itself out in the bedroom as well as our daily life. I was afraid to voice my concerns or displeasure for fear of repercussions, I knew sex could be used as a weapon. But, I was able to stand my ground at times, although he never did respect my boundaries for any length of time, and I eventually gave up trying to get my emotional needs met and instead withdrew inside myself when we made love. (Natalie)

Aside from sexual assault, there are other behaviours by your partner that are unfavourable to healing. For example, pressuring you to speed up your recovery is likely to replicate the dynamics of sexual abuse. Remember that you cannot be rushed through healing. Your partner should not take it upon himself to 'get you over' your fear of sex.

> He requested anal, under some sort of pretext, I think he had decided I ought to get over my phobia – I couldn't bear to be touched in that area. He told me he'd read an article about how good it could be, as long as you used enough lubrication. So he smeared on the Vaseline, and I felt unable to say no. I wasn't in control, I was scared by the repetition. (Emma)

Also be careful that all the sexual problems and the responsibility for fixing them are not heaped on you because you are the abuse survivor. A family therapist told one of us that men often come to counselling with their survivor-partners saying, 'She doesn't like sex.' The counsellor's reply where appropriate is, 'Perhaps it's the sex she's having that she doesn't like.' There may be coercion or physical inconsideration – behaviours that *any* woman, let alone a rape survivor, could not be expected to like. So, changing dysfunctional patterns often involves work by both you and your partner.

Remember that sexual healing is for *you*. You don't need to be in a relationship to reclaim your sexual sense of yourself. Whether you choose to share the process with another person, male or like Helena, female, is up to you.

> I can't help but wonder whether subconsciously I can ever be intimate with a man like that again, and that I've just compensated for that and just kind of shifted, and moved into a different direction.

Mastering automatic reactions

Here's a four-step approach to getting control over sexual automatic reactions:[5]

Becoming aware of triggers. When you find yourself experiencing sudden or irrational feelings, stop and acknowledge them. Is it a trigger to past sexual abuse? Try to determine what triggered it. Some survivors experience a trigger and then disassociate before they have time to be aware of what the trigger was. Try to catch your triggers before numbing out.

While you won't always be able to avoid triggers, there are things you can do to make current and future sexual activity distinct from the sexual violence. This may give you a greater sense of control.

> When you do feel ready to be intimate, the sexual activity should be as different from the rape as it can possibly be. Engage in different sexual behaviour, different positions. If you were raped in the dark, keep the lights on. Focus on his face and constantly remind yourself whom you are with. As difficult as it may be, talk with him beforehand, and let him know where not to touch you, what not to do. Also get assurance from him that he will stop when you ask, should you feel threatened-that he will allow you to be in control of what you do and do not do sexually. If you feel uncomfortable, say so. A caring partner will respect your wishes.[6]

Calm yourself. Tune into your body. What are you feeling? Remind yourself that the trauma isn't happening now. Focus on your breathing. Do something calming.

Affirm your present reality. When your partner assaulted you, your rights were taken away. Now you do have the right to say no or yes, and to be respected. Remind yourself. Recognise that your body belongs to you. Tell yourself that this is now, and now does not hold the same dangers for you.

Choose a new response. You can learn to respond differently. Make a list of responses you can cultivate, or discuss strategies with your counsellor, if you have one.

For instance, practise remaining present. As with any automatic reaction, ask yourself what triggered you to space out or float away? If it's a certain touch or word, speak to your partner about not doing it anymore, or doing things differently.

Notice what is happening with your body. How does it feel? Where are your partner's hands? Do you like them there, or would you rather they were elsewhere? What are your emotions doing? Do you want to *stop*? If you have sexually dissociated for a long time, you'll probably need to work hard at 'reassociating' yourself with sex, your feelings both physical and emotional, and the feel of your partner close to you.

Creating new meanings for sex and your sexuality

Here are some suggestions for creating ideas and meanings about sex that overturn messages imposed upon sex by sexual abuse (and by our society):[7]

Avoid exposure to things that reinforce the sexual abuse mind-set. Be discriminating about television programs, films, books, magazines, websites and other media forms that portray sex as sexual abuse or sexual violence as erotic.

Use new language when referring to sex. If your partner used degrading language for both sex and your body, you may have adopted these descriptions. If you took on a view of sex as dirty, or as just an altogether unpleasant business, you may be caught in a vicious cycle whereby your experiences influence your language, and the language continually reinforces the perception. Give your sexual body parts their correct names or choose your own terminology for them.

Discover more about your sexual attitudes. Make two lists: one for how you see sex, and the other for how you *want* to see it. You can also draw or paint them. What different views do you think you'd have about sex if you hadn't been abused?

You'll need to challenge any social messages (that control women's sexuality) you may have internalised, such as, 'Nice girls aren't openly sexy and if they are, they are inviting rape', or 'Liking sex is dirty'. Sexual healing means rejecting messages such as these and substituting them with new ones such as, 'Sexual desire in either sex is healthy and wonderful. I have a right to be a woman in the fullest sense. My sexuality is not inviting rape.'

Gentle challenges to what we have held to be true about sex can result in positive change.

Learn more about healthy sex. Do you have friends who do not seem to be ashamed of their sexuality? Are you part of a survivor support group, or do you know a survivor who has done some sexual healing? They may be helpful for you to discuss the difference between abusive and non-abusive sex with.

Read books, articles and websites that portray sex as healthy, loving and non-threatening.

Awakening sexual interest

At a certain stage of your healing, you will come to know when you are ready to get in touch with your desires. It may be an extremely emotional time, because your vulnerabilities are laid bare, and the fear that you are opening yourself to more hurt surfaces. To decrease your fear and increase your sense of control, it is good to establish two ground rules that 'relieve interpersonal strain and sexual pressure':

1. Expressing an interest in sex is not a commitment to sexual activity.

2. Declining sex is not an absolute rejection.[8]

As you experience ongoing safe touch and sex, those fears are likely to decrease.

Creating new experiences with touch

If you have suffered a lot of touch and sex that was brutal and abusive, your body may have become used to receiving it that way. Positive touch will be a profound *relearning* experience for you.

Make time to explore touch. You may want to begin by touching *yourself* in ways that feel good, gentle or erotic. Perhaps masturbation was used against you in an abusive way and you may find that it is inseparable from abusive fantasies. However, self-pleasuring can be part of learning to be loving with your body now.

When you feel ready, you may want to lie close to your partner and explore touch. Try to maintain awareness of how something feels for you both physically and emotionally.

Such touching does not have to lead to sexual intercourse if you don't want it to. You can say, 'Let's stop please', at any time.

For some years, I found that I often became scared or defensively prickly when my partner so much as wanted a hug. I saw all physical affection as a prelude to sex, and because I didn't want sex, I rejected physical affection. As I healed sexually and talked this over with my partner instead of becoming defensive, it became possible to have hugs and other exchanges of physical affection, and to learn that they did not have to lead to sexual intercourse, although they could do so if mutually desired. (Rachel)

Massage. This can be relaxing and can help you learn how to enjoy safe and gentle touching. There are lots of women masseurs around. Many masseuses, male or female, are aware that survivors do have specific concerns. If the idea of massage appeals to you, speak to the masseuse first and check out their sensitivity to these issues. A good masseuse is one who will explain what she is doing at every stage, and be amenable to stopping upon request.

Setting sexual limits

Perhaps the sexual violence you experienced has left you with a fear that if you assert your will and say no to sex or a particular act, position or touch, you will be assaulted or otherwise hurt and degraded. Maybe you came away from the abuse feeling as though you don't have any right to make choices about your body. Or, if you were taught that the lack of enjoyment was *your* failing, you may have become adept at being a performer and pretended enjoyment or faked orgasms.

In healing and setting boundaries, it is good practice to make a promise to yourself to break the habit of pretending you are okay with sex, certain touch, or different positions. You have the right not to like something and not to want to do it. These fears are deeply rooted and so dealing with them is not always as simple as intellectually trying to dispel them. It requires practice:

This is a hard issue for me. I have always been the type who was desperate to please, so saying no to any request (not necessarily sexual) has always been difficult. I am learning now that I have the choice, and that it is ok for me to use it. (Emma)

If you continue to have sex that you really don't want, old wounds will reopen because the same dynamics of abuse are being replayed.

As discussed earlier, an important consideration is whether you are in a safe relationship. If you begin to practise saying no to sex you don't want, and your partner responds with anger or withdrawal of affection, this isn't a safe environment for you to heal sexually in. This, however, does not mean that you should continue to have sex to please him. Instead, you may want to think of other ways of addressing the issue. Remember that you are not inadequate because you have sexual wounds; it is his demanding or degrading response that is inadequate.

Hopefully, you will develop a relationship in which your partner is respectful of you and attuned to your desires (or lack thereof). The degree to which you are able to set limits and have them respected will be likely to help the growth of intimacy and sexual safety.

There may be things that happened in the course of sexual assault, such as anal contact or other types of touching, that you need never do again if you don't want to. You have the same right as anybody else to have a preference (or not) for different things. You are now a choice-maker and have a voice.

> Healing happens most quickly when women are careful to avoid stressful sexual situations, and choose sexual activities that feel comfortable. You are the only one who can know and choose … Communicating, making choices about sexual activities, being assertive, and taking time to go slowly contribute to a satisfying sexual experience. As a result of the sexual assault you may want to become more assertive, or be more open about your feelings than you were in the past.[9]

You can say yes and then no. You are allowed to stop sexual activity at any time. You may want to pre-empt this by telling your partner that you don't always know how you are going to react during sex.[10]

You may want to declare a period of rest from sex in order to commit energy to healing. It can be as long as you like. If you have a partner, let him know what touching, if any, you can give at this time; Here are some ideas:

> Tell your partner about these feelings and suggest other ways to be physical: 'I'm not feeling like having sex these days, but I would like to have physical contact with you. What I feel comfortable with are massages, hugs, kisses, holding hands, and sitting close to you when we are watching TV or reading on the couch. I will initiate some of these activities and want you to initiate too.' … Other specific activities may include taking a bath together and taking turns washing each other, cuddling under the covers and gently stroking each other, choosing a warm and

> comfortable room in the house and taking turns touching each other (excluding breasts and genitals), exchanging massages (try some oil or talcum powder) whether deep muscle or light and soothing. Don't forget your favorite music or candles, and pay attention to how it feels to touch and be touched without the pressure to be sexual.[11]

This can be an important time period for healing and learning that you have the right and the power to control your sex life.

Remember this saying: *You can't say yes to sex until you can say no to sex at any time.'*[12]

Reclaiming your sexuality

Sexual violence gave you awful messages about your body, womanhood and sexuality. Healing is a time of weeding out those messages and giving them back to the perpetrator. They belong to him, *not you*.

Here are some things you can do to celebrate your sexuality and give your womanhood the honour it deserves.

Think about what makes you feel sexy. What is sexy for you is an individual thing. It may be a partner's cologne, his lovely rear end, a constricted biceps or a certain look. If there's something your partner can do, let him know. Sometimes, what feels sexy may be something about *you*.

> I dance very provocatively, I know, and when I am in a good mood I am proud of my body (despite what I went through to get it) and I like to show it off. (Emma)

Doing what makes you feel sexy doesn't have to be for anyone else but you. Brush your hair differently in a way that is sensuous to you. Wear a lacy g-string or particular article of clothing because *you* like it and feel good in it. Put on music and move around to the beat because that turns *you* on.

Rebel against your rapist. It is empowering to consider all of the rules the rapist imposed on you as a woman, and then actively challenge them. This can involve everything from how you view yourself sexually, to choosing to reveal your cleavage in a blouse if he used to object. It's your body.

> In reclaiming my sexuality, I knew it was time to break Paul's rules and not let him keep ruling me from a distance of years. He had based much of his sexual violence on labelling my body and my sexuality 'sluttish.' If I wore sexy clothing, he said I

was a whore who was inviting other men to have sex with me – particularly, what angered him were displays of breast.

A helpful counselling technique that assisted my rebellion was one my counsellor called 'Provocation.' She would say things like, 'So Rachel, you're a slut who's asking to be raped if you're sexual, are you? You must be! Didn't Paul say so?' This was a really excellent way to confront and challenge those fears and beliefs. I yelled, 'The hell I am! He does not define who I am or what I do!' At this point, my counsellor would applaud and encourage me: 'Tell him again, Rachel, go on! What can he not define?'

Positive self-talk. Caress your body. Tell it that it is beautiful and that your rapist should never have demeaned it the way he did. Tell yourself that what the perpetrator did to your body and what that implied about it, are *his* issues, and they are *wrong*.

Making friends with your body: Self-exploring. Have a good look at yourself, and note how you feel as you do. If you still experience disgust and shame, you have more work to do. It's all right. In time and with practice, you will learn to appreciate your body without the lenses of abuse.

A sexy dance class? Belly-dancing is one way that abused women can learn to feel comfortable with their bodies and with being sensual. If you like the idea, see if you can find a class near to you. There are other forms of dance that are sensuous. How about some varieties of Latin street-dancing or jazz?

Listen to sexy music. Write down ten to 20 pieces of music that you consider sexy or sensuous, and make yourself a CD or tape. Dance, sway or make love along to it.

Listening to sexy songs by *women* can be an integral part of reclaiming your own sexuality. Nina Simone, Madonna, and some hip-hop women are inspiring because they represent women who aren't afraid to be openly sexual.

Be around other people who affirm your beauty. Although it is important ultimately to be able to validate yourself, it can still be very nice and confidence inspiring when compliments come from others like our friends or from our partner.

My boyfriend is really amazing, always very complimentary. (Adair)

(Mythical) Role-models. Perhaps you know women who are comfortable being sensuous or talking about sex. Women who accept their sexual selves can encourage and teach those of us who are fearful of our sensuality.

You can also find role models in mythology.[13]Because the legends of long ago contain many powerful symbols and healing parallels, they can actively aid your healing by helping to restore strength and pride in your own sexuality and 'woman-ness'. For instance, many goddesses and warrior women of old had no shame about being women and being sexual. The Irish Warrior-Queen Maeve offered the 'friendship of the thighs' to the man who could get her the magical Brown Bull of Ulster, which she desired above all things. Maeve thought her sex was worth offering as a prize for a dangerous mission. What beautiful, sexy confidence and self-esteem!

The progress and path of the healing journey

Healing sexually is the same as the other types of recovery we have looked at in earlier chapters. It involves naming what has happened in the past and what is happening now and facing the memories and feeling the emotions that need to be experienced to cleanse and heal the wounds. The belief systems that reside within and perpetuate the damage rise to the surface, which is actually therapeutic. When these belief systems reveal their roots so powerfully, they can then be challenged and truly overturned – at more than just an intellectual level.

> Everything culminated when I attended a seminar on feminine sexuality in the early 1990s. It was an incredibly healing and empowering experience. For me, I came home and initiated the most wonderful and uninhibited sexual experience of my life.
> (Jill)

Any other sexual assault history, aside from the partner rape(s), is likely to impact on sexual healing. You may have a clear sense of what stems from the sexual abuse by your partner, and what from other traumas, but sometimes, the issues will be similar. With sufficient support, you can address each as it appears.

Like the other areas of healing, it involves regaining control. From deciding if you want to have a sexually intimate relationship to what exactly you feel comfortable doing sexually and when you want to do it, and learning how to trust and communicate, you evolve into a woman of power – a choice-maker.

Through these processes, you can come to recognise that your body is sacred and wonderful, despite what you may have come to believe. In the end, it doesn't matter what your partner's opinion was, or how he may have denigrated the body he was supposed to love. It matters what *you* think. You can heal. You can wipe away the shame his acts inflicted just as you are eradicating it in other parts of your life.

It doesn't happen all at once. For some women, reclaiming their sexuality may be quite rapid; for others, it can take years. It's a part of the other healing we've looked at and accompanies improved self-esteem, feeling your grief, taking control of your life and establishing healthy relationships. It may be something that recycles a number of times over the years, rather than something you go through once. Be proud of any progress you've made in your healing up until now; at the right time, more will follow.

You are a goddess.

We wish you loving, passionate sex that leads you to the awareness that the distance between sex and rape is a vast one.

CHAPTER 20

For Supporters

Many survivors of partner rape find little understanding or validation for their experiences; in fact, we have seen how much secondary wounding takes place. Yet this need not be the case. If you are the friend or significant other of somebody who has been sexually abused in a relationship, your position is an important one and may be invaluable in assisting her journey to safety and healing. Rape, by its nature, often shatters a woman's sense of dignity; your care and respect can help its restoration.

If she is still being abused, your support is particularly crucial yet it could be very distressing for you. We hope that this chapter will help you to handle your thoughts and feelings in ways that ensure that you can continue to be there for her without damaging either her or yourself.

Safety is of course the most important issue – hers and your own. If a disclosure is made to you about a recent rape, first establish if she needs to be taken to a place of safety. Strongly recommend that she go to the hospital for medical treatment even if there are no injuries. She may want to safeguard against pregnancy. Offer to accompany her. Recommend that she contact the local sexual assault service.

If you are helping her physically leave an abusive relationship, *at no time must you put your own safety at risk*. Police intervention may be needed to help get her, or him, out. If you have her stay with you, there's the danger that her partner will come looking for her, which doesn't really help her (or you). It may be better if she is taken to a refuge or other place of safety.

For parents or caregivers of teenagers

This chapter is for you too.

If you find out your daughter is being sexually and perhaps physically abused by her boyfriend, you will naturally be very shocked and angry. You may believe that forcing her to break up with him is a way of keeping her safe. This could be counterproductive as she is likely to see him secretly anyway. Don't underestimate or minimise the bonds that young people forge with their partners, or assume that it is easy for her to 'just break up' with him.[1]

If you yell at her or threaten her partner, she may stop talking to you. You want to keep the communication lines open. The more valued she feels by you, the less likely she is to see the abuser as the only person who cares about her.

Tell her that violence is always unacceptable, and assure her that she doesn't deserve it. Listen to her and believe her. Take her feelings for her partner seriously. Offer to go with her to get legal help or counselling. Get support for yourself too; it's your beloved *child* being harmed and your pain is completely understandable

How do women tell about partner rape?

How a woman tells about partner rape may depend on several factors, including whether she is still in the relationship or to what degree she believes myths that say her rape isn't real. She may have no name to give experiences of sexual assault. She may therefore first disclose physical or other types of abuse, as these are easier for her to label. This may be an attempt to establish whether you are safe enough to tell about other things. In the course of a disclosure of battery or other abuse, you can gently ask if there have been times her partner has made her do sexual things that she didn't want to. Don't be afraid of being wrong. Research indicates that if women are asked about partner rape, they will be more inclined to speak about it.[2] It is better to take the risk and ask in a non-intrusive way.

She may feel relief that the question is out, and open up further. Don't be surprised if she begins shaking or crying. Be prepared to offer comfort. A denial either means that nothing has happened, or that the survivor isn't comfortable talking about it right now. Don't press her but continue to offer support for the other issues she has identified. That you were attuned enough to ask about sexual violence may serve her at a future time.

If you think a woman is hinting at sexual violence by saying something like, 'He gets angry when I don't want to have sex', ask if there have been times she has been forced or coerced into having sex. If she does not want to call her experience rape, respect that. Naming can be painful, and even hinting at what has happened or giving it other names can be a terrifying place to start from, most particularly if it involves branding somebody whom she may love a rapist. The name matters less than the fact that it happened and is hurting her. However, some women *do* want it to be named so that they can know their own perception of what happened is not crazy. If she does seem to be struggling for a definition of what happened to her, you can suggest that it is called rape. You can either share your own experience or tell her about someone else and how that person labelled what happened as rape.

A woman who has been raped by her partner may falteringly say, 'He raped me', and then express embarrassment: 'I know it sounds pretty stupid to call it rape if he was my partner.' A validating response could be, 'It's not silly to call rape by its name. Rape by a partner is as much a rape as that by a stranger.'

If she is able to be more forthright and call it rape without questioning her own reality, you may respond by saying something like, 'Partner rape is a horrible betrayal. I'm sorry that it happened to you, but I'm so glad you feel able to tell me.'

After hearing a disclosure of rape, some people worry about raising the subject again because they don't want to 'upset' the woman. In reality, she may think you are embarrassed or that you believe her rape *is* nothing. While you don't want to ask about it every time you meet, you can say something like, 'How are you after our talk last week?' She is likely to appreciate that you care enough to ask. If she doesn't wish to speak of it, it's not that she is being contrary. Because partner rape is so painful at certain stages, she may be trying to hold the pain down for a little while. She may also be struggling with some guilt about 'betraying' her partner by telling. If she is caught in a cycle of violence, your question may catch her at a time when she needs to believe everything is fine. Don't push her but reiterate that if she needs an ear in future, it will be there. Remember that you were the person she was comfortable enough to come to in the first place. Maybe that first act of helping her break the silence is all she needs from you right now.

However the disclosure comes, be honoured that she trusts you.

Some ways of helping

Be a friend but not a counsellor. Do not try to delve into deeply traumatic issues with her. This is much more appropriate for somebody with training to do. If you are seeing the manifestations of trauma in her life – for example, she calls you often in the middle of the night because she is having nightmares about the rape – it will benefit both of you if you give her the number of a 24-hour crisis line staffed by professionals who are *paid* to deal with trauma. She may present dilemmas to you such as, 'It was my fault I was raped. I went back to him'. You can say, 'Rape is always the choice of the perpetrator and never your fault, but to better understand your decisions to return you may benefit from seeing a counsellor.' Don't feel a failure if you don't know answers. Of course you don't want her to feel bad, but bear in mind that her reactions are normal and as she moves through healing, she will discover answers within herself.

There is no doubt that the feelings invoked by a disclosure of rape can be huge. However, you will need to try and remain as calm as possible.

> … It is important that you attempt to achieve a delicate balance between your being emotionally available and maintaining enough objectivity so as not to be sucked into the same roller coaster of feelings she is experiencing. This balance is what makes it safe for you to go to, what makes for a good anchor … she won't trust you if she has to worry about you freaking out.[3]

If you get visibly upset, the woman may feel guilty for making you sad, and may feel obliged to comfort you. Tell her this is *her* space; assure her that she does not need to comfort you.

Convey respect to her in every way possible. Do not admonish, patronise or negatively judge her. Make and repeat clear statements about her value and rights as a person, such as, 'You don't deserve to be treated that way' and 'No one, not even your husband, has the right to mistreat you.'[4]

> They asked me something about Carl and I don't know what happened but they started saying, 'Liz, Do you realise what's happened? You've gone through your childhood and you're copying the same pattern in your marriage.' And it was like right there in that coffee shop, the light bulb went on and I just went, 'Oh my God I have to get out of this.'

> I knew that he was trying to intimidate me and keep me crazy. They said that I either had to make space for myself, or go some place because they were worried about my safety. (Liz)

Emphasise talents, successes or achievements she has made. Take her some flowers just because you care about her. If the abuser has convinced her that only he really loves her, it can be extremely helpful for her to receive positive regard from others.

Keep her confidence. In order for her to feel safe she needs to know she can trust you not to tell what may be her most painful secret.

Believing her

Believing the woman who discloses a rape to you is the most important starting point in support. Disclosures of partner rape are sometimes harder to hear than disclosures of stranger rape. If you have familial or friendship ties to her partner it may be hard to believe her. Yet being accused of lying – either with a direct statement or in other roundabout ways like, 'I believe you but I wasn't there so I don't really know' – is incredibly painful to a survivor of rape. In order for trust to be built, the survivor will need to know that you believe her. For Sarah, ironically (and sadly) it was the current partner of her violent husband who offered that unconditional belief:

> A few years ago I got a phone call from her. We agreed to meet for coffee, which nobody else thought was a very good idea. It turned out to be the best thing because each of us could start a sentence and the other could finish it. We knew exactly what the other person was thinking. It was the only time I have ever felt that I could say what happened. There were no misunderstandings. She knew exactly what I'd gone through without me having to outline everything and there was complete acceptance of everything I said. Up to that point no one had.

If you do have trouble believing a woman, ask yourself why. Be honest with yourself about your doubts. Do you think she is lying or is it because you know her partner favourably, and don't really want to believe that he would do such a thing? Perhaps you are subscribing to some of the mythology?

Do you not believe her because she seems 'hysterical' while her partner is rational? Does she have issues with substance abuse that you believe lessen her credibility? It may be easier to believe a man who seems to be a model of stability than a nervous or drug-addicted woman, but it's possible that mistreatment has contributed to her condition. Also, women who have had a history of mental instability or substance abuse are not immune from rape.

Has her partner denied raping her? Consider the possibility that he may be manipulating you; abusers manipulate not only their victims, but also family, friends and even trained counsellors. It's also possible that like many partners who rape, he doesn't see the act/s of forced sex he's inflicted as rape.

What are the implications of believing her? Are you related to her partner? If so, you are not asked to turn against him and hate him forever. You can acknowledge your disappointment in him and tell the survivor that even though you care about him, what he did was wrong.

In the end it's your call. If you cannot give the woman sincere belief or you cannot handle the implications of believing her, you will be better to point her towards other support. Your belief can have a powerful impact on her healing.

> I did have one good male friend, Mark, whom I finally told when he took me out for my birthday. I did not disclose the details, but he knew enough about me to believe me, and he was very supportive of me. It was while telling him that I realised how angry I was at Sean for what he had done, and for dismissing my concerns. It was like I needed to see someone else to get angry about it for me to admit my own feelings and see them as valid. (Natalie)

Responding without blaming or minimising

Not blaming her is of equal importance to believing her. Even if you don't like certain choices she has made and you believe they contributed to the rape, recognise that to rape her was her partner's choice, and wasn't her fault. This is not the time to say things like, 'So why did you stay with him?' or 'You must have known what he was like.'

She may self-recriminate with statements like, 'If I hadn't stayed with him, it wouldn't have kept happening.' You cannot take any responsibility for how she feels and therefore it is better not to try and 'convince' her that it wasn't her fault. You can make clear statements such as, 'Whatever you did, nothing justifies you being raped.' Don't worry if this does not appear to make much difference right now. As she goes into healing and begins to understand *why* it was not her fault, the true power of your words will become apparent to her. Just as survivors remember people blaming and hurting them, they also remember those who *didn't* blame them.

Even though you may have no intention to hurt, you may still need to exercise caution. Many a survivor has been hurt by well-intentioned statements that are still basically blame, like, 'Why didn't you come and sleep on my couch?'

Never say or imply such things as, 'at least it's not as bad as if he was a stranger'.

It is important to recognise that she may minimise or downplay the seriousness of the rape. While it won't be helpful for you to insist that she *must* be feeling more than she says she does, you can resist buying into her minimisation. Be honest – tell her that sexual assault in any context is wrong. As she deals with it later, it may begin to hurt very much, and she will need you then.

Listening with affirmation

In general, it will be useful to listen more than you speak. However, it is also important to avoid being entirely silent as this can give the survivor the impression that you are indifferent to her pain. There are nonverbal ways to illustrate that you are hearing her: a squeeze to her hand at certain points (having ascertained that physical contact is acceptable), keeping eye-contact and not looking off into space or at your watch.

Take your cue from her. If she is crying or shaking, tell her that you can see this is very distressing for her. If it is appropriate for your relationship, ask her if she would like to be held. Assure her that you want to hear what she has to tell you. You don't need to walk on eggshells and be so afraid of saying the wrong thing that you say nothing. There are things you can say that are likely to validate and put the woman at greater ease. You could start with, 'Yes. That *is* rape.'

Here are some other helpful responses:[5]

- I believe you.
- I care about you.
- I'm glad you told me.
- You are not alone.
- Violent behaviour towards you is never appropriate or deserved.
- It's okay to be afraid.
- I'm glad you survived.
- It's okay to be angry with your husband.
- You deserve a non-violent life.
- You can change your life.
- You are not responsible for your husband's behaviour.
- You have the right to make choices.
- You are not to blame.
- You have a right to privacy.
- Whatever you did, you didn't deserve to be raped.
- Whatever you are feeling is OK.
- Your responses are totally normal.

'You deserve support' is another particularly affirming comment. If she is ashamed of staying in the relationship, telling on her partner, or she subscribes to myths about partner rape, she may be convinced that she does *not* deserve support.

Hearing her feelings and beliefs

Rather than assuming you know how the survivor feels, ask her. She may appreciate the opportunity to explore and identify her feelings. As you listen to her, you may want to reflect back to her your interpretation of what she seems to be saying. For example, you may say, 'It sounds like you felt betrayed by the rape. Is that right?' Don't be afraid of being wrong. She will either confirm that and possibly want to talk more about it, or she may say, 'Not betrayed exactly … It was more like shock.'

If the woman expresses anger or sadness at what has happened to her, tell her she has a right to be angry or sad. However, even if she feels anger, this may be mixed with positive feelings for the abuser. She may be trying to negotiate her way through an emotional minefield, and will again need to know you accept her and don't judge her feelings. She may say things like, 'You probably think I'm crazy for loving somebody who did that to me.' Assure her that she is not crazy for what she feels. You can tell her that many women who survive partner rape still love their partners; this will help her feel less isolated. Indeed, some women are anxious that their partners not be seen as monsters, and may express guilt for telling about the rape. You may say something like, 'Your need for support doesn't mean you are betraying him. Even though he's good to you in other ways, he doesn't have the right to force sex on you.'

Don't tell her to 'get over it' or suggest that by now her abuse shouldn't be an issue. Healing, even when it involves some pain, *is* 'getting over it'. An empathic and caring response will be a great comfort to her and, since trauma-based fears are often worsened by a sense of aloneness, may even alleviate her fear.

If the woman has religious beliefs that you don't share, don't make light of those concerns. Her beliefs are important to *her;* they may have sustained her through bad times. However, she may now be suffering from a pull between dictates of her beliefs, and the sexual or other violence her partner has perpetrated. Suggest that she seek support from other women of faith who have been raped by partners and who will understand her spiritual concerns.

If the woman is out of the relationship with the perpetrator of her rape, and is well in touch with her anger, it may be appropriate and validating for you to join her in her anger. If you love or value the woman very much, it may be extremely difficult not to express anger at the perpetrator. However, if she still loves him, it will usually be more helpful to focus on the abuse rather than the abuser. One of the worst outcomes of explosions of vitriol at her partner is that she may not feel safe enough to speak with you again. You *can* feel and express your anger to a trusted other; in fact it is probably essential for your emotional wellbeing that you do so. Never confront the perpetrator about what the woman has told you, though; you could expose her to greater danger.

Reflective listening

Objectivity does not mean that you are neutral and have no feelings or opinions. However, it is necessary that you own them as your own without pushing them onto her. For example, let's say you believe that anger is a more appropriate response to partner rape than love, and you are supporting a woman who expresses love for her partner. If you feed those judgments back to her, she is likely to feel wrong, stupid, and certainly not accepted by you.

You can offer her another reality in a positive way that doesn't belittle her experience. This may be particularly helpful if she is accepting the realities presented by her abuser. For example, when she tells you what he says she does to provoke his violence, you can say, 'His violence is not your fault. He has other choices than violence.' Some men who rape their partners excuse it by saying that it is because they are 'highly sexed' and 'lose control'. If she tells you this, you can gently suggest that rape is not the act of a man *losing* control, but a man *having* control. Offering her new ways to look at things outside of the abuser's reality may cause a shift in the beliefs that are keeping her in bondage.

You can present another reality as a question. For instance, if you believe she is being manipulated through guilt, you can ask, 'Does he often say things that you feel guilty about when he thinks you are going to leave? Do you think it could be manipulation?' This gives her the chance to articulate how she sees the problem without being forced to wear the subjective judgment of another person.

Respecting NOT rescuing

'Rescuing' is not respectful. It is often conditional, i.e. 'I'll only help you if we do things my way.' The rescuer gives advice instead of encouraging the survivor to find resources with which to help *herself*. Well-intentioned but forced 'help' is unhelpful and controlling in a way similar to the perpetrator. Trusting bonds are rarely forged with rescuers; a woman knows that the friendship often depends on her obedience to the rescuer.

A supporter who is respectful and not rescuing doesn't take responsibility for the woman's decisions away from her, and continues to value her whether the helper likes her choices or not. Avoid using words like 'You should.' Giving *information* instead of advice offers her a greater sense of having options to choose among. Ask about other potential avenues of support she has. Tell her about services that you know of that assist women in her situation. Help her to explore other options. If she is very confused, she may ask you, 'What should I do?' You can respond by empowering her, 'What do you think you should do?' Then, you can support her answer: 'You are the one who knows your situation best.' You can help her in acting on her choices, as Sarah's group of workmates did:

> Anyway, we'd agreed that we would get divorced but it wasn't a convenient time, so I told the women at work that we'd agreed. After nine months, the women at work said, 'Look it's not going to happen unless you actually make it happen and we need to have a countdown.' So they actually said to pick a date, and that will be the date the marriage ends. So we had a countdown to when I was going to tell him the marriage was over.

You may find yourself being judgmental (and thus disrespectful) of a woman who chooses to remain with the rapist partner. In fact, some women are able to salvage relationships in which rape has occurred either by demanding that sexually abusive behaviour be addressed or by leaving for a period of time and only resuming the relationship when they see evidence that the partner has accepted responsibility for the rape(s). These are not poor choices; they are carefully deliberated.

Even if the relationship is clearly dangerous, it's still wise to take the line of respecting that she knows best. You can say in a non-judgmental way, however, that you don't agree with a choice. Make 'I' rather than 'you' statements; i.e. instead of saying 'You should leave', say, 'I'm worried that if you stay, the violence will get worse.' This articulates your concerns without directing or blaming her.[7] Tell her that you believe her safety needs to be a priority. If she has become used to the abuser's needs coming first, she may not have considered this before. Honesty will foster deeper trust between you and the survivor.

Don't make the mistake of thinking that because she wishes to stay with her partner, the rape hasn't really harmed her. It may hurt very much, and she has a right to seek healing even if she does stay.

Support throughout a legal process

It is important that the survivor regains control over her life and makes the decision of whether to report to the police or not. At no time should she be pushed either way. It's her choice. If you are the parents of a teenager, it may be very hard to hear that your daughter has been raped, and you may want to press charges. Consider that this may not be best for her. Seek advice from a rape crisis centre.

If she does press charges for sexual assault or battery or is seeking a restraining order, she may appreciate you accompanying her to court. She is likely to be frightened throughout these actions, but may also be resolutely sure she is doing the right thing. Tell her she has a right to seek justice and protection. Like Kuriah's friends, you may become advocates for her:

> Some very powerful women in my life went to bat for me and called the system on its lies and the plea bargain was withdrawn.

Ask how you can best help. She may need rides to legal and rape crisis appointments or support while she attends these.

Be aware that although she may want you to accompany her through certain parts of the legal process, she may prefer privacy at times. For example, if she is giving evidence in a trial, she may want you to be at the courthouse but prefer for you not to be in the courtroom. No matter how much she loves or trusts you, there may be details she is too ashamed right now for you to know. Let her lead and give her privacy when she needs it. That will help restore her sense of dignity.

For her partner

For the new partner

You are in an especially powerful place to be an ally in healing.

If she has problems with sexuality or intimacy, it isn't that she doesn't love you or isn't attracted to you. She has been wounded in a very intimate way. She may blame herself for difficulties between you and may be apologetic to you for 'putting up' with her. Assure her that you are not anywhere you don't want to be, and that you know it's not her fault. If you can give her love, patience and gentleness, it may ensure that one day you'll have a very passionate and trusting soul-mate.

You may feel that it is not fair; it was not you who did the abusing and yet you are suffering for it. The impact of sexual abuse on the lives of survivors and significant others most certainly is not fair. Your feelings count, and it may be a good idea if you have somebody you can talk them through with. Couples counselling may also be an option.

Be honest with yourself about your own capacities. If the effects of her trauma are impacting severely on your life with her and she does not want to seek help, you may need to question whether this relationship is for you. Be honest with her; it may provide her with the impetus to make changes. Let her know that you are not rejecting her because she was raped, but because the ongoing nature of the problems combined with the fact that she will not seek help is causing you unhappiness. [8]

For the perpetrator partner

If she has remained with you, it may be hard to watch her pain. Be aware that she may be frightened to share it with you. You probably have a hard time understanding the depth of her devastation, but please try. You can make amends. There are things you can do that *may* help her to feel safe with you again, but this is likely to take time. You need to take full responsibility for any sexual violence perpetrated and genuinely want to make change. This means that you:

- Acknowledge what you've done and that it has hurt her.
- Acknowledge control over your own behaviour. If you continue to say things like, 'I just went crazy', she will wonder when the conditions under which you assaulted her will reoccur.
- Don't minimise what you did. Avoid statements like, 'But I've been good to you, haven't I?'
- Don't invalidate her with statements like, 'That was years ago. Why are you bringing it up now?'
- Don't rationalise that if it wasn't violent, it didn't really hurt her.
- Question any assumptions you may hold about being 'entitled' to sex or that she 'owes' you sex. Recognise that rape of a partner is a crime, not a right.
- Make sure she knows that it was not her fault.
- Give her space to heal. Don't be impatient with the time required.
- Take responsibility for getting help for yourself.

Other ways of increasing her feelings of safety include: stopping all coercive and controlling behaviour both in the bedroom and out of it, not insisting on attending counselling with her if she is not comfortable with this, not demanding to know what she talked about with her counsellor.

If she has chosen to separate to examine what she wants in her future, don't pressure her to return. If she decides not to return, you will need to accept it. At best, you may be safer for other women. If she does return, consider yourself fortunate.

While you don't have to put up with abusive behaviour yourself, be prepared to hear her feelings of anger and disappointment.

Caring for yourself

If you are supporting a woman who has been raped by her partner, your self-care is really important. Remember that at no stage do you and your needs for comfort, peace, support or the things you enjoy become unimportant.

If you offer to do more than you really wish to do or you have begun to feel as if you are expected to drop everything to respond to another crisis, you will end up burnt-out and resentful. Burnout is a very real phenomenon. It is *not* a statement about who you are. You can avoid it with adequate self-care. Do not neglect yourself if you notice signs of burnout such as depression, loss of enjoyment of life, irritability and feeling too tired to care anymore. This may mean saying no to a persn you care about.

You are not responsible for having all the answers or providing all help. If you feel that way, it is possible you've taken on inappropriate responsibility. This will ultimately be harmful since you may begin to distance yourself from her because it has become too hard.

Set limits. It is good for her to seek as many resources as she can.

If you are a survivor of rape, partner rape or other relationship violence, you are equipped with understanding. However, you may find it triggering at times. It will undoubtedly remind you of aspects of your own experience. If you begin to experience flashbacks, panic or other pain related to your own traumas, take steps to get support for yourself. Don't curse yourself for not being 'stronger'. It is not your fault you have been traumatised any more than it is the fault of the person you are supporting.

Emotions and thoughts you could experience

You will probably experience a wide range of emotions. It is important not to suppress them or minimise them; that will not only hurt you but also the woman you are supporting.

Frustration. If the woman you care about is still in danger, you are apt to feel some aggravation. This is only natural. Don't let it boil over onto the woman or other people who are important to you. *Do* talk about it to somebody to who understands relationship abuse and the frustration experienced by helpers. Sound off! For example, tell your support that hearing an abuser excused and justified is driving you to screaming point.

The woman may vacillate between staying and leaving. Sometimes, she may enlist your help in making safety plans, only to remain at the last minute. This can be intensely frustrating especially if you are (consciously or unconsciously) taking responsibility for outcomes.

Helplessness. Somebody you care about has been hurt. If the abuse is current, you may feel overwhelmed by a sense of helplessness or inadequacy. It will benefit you to accept that you cannot change her circumstances; only she can.

If you have shown care to an abused woman, you are doing what you can. If you have let her ask for what she needs from you and then, without going beyond your limits, provided that need, you have made a difference and you are a terrific friend.

Physical and emotional fatigue. Assisting somebody in crisis or listening to her as she shares pain is draining. Physical or mental weariness is a natural product of making energy available for others. It's a very real warning-flag. Rest. Do the things you enjoy. Laugh. Give yourself breaks.

Listened out. While a woman is healing from rape, she may need to talk about it many times. She is trying to make sense of it, and each time she covers what appears to you to be the same ground, she is bringing new lessons away with her. She needs space to do that, but *you* do not have to be the sole provider of that space. She can join a support group or can seek counselling, which may be more appropriate at times.

If she is still in the relationship you may have periods of feeling weary of hearing about something that never seems to change. Tell her that right now, you aren't able to hear her. Honesty is much better than simply changing the subject or avoiding it. Survivors of rape and domestic violence are mostly respectful of the space of others; she may be anxious that you are growing sick of hearing about it and apologetic for needing to talk. Let her know she has nothing to be sorry for.

If you find yourself thinking, 'How dare I complain of being tired after all she has been through', you are asking yourself to be more than you can be.

Anger and sadness. If you love or value the woman who is in an abusive relationship, it may enrage and distress you that she is continuing to be raped or otherwise abused. Many rape crisis services will give support to families and friends of women who have been raped. Find out what exists for you. Find a shoulder to have a good cry on or to sound off to about wanting to wring the perpetrator's neck. Unaddressed anger and sadness can manifest as depression; you don't deserve that.

Self-blame. Many people who care about abused women blame themselves because they couldn't somehow prevent her from being hurt. If she is still in a bad relationship, you may be asking yourself what you aren't doing right to help her be safe.

Remind yourself, whether you are a friend or a relative that you aren't responsible for her choices or for what her abuser chooses to do. She needs to have control of her life.

Vicarious traumatisation (VT). This is different from simply feeling upset or even very distressed by another person's story. With VT, you are taking the horror into yourself and are unable to stop thinking about what you've heard. You are traumatised by the other person's experiences. So, if you should begin to experience symptoms of PTSD (see chapter 10) that are unrelated to any trauma of your own, you should seek support immediately. There's nothing *wrong* with you; you have been affected in a way that even some seasoned counsellors are.[9]

Gestures that mean a lot

> I was alone when my partner hurt me. I have been shown by consistent caring that I'm not alone now. (Rachel)

Supporting gestures don't need to be huge, nor do they always need to involve deep psychological energy. Cook your friend a meal. Offer to take her kids off her hands for a couple of hours. She will feel valued. Survivors of partner rape so often feel as though what happened to them doesn't matter, that *they* don't matter. Caring gestures, from sitting with her as she pulls out memories she may have held down for a long time, to an affectionate e-card, will help her reverse those old messages:

> Some time ago, I was struggling with memories of my experiences of partner rape. I told my wonderful best friend, Helen. After sitting with me for a while, she cooked dinner for me and bought me some bath oils. These gestures hit the mark beautifully. Helen seemed to know what parts of me were feeling drained, lonely and unclean. These gestures affirm that I am worth caring

for and listening to, even when I doubt it myself. Somebody
knows my wounds are real and cares that I have been hurt. These
gestures have actively helped me heal. (Rachel)

In all good relationships, care and support is mutual. Sometimes one
person will need more energy because they are having a hard time but
it's still a two-way thing. Try not to make the mistake of thinking, 'I can't
put anything on her; she has enough on her plate.' Consideration for an
embattled friend surely has a place, but it's also true that people can be
disempowered by feeling like the eternally done *for*. If a friend whom you
have supported through rape or other abuse wants to do something nice
for you or let you cry on *her* shoulder, let her. She'll feel trusted, valued
and empowered.

CHAPTER 21

Breaking Down the Bedroom Door

We have seen the many faces of partner rape and its powerful legacy in survivors' lives. Within the cultural context of false beliefs, sexual violence by partners is still, in many ways, 'in the closet' and the community colludes in the crime through its denial.

Society's silence breeds shame and a concurrent silence by its survivors.

> The shame of having been in an abusive relationship is enough, but the idea of the rape as well makes it worse. It's not something I want to tell anyone.

> I have told very few people of my history: my husband and maybe one friend. (Melina)

We have also seen how society's silence is conducive to victim blaming and secondary wounding.

> There seems to still be a wide range of opinion from a belief that women ask for it, they contribute to it, to 'it is an utter outrage'. There is a perception that alcohol can be a common contributing factor for the man or the woman. (Relationships Australia Counsellor)

> Some women had experienced community condemnation for their inability to protect themselves and their children from the perpetrator. Other family of origin members were often the ones to hold this position. (Canberra Rape Crisis Counsellor)

Thus, it is essential that partner rape is named and confronted. That has of course been one of the primary intents of the first 20 chapters of this book.

Additionally and vitally, the cultural landscape that partner rape inhabits must be remodelled to reduce violence against women and create better conditions for women who are harmed by it.

Rape is about inequality of power. Partner rape epitomises gender inequality in the home. Women's powerless position relative to men must be radically modified. Such a metamorphosis is a prerequisite for ending violence against women. Gender hierarchy in the workplace, politics, and the home needs to be eliminated with activities in the private domain seen as equally important as those performed outside of it.

And, 'equality' means revolutionary changes with the nature of sex roles and relations transformed. Women's freedom from sexual assault by partners has to be the ultimate aim. We deserve nothing less.

> I want an acceptance/recognition of this type of assault so that people like me no longer have to feel the confusion about what happened. Was it rape? Was it assault? Abuse? An overreaction? A figment of my imagination? I want it to be known that husbands/boyfriends/partners are capable of rape. I want it to be made clear that it does happen and that it has to stop. I want nobody else to have to go through what I did. (Emma)

We look next at a few ideas for transformation and make some suggestions for improving support for partner rape victims.

Changing values and attitudes

The positive role that men can play

Some men do collectively or individually challenge rape culture. They campaign to end sexism and to redefine masculinity separate from aggression, violence and sexual conquest. Men who are serious about ending sexual violence of women can encourage other men in the understanding that 'getting it' and not taking no for an answer are not the benchmarks of what is a real man.

Here is one example. It has long been recognised that aggressive and competitive sports such as football are male arenas in which the sexual devaluing of women is encouraged and even glorified. Jim Stynes, an Australian footballer whose wife 'spent considerable time attempting to educate me, and get me to realise how the football sub-culture and society in general, marginalises, silences and disrespects women in the way it talks about them' is challenging that subculture:

> Sexual abuse of any kind can seriously damage the victim, both psychologically and emotionally. As a young male in this culture I didn't posses a critical awareness of these after-effects. Then when I began my work with young women and men I

started hearing their stories of long-term abuse and its impacts. Consequently I became aware of countless numbers of young women falling into deep depression, self-mutilation, becoming suicidal, binging on drugs and alcohol, becoming anorexic or bulimic. The list goes on but in every case, they were just trying to numb the pain and forget.[1]

Terence Crowley writes, 'As long as men link sexual excitement with domination and violence, a rape culture will continue. Until the effects of men's behaviour to women define the moral value of that behaviour, a rape culture will thrive.'[2] In other words, the sexual abuse and degradation of women should be seen not as 'the boys having a bit of fun' – not the behaviour of 'heroes' who, having conquered the playing field, are justified in extending the conquest mentality to women. Rather, because of its effect on women, rape should be viewed as a *disgrace*. Images of consent and mutual desire that are more erotic than images of conquest and power can be generated.

> 'No' is hard to hear. But what about a heartfelt 'Yes!' What about 'more' or 'now!' or 'harder' or 'faster' or any other expressions that we may have longed to hear in our fantasies and dreams of desire. What would it be like to create a space where partners can speak their wishes, express what feels good and tell us how to help pleasure them? Here is communication in a safer space that can be trusted and played with. 'Kiss me this way.' 'Touch me here.' This is information that can bring us closer in sexual intimacy without assault.[3]

Imagine if men stopped supporting their 'brothers' who say, 'What was I to do? She let me kiss her', or 'I went home the other night and rolled the old lady over for a piece of the action. She didn't like it but don't women complain about everything?' Imagine other men instead of validating these comments, saying, 'You have hurt her.' Imagine them calling it rape. Men do have a crucial part to play in 'unmaking' prescribed norms of male behaviour.

Men can recognise that ending the rape culture is not just about not raping, but about not participating in any form of degradation, objectification and control of women. Imagine men sneering disdainfully at other men who think saying, 'Show us your tits' is the height of cool.

Not confronting and challenging is assenting. A man who can stand up in the midst of rape culture and openly challenge it and traditional notions of masculinity is an example of a man exercising true power – unlike a man who forces or coerces a woman into sex.

Empowering our daughters, nieces, grand-daughters, friends …

Our daughters must never feel limited in anything *because* they are female. We need to set an example for them by addressing 'the propaganda of inferiority' that surrounds girls, and on which much of rape culture rests.

> The most important gift anyone can give a girl is a belief in her own power as an individual, her value without reference to gender, her respect as a person with potential.[4]

Because girls are also generally socialised to be submissive and 'nice', they often experience difficulties being assertive. It is sad but true that some teenage girls submit to sexual coercion because they are afraid that their partners will like them less, or withdraw affection altogether. Are rapists responsible for playing on these fears and proceeding to have intercourse without real consent being present? Absolutely. Yet, it is essential that our girls know that what happens to their bodies and when, is a most basic right, and that they have a right to assert what they do and don't want to do. It is naïve and unfair to say that assertiveness would stop *all* rape. But there are times when it *may* cause a potential rapist to back off.[5]

Many teenage girls interpret warning signs of abuse such as jealousy or possessiveness as romantic.

> It's taboo, but admit there's a problem. Provide enough support to allow women to help themselves. Improve education in schools so that young women can identify an abusive relationship. (Charlotte)

Sex education should include information on the signs of an abusive personality and ways of responding before a girl is sucked very deeply into an abusive relationship. It could include realistic information about what sexual violence is and the various scenarios in which it happens, including relationships.

If we can change the way girls view themselves in relation to male power early and increase their knowledge of relationship violence dynamics, they will hopefully be less inclined to go into relationships or marriage believing that the male partner has a right to be boss, and that they must submit to sex in order to keep the peace.

This world is our girls' space too. They are allowed to be in it without contempt and threat because they are female.

It is essential that a girl think of herself as valuable in her own right, as a 'real person', not a toy or a marionette dancing on strings held by the men in her life.[6]

Impacting on our sons, nephews, mates ...

Boys may be exposed to their fathers physically and emotionally abusing their mothers. They witness sexual harassment and bullying. They see females objectified in the media. They hear the banter and jokes that minimise and narrowly define rape. These are strong forces to overcome. However, somehow the generational cycle of sexual violence and misogyny must be broken.

As parents, relatives or mentors, we can provide boys with a different script both as individuals and through lobbying the other principal influences of our children – schools, sports and the media – to change the messages of gender inequity and violence.

Our boys can learn that if they are seeing representations of girls as inferior, these are wrong. We could challenge the labels that equate the feminine with inferiority: 'You pussy', 'You cry-baby girlie.'

We can also help them to redefine masculinity.

If we are serious about significantly decreasing our rape rates, we must move men, and especially young boys away from a definition of masculinity that centers on toughness power, dominance, eagerness to fight, lack of empathy and a callous attitude towards women. For as long as these values ... prevail among many men, rape will continue to be viewed by them as proof that they are 'one of the boys', that they are 'real men.' When dominance and power define masculinity, men rape as a way of putting 'uppity' women in their place.[7]

When they start dating, we can have honest talks with them about consent: what it is and what it isn't. They need to know that a woman lying there passively or submitting after badgering or emotional blackmail is not consenting. They need to know that, 'No' means 'No'.

Keeping an eye on the media

The role of the media is potentially very important as a powerful shaper of social attitudes. Sexual assault has gone through a few 'fashionable' media phases after which any serious coverage lapses into resounding silence unless the accused is a celebrity or there are particularly titillating aspects of the case. The media also plays a vital role in how it portrays men and women and their relationships. Sometimes this is subtle; for instance, media presentations of jealousy and possessiveness work against women learning to recognise such behaviour as a potential warning or precursor to other violent behaviour. Sometimes, it is more direct with women portrayed as actually wanting to be violated. For instance, television, film and news reportage eroticise forced sex in relationships or depict women raped by ex-partners as provocateurs who upset men by choosing to leave them.

Grrl Activistas is an example of a group that formed to combat this. It recognised that much media is inherently sexist and biased against survivors of rape. When inaccurate or biased portrayals of sexual assault in news reportage, on talk shows or in plotlines in soap operas are identified, group members send mass mails to the relevant bodies to protest.

Another example is *The Truth About Rape, a* UK-based group. Its mandate includes combatting media bias. Members demand that the media stop slandering rape victims and fuelling myths.

You can join them. When you see such things, wherever you see them, you could speak up. It's a lot better than silence. We can call the media on its irresponsible coverage of rape. When you see a biased portrayal of rape, and you make yourself heard either individually or as part of a group, you are sowing the seeds of further consideration and change in at least some people.

From the pulpits

Churches have the potential to impact on attitudes about domestic violence and partner rape by making it clear to their congregations in sermon topics that the theology and scripture support neither male superiority[8] nor violence to women. Spiritual leadership should also encourage women to re-evaluate the divine images that they've learned and to reconceptualise a God who does not abandon them or expect them to see submission to repeated rape as their duty. Instead of focusing on saving relationships in which women are unsafe, religious leaders could recognise that divorce can be an opportunity for a new life.[9]

Imagine if religious institutions took the role in calling marital rape a sin not on the part of a non-submissive woman, but on the part of the perpetrator. This *can* happen; some churches have made inroads into addressing domestic and sexual violence in their congregations.

Improving the response to partner rape

Aside from playing a role in changing values about relationships and violence, church leaders can provide better support to survivors. They need to be aware of and alert for signs of violence and offer practical help to women. Leaders could also be more responsive through networking with domestic violence services, doing community outreach in the form of volunteering at these services and raising donations.[10]

It is important that clergy, police, prosecutors and counsellors, whose 'helping' paths may intersect with partner rape victims, not have preconceived notions of how a 'good' victim appears and behaves. If a woman presents as being too 'together', well-spoken and poised, she may not be helped or heard. That has been Jennifer's experience:

> I understand that I, the survivor, need to take responsibility for my own growth. I also understand that no one can 'make things better' for me on an emotional, physical and psychological level other than myself. I do feel that one of the greatest stumbling blocks I have faced is that no one in authority took ownership of my case.

> I was seen as too intelligent, too articulate, too independent and too strong willed. I was told I was capable of doing this, that and the other by myself. I can never describe the incredible feeling of isolation that this gave me.

More resources for survivors

Women who are living with violence are sometimes trapped by financial dependency and by lack of information:

> I'd ask government or community groups to provide information to people to enable them to recognise the abuse. People need to be educated about the things that we tend to think are normal so we can reduce the escalation of the behaviour.

> Also, there is a serious need for the victims to have access to information that may be needed by the survivor. In my case access to financial information is crucial to my survival. There should be freedom of information within a marriage for both parties. (Samantha)

Welfare-type payments more commensurate with the cost of rearing children would be an advantage to women seeking to escape rape or other abuse, and also for those who cannot, due to fear for their lives, collect child support.

Renovating the halls of ' justice'

There is plenty of room for improvement in how the criminal justice system responds to victims of partner rape. For instance, police ignorance (and denial) about the sexual part of domestic violence may contribute to these assaults not being identified and/or reported at the time that other domestic violence is reported.[11]If the sexual assaults are not being picked up or acted upon at the police callout, both the prosecution and the defence may use this later as evidence of a 'discrepancy' or inconsistency by the victim. This contributes to her portrayal as an 'unreliable witness' and leads to prosecutors dropping the matter or in the defence attacking her credibility.

More sensitive police questioning on domestic violence calls could increase both disclosure plus the likelihood of the witness continuing to be keen on prosecution.

Asking discreet and sensitive questions necessitates knowledge about partner rape. Appropriate behaviour by defence lawyers and sound judicial directions and commentary also require an understanding of domestic violence and rape. Therefore, a mandatory part of training for the bench and other criminal justice practitioners should be gaining familiarity with the victims' reality of sexual assault by partners. This may in part protect women from being victimised yet again on the witness stand. More law reform is required too to better protect the victim witnesses from questions that are inappropriate[12]and to facilitate expert testimony to explain about trauma, its impact on memory and about the dynamics of intimate violence.

The court needs to mandate an advocate and a support person to represent the basic human rights of the victim in the trial and to ensure that she knows exactly what is taking place:

> A caseworker needs to be appointed who can then guide and mentor the victim through the process from the initial complaint to final court hearing. Someone who has some authority and the spirit to insist that justice is done. Someone who is not afraid to go to battle for the survivor and can push to make things happen. Someone who can have an impact if there is a perception that the survivor is being treated less than fairly. (Jennifer)

In addition, the wording of evidence law and consent provisions needs to be less grey and more encapsulating of the victim's reality. When evidence of her experiences, like prior violence, is not admitted and the incident is looked at in isolation from the dynamics of the relationship, understanding the woman's lack of consent is problematic. Current legal tests of relevance and reasonableness that are supposedly neutral are born and fit within a context of potent and persistent mythology about women's roles, sexuality, personality traits, rape, violence and relationships with men:[13]

> The law must take care to 'spell out' what is reasonable conduct, and conversely what is not, rather than merely resort to empty vessels into which the jury may pour its discriminatory and prejudiced beliefs.[14]

Whatever laws are enacted they need to be written in a more simple and comprehensible fashion. Aside from simplifying the statutes though, judges need to learn how to communicate concepts such as consent with succinctness and clarity, pitching the message to the level of the jury audience. Further, the public must be able to challenge judicial comment and injustices that put women at further risk in their reinforcement of myths that *approve* the crime of partner rape. The Truth About Rape group, mentioned above, has been active in publicly refuting biased legal comment in rape cases. We can join or put our support behind groups such as this; we can start our own groups or fight as individuals.

In order to create a playing field that levels the myths about domestic violence, sexual assault and their intersection in rape by a male partner, sentencing guidelines need to be created that are based upon non-gender objective standards so that biases or ignorance about harm, and of victim and perpetrator blameworthiness can no longer run amok or implicitly in sentencing:

> I feel this problem is only given 'lip service'. Make the perpetrators accountable for their actions. Heavier penalties and swifter action needs to be implemented. (Jennifer)

Better response by health practitioners

Doctors – GPs or those at the casualty unit – are often the first port of call for a victim of partner rape. They are in a position of trust and therefore can do much good if guided by some empathy and education.

> There seems little doubt that as violence escalates, or as women are supported to redefine their experiences, they will increasingly look to health and other support services for assistance. Health care providers and general practitioners are therefore critical points of intervention in being able to initially screen, respond to, and possibly prevent women's revictimisation.[15]

Unfortunately, physicians who have contact with domestic violence victims are socialised in the same culture as others in the community and are equally likely not to see sexual assault by a partner as 'real' rape. For example, Bergen's book cites a domestic violence worker who accompanied a marital rape victim to the hospital to have a rape kit done. The doctor who attended the victim told her that it wasn't really rape and that it was her fault for staying in the relationship.[16]Indeed some doctors have an unfortunate habit of condescending to abused women, negatively labelling them, blaming them and only medicating the presenting symptoms.

Many doctors have not been trained to recognise the signs of violence against women, or to perceive their role as interventionist, or to understand the dynamics of family violence such as its consequences for victims' self-esteem and their inability to act. These are essential elements in constructing a more effective response. Symptomology, dynamics of abuse, detection and appropriate treatment should be integrated into medical course curricula and taught as part of in-service training programs to improve detection or screening and supportive interaction.

Meeting the unique support needs of partner rape survivors

Because women raped by partners feel isolated and confused about the nature of what happened to them, they often need somebody to ask the right questions and offer them validation and support. As Melina describes below, counselling service providers need to understand the denial that is a part of the victim's experience and the need to ask thoughtful and indirect questions:

> You survive by covering up. If a counsellor asks a question about violence, you have been taught to outright deny any problems from fear and from your warped/damaged view of what is normal. You have learned to accept the abnormal as normal in order to survive. The questions you are asked in order to diagnose/ascertain abuse are coming from the perspective of someone 'outside' in the normal world.
>
> The counsellor asks: 'Have you been raped?'
>
> I answer: 'No'
>
> Questioning needs to be much more subtle and specific, e.g. How does he initiate sex? Do you say no to sex? Can you? Have you? What did he say? What did he do?

Aside from the delicate nature of the initial assessment interview, another issue in service provision is which area of women's services partner rape should fall under.

> ... the gap that currently exists in locating who should respond
> to intimate partner sexual assault within the service sector. If
> domestic violence services view spousal sexual violence as a
> rape issue, and sexual assault services view it as a domestic
> violence issue where does that leave the victim/survivor? [17]

Rape crisis services do have a valuable role to play in providing support
and access to healing for survivors of partner rape, although some argue
that if women identify primarily as victims of domestic violence, then
domestic violence services are more appropriate for them. It is certainly
true that some women raped by partners have safety issues that are
traditionally addressed by domestic violence services. However, if partner
rape were only the province of domestic violence services, women who
have been raped but don't identify as domestic violence survivors would
not be reached. Also, survivors of partner rape who are battered but who
find the *rape* more psychologically disturbing may be further hurt by the
fact that nobody seems to want to help them deal with the rape.

> When treated as battered women, the wounds left by the sexual
> abuse often go unaddressed. [18]

Survivors do have a hard time defining it themselves, and if services don't
specifically mention it they can perpetuate silence around partner rape,
with survivors feeling marginalised as if their rape does not deserve the
response that other rape gets.

> Both sexual assault and domestic violence services have been
> reluctant to name the experience for women in their commitment
> to ensuring victim/survivors retain maximum 'choice and control'
> over the issues they identify during counselling. However, the
> importance of balancing a woman's right to exercise control
> over the issues that she raises in counselling, and the very real
> possibility that she will be struggling to find a language or a
> framework through which to express her broader experience of
> violence, including rape, is critical. [19]

Sexual assault services can make partner rape a clearly defined part of their
outreach and help women define the violence and break the silence. [20] One
way to do this is to make sure that marital/partner rape is clearly defined
in their leaflets, posters or other advertising material. Media outreach is
also extremely helpful because, 'When a subject of this sort is discussed
often enough on television, and in popular magazines, eventually victims

hear about it.'[21] The message, 'We acknowledge partner rape and we offer support for it', will come as a relief to many women.

We know that there is a need for counselling and support groups specifically for *partner* rape.[22] Rape crisis and domestic violence services could work together with clients raped by partners to start and facilitate support groups and develop therapeutic approaches. Such coordinated responses could address both safety and rape-trauma issues.

One example of a coordinated program is 'Understanding and Responding to Disclosures of Sexual Violence' – a one day workshop offered by the Gold Coast Sexual Assault Service in Australia. Here are just a few of its aims: [23]

- Training locates IPSA (Intimate Partner Sexual Assault) in the context of contemporary research and practice in the fields of sexual assault and domestic violence, emphasising the overlap of issues of sexual assault and domestic violence in relation to strategies, legislation and funding.

- Addresses the need for collaboration between domestic violence workers, sexual assault workers and women's refuges …

- Demonstrates a sensitivity towards the barriers faced by victim/survivors in disclosing and reporting sexual assault.

- Demonstrates a capacity for replication (i.e. other services/organisations could adapt/re-model the program for their use).

This is a good 'best practice' initiative and we can hope to see programs like it developed more widely.

Survivors healing in activism

The two themes in this chapter (and aims of the book) have been changing the rape culture and helping survivors. These two intersect when we look at healing and activism.

I once believed that I had to wait until society changed before it was safe for me to speak out. I was afraid of the social stigma of being a rape victim and more afraid of being laughed at for saying partner rape is real rape. However, I came to the view that it was up to me to speak out despite the stigma and ignorance. I decided that I could and would be a part of the change I desired. (Rachel)

Indeed, take action like we have done.

> It is only through feeling the feelings from long ago – the
> sadness, the anger, and maybe most of all the fear – that we
> can go beyond and proceed from awareness through to anger, to
> action and empowerment.[24]

When you take part in a movement outside yourself, you not only stand up for yourself, you also become part of the solution in a broader sense, and this can be immensely satisfying as you work to overthrow the forces that have harmed you.

There are some suggestions in chapter 17. It is true that when women heal, they transform not only their own lives but often also those around them. Imagine legions of women ceasing to be silent and knowing that they deserve better.

The women who contributed to this book, including the authors, are exercising our activism and voices. Thus, *Real Rape, Real Pain* is an example of healing and social change in practice.

> It's been really true to my experience and really true to myself
> and really true to how I feel and there's a part of me that is just
> like thank you so much for letting me speak. There's a part of
> me that's just grateful to the rest of me that I have allowed that
> voice out, and I think I feel more whole and more, there's a lot of
> feelings and stuff and I really feel like it's this sort of vital sort of
> healing thing, so I do feel really grateful for it. (Kate)

> I would love to see awareness and acceptance of partner rape as
> a crime by society in general – that it is not a 'sort-of' rape, that
> the many women who unfortunately are forced to endure this
> trauma can feel safety and support in doing that which is best for
> them without the need to justify their past relationship with their
> assailant. If every word I wrote here or just one of them makes a
> positive impact or empowers only one survivor all of this work
> will have been worth it. (Summer)

About the Women

You have met 30 survivors in this book. We come from a variety of backgrounds and lifestyles: our occupations include psychologist, lawyer, sex worker, teacher, student, public servant, homemaker, social worker, and unemployed pensioner. We range in age from early twenties to late fifties. Some are self-identified alcoholics, recovering alcoholics and addicts, Anglo-Australian, Asian-Australian, American, Canadian, English. Some survived years of physical violence; others were not beaten. Some of us experienced repeated sexual assault, for others the rape was a 'one-off.' For some, the perpetrator was our husband, others an estranged husband, de facto partner or boyfriend.

Different voices with one commonality: each identifies as a survivor of sexual assault by an intimate partner and each wanted to be heard so that their painful experiences and trauma can serve a purpose. In the preceding pages these women opened up their hearts. They revealed their lives to date in as honest a way as they are able to do. They recognised that telling their stories or just identifying has been a part of their healing:

> I wanted to come along and tell my story because my self-expression was so squashed for all of those years. One of the real healing things for me is to express it and to face it and stop internalising it because you get locked in a world and wherever you go to the perpetrator is so strong in his manipulating controlling ways that he somehow has manipulated you into thinking that he doesn't mean it. (Liz)

In alphabetical order

Adair (USA): Thirty-three years old, I live with my boyfriend of ten years and I am the mother of two beautiful girls, ages nine and twelve. We also had a son, Conner Michael, who was stillborn. A true testament of our family's love and strength, Conner forever changed our hearts. In his one brief moment, he forever changed the way we look at life … at living it. As a family we enjoy spending our time outdoors and try to bike ride the beautiful trails around our home as often as the weather allows. I currently am working in elderly care, as a home companion, but one day hope to return to school to receive a degree in teaching. Personally, I enjoy singing and my love of music is more often than not, what can pull me through a bad day, a sad time, a beautiful moment … or just life.

Charlotte (UK): I've just come back to England with my wonderful new husband and baby. We established an incredible link of trust, and I told him everything there was to know about how I became the person I was. He accepted everything. Finally I had met someone that respected me, and treated me right. I'm in my mid-20s and finally, my priorities changed, I had this overwhelming desire to travel and meet people, and be alone … actually get to know myself again. As clichéd as that sounds, it made sense to me. 'Live a good life, die old and leave a beautiful memory.'

Emma (UK): I am 19 and I live in England. I am studying for a degree in law and have just finished my first year. I like to read; my favourite authors include David Eddings. Raymond Feist and Robert Rankin. I love the music of Tori Amos, Bob Dylan and Counting Crows, among others. I work part-time in a record store. I enjoying driving, I have my own car called Percy and he is the same age as me! I enjoy working and playing with computers, and I am (slowly) designing my own website.

Eva Jane (Australia and England): I am in my mid-fifties and have four adult children. I am studying for a higher degree in Theology. After separating from my violent husband almost 20 years ago, I started attending university which really helped my sense of self-esteem. I haven't had a relationship with anyone since my husband but am very active in the Church. I have the best relationship with my children now. I've apologised to them for things I've done through their lives. I've said to them that if they ever need to say anything to me, to say it and I have to deal with it. I'm trying to make up for what I didn't do when they were younger.

Helena (Australia and Africa): My parents and I moved to Australia from Eastern Europe when I was a little girl. I am in my mid-30s, a law student, mother of two and have recently begun a lesbian relationship. I've led a pretty adventurous life so far travelling around the world. I've lived in a number of places in Australia too. My husband was a native African.

Jackie (USA): My interests are reading, activism, and women's rights. I enjoy hanging around my house in my pyjamas until 2 p.m. and spending time with good friends over a good meal. I am close to gaining my degree in counselling.

Jennifer (Australia): I am a physically beautiful woman, literate, career minded, independent, kind, caring, fun-loving, funny and financially astute. Often described as a lady. I am an Information Technology professional employed by Government. I dislike liars, dishonesty, cruelty and bad manners. I like simple pleasures, walks, helping others and witty conversation with trusted friends. The only thing I can't do is that which I have not tried. I love my son and my cat. I honour my friends. I have met another man and am getting married soon – never thought that would happen!

Jill (USA): A psychologist, I have a few undergraduate degrees. I split up with my husband but we've had counselling and are giving the relationship another chance, particularly since we have two children. I don't drink, do drugs and am still active in my Church.

Jodie (Australia): Having grown up on a farm just out of a small country town in NSW, I moved to the city after finishing my HSC to continue my studies at University. I now work for the same university as a researcher in an Institute dedicated to Youth, Education and Community. I also currently work as a counsellor/accommodation worker with women escaping domestic violence and volunteer as a phone counsellor for another support service (women specific). I spend spare time reading, snuggling with my cat and with friends. I hope one day to be able to work either directly or indirectly with women survivors of sexual assault.

Justine (UK): I am aged 32 with one child, a girl, had been with my partner for 12 years. I am a legal secretary for a well-known solicitors in the UK. I like football (watching it) and socialising, music, crosswords and reading. I (strangely) still prefer male company to female. I feel I can relate better to men.

Kate (Australia): In my late 30s, I am studying for another undergraduate degree, which I hope will translate into a 'real' job next year. I am very busy taking care of my two young children and trying to break the cycle of violence. Since leaving the violent partner, I remarried and re-divorced. I am deeply committed to recovery from the abuses I have experienced in my life and from alcohol and codependency. I think that the biggest thing for me too is to teach them boundaries in every day life. I feel like if they've got boundaries in everyday life they'll feel stronger about their sexual life. I really push with them about respecting each other's boundaries, and mine. So I guess that's what I do for them.

Kelly (Australia): I'm a sex worker with a university degree. Bipolar, I self-medicate on cannabis. I used to do amphetamines but I've been clean for about half a year. I have a young child. I vacuum my floor on my hands and knees so I can be sure that every speck is up. I can't ever have it not absolutely perfect because if someone turned up that had never been to my house before, they would just think I was a dirty person and it is extraordinarily important to me that when people walk into my house they have to go, 'Oh my God that's just beautiful.' Like even my shower, not one, not one ever soap stain ever. I windex it every day, plus I scrub it with cleansing powder twice a week.

Kuriah (USA): The daughter of immigrants, I live in Northern California and have several university degrees. I am moving on (after years of battling in the criminal justice system). I have a wonderful young man for a child, an exciting and challenging job. I have friends for the very first time in years. I am living in my own home and am no longer paralysed by the fear of what ifs.

Linda (Luxembourg): Hobbies and interests: reading, walking, gardening (especially vegetables!), and would include riding and travelling if I didn't have so many children, and so little time and money! And writing too, I suppose, though not as much as I would like due to time restraints! I was born in the UK, grew up in Luxembourg, am following Open University course at present. My academic interests include languages, and social issues. I work full-time at the European Court of Justice. Have a long-term partner and six kids between us, which makes holidays fun and noisy and rather messy. Vices include smoking and procrastinating, and spending too much time on the computer when the kitchen needs cleaning, etc.

Liz (Australia): I'm in my mid-thirties and am in early recovery from the violence I experienced with my estranged husband. I spend most of my time as a single Mum with two young sons.

Lisa (Australia): An emigrant from the UK and with a nursing background, I was in a fairly senior position in the Public Service but am currently at a mid-level one. I'm 44 with a six-year-old son. I have been putting all of my energies into him and into trying to get some justice.

Marg (Australia): I started using alcohol when I was in my early teens. I've had at least three physically violent relationships through my 20s. About a year ago, my daughter and I ended up in another refuge. They really helped me to see that I have a problem with depression and with alcoholism. So a couple of months ago we moved into this house. I'm not drinking very much now. We're both seeing a counsellor. I sort of have a boyfriend – a guy that I've been mates with for a long time. We're mostly friends and he's OK to be with.

Maree (Australia): Chronic smoker, ex-heroin and other drug addict, and riddled with ill-health, although I'm only in my mid-40s I'm sure I look older. I have two children and a lovely granddaughter who I adore. I come across as a super tough lady with a twinkle in my eye and I've been told I have a heart of gold within. I'm recently out of prison and trying not to drink but sometimes I just get real down and get drunk.

Melina (Australia): I'm a Queenslander. I am not afraid to be different. I am grateful for my parents both being artists, instilling in me an appreciation of art and design, and a love of nature and the bush. I am now happily married with two daughters.

Natalie (Canada): I am a psychologist who has battled depression throughout my life. I'm in my mid-30s and just recently filed for divorce from my husband (not the perpetrator). I enjoy reading, card games, and dancing, and crocheting. I've just completed my PhD and have two beautiful children. I grew into a woman who takes a care-taking role; one who self-sacrifices and denies her own needs and wants for the sake of others.

Nichole (USA): I am 24 years old. I have three BA's – psychology, liberal arts for the human services, and women's studies. I am about to start my second year of law school. I enjoy trashy novels, foreign travel, and attending Tori Amos concerts. When I grow up, I hope to be a mental health lawyer, or marry into wealth and eat cherries by a swimming pool.

Patricia (USA/Australia): I indirectly convey some of my story of sexual violence by a previous partner through my voice as one of the authors. I've been in recovery for most of my life from various 'isms'. I try to get a daily endorphin high and meditative experience from jogging, cycling or aerobics. Am the mother of four adults – I tried to pickle them but they insisted on growing up.

Rachel (Louise, Australia): I have five gorgeous kids and a husband. I love music and am proud of my enormous and eclectic 750+ CD collection. I love reading, dancing, Guinness, off-colour jokes, the colour pink and absolutely anything Harry Potter oriented. I dislike snobbery and spite and have no time at all for bigots. My passions are rape activism and justice for asylum-seekers.

Sarah (Australia): I'm 32. I am working full time at a mid-level position for the government plus studying for an undergraduate degree. I am very close to my family, especially my sister. It's a major hurdle because I just simply don't trust males. It is getting better. Certainly I wasn't able to buy another house until about three and half years ago because what was the point of acquiring anything and making yourself comfortable if somebody else could walk off with it? I haven't had a relationship since my marriage ended and I don't know how much longer it will be before I am able to not be driven by fear to the extent where I can be comfortable enough around a man.

Samantha (Australia): I am 37 years old and have one teenage daughter. We live in the Northern Territory. I have a Bachelor of Commerce degree but only started working recently since I left my husband.

Shefali (Bangladesh woman in Australia): I moved to Australia from Bangladesh as a young teenager. My parents were fairly traditional Muslims and I was taught to be a good girl. I didn't finish uni but have worked in the public service my adult life. I'm now in my late 30s and have three children. Under the circumstances I think I'm coping very well. I have a house, a car, three beautiful and healthy children, still a permanent job that gives so much leave, my good health, some genuine friends and the best and not the least – my sanity.

Siobhan (Australia): I am in my mid-40s and am on a pension looking after my teenage son. I have a hearing disability. I enjoy a wine or two with dinner and perhaps more when socialising; perhaps more than I should. Sometimes it worries me since it's in the back of my mind, 'Oh my god I hope I don't turn into an alcoholic', because I must say I do like the relaxed feeling. Being a tense person and being shy, in social situations it helps me to relax and talk to people. I may never get into another relationship because I won't trust anybody ever again.

Summer (USA): I am a mother of three teen daughters, ages 17, 15 and 13. To say that they are my life and my sustenance would be a vast understatement. I am currently married but working my way out. Before last year I was employed in a Human Resources position with a contract research organisation specialising in cancer research. Last year I made the decision to take on the responsibility of caring for my elderly grandfather on a full-time basis. It is both challenging and rewarding. I love writing, reading, and spending time with close friends. My greatest love outside of my children is spending time near the ocean. It is close to my home and I go there frequently to think about how far I have come and where I am headed in my life. I suppose you could say that I have a deep reverence for the ocean. I dislike disingenuous people, close-minded people. My life today is precious to me, something that I couldn't say for the longest time, not that long ago. Above all else, I am a survivor and no longer a victim. I truly am blessed despite the bad that was done to me.

Tiffany (US): I'm in my 40s and now live in Australia with my second husband and my 18-year-old son. I have a fairly senior level job with the Government. My relationship with my current husband is affected I think by the violence inflicted by the ex. It does still haunt me. We have quite an active social life and enjoy going to clubs with other couples.

Tracey (Australia): I'm in my mid-20s and work for a tele-communications company. I am a keen role player and travel around Australia, when I can afford to, going to role-playing conventions. I just want to get on with my life. I don't need a man to feel that my life is complete. I'm quite happy just to be me for a while and leave it at that.

APPENDIX 2

If You are Sexually Assaulted

If you want to press charges, don't shower or bathe. While it is understandable you may want to wash, this leads to the loss of evidence. If you are pressing charges, you will need to have a doctor do a rape-kit – that is the gathering of physical evidence that can be used in court. A rape crisis worker can explain the process to you. See chapter 14 for important information about reporting partner rape and the courts.

We recommend that you go to a hospital to have any injuries tended to whether you are pressing charges or not. STD issues may need attention. You will not be required to disclose who raped you. Because post-rape treatment (or the rape-kit process if you are reporting the rape) can feel humiliating and frightening, you can have a rape crisis worker and/or a good friend accompany you.

You can ask for the morning after pill to eradicate a possible conception if you wish. This can be taken up to 72 hours after the assault. Because of the personal philosophies of some doctors or nurses, they may not offer you the morning after pill, but you *do* have a right to have access to it – so do ask if you are not offered it. Also, in some places it is possible to get the morning after pill over the counter from a pharmacy. You don't have to tell anybody why you want it. If you don't want to take the morning after pill, it's most important that you know a rape-related pregnancy puts you under no obligation to return to your ex-partner.

Try to find a practitioner or a place that has expertise in sexual assault so you are not wounded by a health provider's ignorance:

> The only person I went to see that day was the local GP and got the morning after pill and he documented all my bruises and that, but he was too scared to do anything. He kept saying, 'It's not my area of expertise and you shouldn't really be here', and he just wanted to push me out the door. He wasn't interested

and he was flustered. He was just a normal sort of middle-aged
family man GP. (Lisa)

Rape crisis workers usually are aware of doctors who are known to be
sensitive, and may recommend one to you.

Get as much support as you can. You deserve it. Your journey will be made
a little easier with people who are on your side. Rape crisis services are
there for you to use, and can be found by looking in your telephone book.
Please also see Appendix 3 for online resources.

Your self-care is most important at this time. Be very kind to yourself
as you recover, and remember that what has happened to you is not
unimportant.

We wish you healing and strength.

Suggested Reading and Online Resources

Books

Many of the books below can be ordered online through Amazon.

Marital/partner rape

I Never called it Rape, Robin Warshaw, HarperPerennial, New York 1994

Published results of the *MS* magazine study on rape by dates and acquaintances. Much good and relevant material.

License to Rape: Sexual Abuse of Wives, David Finkelhor and Kersti Yllo, The Free Press, New York 1985

This landmark study covers many aspects of rape by husbands, including effects on women and potential strategies for ending it. Also, interviews with husbands who raped their wives – scary, but truly illuminates that it is their problem, their issues around power and not your fault.

Rape in Marriage, Diana E.H. Russell, MacMillan Publishing Company, USA 1990

A must-read for anybody seeking to understand rape by partners. Includes a section on rape by lovers, i.e. boyfriends. Excellent coverage of the view of women as property from historical times.

The Rapist Who Pays the Rent, Ruth Hall, Selma James and Judith Kertesz – A British text which covers women's fight to have rape in marriage recognised as a crime. Can be mail-ordered cheaply from WAR (Women Against Rape, UK) Ph: 02074822496 or email: war@womenagainstrape.net

Voices of the Survivors, Patricia Easteal, Spinifex Press, North Melbourne 1994

An Australian text, this book covers rape in very many settings, including by husbands, boyfriends and estranged partners.

Wife Rape: Understanding the Response of Survivors and Service Providers, Raquel Kennedy Bergen Sage Publications Inc., California 1996

Excellent study with lots of material on the responses and needs of survivors of rape by husbands.

Note: Because some of the above books are published studies, they are costly. See if your library or local women's resource centre stocks them.

For Christian survivors of rape/domestic violence

Hope for the Brokenhearted: Biblical Solutions for Survivors of Abuse and Rape, Todd R. Cook. ACW Press, USA 2004

Keeping the Faith: Guidance for Christian Women Facing Abuse, Marie M. Fortune, HarperCollins Publishers, New York 1987

Reverend Dr Fortune's books about Christians, the clergy and sexual/domestic violence have been revolutionary.

Trauma and healing

Healing the Trauma of Domestic Violence, Edward Kubany, Ph.D., Mari McCaig, MSCP, and Janet R. Laconsay, MA. New Harbinger Publications Inc, California, 2003

Information and writing exercises on domestic-violence related trauma.

I Can't Get Over it: A Handbook for Trauma Survivors, Aphrodite Matsakis PhD. New Harbinger Publications Inc, California, 1992.

Excellent. Explains PTSD thoroughly but without 'textbooky' stodginess. Good sections on domestic violence and rape. Writing exercises and other strategies for healing and taking control of your life again.

Recovering from Rape, Linda E. Ledray R.N. Ph.D, Henry Holt and Company, New York, 1994.

Geared more towards survivors of rape by strangers or acquaintances, but still some good material which helps you understand and master your feelings

Trauma and Recovery: from domestic abuse to political terror, Judith Lewis Herman, BasicBooks, USA, 1992

A classic. Scholarly but very human and compassionate. Dr Herman covers the many reasons why women may find themselves unable to leave abusive relationships, and what the repercussions can be. Discusses safety as it is related to healing.

Sexuality and relationships after abuse

The Sexual Healing Journey: A Guide for Survivors of Sexual Abuse, Wendy Maltz, HarperCollins Publishers Inc., New York, 2001.

Compassionate advice on reclaiming sexuality after sexual abuse. Much focus on child sexual abuse.

Trust After Trauma: A Guide to Relationships for Trauma Survivors and Those Who Love Them, Aphrodite Matsakis PhD, New Harbinger Publications Inc, California, 1998.
Helpful and comprehensive book on overcoming the impact of trauma on relationships.

Escaping abuse

Free Yourself from an Abusive Relationship: Seven Steps to Taking Back Your Life, Andrea Lissette MA, CDVC and Richard Kraus PhD. Hunter House Inc, California, 2000
Good, practical advice on all aspects of leaving an abusive relationship.

Stalking

Stalked: Breaking the Silence on the Crime of Stalking in America, Melita Schaum and Karen Parrish, Pocket Books, New York 1995.
Statistics on stalking, testimonies of survivors, and advice for dealing with stalking.

Rape and law

Balancing the Scales: Rape, Law Reform and Australian Culture, Ed. Patricia Easteal, The Federation Press, NSW 1988
A series of excellent legal essays on aspects of rape law, and inequity in Australia. Much focus on legal stereotypes of what is 'real' rape and directives for change.

Carnal Knowledge: Rape on Trial, Sue Lees, The Women's Press London, 1997
A good UK text which analyses many aspects of rape law. Calls for change.

Rape and the Legal Process, Temkin, J, Sweet and Maxwell, London, 1987.

Real Rape: How the Legal System Victimizes Women who say No, Susan Estrich, President and Fellows of Harvard College, USA, 1987
This is a classic US text which explores inequities in the law contributed to by stereotypical notions of rape.

Rape and society

Against our Will: Men, Women and Rape, Susan Brownmiller, Ballantine Books New York, 1993.
Exploration of historical and contemporary approval of rape as a tool of power over women. Analysis of rape in many settings. Though this classic is almost 30 years old, its power has not diminished.

Transforming a Rape Culture – Eds**.** Emilie Buchwald, Pamela R. Fletcher, Martha Roth Milkweed Editions, Minneapolis, 1995 Beautiful, strong and insightful essays into why rape culture exists and what must be done about it. Survivors of marital rape, please read Carol Adams' essay within.

Online resources

If you have access to the internet, there are some good sites offering information and support. We've listed a selection of sites and online organisations for you to browse.

Important: Internet Safety

Web browsers store a history of all the pages you visit during your time on the internet. If your abuser has access to your computer, we encourage you to read and follow the instructions below to maximise privacy and safety.

Hidden hurt abuse information and support site instructions[i]

Clearing the view history in your web browser

Using the toolbar of your web browser, find the menu selection that gives you view options.

In Microsoft Internet Explorer use the View button, then select Options, then Navigation. In the History section, select Clear History, then OK.

In Netscape Navigator use the Options button, then select Network Preferences, then both Clear Memory Cache and Clear Disk Cache, then OK.

In AOL click on the Members menu, click on Preferences, click on the www icon, select Advanced and then Purge Cache.

Other web browsers should have similar features.

Additionally, you need to make sure that the 'Use Inline Autocomplete' box is *not* checked. This function will complete a partial web address while typing a location in the address bar at the top of the browser.

If you are using Internet Explorer, this box can be found on the MS Internet Explorer Page by clicking on the 'View' icon at the top, then 'Internet Options', and then the 'Advanced' tab. About halfway down there is a 'Use Autocomplete' box that can be checked and unchecked by clicking on it.

Email: If an abuser has access to your email account, he may be able to read your incoming and outgoing mail. If you believe your account is secure, make sure you choose a password he won't be able to guess.

Be aware that this is not foolproof. An observant computer user may notice that the history is gone, and get suspicious.

Message boards

Message boards are good ways of getting support, ideas and validation from other survivors. You may forge supportive friendships with survivors from around the world. It is important though *not* to give out personal details unless you are certain that you can trust those whom you give them to, and don't use your full name at any time. Find out whether forums are private, with Google spidering disabled so that your posts cannot be located by search engines.

In choosing a message board, you need to consider whether it is safely moderated. Anybody can decide to start a survivor message board, but not all are appropriate to be in charge of communities of vulnerable people. Users can be damaged by abusive or unhealed moderators or members, and there is no accountability.

The following two message boards are listed because in our experience, they are responsibly moderated and safe healing communities.

Rape/child sexual abuse support

Pandora's Aquarium: *www.pandys.org*

A thriving and supportive community featuring forums on sexuality, parenting, trauma, relationships and other. Moderated chat room.

Domestic violence support: Artemis Message Forums: http://hiddenhurt. *rhiannon3.net*

Moderated by three wise and healing women.

Rape/domestic violence survivor sites

Marital/partner rape links

Aphrodite Wounded, Help for Women sexually Assaulted by Partners: www.aphroditewounded.org

National Clearinghouse on Marital and Date Rape: *http://members.aol. com/ncmdr/*

Hidden Hurt Marital Rape Article: *www.hiddenhurt.co.uk/Articles/ maritalrape.htm*

Just Keeping the Peace – Australian Partner Rape study: *www.aifs.gov. au/acssa/pubs/issue/i1.html*

Survive UK Marital Rape Article: *http://survive.org.uk/maritalrape.html*

The Wife Rape Information Page: *http://www.wellesley.edu/WCW/projects/mrape.html*

Marital Rape – A US Study: *http://www.thecriminologist.com/new_criminologist/volume1/marital_rape/marital_rape.asp*

Rape help sites

Welcome to Barbados: *www.welcometobarbados.org/*

Surviving to Thriving: *www.survivingtothriving.org/*

Escaping Hades: *www.escapinghades.pandys.org/*

Rape, Abuse and Incest National Network (USA): *www.rainn.org/*

PTSD/Rape Trauma Syndrome

Gift from Within – Several good articles on PTSD: *www.giftfromwithin.org/*

Rape Trauma Syndrome: The Journey to Healing Belongs to Everyone, by Aimee Menna *www.giftfromwithin.org/html/journey.html*

Stress Responses in Sexual Trauma Victims and in Others: Experiencing Overwhelming Events: Helpful Strategies for Self, Children, Supporters, and What Trauma Therapists Really Do by DR. Erwin R. Parson and Luerena K. Bannon: *http://www.giftfromwithin.org/html/strategy.html*

Domestic violence help sites

Hidden Hurt: *www.hiddenhurt.co.uk/*

Rhiannon3: *www.rhiannon3.net/index.html*

Domestic Violence and Incest Resource Centre (DVIRC) Australia: *www.dvirc.org.au*

Domestic violence/rape resources for women of different faiths

What does Islam say of domestic violence?

www.islamherald.com/asp/questions/violence/islam_and_domestic_violence.asp

Islamic Society of North America's (ISNA) Domestic Violence Forum: *www.isna.net/dv/*

(This site contains advice from an Imam).

Jewish Women International: *www.jewishwomen.org*

Articles on Judaism and Domestic Abuse: *http://members.aol.com/agunah/articles.htm*

Christian Reformed Church Abuse Prevention: *www.crcna.org/abuse/*

Hope For Healing: *www.hopeforhealing.org*

Christians for Biblical Equality: *www.cbeinternational.org*

Help for teenagers surviving abusive relationships

GirlHealth: *www.girlhealth.org/test/rape3/facts.html*

Teenwire: *www.teenwire.com/*

Make a Noise: *www.ysp.org.au/*

Trust Betrayed: *www.wvdhhr.org/bph/trust/*

NebFacts – Dating Violence/Assault: *http://ianrpubs.unl.edu/family/ nf244.htm*

Stalking

The Anti-Stalking Website: *www.antistalking.com/*

Stalking Victim's Sanctuary: *www.stalkingvictims.com/*

Wilson's Safety Plan[1]

Safety when preparing to leave

1. Make arrangements to go to a place that is safe. This may be with trusted friends, relatives or a hotel.

2. Keep a bag packed and hidden that contains clothes and personal hygiene items. You should also pack money; extra cheques or a cheque book; charge cards; important papers such as a protection order; birth certificates; marriage licence; children's immunisation records; titles to property or cars; and telephone numbers of friends, relatives or shelters. You may want to pack anything which has personal value to you, such as photographs that you don't want destroyed. If you have space, pack one or two of your children's toys.

3. To avoid jeopardising your safety, hide the bag where it won't be discovered by your partner, perhaps leaving it with trusted friends, relatives or at work.

4. Hide an extra set of house keys and car keys in a place that is easily accessible to you.

Safety during a violent episode

1. Make a safety plan in advance in case you need to leave your home quickly.

2. If an argument seems unavoidable, try to have it in a room from which you can easily get away. Try to stay away from rooms where weapons may be available, including the bathroom, kitchen and bedroom.

3. Identify in advance the doors, windows or stairways that would allow you to get out of your home quickly and safely.

4. Identify trusted neighbours that you can tell about the violence, and ask that they call the police if they hear a disturbance coming from your home.

5. Devise a code-word to use with your children, trusted family members, friends and neighbours when you need them to call the police.

Workplace safety

1. Decide who at work you will inform of your situation. This can include a supervisor, a staff person in the employee assistance program, or human resources department and security personnel.

2. Provide a picture of your batterer to the appropriate persons.

3. Ask for help screening your telephone calls at work.

4. Review your work schedule with your supervisor and ask about changing your work hours.

5. Ask your supervisor about changing your work station.

6. Review the parking situation. If possible, try to park close to the building for easy entry and exit

Ask someone to escort you to and from your vehicle. Ask them to wait until you are safely on your way.

7. Try to use a variety of routes to and from your home. Plan what you would do if something happened while you were going home.

8. Provide your contacts at work with name and telephone number of an emergency contact person in case you can't be reached. This person should be someone other than your abusive partner and should be someone you trust.

9. If you need to take a leave from work, provide your address or telephone number to a trusted company contact person.

10. If you need to permanently leave your community, ask whether your company has a relocation program and how it operates.

APPENDIX 5

About Restraining Orders

Depending on where you live, these may be called something different; for instance in Australia, one can apply for what is called in some states a domestic violence order (DVO) and in others, an Apprehended violence order (AVO).[1] In the US, the past decade has witnessed much movement in domestic violence legislation.

> Legislative attention to the problem of domestic violence has led in the past decade to the enactment of an avalanche of new laws in the 50 states. Between 1997 and 2003 there were over 700 new domestic violence-related enactments, including both amendments of old laws and enactment of new laws, such as the creation of a new crime of domestic violence in 38 states.[2]

In most jurisdictions you don't have to have lived with a man to be eligible for some type of a restraining order. Most places do recognise that women who break up with partners they did not live with may face threats, stalking, rape, and other acts of abuse or intimidation too. For instance in 2004, the *Domestic Violence, Crime and Victims Act* 2004 was enacted in the UK which made 'couples who have never cohabited or been married eligible for non-molestation and occupation orders'.[3] In the US there has also been some accommodation made for single people.[4]

Wherever you are, please check with your local court or domestic violence advocacy service to find out where you stand.

Some women don't seek an Order because they are afraid such action may provoke the abuser, or will be useless. If you have felt that way, perhaps you will be encouraged by the following, written by survivor and counsellor Susan Brewster:

> Most battered women I have counselled are initially terrified to file assault complaints, protective orders, or anything else which their abusive partners won't like. Many women eventually come to recognise, however, that they are in danger either way: they

are being hurt even when they are appeasing their partner's every wish. Many of these women eventually decide that having a protective order is better than having nothing. Though some batterers ignore court orders or other such threats of disciplinary action, many will discontinue (at least temporarily) their violent behaviour when they see that punishment for that behaviour is uncomfortable and inevitable.[5]

While restraining orders cannot offer ironclad guarantees, they are shown to be helpful in a high proportion of cases:

Orders for Protection; New News: Only 20 per cent of women who report partner violence get protection orders – also known as restraining orders – that prohibit their abusers from certain types of contact. While the effectiveness of these orders has been a subject of debate, a new large-scale study suggests that they can and do work. A retrospective study of 2691 victims of partner abuse found that those who received a permanent court-ordered protection order (usually lasting 12 months) had an 80 per cent less risk of further abuse compared with women not receiving a protection order. Women who received temporary protection orders (usually in effect for 2 weeks) were no more likely to experience physical abuse than women without any protection order, although their risk of psychological abuse (harassment. stalking and threats) was far greater. The study was authored by Dr. Mary A. Kernic of the University of Washington and the Harborview Injury Prevention and Research Center in Seattle and published in the Journal of the American Medical Association in August 2002.[6]

Another positive outcome of protection orders can be an increased sense of personal control and self-confidence for you:[7]

The violence and threats to my life worsened; the final straw was when Paul came one night while I was bathing, declared that I was his forever – and pushed my head under the water, holding it there. I decided to act, and got a restraining order. Although there was still verbal harassment, I was grateful for the fact that it did end the physical violence. I wanted to be around to raise my two children. (Rachel)

The burden of proof does vary across jurisdictions and so you need to check with your local domestic violence service. If there hasn't been physical violence with injuries, witnesses or diaries that evidence emotional abuse can be helpful:

> I did successfully obtain an order giving me protection from Ahmad. I had diaries that I'd kept over a period of time, initially they were to be a journal of my pregnancy to give my daughter, but I'd never let her read it now. The order was the only thing that gave me instant peace from my husband's terrorising ... I managed to get a meeting with the police prosecutor on duty that day before court started. If I hadn't, I don't think I would have been granted the order; when in a tight spot Ahmad is incredibly slippery and relies on confusing an issue till you can't make head nor tail of what's going on. I got to give the police prosecutor a little of the history, so once in court he saw him coming. One thing I would like to emphasise here is that I was really shocked at how you usually aren't given a chance to speak to your police prosecutor before you go into the court room. You just hit the ground running with someone who knows nothing about your case, in the hopes of their being able to get you protection from a dangerous man. I think it would make a huge, huge difference if you are given a short interview with your assigned prosecutor before you go into the courtroom. (Melina)

In many places, the onus of prosecution or action is still placed upon the victim:

> I applied by myself at the local women's Domestic Violence support centre. I only did so because I'd been told by two solicitors that what he was doing was domestic violence and he wouldn't stop unless I did something about it. It briefly occurred to me that these people were more sane than I was and they could possibly see things more clearly than I could. Thank God they did say it – no one else around me knew there was anything that could be done ... I had to get the order renewed just as it was coming up for expiration, because he made new threats of violence. I think he had a court case of some kind, and he felt he could frighten me into giving evidence for him or something. This was only renewed for one year. Ahmad got a friend to appear on his behalf in court. This time I went in without getting to see the police prosecutor first, and it was terrifying seeing him struggle to get a grip on the history of the case in a space of seconds. It was so unfair on both of us. (Melina)

Research has shown ambivalence by both the police and magistrates with some of the latter not regarding reasonable fear as sufficient grounds for granting an order:[8]

When I fought for my restraining order, the magistrate stated that I didn't need a weapons inclusion as Maggot had never hurt me with a weapon and that Maggot needed access to weapons to do his job. He didn't need to use a weapon. He silenced me quite effectively with his fists.

The police failed to support me in my application for my restraining order and told me I was quite capable of doing so myself. I feel that their failure to do so made every step in my escape so much more difficult and ridiculously expensive for me. At times I felt like I was totally drowning under the pressure.

They dropped the charge and it looks like the common assault will be dropped too. (Jennifer)

Legal Aid terminated my application since I couldn't provide the financial documentation they required. They did go to court for me though to adjourn the DVO mention until after the criminal charges. I was assured that the DVO would be in place until then. Yet two weeks later I received a letter from Legal Aid stating that the DVO had been revoked. (Samantha)

However, we must note that this does seem to be an area of law that is changing and attempting to meet victims' needs in jurisdictions around the world. In Tasmania, for example, legislation was enacted in April 2005 that allows police officers over the rank of sergeant or above to issue a police family violence order. Economic and emotional abuse or intimidation are included as types of violence along with a test of whether 'the behaviour is calculated to unreasonably control or intimidate its victim'. [9]

Two legal procedures for American women to be cautious of are *forced mediation* and *mutual protection orders*. These assume a level playing field between abuser and abused. You possibly already understand that your ex-partner will lie and manipulate in mediation sessions. As well, if you have been abused, you should not have to experience the trauma of facing your abuser in an environment not designed to maximise your safety. Please talk to your lawyer and/or a domestic violence advocate about how you can get out of mediation if the court has ordered it.

Because a mutual protection order is one that holds that both parties are aggressors, it may lead to police refusal to help you if you have been abused. [10]

What if he violates/breaches the restraining order?

This is a very real concern, because as we know, it happens not infrequently. If you continue to be abused, harassed or threatened in any way after obtaining an order, your ex-partner is committing a criminal act (in most jurisdictions).[11] Be prepared to call the police, and make sure you have a copy of the order with you at all times so that if it is violated, you can produce it straight away.

It is sad but true that women sometimes still receive unhelpful or insulting behaviour from the police when they attempt to report domestic violence or infractions of restraining orders. There is some evidence that police and the courts sometimes minimise the violence and the violent partner is not punished.[12]

> Every time he came to the door and started up I'd have to call the police, and some of them were very supportive. Some of them weren't. They wouldn't arrest him except one time. In the middle of the night he was banging on the windows and yelling. Peter woke up screaming. (Tiffany)

> I had a police chief tell me I was being 'bitchy' because I wanted my batterer arrested for violating the restraining order. They are too quick to place the blame with the victim. They tell you they are overworked and underpaid. They leave out the part of them choosing their profession in justice. (Kuriah)

Also, you may have to prove that the order has been breached. It is good, therefore, to have photos of any injuries and to have witnesses. As Tracey points out, the last can be difficult:

> The other thing that also brings a large amount of impotence to the order is that for me to prove that that actually happened, I would have to convince my friend to take time off work to come into a Magistrates Court to then give a testimony to the Magistrates Court and/or a police officer and give an affidavit. Most people don't want to get involved to that level. So he has complete freedom of movement, can go wherever he wants to go, short of going to where I live or work, and yet every time I'm invited to something, I'm the one having to ask, 'Is this person going to be here? What's going to happen if he turns up? Is someone else going to be the one to say sorry that I have to leave? Am I going to really be comfortable saying no I have to leave. If something happens, do I have someone who is willing to take the time off work to make a statement at the Magistrates Court?'

If you feel that concerns for your safety have not been adequately acted upon, you have the right of complaint. Your safety matters.

End Notes

Preface

[1] Patricia Easteal, *Killing the Beloved*: *Homicide Between Adult Sexual Intimates in Australia*, Canberra: Australian Institute of Criminology.

[2] *R v Robyn Bella Kina* (1993) 79 ACR 109, per the President and Davies JA.

[3] Patricia Easteal, *Voices of the Survivors*, Melbourne, Spinifex Press.

Chapter 1

[1] Aphrodite Matsakis, *I Can't get Over It*: *A handbook for trauma survivors*, New Harbinger Publications Inc, California, 1992, p. 79.

[2] Linda Ledray, *Recovering from Rape* Henry Holt and Company, New York, 1994, p. 132.

[3] A Matsakis, 1992, p. xvii.

[4] A Matsakis, 1992, p. xix.

[5] Judith Herman, *Trauma and Recovery*: *From domestic abuse to political terror*, BasicBooks, USA, 1992, p. 212.

Chapter 2

[1] Melanie Heenan, 'Just 'keeping the peace': A reluctance to respond to male partner sexual violence' (2004) 1 Issues Australia Study for the Centre of Sexual Assault citing P Mahoney and L M Williams (1998), 'Sexual assault in marriage: Prevalence, consequences, and treatment of wife rape,' in Jana L Jasinski and Linda M Williams (eds) Partner Violence: A Comprehensive Review of 20 Years of Research, Sage Publications, Thousand Oaks, USA.

[2] David Finkelhor and Kersti Yllo, *Licence to Rape*: *Sexual Abuse of Wives* Holt, 1985, p. 30.

[3] Diana Russell, *Rape in Marriage*, MacMillan Publishing Company, USA, 1990, p. 86.

4   Raquel Bergen, *Wife Rape: Understanding the response of survivors and service providers*, Sage Publications Inc, California, 1996.

5   Judith Herman, *Trauma and Recovery: From domestic abuse to political terror*, BasicBooks, USA, 1992, p. 80.

6   ibid and D Finkelhor and K Yllo, 1985.

7   US Department of Justice, *Marital Rape: A US Study*, The New Criminologist at http://www.thecriminologist.com/new_criminologist/volume1/marital_rape/marital_rape.asp citing I Johnson, I, and R Sigler (1997). Forced sexual intercourse in intimate relationships. Dartmouth/Ashgate and RK Bergen (1996). Wife rape: Understanding the response of survivors and service providers. Thousand Oaks, CA: Sage.

8   Walter S DeKeseredy, Carolyn Joseph, Jessica Edgar, *Understanding Separation/Divorce Sexual Assault in Rural Communities: The Contributions of an Exploratory Oho Study*, Paper presented at the 2003 National Institute of Justice Conference on Criminal Justice Research and Evaluation, Washington, DC, at February 2004.

9   'Marital Rape' Battered Women's Justice project at www.bwjp.org/documents/Marital per cent 20Rape per cent 20Word.doc.

10   D Finkelhor and K Yllo, 1985.

11   D Russell,1990, p. 201.

12   D Finkelhor and K Yllo, 1985.

13   Patricia Easteal, *Voices of the Survivors*, Spinifex, 1994.

14   Patricia Easteal, *Shattered Dreams*, BIMPR, 1996.

Chapter 3

1   Raquel Bergen, *Wife Rape: Understanding the response of survivors and service providers*, Sage Publications Inc, California, 1996, p. 104.

2   D Russell,1990.

3   Patricia Easteal, *Voices of the Survivors*, Spinifex, Melbourne, 1994.

4   Australian Bureau of Statistics, *Women's Safety Survey* (1996), p. 14. Both P Easteal *Less Than Equal*, Butterworths, Sydney and Melanie Heenan 'Just "keeping the peace": A reluctance to respond to male partner sexual violence' (2004) 1 *Issues Australia Study for the Centre of Sexual Assault* argue that these figures are no doubt conservative.

5   K J Wilson, *When Violence Begins at Home: A comprehensive guide to understanding and ending domestic violence,* Hunter House Inc, California, 1997.

6   D Finkelhor and K Yllo, *License to Rape: Sexual Abuse of Wives*, The Free Press, New York, 1985.

7   K Painter, Wife Rape, Marriage and Law: Survey Report, Key Findings and Recommendations, 1991, as provided on the Rape Crisis Federation, Wales and England,website at http://www.cambridgerapecrisis.org.uk/rcf-archive/statistics.htm.

8   A worker, Cattis, went through the 'face sheets' in order to collect the data and ensure client confidentiality. Of the 712 files from 1995 through 2002, in 172 the relationship of victim to perpetrator was not mentioned on the cover sheet.

9   Patricia Easteal, *Less Than Equal: Women and the Australian Legal System*, Sydney: Butterworths, 2001, pp. 139-60 for Australian statistics and discussion.

10   D Shapcott, *The Face of the Rapist*, Penguin Books, Auckland, 1988, pp. 37, 108.

11   D Shapcott, 1988, p. 102.

12   D Shapcott, 1988, p. 36.

13   D Russell,1990, p. 18.

14   D Finkelhor and K Yllo, 1985.

15   D Russell, 1990, p. 261.

16   See Alison Young 'The Wasteland of the Law, the Wordless Song of the Rape Victim' 22 (1998) *Melbourne University Law Review*, pp. 445-6. She writes that woman's 'signal quality exists through the projection of femininity from her bodily surfaces' and that this idea is conveyed to or through the law in rape trials. Empirical research of juries has shown that evidence of apparently precipitating conduct on the part of the complainant as well as jurors' perceptions of her sexual character can be crucial in their decision-making. See for instance, H Kalven and H Zeisel, 1966, *The American Jury*, Little, Brown & Co, Boston,; C Jones and E Aronson, 1973, 'Attribution of Fault to a Rape Victim as a Function of Respectability of the Victim', *Journal of Personality and Social Psychology*, 26, p. 415.

17   Anne Summers, *The End of Equality: Work babies and women's choices in 21st century Australia* Random House, Milsons Point, 2003, p. 93.

18   Rae Kaspiew, 'Rape Lore: Legal Narrative and Sexual Violence' 20 (1995) *Melbourne University Law Review*, p. 355.

19   D Finkelhor and K Yllo, 1985, p. 86: M Victory, *For Better or Worse: Family Violence in Australia*, Victoria, 1993, p. 28.

20   Carol Adams 'I just raped my wife! What are you going to do about it, Pastor?' The church and sexual violence', in *Transforming a Rape Culture*, eds E Buchwald, P Fletcher and M Roth, Milkweed Editions, Minneapolis, 1995, p. 64.

[21] Helen Benedict, *Virgin or Vamp: How the press covers sex crimes*, Oxford University Press, New York, 1992, p. 3.

[22] H Benedict, 1992, pp. 86-7.

[23] R Warshaw, *I Never Called It Rape: The MS. Report on recognizing, fighting and surviving date and acquaintance rape*, HarperPerennial, New York, 1994, p. 63.

[24] R Bergen, 1996, p. 66.

Chapter 4

[1] Aphrodite Matsakis, *I Can't get Over It: A handbook for trauma survivors*, New Harbinger Publications Inc, California, 1992, p. 293.

[2] Aphrodite Matsakis 1992, p. 268.

[3] D Russell 1975, p. 267.

[4] D Finkelhor and K Yllo, *License to Rape: Sexual Abuse of Wives*, The Free Press, New York, 1985, p. 25; Patricia Easteal Voices of the Survivors, Spinifex Press, 1994, p. 74.

[5] Finkelhor and Yllo, 1985, p. 91.

[6] Finkelhor and Yllo, 1985, p. 90.

[7] Matsakis, 1992, p. 78.

Chapter 5

[1] Judith Herman, *Trauma and Recovery: From domestic abuse to political terror*, BasicBooks, USA, 1992, p. 112.

[2] J Herman 1992, p. 111.

[3] J Herman 1992, p. 112.

[4] Y Darlington, *Moving On: Women's Experiences of Childhood Sexual Abuse and Beyond*, The Federation Press Pty Ltd Sydney 1996, p. 67.

Chapter 6

[1] Carol Adams, 'I just raped my wife! What are you going to do about it, Pastor?' The church and sexual violence, in *Transforming a Rape Culture*, eds E Buchwald, P Fletcher and M Roth, Milkweed Editions, Minneapolis, 1995, p. 63-4.

[2] These reasons are drawn from D Finkelhor and K Yllo, *License to Rape: Sexual Abuse of Wives*, The Free Press, New York, 1985, pp. 65, 80, 79, 66, 81 and 76.

[3] Reasons for stranger rape are drawn from Diana Russell, *The Politics of Rape: The Victim's Perspective*, Stein and Day, 1975, New York, pp. 244, 253, 252, 246, 245.

4   Researcher Nicholas Groth studied jailed sex-offenders and identified three categories of rapist motivation: Power, Anger and Sadism. These categories are a useful contribution to an understanding of perpetrator mindset. We will explore them, with some examples of how they work.

5   Nicholas Groth, with H Jean Birnbaum, *Men Who Rape: The Psychology of the offender*, Plenum Press, New York, 1979, p. 25-8.

6   D Shapcott, *The Face of the Rapist*, Penguin Books, Auckland, 1988, p. 44.

7   N Groth, 1979, p. 25.

8   Diana Russell, 1990, p. 153.

9   D Shapcott, 1988, p. 38.

10   N Groth, 1979, p. 3.

11   D Shapcott, 1988, p. 39.

12   N Groth, 1979, p. 3.

13   D Shapcott, 1988, p. 39.

14   N Groth, 1979, pp. 4, 16.

15   D Finkelhor and K Yllo, 1985, pp. 54-5.

16   N Groth, 1979.

17   Studies certainly bear this out, e.g. D Finkelhor and K Yllo,1985, p. 55; D Russell, 1990, p. 46.

18   D Finkelhor and K Yllo, 1985, pp. 50, 55.

19   C Adams, 1995, p. 68.

20   S Hite, *The Hite Report on Male Sexuality: How men feel about love, sex and relationships*, Ballantine Books, New York, 1982, p. 776.

21   Respondent in Hite, 1981, p. 749.

22   Cited in B Toner, *The Facts of Rape*, Arrow Books Ltd, London, 1977, p. 80.

23   D Russell, 1975, p. 110-11.

Chapter 7

1   K J Wilson, *When Violence Begins at Home: A comprehensive guide to understanding and ending domestic violence*, Hunter House Inc, California, 1997, pp. 23, 25.

2   For an overview of the types of violence, dynamics and effects, see Patricia Easteal, 'Violence against women in the home: Kaleidoscopes on a collision course?', *QUT Law and Justice Journal* Vol 3 No 2 2003, at http://www.law.qut.edu.au/about/ljj/editions/v3n2/easteal_full.jsp.

3   K J Wilson, 1997, p. 10.

Chapter 8

[1]   Carol Adams 'I just raped my wife! What are you going to do about it, Pastor?' The church and sexual violence, in *Transforming a Rape Culture*, eds E Buchwald, P Fletcher and M Roth, Milkweed Editions, Minneapolis, 1995, p. 63.

[2]   We are using K J Wilson, *When Violence Begins at Home: A comprehensive guide to understanding and ending domestic violence*, Hunter House Inc, California, 1997 for excuses that violent partners commonly use (1997, p. 22). We have adapted them to fit sexual violence.

[3]   D Shapcott, *The Face of the Rapist*, Penguin Books, Auckland, 1988, p. 31-2.

[4]   D Finkelhor and K Yllo, *License to Rape: Sexual Abuse of Wives*, The Free Press, New York, 1985, p. 115; Raquel Bergen *Wife Rape: Understanding the response of survivors and service providers*, Sage Publications Inc, California, 1996, p. 26.

[5]   R Warshaw, I Never Called It Rape: The MS. Report on recognizing, fighting and surviving date and acquaintance rape, HarperPerennial, New York, 1994, p.63.

[6]   R Bergen, 1996, p. 34.

[7]   R Bergen, 1996, p. 30.

[8]   Patricia Easteal, *Voices of the Survivors*, Melbourne: Spinifex, 1994, p. 60.

[9]   R Bergen, 1996, p. 26-9.

[10]   R Bergen, 1996, p. 49.

Chapter 9

[1] D Finkelhor and K Yllo, *License to Rape: Sexual Abuse of Wives*, The Free Press, New York, 1985, p. 137-8.

[2]   Raquel Bergen, *Wife Rape: Understanding the response of survivors and service providers*, Sage Publications Inc, California, 1996, p. 60.

[3]   Judith Herman, *Trauma and Recovery: From domestic abuse to political terror*, BasicBooks, USA, 1992, p. 91.

[4]   Carol Adams 'I just raped my wife! What are you going to do about it, Pastor?' The church and sexual violence', in *Transforming a Rape Culture*, eds E Buchwald, P Fletcher and M Roth, Milkweed Editions, Minneapolis, 1995, p. 63.

[5]   R Bergen, 1996, p. 23 and Angela Taft, 'Violence against women in pregnancy and after childbirth' (2002) 6 *Australian Domestic and Family Violence Clearinghouse Issues Paper*. In the Australian Bureau of statistics,

Women's Safety Survey 1996 at http://www.abs.gov.au/Ausstats/abs@.nsf/0/ b62deb3ac52a2574ca2568a900139340?OpenDocument April 2005 – of those who had experienced violence by a previous partner, violence took place during pregnancy for 41.7 per cent , for just about half of these, it began during that time.

6   K J Wilson, *When Violence Begins at Home: A comprehensive guide to understanding and ending domestic violence*, Hunter House Inc, California, 1997, p. 166.

7   K J Wilson, 1997, p. 70.

8   K J Wilson, 1997, p. 48.

Chapter 10

1   In the ABS *Women's Safety Survey* (1996). http://www.abs.gov.au/Ausstats/ abs@.nsf/0/b62deb3ac52a2574ca2568a900139340?OpenDocument   of those who had experienced violence by a previous partner, for more than one third (35.1 per cent) the violence continued after separation. For some, it begins at that time. One only has to look at the frequency of breaches to domestic violence orders or restraining orders to know that not even legal intervention may deter the desire for control. Almost half of spousal homicides committed by men targeted the killing of women who had left them, or were attempting to leave them (Patricia Easteal, *Killing the Beloved: Homicide between Adult Sexual Intimates* 1993).

2   We've combined the work of Ann Wolbert Burgess and Linda Lytle Holmstrom, who studied the short- and longer-term impact of rape on a group of victims, and described their findings as Rape Trauma Syndrome as discussed in D Shapcott, *The Face of the Rapist*, Penguin Books, Auckland, 1988 with work on PTSD by Judith Herman, *Trauma and Recovery: From domestic abuse to political terror*, BasicBooks, USA, 1992, and A Matsakis, *I Can't get Over It: A handbook for trauma survivors*, New Harbinger Publications Inc, California, 1992.

3   Linda Ledray, Recovering from Rape, Henry Holt and Company, New York, 1994, p. 82.

4   A Matsakis, 1992, p. 9.

5   A Matsakis, 1992, p. 277.

6   A Matsakis, 1992, p. 13.

7   We are relying heavily on A Matsakis, 1992 for the description of these symptoms.

8   A Matsakis, 1992, p. 14.

9   J Herman, 1992, pp. 50-1.

[10] J Herman, 1992, p. 109.

[11] J Herman, 1992, p. 119.

Chapter 11

[1] Diana Russell, Rape in Marriage, MacMillan Publishing Company, USA, 1990, pp. 219-20.

[2] Coined from an incident that happened almost 30 years ago in Stockholm, Sweden in which an armed robber held a woman hostage in a bank vault. By combining terrorisation with the granting of small concessions, he established powerful psychological control over his victim. Ochberg, www. giftfromwithin.org/html/spousal.html.

[3] This is described by Judith Herman, *Trauma and Recovery: From domestic abuse to political terror*, BasicBooks, USA, 1992, pp. 77, 78.

[4] Dr Frank Ochberg (www.giftfromwithin.org/html/spousal.html).

[5] J Herman 1992, p. 79.

[6] A Lissette and R Kraus, *Free Yourself from an Abusive Relationship*, Hunter House Inc, California, 2000, p. 73.

[7] K J Wilson, When Violence Begins at Home: A comprehensive guide to understanding and ending domestic violence, Hunter House Inc, California, 1997, p. 183.

[8] Carol Adams 'I just raped my wife! What are you going to do about it, Pastor?' The church and sexual violence, in Transforming a Rape Culture, eds E Buchwald, P Fletcher and M Roth, Milkweed Editions, Minneapolis, 1995, pp. 82-3.

[9] D Russell 1990, p. 247.

[10] R Warshaw, *I Never Called It Rape: The MS. Report on recognizing, fighting and surviving date and acquaintance rape*, HarperPerennial, New York, 1994, p. 63.

[11] D Russell 1990, p. 220.

[12] A Lissette and R Krause 2000, p. 197.

[13] K J Wilson, 1997, p. 102-4 and Patricia Easteal, *Shattered Dreams: Domestic Violence Among the Overseas Born in Australia*, BIMPR, Melbourne, 1996.

[14] P Easteal 1996.

[15] A Lissette and R Kraus, 2000, pp. 90-1.

[16] D Russell 1990, p. 221.

[17] Margaret Atwood novel, *Cat's Eye*, 1989, p. 20.

[18] Witnessing is a form of violence. See Lesley Laing, 'Children, young people and domestic violence' (2000) 2 *Domestic and Family Violence Clearinghouse Issues Paper* for reviews of the literature and Adam M Tomison, 'Exploring family violence: links between child maltreatment and domestic violence' (2000) and Jeff Edleson 'Children's witnessing of adult domestic violence' (1999) 14 (4) *Journal of Interpersonal Violence* 839 and M Suderman and P Jaffe, 'Children and youth who witness violence: New directions in intervention and prevention', in D A Wolfe, R.J. McMahon and R DeV Peters (eds), *Child Abuse: New Directions in Prevention and Treatment across the Lifespan* (1997).

[19] K J Wilson, 1997, p. 42.

[20] K J Wilson, 1997, p. 42-4.

[21] A Lissette and R Kraus, 2000, p. 199.

[22] Reproduced by permission of The Paladin Group's Domestic Violence Web Page, www.silcom.com/~paladin/madv/.

Chapter 12

[1] K J Wilson, When Violence Begins at Home: A comprehensive guide to understanding and ending domestic violence, Hunter House Inc, California, 1997, pp. 294-5.

[2] K J Wilson, 1997, pp. 143-4, 294.

[3] These are taken from K J Wilson, 1997. See Appendix 4.

[4] A Lissette and R Kraus, Free *Yourself from an Abusive Relationship*, Hunter House Inc, California, 2000, p. 130.

[5] D Finkelhor and K Yllo, *License to Rape: Sexual Abuse of Wives*, The Free Press, New York, 1985, p. 197.

[6] Raquel Bergen, *Wife Rape: Understanding the response of survivors and service providers*, Sage Publications Inc, California, 1996, p. 43.

[7] M Schaum and K Parrish, *Stalked: Breaking the Silence on the crime of stalking in America*, Pocket Books, New York, 1995, p. 56.

[8] M Schaum and K Parrish, 1995, p. 64.

[9] Most of these suggestions come from M Schaum and K Parrish, 1995, pp. 134-5.

[10] A Lissette and R Kraus, 2000, p. 129.

[11] See for instance Hayley Katzen 'It's a Family Matter, not a Police Matter: The Enforcement of Protection Orders' (2000) 14 *Australian Family Law Journal* 119.

[12] A Lissette and R Kraus, 2000, p. 176.

¹³ Judith Herman, *Trauma and Recovery: From domestic abuse to political terror*, BasicBooks, USA, 1992, p. 91.

¹⁴ Psychiatrist Frank Ochberg's article found at <http://www.giftfromwithin. org/html/spousal.html>http://www.giftfromwithin.org/html/spousal.html.

Chapter 13

¹ The ideas in the chapter are largely derived from the work of Aphrodite Matsakis, *I Can't get Over It: A handbook for trauma survivors*, New Harbinger Publications Inc, California, 1992.

² Sometimes somebody will use a woman's trauma against her because they *want* to hurt her. In writing about cruelty as a source of secondary wounding, Aphrodite Matsakis says, 'In the absence of a trauma, they would have found something else to use as a weapon against you.' (1992, p. 91).

³ Raquel Bergen, *Wife Rape: Understanding the response of survivors and service providers*, Sage Publications Inc, California, 1996, p. 80.

⁴ For instance in September 2004, National Conference on Domestic Violence and Sexual Assault was convened in Melbourne.

⁵ A Matsakis, 1992, p. 86.

⁶ Drawn from A Maatsakis, 1992, p. 94.

Chapter 14

¹ Denise Lievore, 'Intimate Partner Sexual Assault: The Impact of Competing Demands on Victims' Decisions to Seek Criminal Justice Solutions' (2003) on Australian Institute of Criminology <http://www.aic.gov.au/conferences/ other/lievore_denise/2003-02-AIFS.html> at May 2004 using the ABS 1999 Crime and Safety Survey, at May 2004. Conforms to earlier surveys such as NSW Sexual Assault Committee, Sexual Assault Phone-In Report (1993) and Patricia Easteal, *Voices of the Survivors*, Spinifex, Melbourne, 1994.

² This is despite legislation in some jurisdictions that prohibits such a direction. Laws are very grey; they have an open-plan construction with supporting beams of judicial interpretation and discretion. Moreover, although law reform may appear to remove a concept, it does not stop judges from raising the subject in their remarks to the jury or in their sentencing. See Simon Bronitt 'The rules of recent complaint: Rape myths and the legal construction of the "reasonable' rape victim"', in P. Easteal (ed.) *Balancing the Scales: Rape, Law Reform and Australian Culture* (Sydney: Federation Press, 1998.

³ *Crimes Act 1900* (ACT) s92R; *Crimes (Sexual Assault) Amendment Act 1981* (NSW); *Criminal Code* (NT) s192 as amended in 1994; *Criminal*

Code (Qld) s347 as amended in 1989; *Criminal Law Consolidation Act Amendment Act* (1992); *Criminal Code* (Tas) s185(1) as amended in 1987; *Crimes Act 1958* (Vic) s62(2) as amended by *Crimes Act Amendment Act 1985* and *Crimes (Sexual Offences) Act 1991*; *Criminal Code 1913* (WA) s325 was repealed by Act No. 74 *Acts Amendment (Sexual Assault) Act 1985.*

4   See Neal Miller, Domestic Violence: A Review of State Legislation Defining Police and Prosecution Duties and Powers, June 2004, for a state by state description, June 2004, at http://www.ilj.org/dv/index.htm April 2005.

5   Robbie Sherwood, *The Arizona Republic*, Mar. 10, 2005.

6   Patricia Easteal 'Rape in Marriage: Has the License Lapsed?', in Patricia Easteal (ed), *Balancing the Scales*: *Rape, Law Reform and Australian Culture* (1998).

7   *DPP v Cowey* (Unreported, South Australia Court of Criminal Appeal, Cox, Prior, Lander, 18 July 1995).

8   *R v Johns* [1992] South Australia Supreme Court (Unreported, Bollen J, 26 August 1992).

9   Anne Summers *The End of Equality*: *Work babies and women's choices in 21st century Australia* Random House, Milsons Point, 2003, p. 111.

10   These were at the ACT Director of Public Prosecutions. More discussion about them can be found in two publications currently in press: Patricia Easteal and Miriam Gani, 'Sexual Assault by Male Partners: A Study of Sentencing Variables' (2205), *Southern Cross University Law Review,* 9 39-72; P Easteal and C Feerick, 'Sexual Assault by Male Partners: Is the License Still Valid?' (2005) *Flinders Journal of Law Reform*, 8 (2) 185-207.

11   For instance, Jessica Harris and Sharon Grace *A Question of Evidence? Investigating and Prosecuting Rape in the 1990s* (1999) at 21 <http://www. aifs.gov.au/acssa/onlinedocs/lawpolicy.html> June 2004 found that in the UK.

12   In looking at five Australian jurisdictions, Denise Lievore found that 38 per cent of the prosecutions in sexual assault were dropped; prosecutorial decisions in adult sexual assault cases, *Trends and Issues in Crime and Criminal Justice*, number 291, January 2005 at http://www.aic.gov.au/publications/tandi2/tandi291t.html.

13   In P Easteal and C Feerick, 2005; 10 of the 21 cases of partner rape were dropped.

14   We refer of course to Lord Matthew Hale pronouncement in the 17th century that subsequently became the most cited authority in marital rape

cases in countries with English common law foundations: 'The husband cannot be guilty of a rape committed by himself upon his lawful wife, for by their mutual matrimonial consent and contract, the wife hath given up herself in this kind unto her husband which she cannot retract' *History of the Pleas of the Crown*, 1736 (S Emlin ed), Vol, p. 629.

[15] King CJ in *Case Stated by the (South Australia) DPP* (No 1 of 1993) (1993) 66 *Australian Criminal Reports* at 259 and discussed by Sally Kift, 'That all Rape is Rape even if not by a Stranger' (1995) 4(1) *Griffith Law Review*, 60-111, p. 64.

[16] In P Easteal and C Feerick, 2005, seven of the 10 discontinuances were at the victim's initiative.

[17] See P Easteal and C Feerick for further discussion of the reasons that victims give for not wanting to continue with the proceedings.

[18] *R v An* [2000] 117 Australian Criminal Reports 176. Compares Hunt CJ at CL in *Beserick* at 522; 429.

[19] P Easteal And C Feerick, 2005.

[20] In over half (54 per cent) of the trials studied by Pia van deZandt 'Heroines of Fortitude' (ed. Patricia Easteal) in *Balancing the Scales*: *Rape, Law Reform and Australian Culture* (1998) 124, 130 the complainant was cross-examined about a possible motive for making a false report to the police.

[21] M Heenan, 'Just "keeping the peace": A reluctance to respond to male partner sexual violence' (2004) 1 *Australian Centre for the Study of Sexual Assault* 1, citing work from her 2001 unpublished Monash University PhD thesis: 'Trial and Error: Rape, Law Reform and Feminism' Download from http://www.aifs.gov.au/acssa/pubs/issue/i1.html.

[22] M Heenan, 2004.

[23] M Heenan, 2004.

[24] P Easteal and C Feerick, 2005.

[25] 61 per cent acquitted in contrast to 43 per cent across all principal offences. Australian Bureau of Statistics, *4513.0 Criminal Courts*, Australia, 11/02/05, http://www.abs.gov.au/Ausstats/abs@.nsf/0/62e9baff94dad459ca2568a900 1393fe?OpenDocument March 2005.

[26] In the ACT DPP sample, of those who went to trial, there were no jury findings of guilt; six defendants pleaded guilty, three were acquitted and in two trials there were hung juries.

[27] S Lees Ruling Passions: Sexual Violence, Reputation and the Law, Open University Press, Buckingham, 1997, p. 123. Phil Rumney 'When rape isn't rape: Court Of Appeal sentencing practice in cases of marital and relationship rape', *Oxford Journal of Legal Studies* (1999) 19, 243 and Harris J and

Grace, S 'A Question of Evidence? Investigating and Prosecuting Rape in the 1990s', Home Office Research Study No. 196, Home Office, London, 1999.

[28]   Stockwell (1984) 6 Cr App R 84 as discussed in J Temkin *Rape and the Legal Process*, Sweet and Maxwell, London, 1987, p. 43.

Chapter 15

[1]   David Finkelhor and Kersti Yllo, *Licence to Rape: Sexual Abuse of Wives* Holt, 1985, p. 115.

[2]   According to Diana Russell, *Rape in Marriage*, MacMillan Publishing Company, USA, 1990, p. 53, where there is a power imbalance in a relationship, a woman may accept her partner's view of the sexual violence.

[3]   Carol Adams, 'I just raped my wife! What are you going to do about it, Pastor?' The church and sexual violence, in *Transforming a Rape Culture*, eds E Buchwald, P Fletcher and M Roth, Milkweed Editions, Minneapolis, 1995, p. 63.

[4]   D Finkelhor and K Yllo, 1985, p. 115.

[5]   Aphrodite Matsakis, *I Can't Get Over It: A handbook for trauma survivors*, New Harbinger Publications Inc, California, 1992, p. 272.

[6]   D Finkelhor and K Yllo, 1985, p. 125.

[7]   A Matsakis, 1992, p. 73.

[8]   *R v Salter* [2002] VSCA 128 (Unreported, Winneke P, Buchanan JA and O'Bryan AJA, 22 August 2002) [4] Winneke P; Buchanan agreed with Winneke P.

[9]   Raquel Bergen, *Wife Rape: Understanding the response of survivors and service providers*, Sage Publications Inc, California, 1996, p. 46.

[10]   For instance, in Patricia Easteal, *Voices of the Survivors*, Spinifex, Melbourne 1994, p. 229, women raped by estranged husbands or de factos were the second most likely group, after victims of stranger rape, to report the rapes to the police. 29.2 per cent reported compared with 13 per cent, or less than half that, of women who reported husbands or de factos with whom they had been living at the time of the rapes.

[11]   R Bergen, 1996.

[12]   R Bergen, 1996, p. 45.

[13]   Patricia Weaver Francisco, *Telling* Cliff Street Books/HarperCollins, 1999, p. 219.

Chapter 16

[1] If you worry that there are things you cannot remember, there are memory aids you can try. Please discuss this with your therapist.

[2] D Finkelhor and K Yllo, *License to Rape: Sexual Abuse of Wives*, The Free Press, New York, 1985, pp. 118-19.

[3] Aphrodite Matsakis, *I Can't get Over It: A handbook for trauma survivors*, New Harbinger Publications Inc, California, 1992, p. 189.

[4] Linda Ledray, *Recovering from Rape*, Henry Holt and Company, New York, 1994, p. 125.

[5] L Ledray, 1994, p. 118.

[6] L Ledray, 1994, p. 119.

Chapter 17

[1] Aphrodite Matsakis *I Can't get Over It: A handbook for trauma survivors*, New Harbinger Publications Inc, California, 1992, p. 217.

[2] Melody Beattie, *Beyond Codependency*, Collins Dove, Burwood, 1989, p. 175.

[3] Melody Beattie has written many books on this topic such as *Codependent No More*, Hazelden, Minnesota, 1987; *Beyond Codependency*, Collins Dove, Burwood, 1989. She also has published several daily meditation books such as *The Language of Letting Go*, Hazelden, 1990 that can be very helpful.

[4] Judith Herman, *Trauma and Recovery: From domestic abuse to political terror*, BasicBooks, USA, 1992, p. 196.

[5] A Lissette and R Kraus, Free *Yourself from an Abusive Relationship*, Hunter House Inc, California, 2000, p. 241.

[6] Raquel Bergen, *Wife Rape: Understanding the response of survivors and service providers*, Sage Publications Inc, California, 1996, p. 62.

[7] A Matsakis, 1992, p. 274-5.

[8] A Matsakis, 1992, p. 25.

[9] As described in Alcoholics Anonymous (AA) literature.

Chapter 18

[1] Melody Beattie, Beyond Codependency, Collins Dove, Burwood, 1989, p. 186.

[2] List is partly derived from A Lissette and R Kraus, Free *Yourself from an Abusive Relationship*, Hunter House Inc, California, 2000, pp. 238-9.

3   Some of the questions in this list come from A Lissette and R Kraus, 2000, pp. 263-4.

4   Ann Jones in K J Wilson, *When Violence Begins at Home: A comprehensive guide to understanding and ending domestic violence,* Hunter House Inc, California, 1997, p. 145.

5   Reproduced in part with the kind permission of Will H, Recovery-Man.com Webmaster Minor.

6   M Beattie 1989, pp. 141-90.

Chapter 19

1   We draw heavily on an excellent and comprehensive book written by sexual trauma expert Wendy Maltz, *The Sexual Healing Journey: a Guide for Survivors of Sexual Abuse,* HarperCollins Publishers Inc, New York, 2001 and recommend that you read it in its entirety.

2   W Maltz, 2001, p. 85.

3   W Maltz, 2001, p. 134-8.

4   W Maltz, 2001, p. 176.

5   W Maltz, 2001, pp. 154-5.

6   Linda Ledray, *Recovering from Rape,* Henry Holt and Company, New York, 1994, p. 131.

7   W Maltz, 2001, p. 100-2.

8   W Maltz, 2001, p. 284.

9   Advice from Seattle Institute for Sex Therapy, Education, and Research, 'Recovering from Rape: Healing Your Sexuality' at http://www.sextx.com/rape.html April 2005.

10   Advice from Seattle Institute for Sex Therapy, Education, and Research, 'Recovering from Rape: Healing Your Sexuality' at http://www.sextx.com/rape.html April 2005.

11   Advice from Seattle Institute for Sex Therapy, Education, and Research, 'Recovering from Rape: Healing Your Sexuality' at http://www.sextx.com/rape.html April 2005.

12   W Maltz, 2001, p. 197.

13   Another example: If you've ever seen any rendering of the ancient goddess Sheela-na-Gig, you'll know that this is a lass with no inhibitions whatsoever about prideful displays of pudenda. There she sits, proudly holding open her bowl-shaped vagina for all who want to see. See Aphrodite Wounded website, www.aphroditewounded.org for more information about mythology and female sexuality.

Chapter 20

[1] K J Wilson, *When Violence Begins at Home*: *A comprehensive guide to understanding and ending domestic violence*, Hunter House Inc, California, 1997, p. 54.

[2] Raquel Bergen, *Wife Rape*: *Understanding the response of survivors and service providers*, Sage Publications Inc, California, 1996, p. 102.

[3] Susan Brewster, *To be an Anchor in the Storm*: *A guide for families and friends of abused women*, Ballantine Books, New York, 1997, p. 145.

[4] K J Wilson, 1997, p. 138.

[5] This is a secularised sub-list from Carol Adams's list for women of faith raped by husbands. Carol Adams 'I just raped my wife! What are you going to do about it, Pastor?' The church and sexual violence, in *Transforming a Rape Culture*, eds E Buchwald, P Fletcher and M Roth, Milkweed Editions, Minneapolis, 1995.

[6] K J Wilson, 1997, p. 136.

[7] K J Wilson, 1997, p. 142.

[8] Linda Ledray, *Recovering from Rape*, Henry Holt and Company, New York, 1994, p. 170.

[9] Judith Herman, *Trauma and Recovery*: *From domestic abuse to political terror*, BasicBooks, USA, 1992, p. 140-1.

Chapter 21

[1] Jim Stynes, 'Footy's silent victims', *Herald Sun*, 1 April 2004, p. 19.

[2] Terence Crowley, 'The lie of entitlement', *Transforming a Rape Culture* eds. E Buchwald, P Fletcher and M Roth, 1995, pp. 344, 347.

[3] J Weinberg and M Biernbaum, 'Conversations of consent: Sexual intimacy without sexual assault', *Transforming a Rape Culture*, eds. E Buchwald, P Fletcher and M Roth, 1995, p. 98.

[4] E Buchwald, 'Raising girls for the 21st century', *Transforming a Rape Culture*, eds. E Buchwald, P Fletcher and M Roth, 1995, p. 191.

[5] Elizabeth Powell, 'I thought you didn't mind', *Transforming a Rape Culture*, eds. E Buchwald, P Fletcher and M Roth, 1995, pp. 109-11.

[6] E Buchwald 1995, p. 191.

[7] Myriam Miedzian, 'How rape is encouraged in American boys and what we can do to stop it', Transforming a Rape Culture, eds. E Buchwald, P Fletcher and M Roth, 1995, p. 155.

[8] C Adams, 'I just raped my wife! What are you going to do about it, Pastor?' The Church and Sexual Violence', *Transforming a Rape Culture*, eds. E

Buchwald, P Fletcher and M Roth, 1995, p. 82.

9   K J Wilson, *When Violence Begins at Home*: *A comprehensive guide to understanding and ending domestic violence*, Hunter House Inc, California, 1997, pp. 184-7.

10 K J Wilson, 1997, pp. 184-7.

11 Melanie Heenan 'Just 'keeping the peace': A reluctance to respond to male partner sexual violence' (2004) 1 Issues Australia Study for the Centre of Sexual Assault at http://www.aifs.gov.au/acssa/pubs/issue/i1.html cites Kersti Yllo, 'The silence surrounding sexual violence.' 'The issue of marital rape and the challenge it poses for the Duluth model', in M. Shepard and E. Pence (eds) Coordinating Community Responses to Domestic Violence: Lessons from Duluth and Beyond (1999), shows that with the Duluth integrated response model to domestic violence, the sexual assault can be ignored.

12 Terese Henning and Simon Bronitt, 'Rape victims on trial: Regulating the use and abuse of sexual history evidence', in *Balancing the Scales*: *Rape, Law Reform and Australian Culture*, ed. P Easteal, 1998, p. 76.

13 See Patricia Easteal 'Women, Law and Cultural Contexts: Kaleidoscopes of Reality' (1999/2000) *Contemporary Issues in Law*, p. 213.

14 Patricia Easteal 'Beyond Balancing' in *Balancing the Scales*: *Rape, Law Reform and Australian Culture*, ed. P Easteal, 1998, p. 205.

15 M Heenan, 2004 at http://www.aifs.gov.au/acssa/pubs/issue/i1.html.

16 Raquel Bergen, *Wife Rape*: *Understanding the Response of Survivors and Service Providers*, Sage Publications Inc, California, 1996, p. 85.

17 Good Practice Programs, Understanding and Responding to Disclosures of Sexual Violence http://www.aifs.gov.au/acssa/gpdb/ipsagoldcoast.html.

18 R Bergen, 1996, p. 90.

19 M Heenan, 2004 at http://www.aifs.gov.au/acssa/pubs/issue/i1.html.

20 R Bergen, 1996, pp. 87, 99.

21 D Finkelhor and K Yllo, *License to Rape*: *Sexual Abuse of Wives*, The Free Press, New York, 1985, p. 188.

22 D Finkelhor and K Yllo, 1985, p. 192; R Bergen, 1996, p. 105.

23 http://www.aifs.gov.au/acssa/gpdb/ipsagoldcoast.html.

24 Patricia Easteal, *Voices of the Survivors*, Spinifex Press, Melbourne, 1994.

Appendix 3

1   http://www.hiddenhurt.co.uk/internet_safety.htm.

Appendix 4

[1] KJ Wilson, *When Violence Begins at Home: A comprehensive guide to understanding and ending domestic violence*, Hunter House Inc, California, 1997, p. 294-5.

Appendix 5

[1] See Renata Paulander, *Domestic Violence in Australia – The Legal Response*, Federation Press, Sydney, 2002 for an overview of relevant laws.

[2] Neal Miller, Domestic Violence: A Review of State Legislation Defining Police and Prosecution Duties and Powers, June 2004, accessed from at http://66.102.7.104/search?q=cache:Kp0syjay8a4J:www.ilj.org/dv/Papers/DV_Legislation-3.pdf+Neal+Miller,+Domestic+Violence:+A+Review+of+State+Legislation+Defining+Police+and+Prosecution+Duties+and+Powers&hl=en&ie=UTF-8 April 2005.

[3] http://www.legislation.hmso.gov.uk/acts/acts2004/20040028.htm.

[4] In the US, for instance, the category of people who can seek protection from the Courts was broadened in *Violence Against Women Act* to include unmarried. This, in turn, has led to some state legislative reform as discussed in Neal Miller, 2004.

[5] Susan Brewster, *To be an Anchor in the Storm: A guide for families and friends of abused women*, Ballantine Books, New York, 1997, p. 190.

[6] Newsletter, Silent Witness National Initiative, Nov. 2002.

[7] KJ Wilson, *When Violence Begins at Home: A comprehensive guide to understanding and ending domestic violence*, Hunter House Inc, California, 1997, p. 79.

[8] See for example Belinda Carpenter, Sue Currie and Rachael Field, 'Domestic Violence: Views of Queensland Magistrates' (2001) 3 *Nuance* 15 and Jennifer Hickey and Stephen Cumines, *Apprehended Violence Orders A Survey of Magistrates*, Judicial Commission of NSW, Sydney, 1999.

[9] *Family Violence Act* (2004).

[10] KJ Wilson 1997, pp. 85-6.

[11] For instance, in the UK in 2004 with the new Domestic Violence, Crime and Victims Act breach of a non-molestation order became a criminal offence punishable by up to five years' imprisonment. A police officer can arrest without a warrant.

[12] Studies in Australia that have looked at this issue are discussed in Patricia Easteal, 'Violence against women in the home: Kaleidoscopes on a collision course?' *QUT Law and Justice Journal* Vol 3 No 2 2003, at http://www.law.qut.edu.au/about/ljj/editions/v3n2/easteal_full.jsp.

Breinigsville, PA USA
19 August 2010
243818BV00001BA/20/A